G. K. Chesterton

Dickens by Chesterton

e-artnow 2020

G. K. Chesterton

Dickens by Chesterton

Critical Study, Biography, Appreciations & Criticisms of the Works by Charles Dickens

e-artnow, 2020
Contact: info@e-artnow.org

ISBN 978-80-273-0634-3

Contents

Charles Dickens	13
Charles Dickens	15
Charles Dickens — A Biographical Sketch	19
Charles Dickens - Critical Study	25
Chapter 1. The Dickens Period	26
Chapter 2. The Boyhood of Dickens	33
Chapter 3. The Youth of Dickens	39
Chapter 4. "The Pickwick Papers"	47
Chapter 5. The great Popularity	55
Chapter 6. Dickens and America	63
Chapter 7. Dickens and Christmas	71
Chapter 8. The Time of Transition	78
Chapter 9. Later Life and works	87
Chapter 10. The Great Dickens Characters	96
Chapter 11. On the Alleged Optimism of Dickens	102
Chapter 12. A Note on the Future of Dickens	109
Appreciations and Criticisms of the Works of Charles Dickens	113
Introduction	115
Sketches by Boz	129
Pickwick Papers	133
Nicholas Nickleby	138
Oliver Twist	142
Old Curiosity Shop	146
Barnaby Rudge	151
American Notes	156
Pictures from Italy	160
Martin Chuzzlewit	162
Christmas Books	167
Dombey and Son	171
David Copperfield	177
Christmas Stories	181
Bleak House	184
Child's History of England	188
Hard times	192
Little Dorrit	196
A Tale of Two Cities	200

Great Expectations	204
Our Mutual Friend	208
Edwin Drood	213
Master Humphrey's Clock	217
Reprinted Pieces	221

Charles Dickens

CHARLES DICKENS

Charles Dickens

Considered merely as literary fashions, romanticism and realism are both tricks, and tricks alone. The only advantage lies with romanticism, which is a little less artificial and technical than realism. For the great majority of people here and now do naturally write romanticism, as we see it in a love- letter, or a diary, or a quarrel, and nobody on earth naturally writes realism as we see it in a description by Flaubert. But both are technical dodges and realism only the more eccentric. It is a trick to make things happen harmoniously always, and it is a trick to make them always happen discordantly. It is a trick to make a heroine, in the act of accepting a lover, suddenly aureoled by a chance burst of sunshine, and then to call it romance. But it is quite as much of a trick to make her, in the act of accepting a lover, drop her umbrella, or trip over a hassock, and then call it the bold plain realism of life. If any one wishes to satisfy himself as to how excessively little this technical realism has to do, I do not say with profound reality, but even with casual truth to life, let him make a simple experiment offered to him by the history of literature. Let him ask what is of all English books the book most full of this masterly technical realism, most full of all these arresting details, all these convincing irrelevancies, all these impedimenta of prosaic life; and then as far as truth to life is concerned he will find that it is a story about men as big as houses and men as small as dandelions, about horses with human souls and an island that flew like a balloon.

"BOZ" (CHARLES DICKENS)

We can never understand a writer of the old romantic school, even if he is as great and splendid as Dickens is great and splendid, until we realise this preliminary fact to which I have drawn attention. The fact that these merely technical changes are merely technical, and have nothing whatever to do with the force and truth behind. We are bound to find a considerable amount of Dickens's work, especially the pathetic and heroic passages, artificial and pompous. But that is only because we are far enough off his trick or device to see that it is such. Our own trick and device we believe to be as natural as the eternal hills.

It is no more natural, even when compared with the Dickens devices, than a rockery is natural, even when compared with a Dutch flower bed. The time will come when the wildest upheaval of Zolaism, when the most abrupt and colloquial dialogue of Norwegian drama, will appear a fine old piece of charming affectation, a stilted minuet of literature, like little Nell in the churchyard, or the repentance of the white-haired Dombey. All their catchwords will have become catchwords; the professor's explanations of heredity will have the mellow, foolish sound of the villain's curses against destiny. And in that time men will for the first time become aware of the real truth and magnificence of Zola and Ibsen, just as we, if we are wise, are now becoming aware of the real truth and magnificence of Dickens.

This is even more true if we look first at that fundamental optimistic feeling about life, which as it has been often and truly said is the main essence of Dickens. If Dickens's optimism had merely been a matter of happy endings, reconciliations, and orange flowers, it would be a mere superficial art or craft. But it would not, as in the case discussed above, be in any way more superficial than the pessimism of the modern episode, or short story, which is an affair of bad endings, disillusionments, and arsenic. The truth about life is that joy and sorrow are mingled in an almost rhythmical alternation like day and night. The whole of optimistic technique consists in the dodge of breaking off the story at dawn, and the whole of pessimistic technique in the art of breaking off the story at dusk. But wherever and whenever mere artists choose to consider the matter ended, the matter is never ended, and trouble and exultation go on in a design larger than any of ours, neither vanishing at all. Beyond our greatest happiness there lie dangers, and after our greatest dangers there remaineth a rest.

But the element in Dickens which we are forced to call by the foolish and unmanageable word optimism is a very much deeper and more real matter than any question of plot and conclusion. If Mr. Pickwick had been drowned when he fell through the ice; if Mr. Dick Swiveller had never recovered from the fever, these catastrophes might have been artistically inappropriate, but they would not have sufficed to make the stories sad. If Sam Weller had committed suicide from religious difficulties, if Florence Dombey had been murdered (most justly murdered) by Captain Cuttle, the stories would still be the happiest stories in the world. For their happiness is a state of the soul; a state in which our natures are full of the wine of an ancient youth, in which banquets last for ever, and roads lead everywhere, where all things are under the exuberant leadership of faith, hope, and charity, the three gayest of the virtues.

There is, of course, an optimism which is evil and debasing, and to this it must be confessed that Dickens sometimes descends. The worst optimism is that which, in making things comfortable, prevents them from becoming joyful; it bears the same relation to an essential and true optimism that the pleasure of sitting in an arm-chair bears to the pleasure of sitting on a galloping horse. It is the optimism which denies that burning hurts a martyr. More profoundly considered, it may be called the optimism which, in order to give a being more life, denies him his individual life; in order to give him more pleasure, denies him his especial pleasure. It offers the hunter repose, and the student pleasure, and the poet an explanation. Dickens, as I have said, sometimes fell into this.

Nothing could be more atrocious for instance, than his course of action in concluding "David Copperfield" with an account of the great Micawber at last finding wealth and success as a mayor in Australia. Micawber would never succeed; never ought to succeed; his kingdom was not of this world. His mind to him a kingdom was; he was one of those splendid and triumphant poor, who have the faculty of capturing, without a coin of money or a stroke of work, that ultimate sense of possessing wealth and luxury, which is the only reward of the toils and crimes of the rich. It is but a sentiment after all, this idea of money, and a poor man who is also a poet, like Micawber, may find a short cut to it. To make such a man, after a million mental triumphs over material circumstances, become the mere pauper and dependant of material success, is something more than an artistic blunder: it is a moral lapse; it is a wicked and blasphemous thing to have done. The end of "David Copperfield" is not a happy ending; it is a very miserable ending. To make Micawber a mayor is about as satisfying a termination as it would be to make

Sir Lancelot after Arthur's death become a pork butcher or a millionaire, or to make Enoch Arden grow fat and marry an heiress. There is a satisfaction that is far more depressing than any tragedy. And the essence of it, as I have said, lies in the fact that it violates the real and profound philosophical optimism of the universe, which has given to each thing its inconmiunicable air and its strange reason for living. It offers instead, another joy or peace which is alien and nauseous; it offers grass to the dog and fire to the fishes. It is, indeed, in the same tradition as that cruel and detestable kindness to animals, which has been one of the disgraces of humanity: from the modern lady who pulls a fat dog on a chain through a crowded highway, back to the Roman Caesar who fed his horse on wine, and made it a political magistrate.

The same error in an even more irreverent form occurs, of course, in the same book. The essence of the Dickens genius was exaggeration, and in that general sense Dora, in "David Copperfield," may be called an exaggerated character; but she is an extremely real and an extremely agreeable character for all that. She is supposed to be very weak and ineffectual, but she has about a hundred times more personal character than all Dickens's waxwork heroines put together, the unendurable Agnes by no means excluded.

It almost passes comprehension how a man who could conceive such a character should so insult it, as Dickens does, in making Dora recommend her husband's second marriage with Agnes. Dora, who stands for the profound and exquisite irrationality of simple affection, is made the author of a piece of priggish and dehumanised rationalism which is worthy of Miss Agnes herself. One could easily respect such a husband when he married again, but surely not such a wife when she desired it.

The truth is, of course, that here again Dickens is following his evil genius which bade him make those he loved comfortable instead of happy. It may seem at first sight a paradox to say that the special fault of optimism is a lack of faith in God: but so it is. There are some whom we should not seek to make comfortable: their appeasement is in more awful hands. There are conflicts, the reconciliation of which lies beyond the powers not only of human effort but of human rational conception. One of them is the reconciliation between good and evil themselves in the scheme of nature; another is the reconciliation of Dora and Agnes. To say that we know they will be reconciled is faith: to say that we see that they wall be reconciled is blasphemy.

Dickens was, of course, as is repeated *ad nauseum*, a caricaturist, and when we have understood this word we have understood the whole matter; but in truth the word, caricaturist, is commonly misunderstood; it is even, in the case of men like Dickens, used as implying a reproach. Whereas it has no more reproach in it than the word organist. Caricature is not merely an important form of art: it is a form of art which is often most useful for purposes of profound philosophy and powerful symbolism. The age of scepticism put caricature into ephemeral feuilletons: but the ages of faith built caricatures into their churches of everlasting stone.

One extraordinary idea has been constantly repeated, the idea that it is very easy to make a mere caricature of anything. As a matter of fact it is extraordinarily difficult, for it implies a knowledge of what part of a thing to caricature. To reproduce the proportions of a face, exactly as they are, is a comparatively safe adventure; to arrange those features in an entirely new proportion, and yet retain a resemblance, argues a very delicate instinct for what features are really the characteristic and essential ones.

Caricature is only easy when it so happens that the people depicted, like Cyrano de Bergerac, are more or less caricatures themselves. In other words caricature is only easy when it does not caricature very much. But to see an ordinary intelligent face in the street, and to know that, with the nose three times as long and the head twice as broad, it will still be a startling likeness, argues a profound insight into truth.

"Caricature," said Sir Willoughby Patterne, in his fatuous way, "is rough truth." It is not: it is subtle truth. This is what gives Dickens his unquestionable place among artists.

He realised thoroughly a certain phase or atmosphere of existence, and he knew the precise strokes and touches that would bring it home to the reader. That Dickens phase or atmosphere may be roughly defined as the phase of a vivid sociability in which every man becomes unusually and startlingly himself. A good caricature will sometimes seem more like the original than the original: so it is in the greatest moments of social life. He is an unfortunate man, a man unfitted to value life and certainly unfitted to value Dickens, who has not sat at some table or talked in some company in which every one was in character, each a beautiful caricature of himself.

Charles Dickens — A Biographical Sketch

The Asseveration that "Dickens" is "a name to conjure with" seems almost a truism. The innumerable editions of his works so constantly pouring from the press abundantly testify to the continued and unabated popularity of the most famous writer of fiction of the Victorian epoch. As regards the circumstances appertaining to his career-the start in life under harassing conditions, the brilliant success attending his initial efforts in authorship, the manner in which he took the world by storm and retained his grip of the public by the sheer force of genius there is, I venture to believe, no parallel in the history of literature.

Born in a humble station of life, his early years spent in the midst of an uncongenial (not to say demoralising) environment, his natural gifts, combined with almost superhuman powers of perseverance, enabled him to overcome obstacles which would have deterred ordinary men, with the result that he rapidly attained the topmost rung of the ladder of fame, and remained there.

Although the leading incidents in the life of Charles Dickens are generally familiar, thanks to the various biographies of him published from time to time, a few facts, briefly stated, will not, I hope, be devoid of interest. The novelist first saw the light at No, 387, Commercial Road, Mile End, Landport, in the Island of Portsea. Like David Copperfield, he was born on a Friday, the natal day being February 7th, 1812. The baptismal register of Portsea Parish Church (St. Mary's, Kingston), where he was christened, records that three names were bestowed upon him, Charles John Huffam, the second being that of his father, and the third the cognomen of his godfather, Christopher Huffam, a "Rigger to his Majesty's Navy," who lived at Limehouse Hole, on the north bank of the Thames. The birthplace in Landport-still existing-is an unpretentious tenement of two storeys, surmounted by a dormer window, and fronted by a small railed-in garden.

John Dickens, the father of Charles, had filled a clerical position in the Navy Pay Office, Somerset House, whence he was transferred to a similar post at Portsea. About four years after the birth of Charles (the second child), the Dickens family removed to Chatham, residing there until the boy was eleven years old. It was at Chatham where he first went to school, and where he, being endowed with exceptional powers of observation, imbibed his earliest impressions of humanity, to be subsequently made available as material for his inimitable sketches.

London, however, was again to be the home of John Dickens-the mighty metropolis which, with its phantasmagoria of life in its every aspect, its human comedies and tragedies, ever attracted the great writer, whose magic pen revelled in the delineation of them. It was in 1823 that the Dickens family took up their residence in Bayham Street, Camden Town-then the poorest part of the London suburbs. There had come a crisis in the affairs of the elder Dickens which necessitated the strictest economy, and the house in Bayham Street (which may still be seen at No. 141) was nothing but "a mean tenement, with a wretched little back garden abutting on a squalid court." This was the beginning of a sad and bitter experience in the life of Charles Dickens. Here he seemed to fall into a solitary condition, apart from all other boys of his own age, and, recalling the circumstances in after years, he observed to Forster: "As I thought, in the little back-garret in Bayham Street, of all I had lost in losing Chatham, what would I have given, if I had had anything to give, to have been sent back to any other school, to have been taught something anywhere?"

Not only did the exceptionally intelligent lad miss the pleasures of association with his schoolfellows and playmates at Chatham, but he no longer had recourse to the famous books whose acquaintance he had made there "Don Quixote," "Robinson Crusoe," "The Arabian Nights," *et hoc genus omne* —which, as admirers of his works will remember, he was so fond of quoting. The account given by Forster of the Bayham Street days is painful reading, and we are told that, thus living under circumstances of a hopeless and struggling poverty, the extreme sensitiveness of the boy caused him to experience acute mental suffering.

After a short residence in Bayham Street, the family removed their belongings to Gower Street North (the identical house was demolished a few years ago), and an effort was made to bring grist to the mill by an attempt on the part of Mrs. Dickens to start a school for young ladies; but the venture proved abortive, notwithstanding the fact that Charles did his utmost to aid the project by leaving "at a great many doors, a great many circulars," calling attention to the advantages of the establishment.

John Dickens's financial difficulties increased, tradesmen became pertinacious in their claims for a settlement of long-standing debts, which could not be met, until at last the father was arrested, and lodged in a debtors' prison events which the novelist afterwards vividly recalled, and which will be found duly set forth in "David Copperfield."

It was at this awkward juncture that some relatives of the family, named Lambert, realising that an opportunity should be given to the poor neglected lad of earning a livelihood, found him an occupation in their blacking- manufactory (started in opposition to the famous Warren), and here he earned a few shillings a week by covering and labelling pots of paste blacking! While infinitely preferable to a state of enforced idleness under demoralising conditions, the boy's experience during what is usually referred to as "the blacking-bottle period," for ever remained a terrible nightmare, and the novelist pointedly referred to that unhappy time when in "David Copperfield" he observed that no one could express "the secret agony" of his soul as he sank into the companionship of those by whom he was then surrounded, and felt his "early hopes of growing up to be a learned and distinguished man" crushed in his breast. In respect of a miserable and neglected boyhood, Alphonse Daudet suffered as did Charles Dickens, and, phoenix-like, both emerged triumphantly from the ashes of what to them appeared to be a cruel conflagration of their desires and aspirations.

There is no doubt that the ordeal of poverty, with its unhappy accompaniments, had counter-acting advantages in the case of Charles Dickens: his natural abilities were sharpened, as well as his powers of observation, his excellent memory enabling him in after years to record those actualities of life which render his books a perpetual joy and delight. Fortunately, brighter days were in store. The elder Dickens (in whom it is easy to detect glimpses of Mr. Micawber) was in a position to send Charles to a reputable school in the Hampstead Road, known as Wellington House Academy (still standing), where he remained two years, and on leaving it he entered another scholastic establishment near Brunswick Square, there completing his studies, rudimentary at the best.

The year 1827 proved a memorable one for the subject of this sketch, for then it was that he, in his fifteenth year, "began life," first as a clerk in a lawyer's office in Lincoln's Inn, and then acting in a similar capacity for a firm of attorneys in Gray's Inn, where his weekly salary amounted to something under a sovereign. As was his wont, he made mental memoranda of his environment, noting the manners, customs, and peculiarities of lawyers, their clerks and clients, for the result of which one needs only to turn to the pages of the immortal "Pickwick." His father, who had left the Navy Pay Office, turned his attention to journalism, and at this time had become a newspaper parliamentary reporter. Charles, craving for a similar occupation, in which he believed there might be an opening for greater things, resolutely determined to study shorthand, and became an assiduous attendant at the British Museum.

His persevering struggle with the mysteries of stenography was recalled when recording David Copperfield's experience—a struggle resulting in ultimate victory. Following in his fathers footsteps, he, at the age of nineteen, succeeded in obtaining an appointment as a reporter in the Press Gallery at the House of Commons, where he was presently acknowledged to be the most skilful shorthand writer among the many so engaged there.

Dickens had just attained his majority when, in 1833, he essayed to venture into the realm of fiction. He has himself related how, one evening at twilight, he stealthily entered "a dark court" in Fleet Street (it was Johnsons Court), and with fear and trembling dropped into "a dark letter-box" the manuscript of his first paper—a humorous sketch entitled "A Dinner at Poplar Walk," (afterwards called "Mr. Minns and his Cousin"); and how, when it "appeared in all the glory of print," he walked down to Westminster Hall, and turned into it for half an hour, because (he explains) his eyes "were so dimmed with joy and pride, that they could not bear the street, and were not fit to be seen there." To this initial effort (which was published in the old *Monthly Magazine*, December. 1833) there is a slight reference in the forty-second chapter of "David Copperfield," where the youthful hero intimates that he "wrote a little something", in secret, and sent it to a magazine, and it was published in the magazine."

His journeys across country by coach or postchaise, when reporting for his newspaper (the *Morning Chronicle*), proved invaluable from a literary standpoint, inasmuch as those expeditions by day and night and in all seasons afforded him special opportunities of studying human idiosyncrasies, as he necessarily came into contact with "all sorts and conditions of men."

The success of his little paper in the *Monthly Magazine* induced him to try his hand at others, for gratuitous publication in the same journal. They bore no signature until the sixth sketch appeared, when he adopted the curious pseudonym of "Boz": this had for some time been to him a familiar household word, as it was the nickname of his youngest brother, Augustus, whom (in honour of "The Vicar of Wakefield," one of his favourite books) he had dubbed Moses, which, being facetiously pronounced through the nose, became Boses, and being shortened became Boz.

The time had now arrived when he considered himself justified in endeavouring to increase his stipend as a reporter for the *Morning Chronicle* by offering to contribute to its pages a similar series of sketches, for which he should be remunerated, and the proposal was acceded to. Accordingly we find several papers signed "Boz" in the *Evening Chronicle*, an offshoot of the *Morning Chronicle*. Some of his sketches of "Scenes and Characters" (signed "Tibbs") appeared simultaneously in *Bell's Life in London*, and a couple also in "The Library of Fiction," edited by Charles Whitehead. Early in 1836 Dickens collected together a number of these bright little articles and stories, and sold the copyright for £100 to Macrone, who published them in two volumes under the title of "Sketches by Boz."

Although remarkable for their humour and originality, the "Boz" sketches were presently to be eclipsed by a work which immediately took the world by storm, and upon which the reputation of Dickens securely rests. I allude to the ever fascinating "Pickwick Papers," and perhaps the most extraordinary circumstance in connection therewith is the fact that the author was then only three-and-twenty, his book rapidly achieving a degree of popularity which we cannot but regard as astounding even in these days of large editions.

The "Pickwick Papers" originated in this way. The junior partner of what was then a young publishing house, Messrs. Chapman & Hall (now a leading London firm), called upon the rising author at his rooms in Furnivals Inn with a proposition that he should furnish the letterpress for a "monthly something" that should be a vehicle for certain sporting-plates by a humorous draughtsman named Seymour. The first idea of a sort of Nimrod Club did not appeal to Dickens, for the excellent reason that he was no sportsman, and it was therefore eventually decided that, having agreed to supply the text, he should exercise a free hand, allowing the illustrations to arise naturally from the text. To give a complete history of the "Pickwick Papers" would occupy considerable space. Suffice it to say that the book was issued in shilling monthly parts (1836-37), then a favourite method of publishing novels, and consistently adopted by Dickens; that it was illustrated by means of etchings; that the sale of the first few numbers was so small that both publishers and author were in despair; and that the success of the work was assured as soon as Sam Weller made his first bow to the public —a character which, by reason of its freshness and originality, called forth such admiration that the sale of ensuing numbers increased until a circulation of forty thousand copies was attained!

The creation of Sam Weller, therefore, was the turning-point in Dickens's fortune, and so great became the popularity of the book that the name of "Pickwick" was bestowed by enterprising tradesmen upon their newest goods, while portraits of Dickens himself were in the ascendant. People of every degree, young and old, revelled in the pages of the "Pickwick Papers" —judges on the bench as well as boys in the street; and we are reminded of Carlyle's anecdote of a solemn clergyman who, as he left the room of a sick person to whom he had been administering ghostly consolation, heard the invalid ejaculate, "Well, thank God, 'Pickwick' (the monthly number) will be out in ten days, anyway!"

The identity of the author of "Pickwick," by-the-bye, was not disclosed until that work was nearly completed. It had given rise to much conjecture until the name of the young writer was at length revealed, when the following "Impromptu" appeared in *Bentley's Miscellany*: —

> Who the *dickens* "Boz" could be
> Puzzled many a learned elf,
> Till time revealed the mystery,
> And "Boz" appeared as Dickens' self.

As soon as the first number of the "Pickwick Papers" was launched (that is, in April, 1836), its author took unto himself a wife, the bride being Miss Catherine Thomson Hogarth, eldest daughter of Mr. George Hogarth, his fellow-worker on the *Morning Chronicle*. By her he had several children, and among those surviving are Mrs. Kate Perugini, a clever painter, and Mr. Henry Fielding Dickens, the eminent K.C. Mrs. Dickens survived her husband nine years and five months.

Before the last of the twenty numbers of "Pickwick" was launched, the author became a public favourite. Certain sage prophets foretold that as "Boz" had risen like a rocket, he would of a surety fall like the stick. But, as events proved, they were wrong, for Dickens not only became the most popular novelist of the 'thirties and 'forties, but, by the sheer strength of his genius, maintained that supremacy. Story after story flowed from his pen, each characterised by originality of conception, each instinct with a love of humanity in its humblest form, each noteworthy for its humour and its pathos, and nearly every one "a novel with a purpose," having in view the exposure of some great social evil and its ultimate suppression.

Following "Pickwick" came "Oliver Twist," attacking the Poor laws and "Bumbledom"; "Nicholas Nickleby," marking down the cheap boarding-schools of Yorkshire; "The Old Curiosity Shop" and "Barnaby Rudge"; "Martin Cluzzlewit"; "Dombey & Son"; "David Copperfield"; "Bleak House," holding up to ridicule and contempt the abuse of Chancery practice; "Little Dorrit"; "A Tale of Two Cities"; "Great Expectations"; "Our Mutual Friend"; and, finally, the unfinished fragment of "The Mystery of Edwin Drood," to which Longfellow referred as "certainly one of his most beautiful works, if not the most beautiful of all."

Of his many minor writings, special mention should be made of the attractive series of Christmas Books, the first of which, "A Christmas Carol," has become almost a text-book; and we know that, by the reading aloud of this touching little allegory to enthusiastic audiences. Sir Squire Bancroft has afforded substantial aid to many deserving charities. Dickens is appropriately termed "the Apostle of Christmas," and it is undoubtedly true that his Yuletide stories were the pioneers of Christmas literature.

Having thus briefly reviewed the literary career of Charles Dickens, it becomes almost essential to consider him from a personal and social point of view, in order to thoroughly realise what manner of man he was. Referring to his personal characteristics, Forster says that to his friends (and their name was legion) Dickens was "the pleasantest of companions, with whom they forgot that he had ever written anything, and felt only the charm which a nature of such capacity for supreme enjoyment causes every one around it to enjoy. His talk was unaffected and natural, never bookish in the smallest degree. He was quite up to the average of well-read men: but as there was no ostentation of it in his writing, so neither was there in his conversation. This was so attractive because so keenly observant, and lighted up with so many touches of humorous fancy; but with every possible thing to give relish to it, there were not many things to bring away." He thoroughly endorsed the axiom that "what is worth doing at all is worth doing well." He was most methodical in his habits, and energetic to a degree. "In quick and varied sympathy, in ready adaptation to every whim and humour, in help to any mirth or game, he stood for a dozen men...His versatility made him unique."

Concerning the novelist's personality, the following testimony has recently been placed on record by Mr. Percy Fitzgerald, a surviving member of the "Dickens Brigade" of young men who revered him as "the Master": "I say advisedly, there (never?) was, and never could be, so genial, amiable, unaffected, and untiring a person in his treatment of friends and guests. He was always eager to listen rather than to speak-to take a second or third place; more anxious to hear, rather than to tell, an amusing story. His very presence was enough, with the bright, radiant face, the glowing, searching eyes, which had a language of their own, and the expressive mouth. You could see the gleam of a humourous thought, first twinkling there, and had a certain foretaste and even understanding of what was coming: then it spread downwards-the mobile muscles of his cheek began to quiver: then it came lower, to the expressive mouth, working under shelter of the grizzled moustache; then, finally, thus prepared for, came the humorous utterance itself!"

Dickens was intensely fond of the Drama, as evidenced not only by the frequent reference in his writings to theatres and actors, but by the fact that he himself was an actor of an exceptionally high order, and it is conceded that had he adopted the stage as a profession he would have attained first rank. Indeed, it was by the merest accident that he did not enter the profession, for when he was about twenty he applied for an engagement to the stage-manager at Covent Garden Theatre, and an appointment was made, which Dickens failed to keep on account of a terribly bad cold. After that he never resumed the idea. In later years he became the leading spirit of a wonderful company of amateur actors, who, on one occasion, performed before her late Majesty Queen Victoria, by special request. Sir John Tenniel is now the sole survivor of that merry confraternity.

As a reader, too, Dickens stood pre-eminent. It has lately transpired that his very first public reading took place, early in the 'fifties, at Chatham, in aid of the Rochester and Chatham Mechanics' Institution, and the subject of the reading was the "Christmas Carol." He gave public readings from his own works both in Great Britain and America, and an entertaining account of these tours may be found in Mr. George Dolby's volume, "Charles Dickens as I Knew Him." There can be no doubt that the mental tension caused by these readings (which covered a period of some fifteen years), supplemented by the strain of literary and editorial labours, curtailed the brilliant career of England's greatest novelist. It was at his charming rural retreat, Gad's Hill Place, near Rochester (his home from 1856), that Charles Dickens breathed his last, on June 9th, 1870, in his fifty-ninth year. "Before the news of his death even reached the remoter parts of England," says Forster, "it had been flashed across Europe; was known in the distant continents of India, Australia, and America; and not in English-speaking communities only, but in every country of the civilised earth, had awakened grief and sympathy. In his own land it was as if a personal bereavement had befallen everyone." Although he himself would have preferred to lie in the small graveyard under the ancient wall of Rochester Castle, or in the pretty Kentish churchyard of Cobham or Shorne, public sentiment favoured the suggestion that the mortal remains of Charles Dickens should be interred in Westminster Abbey; and there, in Poets' Corner, they were laid to rest, quietly and unostentatiously. What Carlyle said of him, a few days later, will meet with universal acceptance: —

"The good, the gentle, high gifted, ever friendly, noble Dickens, —every inch of him an Honest Man."

Charles Dickens - Critical Study

Chapter 1
The Dickens Period

Much of our modern difficulty, in religion and other things, arises merely from this: that we confuse the word "indefinable" with the word "vague." If some one speaks of a spiritual fact as "indefinable" we promptly picture something misty, a cloud with indeterminate edges. But this is an error even in commonplace logic. The thing that cannot be defined is the first thing; the primary fact. It is our arms and legs, our pots and pans, that are indefinable. The indefinable is the indisputable. The man next door is indefinable, because he is too actual to be defined. And there are some to whom spiritual things have the same fierce and practical proximity; some to whom God is too actual to be defined.

But there is a third class of primary terms. There are popular expressions which every one uses and no one can explain; which the wise man will accept and reverence, as he reverences desire or darkness or any elemental thing. The prigs of the debating club will demand that he should define his terms. And, being a wise man, he will flatly refuse. This first inexplicable term is the most important term of all. The word that has no definition is the word that has no substitute. If a man falls back again and again on some such word as "vulgar" or "manly," do not suppose that the word means nothing because he cannot say what it means. If he could say what the word means he would say what it means instead of saying the word. When the Game Chicken (that fine thinker) kept on saying to Mr. Toots, "It's mean. That's what it is-it's mean," he was using language in the wisest possible way. For what else could he say? There is no word for mean except mean. A man must be very mean himself before he comes to defining meanness. Precisely because the word is indefinable, the word is indispensable.

In everyday talk, or in any of our journals, we may find the loose but important phrase, "Why have we no great men today? Why have we no great men like Thackeray, or Carlyle, or Dickens?" Do not let us dismiss this expression, because it appears loose or arbitrary. "Great" does mean something, and the test of its actuality is to be found by noting how instinctively and decisively we do apply it to some men and not to others; above all, how instinctively and decisively we do apply it to four or five men in the Victorian era, four or five men of whom Dickens was not the least. The term is found to fit a definite thing. Whatever the word "great" means, Dickens was what it means. Even the fastidious and unhappy who cannot read his books without a continuous critical exasperation, would use the word of him without stopping to think. They feel that Dickens is a great writer even if he is not a good writer. He is treated as a classic; that is, as a king who may now be deserted, but who cannot now be dethroned. The atmosphere of this word clings to him; and the curious thing is that we cannot get it to cling to any of the men of our own generation. "Great" is the first adjective which the most supercilious modern critic would apply to Dickens. And "great" is the last adjective that the most supercilious modern critic would apply to himself We dare not claim to be great men, even when we claim to be superior to them.

Is there, then, any vital meaning in this idea of "greatness" or in our laments over its absence in our own time? Some people say, indeed, that this sense of mass is but a mirage of distance, and that men always think dead men great and live men small. They seem to think that the law of perspective in the mental world is the precise opposite to the law of perspective in the physical world. They think that figures grow larger as they walk away. But this theory cannot be made to correspond with the facts. We do not lack great men in our own day because we decline to look for them in our own day; on the contrary, we are looking for them all day long. We are not, as a matter of fact, mere examples of those who stone the prophets and leave it to their posterity to build their sepulchres. If the world would only produce our perfect prophet, solemn, searching, universal, nothing would give us keener pleasure than to build his sepulchre. In our eagerness we might even bury him alive. Nor is it true that the great men of the Victorian era were not called great in their own time. By many they were called great from the first. Charlotte Brontë held this heroic language about Thackeray. Ruskin held it about Carlyle. A definite school regarded Dickens as a great man from the first days of his fame: Dickens certainly belonged to this school.

In reply to this question, "Why have we no great men today?" many modern explanations are offered. Advertisement, cigarette-smoking, the decay of religion, the decay of agriculture, too much humanitarianism, too little humanitarianism, the fact that people are educated insufficiently, the fact that they are educated at all, all these are reasons given. If I give my own explanation, it is not for its intrinsic value; it is because my answer to the question, "Why have we no great men?" is a short way of stating the deepest and most catastrophic difference between the age in which we live and the early nineteenth century; the age under the shadow of the French Revolution, the age in which Dickens was born.

The soundest of the Dickens critics, a man of genius, Mr. George Gissing, opens his criticism by remarking that the world in which Dickens grew up was a hard and cruel world. He notes its gross feeding, its fierce sports, its fighting and foul humour, and all this he summarises in the words hard and cruel. It is curious how different are the impressions of men. To me this old English world seems infinitely less hard and cruel than the world described in Gissing's own novels. Coarse external customs are merely relative, and easily assimilated. A man soon learnt to harden his hands and harden his head. Faced with the world of Gissing, he can do little but harden his heart. But the fundamental difference between the beginning of the nineteenth century and the end of it is a difference simple but enormous. The first period was full of evil things, but it was full of hope. The second period, the fin de siécle, was even full (in some sense) of good things. But it was occupied in asking what was the good of good things. Joy itself became joyless; and the fighting of Cobbett was happier than the feasting of Walter Pater. The men of Cobbett's day were sturdy enough to endure and inflict brutality; but they were also sturdy enough to alter it. This "hard and cruel" age was, after all, the age of reform. The gibbet stood up black above them; but it was black against the dawn.

This dawn, against which the gibbet and all the old cruelties stood out so black and clear, was the developing idea of liberalism, the French Revolution. It was a clear and a happy philosophy. And only against such philosophies do evils appear evident at all. The optimist is a better reformer than the pessimist; and the man who believes life to be excellent is the man who alters it most. It seems a paradox, yet the reason of it is very plain. The pessimist can be enraged at evil. But only the optimist can be surprised at it. From the reformer is required a simplicity of surprise. He must have the faculty of a violent and virgin astonishment. It is not enough that he should think injustice distressing; he must think injustice absurd, an anomaly in existence, a matter less for tears than for a shattering laughter. On the other hand, the pessimists at the end of the century could hardly curse even the blackest thing; for they could hardly see it against its black and eternal background. Nothing was bad, because everything was bad. Life in prison was infamous-like life anywhere else. The fires of persecution were vile-like the stars. We perpetually find this paradox of a contented discontent. Dr. Johnson takes too sad a view of humanity, but he is also too satisfied a Conservative. Rousseau takes too rosy a view of humanity, but he causes a revolution. Swift is angry, but a Tory. Shelley is happy, and a rebel. Dickens, the optimist, satirises the Fleet, and the Fleet is gone. Gissing, the pessimist, satirises Suburbia, and Suburbia remains.

Mr. Gissing's error, then, about the early Dickens period we may put thus: in calling it hard and cruel he omits the wind of hope and humanity that was blowing through it. It may have been full of inhuman institutions, but it was full of humanitarian people. And this humanitarianism was very much the better (in my view) because it was a rough and even rowdy humanitarianism. It was free from all the faults that cling to the name. It was, if you will, a coarse humanitarianism. It was a shouting, fighting, drinking philanthropy—a noble thing. But, in any case, this atmosphere was the atmosphere of the Revolution; and its main idea was the idea of human equality. I am not concerned here to defend the egalitarian idea against the solemn and babyish attacks made upon it by the rich and learned of today. I am merely concerned to state one of its practical consequences. One of the actual and certain consequences of the idea that all men are equal is immediately to produce very great men. I would say superior men, only that the hero thinks of himself as great, but not as superior. This has been hidden from us of late by a foolish worship of sinister and exceptional men, men without comrade-ship, or any infectious virtue. This type of Caesar does exist. There is a great man who makes every man feel small. But the real great man is the man who makes every man feel great.

The spirit of the early century produced great men, because it believed that men were great. It made strong men by encouraging weak men. Its education, its public habits, its rhetoric, were all addressed towards encouraging the greatness in everybody. And by encouraging the greatness in everybody, it naturally encouraged superlative greatness in some. Superiority came out of the high rapture of equality. It is precisely in this sort of passionate unconsciousness and bewildering community of thought that men do become more than themselves. No man by taking thought can add one cubit to his stature; but a man may add many cubits to his stature by not taking thought. The best men of the Revolution were simply common men at their best. This is why our age can never understand Napoleon. Because he was something great and triumphant, we suppose that he must have been something extraordinary, something inhuman. Some say he was the Devil; some say he was the Superman. Was he a very, very bad man? Was he a good man with some greater moral code? We strive in vain to invent the mysteries behind that immortal mask of brass. The modern world with all its subtleness will never guess his strange secret; for his strange secret was that he was very like other people.

And almost without exception all the great men have come out of this atmosphere of equality. Great men may make despotisms; but democracies make great men. The other main factory of heroes besides a revolution is a religion. And a religion again, is a thing which, by its nature, does not think of men as more or less valuable, but of men as all intensely and painfully valuable, a democracy of eternal danger. For religion all men are equal, as all pennies are equal, because the only value in any of them is that they bear the image of the King. This fact has been quite insufficiently observed in the study of religious heroes. Piety produces intellectual greatness precisely because piety in itself is quite indifferent to intellectual greatness. The strength of Cromwell was that he cared for religion. But the strength of religion was that it did not care for Cromwell; did not care for him, that is, any more than for anybody else. He and his footman were equally welcomed to warm places in the hospitality of hell. It has often been said, very truly, that religion is the thing that makes the ordinary man feel extraordinary; it is an equally important truth that religion is the thing that makes the extraordinary man feel ordinary.

Carlyle killed the heroes; there have been none since his time. He killed the heroic (which he sincerely loved) by forcing upon each man this question: "Am I strong or weak?" To which the answer from any honest man whatever (yes, from Caesar or Bismarck) would "weak." He asked for candidates for a definite aristocracy, for men who should hold themselves consciously above their fellows. He advertised for them, so to speak; he promised them glory; he promised them omnipotence. They have not appeared yet. They never will. For the real heroes of whom he wrote had appeared out of an ecstacy of the ordinary. I have already instanced such a case as Cromwell. But there is no need to go through all the great men of Carlyle. Carlyle himself was as great as any of them; and if ever there was a typical child of the French Revolution, it was he. He began with the wildest hopes from the Reform Bill, and although he soured afterwards, he had been made and moulded by those hopes. He was disappointed with Equality; but Equality was not disappointed with him. Equality is justified of all her children.

But we, in the post-Carlylean period, have become fastidious about great men. Every man examines himself, every man examines his neighbours, to see whether they or he quite come up to the exact line of greatness. The answer is, naturally, "No." And many a man calls himself contentedly "a minor poet" who would then have been inspired to be a major prophet. We are hard to please and of little faith. We can hardly believe that there is such a thing as a great man. They could hardly believe there was such a thing as a small one. But we are always praying that our eyes may behold greatness, instead of praying that our hearts may be filled with it. Thus, for instance, the Liberal party (to which I belong) was, in its period of exile, always saying, "O for a Gladstone!" and such things. We were always asking that it might be strengthened from above, instead of ourselves strengthening it from below, with our hope and our anger and our youth. Every man was waiting for a leader. Every man ought to be waiting for a chance to lead. If a god does come upon the earth, he will descend at the sight of the brave. Our prostrations and litanies are of no avail; our new moons and our sabbaths are an abomination. The great man will come when all of us are feeling great, not when all of us are feeling small. He will ride in at some splendid moment when we all feel that we could do without him.

We are then able to answer in some manner the question, "Why have we no great men?" We have no great men chiefly because we are always looking for them. We are connoisseurs of greatness, and connoisseurs can never be great; we are fastidious, that is, we are small. When Diogenes went about with a lantern looking for an honest man, I am afraid he had very little time to be honest himself And when anybody goes about on his hands and knees looking for a great man to worship, he is making sure that one man at any rate shall not be great. Now, the error of Diogenes is evident. The error of Diogenes lay in the fact that he omitted to notice that every man is both an honest man and a dishonest man. Diogenes looked for his honest man inside every crypt and cavern; but he never thought of looking inside the thief And that is where the Founder of Christianity found the honest man; He found him on a gibbet and promised him Paradise. Just as Christianity looked for the honest man inside the thief, democracy looked for the wise man inside the fool. It encouraged the fool to be wise. We can call this thing sometimes optimism, sometimes equality; the nearest name for it is encouragement. It had its exaggerations-failure to understand original sin, notions that education would make all men good, the childlike yet pedantic philosophies of human perfectibility. But the whole was full of a faith in the infinity of human souls, which is in itself not only Christian but orthodox; and this we have lost amid the limitations of a pessimistic science. Christianity said that any man could be a saint if he chose; democracy, that any man could be a citizen if he chose. The note of the last few decades in art and ethics has been that a man is stamped with an irrevocable psychology, and is cramped for perpetuity in the prison of his skull. It was a world that expected everything of everybody. It was a world that encouraged anybody to be anything. And in England and literature its living expression was Dickens.

We shall consider Dickens in many other capacities, but let us put this one first. He was the voice in England of this humane intoxication and expansion, this encouraging of anybody to be anything. His best books are a carnival of liberty, and there is more of the real spirit of the French Revolution in "Nicholas Nickleby" than in "The Tale of Two Cities." His work has the great glory of the Revolution, the bidding of every man to be himself; it has also the revolutionary deficiency: it seems to think that this mere emancipation is enough. No man encouraged his characters so much as Dickens. "I am an affectionate father," he says, "to every child of my fancy." He was not only an affectionate father, he was an over-indulgent father. The children of his fancy are spoilt children. They shake the house like heavy and shouting schoolboys; they smash the story to pieces like so much furniture. When we moderns write stories our characters are better controlled. But, alas! our characters are rather easier to control. We are in no danger from the gigantic gambols of creatures like Mantalini and Micawber. We are in no danger of giving our readers too much Weller or Wegg. We have not got it to give. When we experience the ungovernable sense of life which goes along with the old Dickens sense of liberty, we experience the best of the revolution. We are filled with the first of all democratic doctrines, that all men are interesting; Dickens tried to make some of his people appear dull people, but he could not keep them dull. He could not make a monotonous man. The bores in his books are brighter than the wits in other books.

I have put this position first for a defined reason. It is useless for us to attempt to imagine Dickens and his life unless we are able at least to imagine this old atmosphere of a democratic optimism —a confidence in common men. Dickens depends upon such a comprehension in a rather unusual manner, a manner worth explanation, or at least remark.

The disadvantage under which Dickens has fallen, both as an artist and a moralist, is very plain. His misfortune is that neither of the two last movements in literary criticism has done him any good. He has suffered alike from his enemies, and from the enemies of his enemies. The facts to which I refer are familiar. When the world first awoke from the mere hypnotism of Dickens, from the direct tyranny of his temperament, there was, of course, a reaction. At the head of it came the Realists, with their documents, like Miss Flite. They declared that scenes and types in Dickens were wholly impossible (in which they were perfectly right), and on this rather paradoxical ground objected to them as literature. They were not "like life," and there, they thought, was an end of the matter. The realist for a time prevailed. But Realists did not enjoy their victory (if they enjoyed anything) very long. A more symbolic school of criticism soon arose. Men saw that it was necessary to give a much deeper and more delicate meaning to the expression "like life." Streets are not life, cities and civilisations are not life, faces even and voices are not life itself Life is within, and no man hath seen it at any time. As for our meals, and our manners, and our daily dress, these are things exactly like sonnets; they are random symbols of the soul. One man tries to express himself in books, another in boots; both probably fail. Our solid houses and square meals are in the strict sense fiction. They are things made up to typify our thoughts. The coat a man wears may be wholly fictitious; the movement of his hands may be quite unlike life.

This much the intelligence of men soon perceived. And by this much Dickens's fame should have greatly profited. For Dickens is "like life" in the truer sense, in the sense that he is akin to the living principle in us and in the universe; he is like life, at least in this detail, that he is alive. His art is like life, because, like life, it cares for nothing outside itself, and goes on its way rejoicing. Both produce monsters with a kind of carelessness, like enormous by-products; life producing the rhinoceros, and art Mr. Bunsby. Art indeed copies life in not copying life, for life copies nothing. Dickens's art is like life because, like life, it is irresponsible, because, like life, it is incredible.

Yet the return of this realisation has not greatly profited Dickens, the return of romance has been almost useless to this great romantic. He has gained as little from the fall of the realists as from their triumph; there has been a revolution, there has been a counter revolution, there has been no restoration. And the reason of this brings us back to that atmosphere of popular optimism of which I spoke. And the shortest way of expressing the more recent neglect of Dickens is to say that for our time and taste he exaggerates the wrong thing.

Exaggeration is the definition of art. That both Dickens and the Moderns understood. Art is, in its inmost nature, fantastic. Time brings queer revenges, and while the realists were yet living, the art of Dickens was justified by Aubrey Beardsley. But men like Aubrey Beardsley were allowed to be fantastic, because the mood which they overstrained and overstated was a mood which their period understood. Dickens overstrains and overstates a mood our period does not understand. The truth he exaggerates is exactly this old Revolution sense of infinite opportunity and boisterous brotherhood. And we resent his undue sense of it, because we ourselves have not even a due sense of it. We feel troubled with too much where we have too little; we wish he would keep it within bounds. For we are all exact and scientific on the subjects we do not care about. We all immediately detect exaggeration in an exposition of Mormonism or a patriotic speech from Paraguay. We all require sobriety on the subject of the sea-serpent. But the moment we begin to believe a thing ourselves, that moment we begin easily to overstate it; and the moment our souls become serious, our words become a little wild. And certain moderns are thus placed towards exaggeration. They permit any writer to emphasise doubts for instance, for doubts are their religion, but they permit no man to emphasise dogmas. If a man be the mildest Christian, they smell "cant;" but he can be a raving windmill of pessimism, "and they call it 'temperament." If a moralist paints a wild picture of immorality, they doubt its truth, they say that devils are not so black as they are painted. But if a pessimist paints a wild picture of melancholy, they accept the whole horrible psychology, and they never ask if devils are as blue as they are painted.

It is evident, in short, why even those who admire exaggeration do not admire Dickens. He is exaggerating the wrong thing. They know what it is to feel a sadness so strange and deep that only impossible characters can express it: they do not know what it is to feel a joy so vital and violent that only impossible characters can express that. They know that the soul can be so sad as to dream naturally of the blue faces of the corpses of Baudelaire: they do not know that the soul can be so cheerful as to dream naturally of the blue face of Major Bagstock. They know that there is a point of depression at which one believes in Tintagiles: they do not know that there is a point of exhilaration at which one believes in Mr. Wegg. To them the impossibilities of Dickens seem much more impossible than they really are, because they are already attuned to the opposite impossibilities of Maeterlinck. For every mood there is an appropriate impossibility —a decent and tactful impossibility-fitted to the frame of mind. Every train of thought may end in an ecstasy, and all roads lead to Elfland. But few now walk far enough along the street of Dickens to find the place where the cockney villas grow so comic that they become poetical. People do not know how far mere good spirits will go. For instance, we never think (as the old folk-lore did) of good spirits reaching to the spiritual world. We see this in the complete absence from modern, popular supernaturalism of the old popular mirth. We hear plenty today of the wisdom of the spiritual world; but we do not hear, as our fathers did, of the folly of the spiritual world, of the tricks of the gods, and the jokes of the patron saints. Our popular tales tell us of a man who is so wise that he touches the supernatural, like Dr. Nikola; but they never tell us (like the popular tales of the past) of a man who was so silly that he touched the supernatural, like Bottom the Weaver. We do not understand the dark and transcendental sympathy between fairies and fools. We understand a devout occultism, an evil occultism, a tragic occultism, but a farcical occultism is beyond us. Yet a farcical occultism is the very essence of "The Midsummer Night's Dream." It is also the right and credible essence of "The Christmas Carol." Whether we understand it depends upon whether we can understand that exhilaration is not a physical accident, but a mystical fact; that exhilaration can be infinite, like sorrow; that a joke can be so big that it breaks the roof of the stars. By simply going on being absurd, a thing can become godlike; there is but one step from the ridiculous to the sublime.

Dickens was great because he was immoderately possessed with all this; if we are to understand him at all we must also be moderately possessed with it. We must understand this old limitless hilarity and human confidence, at least enough to be able to endure it when it is pushed a great deal too far. For Dickens did push it too far; he did push the hilarity to the point of incredible character-drawing; he did push the human confidence to the point of an unconvincing sentimentalism. You can trace, if you will, the revolutionary joy till it reaches the incredible Sapsea epitaph; you can trace the revolutionary hope till it reaches the repentance of Dombey. There is plenty to carp at in this man if you are inclined to carp; you may easily find him vulgar if you cannot see that he is divine; and if you cannot laugh with Dickens, undoubtedly you can laugh at him.

I believe myself that this braver world of his will certainly return; for I believe that it is bound up with the realities, like morning and the spring. But for those who beyond remedy regard it as an error, I put this appeal before any other observations on Dickens. First let us sympathise, if only for an instant, with the hopes of the Dickens period, with that cheerful trouble of change. If democracy has disappointed you, do not think of it as a burst bubble, but at least as a broken heart, an old love-affair. Do not sneer at the time when the creed of humanity was on its honeymoon; treat it with the dreadful reverence that is due to youth. For you, perhaps, a drearier philosophy has covered and eclipsed the earth. The fierce poet of the Middle Ages wrote, "Abandon hope, all ye who enter here," over the gates of the lower world. The emancipated poets of today have written it over the gates of this world. But if we are to understand the story which follows, we must erase that apocalyptic writing, if only for an hour. We must recreate the faith of our fathers, if only as an artistic atmosphere If, then, you are a pessimist, in reading this story, forego for a little the pleasures of pessimism. Dream for one mad moment that the grass is green. Unlearn that sinister learning that you think so clear; deny that deadly knowledge that you think you know. Surrender the very flower of your culture; give up the very jewel of your pride; abandon hopelessness, all ye who enter here.

Chapter 2
The Boyhood of Dickens

Charles Dickens was born at Landport, in Portsea, on February 7, 1812. His father was a clerk in the Navy Pay-office, and was temporarily on duty in the neighbourhood. Very soon after the birth of Charles Dickens, however, the family moved for a short period to Norfolk Street, Bloomsbury, and then for a long period to Chatham, which thus became the real home, and for all serious purposes, the native place of Dickens. The whole story of his life moves like a Canterbury pilgrimage along the great roads of Kent.

John Dickens, his father, was, as stated, a clerk; but such mere terms of trade tell us little of the tone or status of a family. Browning's father (to take an instance at random) would also be described as a clerk and a man of the middle class; but the Browning family and the Dickens family have the colour of two different civilisations. The difference cannot be conveyed merely by saying that Browning stood many strata above Dickens. It must also be conveyed that Browning belonged to that section of the middle class which tends (in the small social sense) to rise; the Dickenses to that section which tends in the same sense to fall. If Browning had not been a poet, he would have been a better clerk than his father, and his son probably a better and richer clerk than he. But if they had not been lifted in the air by the enormous accident of a man of genius, the Dickenses, I fancy, would have appeared in poorer and poorer places, as inventory clerks, as caretakers, as addressers of envelopes, until they melted into the masses of the poor.

Yet at the time of Dickens's birth and childhood this weakness in their worldly destiny was in no way apparent; especially it was not apparent to the little Charles himself. He was born and grew up in a paradise of small prosperity. He fell into the family, so to speak, during one of its comfortable periods, and he never in those early days thought of himself as anything but as a comfortable middle-class child, the son of a comfortable middle-class man. The father whom he found provided for him, was one from whom comfort drew forth his most pleasant and reassuring qualities, though not perhaps his most interesting and peculiar. John Dickens seemed, most probably, a hearty and kindly character, a little florid of speech, a little careless of duty in some details, notably in the detail of education. His neglect of his son's mental training in later and more trying times was a piece of unconscious selfishness which remained a little acrimoniously in his son's mind through life. But even in this earlier and easier period what records there are of John Dickens give out the air of a somewhat idle and irresponsible fatherhood. He exhibited towards his son that contradiction in conduct which is always shown by the too thoughtless parent to the too thoughtful child. He contrived at once to neglect his mind, and also to over-stimulate it.

There are many recorded tales and traits of the author's infancy, but one small fact seems to me more than any other to strike the note and give the key to his whole strange character. His father found it more amusing to be an audience than to be an instructor; and instead of giving the child intellectual pleasure, called upon him, almost before he was out of petticoats, to provide it. Some of the earliest glimpses we have of Charles Dickens show him to us perched on some chair or table singing comic songs in an atmosphere of perpetual applause. So, almost as soon as he can toddle, he steps into the glare of the footlights. He never stepped out of it until he died. He was a good man, as men go in this bewildering world of ours, brave, transparent, tender-hearted, scrupulously independent and honourable; he was not a man whose weaknesses should be spoken of without some delicacy and doubt. But there did mingle with his merits all his life this theatrical quality, this atmosphere of being shown off—a sort of hilarious self-consciousness. His literary life was a triumphal procession; he died drunken with glory. And behind all this nine years' wonder that filled the world, behind his gigantic tours and his ten thousand editions, the crowded lectures and the crashing brass, behind all the thing we really see is the flushed face of a little boy singing music-hall songs to a circle of aunts and uncles. And this precocious pleasure explains much, too, in the moral way. Dickens had all his life the faults of the little boy who is kept up too late at night. The boy in such a case exhibits a psychological paradox; he is a little too irritable because he is a little too happy. Dickens was always a little too irritable because he was a little too happy. Like the overwrought child in society, he was splendidly sociable, and yet suddenly quarrelsome. In all the practical relations of his life he was what the child is in the last hours of an evening party, genuinely delighted, genuinely delightful, genuinely affectionate and happy, and yet in some strange way fundamentally exasperated and dangerously close to tears.

There was another touch about the boy which made his case more peculiar, and perhaps his intelligence more fervid; the touch of ill-health. It could not be called more than a touch, for he suffered from no formidable malady and could always through life endure a great degree of exertion, even if it was only the exertion of walking violently all night. Still the streak of sickness was sufficient to take him out of the common unconscious life of the community of boys; and for good or evil that withdrawal is always a matter of deadly importance to the mind. He was thrown back perpetually upon the pleasures of the intelligence, and these began to burn in his head like a pent and painful furnace. In his own unvaryingly vivid way he has described how he crawled up into an unconsidered garret, and there found, in a dusty heap, the undying literature of England. The books he mentions chiefly are "Humphrey Clinker" and "Tom Jones." When he opened those two books in the garret he caught hold of the only past with which he is at all connected, the great comic writers of England of whom he was destined to be the last.

It must be remembered (as I have suggested before) that there was something about the county in which he lived, and the great roads along which he travelled that sympathised with and stimulated his pleasure in this old picaresque literature. The groups that came along the road, that passed through his town and out of it, were of the motley laughable type that tumbled into ditches or beat down the doors of taverns under the escort of Smollett and Fielding. In our time the main roads of Kent have upon them very often a perpetual procession of tramps and tinkers unknown on the quiet hills of Sussex; and it may have been so also in Dickens's boyhood. In his neighbourhood were definite memorials of yet older and yet greater English comedy. From the height of Gads-hill at which he stared unceasingly there looked down upon him the monstrous ghost of Falstaff, Falstaff who might well have been the spiritual father of all Dickens's adorable knaves, Falstaff the great mountain of English laughter and English sentimentalism, the great, healthy, humane English humbug, not to be matched among the nations.

At this eminence of Gads-hill Dickens used to stare even as a boy with the steady purpose of some day making it his own. It is characteristic of the consistency which underlies the superficially erratic career of Dickens that he actually did live to make it his own. The truth is that he was a precocious child, precocious not only on the more poetical but on the more prosaic side of life. He was ambitious as well as enthusiastic. No one can ever know what visions they were that crowded into the head of the clever little brat as he ran about the streets of Chatham or stood glowering at Gads-hill. But I think that quite mundane visions had a very considerable share in the matter. He longed to go to school (a strange wish), to go to college, to make a name, nor did he merely aspire to these things; the great number of them he also expected. He regarded himself as a child of good position just about to enter on a life of good luck. He thought his home and family a very good spring-board or jumping-off place from which to fling himself to the positions which he desired to reach. And almost as he was about to spring the whole structure broke under him, and he and all that belonged to him disappeared into a darkness far below.

Everything had been struck down as with the finality of a thunder-bolt. His lordly father was a bankrupt, and in the Marshalsea prison. His mother was in a mean home in the north of London, wildly proclaiming herself the principal of a girl's school, a girl's school to which nobody would go. And he himself, the conqueror of the world and the prospective purchaser of Gads-hill, passed some distracted and bewildering days in pawning the household necessities to Fagins in foul shops, and then found himself somehow or other one of a row of ragged boys in a great dreary factory, pasting the same kinds of labels on to the same kinds of blacking-bottles from morning till night.

Although it seemed sudden enough to him, the disintegration had, as a matter of fact, of course, been going on for a long time. He had only heard from his father dark and melodramatic allusions to a "deed" which, from the way it was mentioned, might have been a claim to the crown or a compact with the devil, but which was in truth an unsuccessful documentary attempt on the part of John Dickens to come to a composition with his creditors. And now, in the lurid light of his sunset, the character of John Dickens began to take on those purple colours which have made him under another name absurd and immortal. It required a tragedy to bring out this man's comedy. So long as John Dickens was in easy circumstances, he seemed only an easy man, a little long and luxuriant in his phrases, a little careless in his business routine. He seemed only a wordy man, who lived on bread and beef like his neighbours; but as bread and beef were successively taken away from him, it was discovered that he lived on words. For him to be involved in a calamity only meant to be cast for the first part in a tragedy. For him blank ruin was only a subject for blank verse. Henceforth we feel scarcely inclined to call him John Dickens at all; we feel inclined to call him by the name through which his son celebrated this preposterous and sublime victory of the human spirit over circumstances. Dickens, in "David Copperfield," called him Wilkins Micawber. In his personal correspondence he called him the Prodigal Father.

Young Charles had been hurriedly flung into the factory by the more or less careless good-nature of James Lamert, a relation of his mother's; it was a blacking factory, supposed to be run as a rival to Warren's by another and "original" Warren, both practically conducted by another of the Lamerts. It was situated near Hungerford Market. Dickens worked there drearily, like one stunned with disappointment. To a child excessively intellectualised, and at this time, I fear, excessively egotistical, the coarseness of the whole thing-the work, the rooms, the boys, the language-was a sort of bestial nightmare. Not only did he scarcely speak of it then, but he scarcely spoke of it afterwards. Years later, in the fulness of his fame, he heard from Forster that a man had spoken of knowing him. On hearing the name, he somewhat curtly acknowledged it, and spoke of having seen the man once. Forster, in his innocence, answered that the man said he had seen Dickens many times in a factory by Hungerford Market. Dickens was suddenly struck with a long and extraordinary silence. Then he invited Forster, as his best friend, to a particular interview, and, with every appearance of difficulty and distress, told him the whole story for the first and the last time. A long while after that he told the world some part of the matter in the account of Murdstone and Grinby's in "David Copperfield." He never spoke of the whole experience except once or twice, and he never spoke of it otherwise than as a man might speak of hell.

It need not be suggested, I think, that this agony in the child was exaggerated by the man. It is true that he was not incapable of the vice of exaggeration, if it be a vice. There was about him much vanity and a certain virulence in his version of many things. Upon the whole, indeed, it would hardly be too much to say that he would have exaggerated any sorrow he talked about. But this was a sorrow with a very strange position in Dickens's life; it was a sorrow he did not talk about. Upon this particular dark spot he kept a sort of deadly silence for twenty years. An accident revealed part of the truth to the dearest of all his friends. He then told the whole truth to the dearest of all his friends. He never told anybody else. I do not think that this arose from any social sense of disgrace; if he had it slightly at the time, he was far too self-satisfied a man to have taken it seriously in after life. I really think that his pain at this time was so real and ugly that the thought of it filled him with that sort of impersonal but unbearable shame with which we are filled, for instance, by the notion of physical torture, of something that humiliates humanity. He felt that such agony was something obscene. Moreover there are two other good reasons for thinking that his sense of hopelessness was very genuine. First of all, this starless outlook is common in the calamities of boyhood. The bitterness of boyish distresses does not lie in the fact that they are large; it lies in the fact that we do not know that they are small. About any early disaster there is a dreadful finality; a lost child can suffer like a lost soul.

It is currently said that hope goes with youth, and lends to youth its wings of a butterfly; but I fancy that hope is the last gift given to man, and the only gift not given to youth. Youth is preeminently the period in which a man can be lyric, fanatical, poetic; but youth is the period in which a man can be hopeless. The end of every episode is the end of the world. But the power of hoping through everything, the knowledge that the soul survives its adventures, that great inspiration comes to the middle-aged; God has kept that good wine until now. It is from the backs of the elderly gentlemen that the wings of the butterfly should burst. There is nothing that so much mystifies the young as the consistent frivolity of the old. They have discovered their indestructibility. They are in their second and clearer childhood, and there is a meaning in the merriment of their eyes. They have seen the end of the End of the World.

First, then, the desolate finality of Dickens's childish mood makes me think it was a real one. And there is another thing to be remembered. Dickens was not a saintly child, after the style of Little Dorrit or Little Nell. He had not, at this time at any rate, set his heart wholly upon higher things, even upon things such as personal tenderness or loyalty. He had been, and was, unless I am very much mistaken, sincerely, stubbornly, bitterly ambitious. He had, I fancy, a fairly clear idea previous to the downfall of all his family's hopes of what he wanted to do in the world, and of the mark that he meant to make there. In no dishonourable sense, but still in a definite sense, he might, in early life, be called worldly; and the children of this world are in their generation infinitely more sensitive than the children of light. A saint after repentance will forgive himself for a sin; a man about town will never forgive himself for a faux pas. There are ways of getting absolved for murder; there are no ways of getting absolved for upsetting the soup. This thin-skinned quality in all very mundane people is a thing too little remembered; and it must not be wholly forgotten in connection with a clever, restless lad who dreamed of a destiny. That part of his distress which concerned himself and his social standing was among the other parts of it the least noble; but perhaps it was the most painful. For pride is not only, as the modern world fails to understand, a sin to be condemned; it is also (as it understands even less) a weakness to be very much commiserated. A very vitalising touch is given in one of his own reminiscences. His most unendurable moment did not come in any bullying in the factory or any famine in the streets. It came when he went to see his sister Fanny take a prize at the Royal Academy of Music. "I could not bear to think of myself-beyond the reach of all such honourable emulation and success. The tears ran down my face. I felt as if my heart were rent. I prayed when I went to bed that night to be lifted out of the humiliation and neglect in which I was. I never had suffered so much before. There was no envy in this." I do not think that there was, though the poor little wretch could hardly have been blamed if there had been. There was only a furious sense of frustration; a spirit like a wild beast in a cage. It was only a small matter in the external and obvious sense; it was only Dickens prevented from being Dickens.

If we put these facts together, that the tragedy seemed final, and that the tragedy was concerned with the supersensitive matters of the ego and the gentleman, I think we can imagine a pretty genuine case of internal depression. And when we add to the case of internal depression the case of the external oppression, the case of the material circumstances by which he was surrounded, we have reached a sort of midnight. All day he worked on insufficient food at a factory. It is sufficient to say that it afterwards appeared in his works as Murdstone and Grinby's. At night he returned disconsolately to a lodging-house for such lads, kept by an old lady. It is sufficient to say that she appeared afterwards as Mrs. Pipchin. Once a week only he saw anybody for whom he cared a straw; that was when he went to the Marshalsea prison, and that gave his juvenile pride, half manly and half snobbish, bitter annoyance of another kind. Add to this, finally, that physically he was always very weak and never very well. Once he was struck down in the middle of his work with sudden bodily pain. The boy who worked next to him, a coarse and heavy lad named Bob Fagin, who had often attacked Dickens on the not unreasonable ground of his being a "gentleman," suddenly showed that enduring sanity of compassion which Dickens had destined to show so often in the characters of the common and unclean. Fagin made a bed for his sick companion out of the straw in the workroom, and filled empty blacking bottles with hot water all day. When the evening came, and Dickens was somewhat recovered, Bob Fagin insisted on escorting the boy home to his father. The situation was as poignant as a sort of tragic farce. Fagin in his wooden-headed chivalry would have died in order to take Dickens to his family; Dickens in his bitter gentility would have died rather than let Fagin know that his family were in the Marshalsea. So these two young idiots tramped the tedious streets, both stubborn, both suffering for an idea. The advantage certainly was with Fagin, who was suffering for a Christian compassion, while Dickens was suffering for a pagan pride. At last Dickens flung off his friend with desperate farewell and thanks, and dashed up the steps of a strange house on the Surrey side. He knocked and rang as Bob Fagin, his benefactor and his incubus, disappeared round the corner. And when the servant came to open the door, he asked, apparently with gravity, whether Mr. Robert Fagin lived there. It is a strange touch. The immortal Dickens woke in him for an instant in that last wild joke of that weary evening. Next morning, however, he was again well enough to make himself ill again, and the wheels of the great factory went on. They manufactured a number of bottles of Warren's Blacking, and in the course of the process they manufactured also the greatest optimist of the nineteenth century.

This boy who dropped down groaning at his work, who was hungry four or five times a week, whose best feelings and worst feelings were alike flayed alive, was the man on whom two generations of comfortable critics have visited the complaint that his view of life was too rosy to be anything but unreal. Afterwards, and in its proper place, I shall speak of what is called the optimism of Dickens, and of whether it was really too cheerful or too smooth. But this boyhood of his may be recorded now as a mere fact. If he was too happy, this was where he learnt it. If his school of thought was a vulgar optimism, this is where he went to school. If he learnt to whitewash the universe, it was in a blacking factory that he learnt it.

As a fact, there is no shred of evidence to show that those who have had sad experiences tend to have a sad philosophy. There are numberless points upon which Dickens is spiritually at one with the poor, that is, with the great mass of mankind. But there is no point in which he is more perfectly at one with them than in showing that there is no kind of connection between a man being unhappy and a man being pessimistic. Sorrow and pessimism are indeed, in a sense, opposite things, since sorrow is founded on the value of something, and pessimism upon the value of nothing. And in practice we find that those poets or political leaders who come from the people, and whose experiences have really been searching and cruel, are the most sanguine people in the world. These men out of the old agony are always optimists; they are sometimes offensive optimists. A man like Robert Burns, whose father (like Dickens's father) goes bankrupt, whose whole life is a struggle against miserable external powers and internal weaknesses yet more miserable —a man whose life begins grey and ends black-Burns does not merely sing about the goodness of life, he positively rants and cants about it. Rousseau, whom all his friends and acquaintances treated almost as badly as he treated them-Rousseau does not grow merely eloquent, he grows gushing and sentimental, about the inherent goodness of human nature. Charles Dickens, who was most miserable at the receptive age when most people are most happy, is afterwards happy when all men weep. Circumstances break men's bones; it has never been shown that they break men's optimism. These great popular leaders do all kinds of desperate things under the immediate scourge of tragedy. They become drunkards; they become demagogues; they become morphomaniacs. They never become pessimists. Most unquestionably there are ragged and unhappy men whom we could easily understand being pessimists. But as a matter of fact they are not pessimists. Most unquestionably there are whole dim hordes of humanity whom we should promptly pardon if they cursed God. But they don't. The pessimists are aristocrats like Byron; the men who curse God are aristocrats like Swinburne. But when those who starve and suffer speak for a moment, they do not profess merely an optimism, they profess a cheap optimism; they are too poor to afford a dear one. They cannot indulge in any detailed or merely logical defence of life; that would be to delay the enjoyment of it. These higher optimists, of whom Dickens was one, do not approve of the universe; they do not even admire the universe; they fall in love with it. They embrace life too close to criticise or even to see it. Existence to such men has the wild beauty of a woman, and those love her with most intensity who love her with least cause.

Chapter 3
The Youth of Dickens

There are popular phrases so picturesque that even when they are intentionally funny they are unintentionally poetical. I remember, to take one instance out of many, hearing a heated Secularist in Hyde Park apply to some parson or other the exquisite expression, "a sky-pilot." Subsequent inquiry has taught me that the term is intended to be comic and even contemptuous; but in the first freshness of it I went home repeating it to myself like a new poem. Few of the pious legends have conceived so strange and yet celestial a picture as this of a pilot in the sky, leaning on his helm above the empty heavens, and carrying his cargo of souls higher than the loneliest cloud. The phrase is like a lyric of Shelley. Or, to take another instance from another language, the French have an incomparable idiom for a boy playing truant; "Il fait l'école buissonnière" —he goes to the bushy school, or the school among the bushes. How admirably this accidental expression, "the bushy school" (not to be lightly confounded with the Art School at Bushey) —how admirably this "bushy school" expresses half the modern notions of a more natural education! The two words express the whole poetry of Wordsworth, the whole philosophy of Thoreau, and are quite as good literature as either.

Now, among a million of such scraps of inspired slang there is one which describes a certain side of Dickens better than pages of explanation. The phrase, appropriately enough, occurs at least once in his works, and that on a fitting occasion. When Job Trotter is sent by Sam on a wild chase after Mr. Perker, the solicitor, Mr. Perker's clerk condoles with Job upon the lateness of the hour, and the fact that all habitable places are shut up. "My friend," says Mr. Perker's clerk, "you've got the key of the street." Mr. Perker's clerk, who was a flippant and scornful young man, may perhaps be pardoned if he used this expression in a flippant and scornful sense; but let us hope that Dickens did not. Let us hope that Dickens saw the strange, yet satisfying, imaginative justice of the words; for Dickens himself had, in the most sacred and serious sense of the term, the key of the street. When we shut 'out anything, we are shut out of that thing. When we shut out the street, we are shut out of the street. Few of us understand the street. Even when we step into it, as into a house or room of strangers. Few of us see through the shining riddle of the street, the strange folk that belong to the street only-the street-walker or the street-arab, the nomads who, generation after generation, have kept their ancient secrets in the full blaze of the sun. Of the street at night many of us know even less. The street at night is a great house locked up. But Dickens had, if ever man had, the key of the street; his stars were the lamps of the street; his hero was the man in the street. He could open the inmost door of his house-the door that leads into that secret passage which is lined with houses and roofed with stars.

This silent transformation into a citizen of the street took place during those dark days of boyhood, when Dickens was drudging at the factory. When ever he had done drudging, he had no other resource but drifting, and he drifted over half London. He was a dreamy child, thinking mostly of his own dreary prospects. Yet he saw and remembered much of the streets and squares he passed. Indeed, as a matter of fact, he went the right way to work unconsciously to do so. He did not go in for "observation," a priggish habit; he did not look at Charing Cross to improve his mind or count the lamp-posts in Holborn to practise his arithmetic. But unconsciously he made all these places the scenes of the monstrous drama in his miserable little soul. He walked in darkness under the lamps of Holborn, and was crucified at Charing Cross. So for him ever afterwards these places had the beauty that only belongs to battlefields. For our memory never fixes the facts which we have merely observed. The only way to remember a place for ever is to live in the place for an hour; and the only way to live in the place for an hour is to forget the place for an hour. The undying scenes we can all see if we shut our eyes are not the scenes that we have stared at under the direction of guide-books; the scenes we see are the scenes at which we did not look at all-the scenes in which we walked when we were thinking about something else-about a sin, or a love affair, or some childish sorrow. We can see the background now because we did not see it then. So Dickens did not stamp these places on his mind; he stamped his mind on these places. For him ever afterwards these streets were mortally romantic; they were dipped in the purple dyes of youth and its tragedy, and rich with irrevocable sunsets.

Herein is the whole secret of that eerie realism with which Dickens could always vitalise some dark or dull corner of London. There are details in the Dickens descriptions—a window, or a railing, or the keyhole of a door-which he endows with demoniac life. The things seem more actual than things really are. Indeed, that degree of realism does not exist in reality; it is the unbearable realism of a dream. And this kind of realism can only be gained by walking dreamily in a place; it cannot be gained by walking observantly. Dickens himself has given a perfect instance of how these nightmare minutiae grew upon him in his trance of abstraction. He mentions among the coffee-shops into which he crept in those wretched days one in St. Martin's Lane, "of which I only recollect it stood near the church, and that in the door there was an oval glass plate with 'COFFEE ROOM' painted on it, addressed towards the street. If I ever find myself in a very different kind of coffee-room now, but where there is an inscription on glass, and read it backwards on the wrong side, MOOR EEFFOC (as I often used to do then in a dismal reverie), a shock goes through my blood." That wild word, "Moor Eeffoc," is the motto of all effective realism; it is the masterpiece of the good realistic principle-the principle that the most fantastic thing of all is often the precise fact. And that elfish kind of realism Dickens adopted everywhere. His world was alive with inanimate object. The date on the door danced over Mr. Grewgious's, the knocker grinned at Mr. Scrooge, the Roman on the ceiling pointed down at Mr. Tulkinghorn, the elderly armchair leered at Tom Smart-these are all moor eeffocish things. A man sees them because he does not look at them.

And so the little Dickens Dickensised London. He prepared the way for all his personages. Into whatever cranny of our city his characters might crawl, Dickens had been there before them. However wild were the events he narrated as outside him, they could not be wilder than the things that had gone on within. However queer a character of Dickens might be, he could hardly be queerer than Dickens was. The whole secret of his after-writings is sealed up in those silent years of which no written word remains. Those years did him harm perhaps, as his biographer, Forster, has thoughtfully suggested, by sharpening a certain fierce individualism in him which once or twice during his genial life flashed like a half-hidden knife. He was always generous; but things had gone too hardly with him for him to be always easy-going. He was always kind-hearted; he was not always good-humoured. Those years may also, in their strange mixture of morbidity and reality, have increased in him his tendency to exaggeration. But we can scarcely lament this in a literary sense; exaggeration is almost the definition of art-and it is entirely the definition of Dickens's art. Those years may have given him many moral and mental wounds, from which he never recovered. But they gave him the key of the street.

There is a weird contradiction in the soul of the born optimist. He can be happy and unhappy at the same time. With Dickens the practical depression of his life at this time did nothing to prevent him from laying up those hilarious memories of which all his books are made. No doubt he was genuinely unhappy in the poor place where his mother kept school. Nevertheless it was there that he noticed the unfathomable quaintness of the little servant whom he made into the Marchioness. No doubt he was comfortless enough at the boarding-house of Mrs. Roylance; but he perceived with a dreadful joy that Mrs. Roylance's name was Pipchin. There seems to be no incompatibility between taking in tragedy and giving out comedy; they are able to run parallel in the same personality. One incident which he described in his unfinished "autobiography," and which he afterwards transferred almost verbatim to David Copperfield, was peculiarly rich and impressive. It was the inauguration of a petition to the King for a bounty, drawn up by a committee of the prisoners in the Marshalsea, a committee of which Dickens's father was the president, no doubt in virtue of his oratory, and also the scribe no doubt in virtue of his genuine love of literary flights.

"As many of the principal officers of this body as could be got into a small room without filling it up, supported him in front of the petition; and my old friend, Captain Porter (who had washed himself to do honour to so solemn an occasion), stationed himself close to it, to read it to all who were unacquainted with its contents. The door was then thrown open, and they began to come in in a long file; several waiting on the landing outside, while one entered, affixed his signature, and went out. To everybody in succession Captain Porter said, 'Would you like to hear it read?' If he weakly showed the least disposition to hear it, Captain Porter in a loud sonorous voice gave him every word of it. I remember a certain luscious roll he gave to such words as 'Majesty-Gracious Majesty-Your Gracious Majesty's unfortunate subjects-Your Majesty's well-known munificence,' as if the words were something real in his mouth and delicious to taste: my poor father meanwhile listening with a little of an author's vanity and contemplating (not severely) the spike on the opposite wall. Whatever was comical or pathetic in this scene, I sincerely believe I perceived in my corner, whether I demonstrated it or not, quite as well as I should perceive it now. I made out my own little character and story for every man who put his name to the sheet of paper."

Here we see very plainly that Dickens did not merely look back in after days and see that these humours had been delightful. He was delighted at the same moment that he was desperate. The two opposite things existed in him simultaneously, and each in its full strength. His soul was not a mixed colour like grey and purple, caused by no component colour being quite itself. His soul was like a shot silk of black and crimson, a shot silk of misery and joy.

Seen from the outside, his little pleasures and extravagances seem more pathetic than his grief. Once the solemn little figure went into a public-house in Parliament Street, and addressed the man behind the bar in the following terms:—"What is your very best-the VERY best ale a glass?" The man replied, "Twopence." "Then," said the infant, "just draw me a glass of that, if you please, with a good head to it." "The landlord," says Dickens, in telling the story, "looked at me in return over the bar from head to foot with a strange smile on his face; and instead of drawing the beer looked round the screen and said something to his wife, who came out from behind it with her work in her hand and joined him in surveying me . . . They asked me a good many questions as to what my name was, how old I was, where I lived, howl was employed, etc., etc. To all of which, that I might commit nobody, I invented appropriate answers. They served me with the ale, though I suspect it was not the strongest on the premises; and the landlord's wife, opening the little half-door, and bending down, gave me a kiss." Here he touches that other side of common life which he was chiefly to champion; he was to show that there is no ale like the ale of a poor man's festival, and no pleasures like the pleasures of the poor. At other places of refreshment he was yet more majestic. "I remember," he says, "tucking my own bread (which I had brought from home in the morning) under my arm, wrapt up in a piece of paper like a book, and going into the best dining-room in Johnson's Alamode Beef House in Clare Court, Drury Lane, and magnificently ordering a small plate of à-la-mode beef to eat with it. What the waiter thought of such a strange little apparition coming in all alone I don't know; but I can see him now staring at me as I ate my dinner, and bringing up the other waiter to look. I gave him a halfpenny, and I wish, now, that he hadn't taken it."

For the boy individually the prospect seemed to be growing drearier and drearier. This phrase indeed hardly expresses the fact; for, as he felt it, it was not so much a run of worsening luck as the closing in of a certain and quiet calamity like the coming on of twilight and dark. He felt that he would die and be buried in blacking. Through all this he does not seem to have said much to his parents of his distress. They who were in prison had certainly a much jollier time than he who was free. But of all the strange ways in which the human being proves that he is not a rational being, whatever else he is, no case is so mysterious and unaccountable as the secrecy of childhood. We learn of the cruelty of some school or child-factory from journalists; we learn it from inspectors, we learn it from doctors, we learn it even from shame-stricken schoolmasters and repentant sweaters; but we never learn it from the children; we never learn it from the victims. It would seem as if a living creature had to be taught, like an art of culture, the art of crying out when it is hurt. It would seem as if patience were the natural thing; it would seem as if impatience were an accomplishment like whist. However this may be, it is wholly certain that Dickens might have drudged and died drudging, and buried the unborn Pickwick, but for an external accident.

He was, as has been said, in the habit of visiting his father at the Marshalsea every week. The talks between the two must have been a comedy at once more cruel and more delicate than Dickens ever described. Meredith might picture the comparison between the child whose troubles were so childish, but who felt them like a damned spirit, and the middle-aged man whose trouble was final ruin, and who felt it no more than a baby. Once, it would appear, the boy broke down altogether-perhaps under the unbearable buoyancy of his oratorical papa-and implored to be freed from the factory-implored it, I fear, with a precocious and almost horrible eloquence. The old optimist was astounded-too much astounded to do anything in particular. Whether the incident had really anything to do with what followed cannot be decided, but ostensibly it had not. Ostensibly the cause of Charles's ultimate liberation was a quarrel between his father and Lamert, the head of the factory. Dickens the elder (who had at last left the Marshalsea) could no doubt conduct a quarrel with the magnificence of Micawber; the result of this talent, at any rate, was to leave Mr. Lamert in a towering rage. He had a stormy interview with Charles, in which he tried to be good-tempered to the boy, but could hardly master his tongue about the boy's father. Finally he told him he must go, and with every observance the little creature was solemnly expelled from hell.

His mother, with a touch of strange harshness, was for patching up the quarrel and sending him back. Perhaps, with the fierce feminine responsibility, she felt that the first necessity was to keep the family out of debt. But old John Dickens put his foot down here-put his foot down with that ringing but very rare decision with which (once in ten years, and often on some trivial matter) the weakest man will overwhelm the strongest woman. The boy was miserable; the boy was clever; the boy should go to school. The boy went to school; he went to the Wellington House Academy, Mornington Place. It was an odd experience for anyone to go from the world to a school, instead of going from school to the world. Dickens, we may say, had his boyhood after his youth. He had seen life at its coarsest before he began his training for it, and knew the worst words in the English language probably before the best. This odd chronology, it will be remembered, he retained in his semi-autobiographical account of the adventures of David Copperfield, who went into the business of Murdstone and Grinby's before he went to the school kept by Dr. Strong. David Copperfield, also, went to be carefully prepared for a world that he had seen already. Outside David Copperfield, the records of Dickens at this time reduce themselves to a few glimpses provided by accidental companions of his schooldays, and little can be deduced from them about his personality beyond a general impression of sharpness and, perhaps, of bravado, of bright eyes and bright speeches. Probably the young creature was recuperating himself for his misfortunes, was making the most of his liberty, was flapping the wings of that wild spirit that had just not been broken. We hear of things that sound suddenly juvenile after his maturer troubles, of a secret language sounding like mere gibberish, and of a small theatre, with paint and red fire; such as that which Stevenson loved. It was not an accident that Dickens and Stevenson loved it. It is a stage unsuited for psychological realism; the cardboard characters cannot analyze each other with any effect. But it is a stage almost divinely suited for making surroundings, for making that situation and background which belongs peculiarly to romance. A toy theatre, in fact, is the opposite of private theatricals. In the latter you can do anything with the people if you do not ask much from the scenery; in the former you can do anything in scenery if you do not ask much from the people. In a toy theatre you could hardly manage a modern dialogue on marriage, but the Day of Judgment would be quite easy.

After leaving school, Dickens found employment as a clerk to Mr. Blackmore, a solicitor, as one of those inconspicuous under-clerks whom he afterwards turned to many grotesque uses. Here, no doubt, he met Lowten and Swiveller, Chuckster and Wobbler, in so far as such sacred creatures ever had embodiments on this lower earth. But it is typical of him that he had no fancy at all to remain a solicitor's clerk. The resolution to rise which had glowed in him even as a dawdling boy, when he gazed at Gads-hill, which had been darkened but not quite destroyed by his fall into the factory routine, which had been released again by his return to normal boyhood and the boundaries of school, was not likely to content itself now with the copying out of agreements. He set to work, without any advice or help, to learn to be a reporter. He worked all day at law, and all night at shorthand. It is an art which can only be effected by time, and he had to effect it by overtime. But learning the thing under every disadvantage, without a teacher, without the possibility of concentration or complete mental force without ordinary human sleep, he made himself one of the most rapid reporters then alive. There is a curious contrast between the casualness of the mental training to which his parents and others subjected him and the savage seriousness of the training to which he subjected himself. Somebody once asked old John Dickens where his son Charles was educated. "Well, really," said the great creature, in his spacious way, "he may be said-ah-to have educated himself." He might indeed.

This practical intensity of Dickens is worth our dwelling on, because it illustrates an elementary antithesis in his character, or what appears as an antithesis in our modern popular psychology. We are always talking about strong men against weak men; but Dickens was not only both a weak man and a strong man, he was a very weak man and also a very strong man. He was everything that we currently call a weak man; he was a man hung on wires; he was a man who might at any moment cry like a child; he was so sensitive to criticism that one may say that he lacked a skin; he was so nervous that he allowed great tragedies in his life to arise only out of nerves. But in the matter where all ordinary strong men are miserably weak-in the matter of concentrated toil and clear purpose and unconquerable worldly courage-he was like a straight sword. Mrs. Carlyle, who in her human epithets often hit the right nail so that it rang, said of him once, "He has a face made of steel." This was probably felt in a flash when she saw, in some social crowd, the clear, eager face of Dickens cutting through those near him like a knife. Any people who had met him from year to year would each year have found a man weakly troubled about his worldly decline; and each year they would have found him higher up in the world. His was a character very hard for any man of slow and placable temperament to understand; he was the character whom anybody can hurt and nobody can kill.

When he began to report in the House of Commons he was still only nineteen. His father, who had been released from his prison a short time before Charles had been released from his, had also become, among many other things, a reporter. But old John Dickens could enjoy doing anything without any particular aspiration after doing it well. But Charles was of a very different temper. He was, as I have said, consumed with an enduring and almost angry thirst to excel. He learnt shorthand with a dark self-devotion as if it were a sacred hieroglyph. Of this self-instruction, as of everything else, he has left humorous and illuminating phrases. He describes how, after he had learnt the whole exact alphabet, "there then appeared a procession of new horrors, called arbitrary characters-the most despotic characters I have ever known; who insisted for instance, that a thing like the beginning of a cobweb meant 'expectation,' and that a pen-and-ink sky rocket stood for 'disadvantageous.'" He concludes, "It was almost heartbreaking." But it is significant that somebody else, a colleague of his, concluded, "There never was such a shorthand writer."

Dickens succeeded in becoming a shorthand writer; succeeded in becoming a reporter; succeeded ultimately in becoming a highly effective journalist. He was appointed as a reporter of the speeches in Parliament, first by The True Son, then by The Mirror of Parliament, and last by The Morning Chronicle. He reported the speeches very well, and if we must analyze his internal opinions, much better than they deserved. For it must be remembered that this lad went into the reporter's gallery full of the triumphant Radicalism which was then the rising tide of the world. He was, it must be confessed, very little overpowered by the dignity of the Mother of Parliaments; he regarded the House of Commons much as he regarded the House of Lords, as a sort of venerable joke. It was, perhaps, while he watched, pale with weariness from the reporter's gallery, that there sank into him a thing that never left him, his unfathomable contempt for the British Constitution. Then perhaps he heard from the Government benches the immortal apologies of the Circumlocution Office. "Then would the noble lord or right honourable gentleman, in whose department it was to defend the Circumlocution Office, put an orange in his pocket, and make a regular field-day of the occasion. Then would he come down to that house with a slap upon the table and meet the honourable gentleman foot to foot. Then would he be there to tell that honourable gentleman that the Circumlocution Office was not only blameless in this matter, but was commendable in this matter, was extollable to the skies in this matter. Then would he be there to tell that honourable gentleman that although the Circumlocution Office was invariably right, and wholly right, it never was so right in this matter. Then would he be there to tell the honourable gentleman that it would have been more to his honour, more to his credit, more to his good taste, more to his good sense, more to half the dictionary of common places if he had left the Circumlocution Office alone and never approached this matter. Then would he keep one eye upon a coach or crammer from the Circumlocution Office below the bar, and smash the honourable gentleman with the Circumlocution Office account of this matter. And although one of two things always happened; namely, either that the Circumlocution Office had nothing to say, and said it, or that it had something to say of which the noble lord or right honourable gentleman blundered one half and forgot the other; the Circumlocution Office was always voted immaculate by an accommodating majority." We are now generally told that Dickens has destroyed these abuses, and that this is no longer a true picture of public life. Such, at any rate; is the Circumlocution Office account of this matter. But Dickens as a good Radical would, I fancy, much prefer that we should continue his battle than that we should celebrate his triumph; especially when it has not come. England is still ruled by the great Barnacle family. Parliament is still ruled by the great Barnacle trinity-the solemn old Barnacle who knew that the Circumlocution Office was protection, the sprightly young Barnacle who knew that it was a fraud, and the bewildered young Barnacle who knew nothing about it. From these three types our Cabinets are still exclusively recruited. People talk of the tyrannies and anomalies which Dickens denounced as things of the past like the Star Chamber. They believe that the days of the old stupid optimism and the old brutal indifference are gone for ever. In truth, this very belief is only the countenance of the old stupid optimism and the old brutal indifference. We believe in a free England and a pure England, because we still believe in the Circumlocution Office account of this matter. Undoubtedly our serenity is wide-spread. We believe that England is really reformed, we believe that England is really democratic, we believe that English politics are free from corruption. But this general satisfaction of ours does not show that Dickens has beaten the Barnacles. It only shows that the Barnacles have beaten Dickens.

It cannot be too often said, then, that we must read into young Dickens and his works this old Radical tone towards institutions. That tone was a sort of happy impatience. And when Dickens had to listen for hours to the speech of the noble lord in defence of the Circumlocution Office, when, that is, he had to listen to what he regarded as the last vapourings of a vanishing oligarchy, the impatience rather predominated over the happiness. His incurably restless nature found more pleasure in the wandering side of journalism. He went about wildly in post-chaises to report political meetings for the Morning Chronicle. "And what gentlemen they were to serve," he exclaimed, "in such things at the old Morning Chronicle. Great or small it did not matter. I have had to charge for half a dozen breakdowns in half a dozen times as many miles. I have had to charge for the damage of a great-coat from the drippings of a blazing wax candle, in writing through the smallest hours of the night in a swift flying carriage and pair." And again, "I have often transcribed for the printer from my shorthand notes important public speeches in which the strictest accuracy was required, and a mistake in which would have been to a young man severely compromising, writing on the palm of my hand, by the light of a dark lantern, in a post-chaise and four, galloping through a wild country and through the dead of the night, at the then surprising rate of fifteen miles an hour." The whole of Dickens's life goes with the throb of that nocturnal gallop. All its real wildness shot through with an imaginative wickedness he afterwards uttered in the drive of Jonas Chuzzlewit through the storm.

All this time, and indeed, from a time of which no measure can be taken, the creative part of his mind had been in a stir or even a fever. While still a small boy he had written for his own amusement some sketches of queer people he had met; notably, one of his uncle's barber, whose principal hobby was pointing out what Napoleon ought to have done in the matter of military tactics. He had a note-book full of such sketches. He had sketches not only of persons, but of places, which were to him almost more personal than persons. In the December of 1833 he published one of these fragments in the Old Monthly Magazine. This was followed by nine others in the same paper, and when the paper (which was a romantically Radical venture, run by a veteran soldier of Bolivar) itself collapsed, Dickens continued the series in the Evening Chronicle, an offshoot of the morning paper of the same name. These were the pieces afterwards published and known as the "Sketches by Boz"; and with them Dickens enters literature. He also enters upon many things about this time; he enters manhood, and among other things marriage. A friend of his on the Chronicle, George Hogarth, had several daughters. With all of them Dickens appears to have been on terms of great affection. This sketch is wholly literary, and I do not feel it necessary to do more than touch upon such incidents as his marriage, just I shall do no more than touch upon the tragedy that ultimately overtook it. But it may be suggested here that the final misfortunes were in some degree due to the circumstances attending the original action. A very young man fighting his way, and excessively poor, with no memories for years past that were not monotonous and mean, and with his strongest and most personal memories quite ignominious and unendurable, was suddenly thrown into the society of a whole family of girls. I think it does not overstate his weakness, and I think it partly constitutes his excuse, to say that he fell in love with the chance of love. As sometimes happens in the undeveloped youth, an abstract femininity simply intoxicated him. In what came afterwards he was enormously to blame. But I do not think that his was a case of cold division from a woman whom he had once seriously and singly loved. He had been bewildered in a burning haze, I will not say even of first love, but of first flirtations. The whole family stimulated him before he fell in love with one of them; and it continued to stimulate him long after he had quarrelled with her for causes that did not even destroy his affection for her. This view is strikingly supported by all the details of his attitude towards all the other members of the sacred house of Hogarth. One of the sisters remained, of course, his dearest friend till death. Another who had died, he worshipped like a saint, and he always asked to be buried in her grave. He was married on April 2, 1836. Forster remarks that a few days before the announcement of their marriage in the Times, the same paper contained another announcement that on the 31st would be published the first number of a work called "The Posthumous Papers of the Pickwick Club." It is the beginning of his career.

The "Sketches," apart from splendid splashes of humour here and there, are not manifestations of the man of genius. We might almost say that this book is one of the few books by Dickens which would not, standing alone, have made his fame. And yet standing alone it did make his fame. His contemporaries could see a new spirit in it, where we, familiar with the larger fruits of that spirit, can only see a continuation of the prosaic and almost wooden wit of the comic books of that day. But in any case we should hardly look in the man's first book for the fulness of his contribution to letters. Youth is almost everything else, but it is hardly ever original. We read of young men bursting on the old world with a new message. But youth in actual experience is the period of imitation and even of obedience. Subjectively its emotions may be furious and headlong; but its only external outcome is a furious imitation and a headlong obedience. As we grow older we learn the special thing we have to do. As a man goes on towards the grave he discovers gradually a philosophy he can really call fresh, a style he can really call his own, and as he becomes an older man he becomes a new writer. Ibsen, in his youth, wrote almost classic plays about vikings; it was in his old age that he began to break windows and throw fireworks. The only fault, it was said, of Browning's first poems was that they had "too much beauty of imagery, and too little wealth of thought." The only fault, that is, of Browning's first poems, was that they were not Browning's.

In one way, however, the "Sketches by Boz" do stand out very symbolically in the life of Dickens. They constitute in a manner the dedication of him to his especial task; the sympathetic and yet exaggerated painting of the poorer middle-class. He was to make men feel that this dull middle-class was actually a kind of elf-land. But here, again, the work is rude and undeveloped; and this is shown in the fact that it is a great deal more exaggerative than it is sympathetic. We are not, of course, concerned with the kind of people who say that they wish that Dickens was more refined. If those people are ever refined it will be by fire. But there is in this earliest work, an element which almost vanished in the later ones, an element which is typical of the middle-classes in England, and which is in a more real sense to be called vulgar. I mean that in these little farces there is a trace in the author as well as in the characters, of that petty sense of social precedence, that hubbub of little unheard-of oligarchies, which is the only serious sin of bourgeoisie of Britain. It may seem pragmatical, for example, to instance such rowdy farce as the story of Horatio Sparkins, which tells how a tuft-hunting family entertained a rhetorical youth thinking he was a lord, and found he was a draper's assistant. No doubt they were very snobbish in thinking that a lord must be eloquent; but we cannot help feeling that Dickens is almost equally snobbish in feeling it so very funny that a draper's assistant should be eloquent. A free man, one would think, would despise the family quite as much if Horatio had been a peer. Here, and here only, there is just a touch of the vulgarity, of the only vulgarity of the world out of which Dickens came. For the only element of lowness that there really is in our populace is exactly that they are full of superiorities and very conscious of class. Shades, imperceptible to the eyes of others, but as hard and haughty as a Brahmin caste, separate one kind of charwoman from another kind of charwoman. Dickens was destined to show with inspired symbolism all the immense virtues of the democracy. He was to show them as the most humorous part of our civilisation; which they certainly are. He was to show them as the most promptly and practically compassionate part of our civilisation; which they certainly are. The democracy has a hundred exuberant good qualities; the democracy has only one outstanding sin-it is not democratic.

Chapter 4
"The Pickwick Papers"

Round the birth of "Pickwick" broke one of those literary quarrels that were too common in the life of Dickens. Such quarrels indeed generally arose from some definite mistake or misdemeanour on the part of somebody else; but they were also made possible by an indefinite touchiness and susceptibility in Dickens himself. He was so sensitive on points of personal authorship that even his sacred sense of humour deserted him. He turned people into mortal enemies whom he might have turned very easily into immortal jokes. It was not that he was lawless; in a sense it was that he was too legal; but he did not understand the principle of de minimis non curat lex. Anybody could draw him; any fool could make a fool of him. Any obscure madman who chose to say that he had written the whole of "Martin Chuzzlewit"; any penny-a-liner who chose to say that Dickens wore no shirt-collar, could call forth the most passionate and public denials as of a man pleading "not guilty" to witchcraft or high treason. Hence the letters of Dickens are filled with a certain singular type of quarrels and complaints, quarrels and complaints in which one cannot say that he was on the wrong side, but that merely even in being on the right side he was in the wrong place. He was not only a generous man, he was even a just man; to have made against anybody a charge or claim which was unfair would have been insupportable to him. His weakness was that he found the unfair claim or charge, however small, equally insupportable when brought against himself. No one can say of him that he was often wrong; we can only say of him as of many pugnacious people, that he was too often right.

The incidents attending the inauguration of "The Pickwick Papers" are not, perhaps, a perfect example of this trait, because Dickens was here a hand-to-mouth journalist, and the blow might possibly have been more disabling than those struck at him in his days of triumph. But all through those days of triumph, and to the day of his death, Dickens took this old tea-cup tempest with the most terrible gravity, drew up declarations, called witnesses, preserved pulverising documents, and handed on to his children the forgotten folly as if it had been a Highland feud. Yet the unjust claim made on him was so much more ridiculous even than it was unjust, that it seems strange that he should have remembered it for a month except for his amusement. The facts are simple and familiar to most people. The publishers-Chapman & Hall-wished to produce some kind of serial with comic illustrations by a popular caricaturist named Seymour. This artist was chiefly famous for his rendering of the farcical side of sport, and to suit this speciality it was very vaguely suggested to Dickens by the publishers that he should write about a Nimrod Club, or some such thing, a club of amateur sportsmen, foredoomed to perpetual ignominies. Dickens objected in substance upon two very sensible grounds-first, that sporting sketches were stale; and second, that he knew nothing about sport. He changed the idea to that of a general club for travel and investigation, the Pickwick Club, and only retained one fated sportsman, Mr. Winkle, the melancholy remnant of the Nimrod Club that never was. The first seven pictures appeared with the signature of Seymour and the letter press of Dickens, and in them Winkle and his woes were fairly, but not extraordinarily prominent. Before the eighth picture appeared Seymour had blown his brains out. After a brief interval of the employment of a man named Buss, Dickens obtained the assistance of Hablot K. Browne, whom we all call "Phiz," and may almost, in a certain sense, be said to have gone into partnership with him. They were as suited to each other and to the common creation of a unique thing as Gilbert and Sullivan. No other illustrator ever created the true Dickens characters with the precise and correct quantum of exaggeration. No other illustrator ever breathed the true Dickens atmosphere, in which clerks are clerks and yet at the same time elves.

To the tame mind the above affair does not seem to offer anything very promising in the way of a row. But Seymour's widow managed to evolve out of it the proposition that somehow or other her husband had written "Pickwick," or, at least, had been responsible for the genius and success of it. It does not appear that she had anything at all resembling a reason for this opinion except the unquestionable fact that the publishers had started with the idea of employing Seymour. This was quite true, and Dickens (who over and above his honesty was far too quarrelsome a man not to try and keep in the right, and who showed a sort of fierce carefulness in telling the truth in such cases) never denied it or attempted to conceal it. It was quite true, that at the beginning, instead of Seymour being employed to illustrate Dickens, Dickens may be said to have been employed to illustrate Seymour. But that Seymour invented anything in the letterpress large or small, that he invented either the outline of Mr. Pickwick's character, or the number of Mr. Pickwick's cabman, that he invented either the story, or so much as a semi-colon in the story was not only never proved, but was never very lucidly alleged. Dickens fills his letters with all that there is to be said against Mrs. Seymour's idea; it is not very clear whether there was anything definitely said for it.

Upon the mere superficial fact and law of the affair, Dickens ought to have been superior to this silly business. But in a much deeper and a much more real sense he ought to have been superior to it. It did not really touch him or his greatness at all, even as an abstract allegation. If Seymour had started the story, had provided Dickens with his puppets, Tupman or Jingle, Dickens would still have been Dickens and Seymour only Seymour. As a matter of fact, it happened to be a contemptible lie, but it would have been an equally contemptible truth. For the fact is that the greatness of Dickens and especially the greatness of Pickwick is not of a kind that could be affected by somebody else suggesting the first idea. It could not be affected by somebody else writing the first chapter. If it could be shown that another man had suggested to Hawthorne (let us say) the primary conception of "The Scarlet Letter," Hawthorne who worked it out would still be an exquisite workman; but he would be by so much less a creator. But in a case like Pickwick there is a simple test. If Seymour gave Dickens the main idea of Pickwick, what was it? There is no primary conception of Pickwick for anyone to suggest. Dickens not only did not get the general plan from Seymour, he did not get it at all. In Pickwick, and, indeed, in Dickens, generally it is in the details that the author is creative, it is in the details that he is vast. The power of the book lies in the perpetual torrent of ingenious and inventive treatment; the theme (at least at the beginning) simply does not exist. The idea of Tupman, the fat lady-killer, is in itself quite dreary and vulgar; it is the detailed Tupman, as he is developed, who is unexpectedly amusing. The idea of Winkle, the clumsy sportsman, is in itself quite stale; it is as he goes on repeating himself that he becomes original. We hear of men whose imagination can touch with magic the dull facts of our life, but Dickens's yet more indomitable fancy could touch with magic even our dull fiction. Before we are half-way through the book the stock characters of dead and damned farces astonish us like splendid strangers.

Seymour's claim, then, viewed symbolically, was even a compliment. It was true in spirit that Dickens obtained (or might have obtained) the start of Pickwick from somebody else, from anybody else. For he had a more gigantic energy than the energy of the intense artist, the energy which is prepared to write something. He had the energy which is prepared to write anything. He could have finished any man's tale. He could have breathed a mad life into any man's characters. If it had been true that Seymour had planned out Pickwick, if Seymour had fixed the chapters and named and numbered the characters, his slave would have shown even in these shackles such a freedom as would have shaken the world. If Dickens had been forced to make his incidents out of a chapter in a child's reading-book, or the names in a scrap of newspaper, he would have turned them in ten pages into creatures of his own. Seymour, as I say, was in a manner right in spirit. Dickens would at this time get his materials from anywhere, in the sense that he cared little what materials they were. He would not have stolen; but if he had stolen he would never have imitated. The power which he proceeded at once to exhibit was the one power in letters which literally cannot be imitated, the primary inexhaustible creative energy, the enormous prodigality of genius which no one but another genius could parody. To claim to have originated an idea of Dickens is like claiming to have contributed one glass of water to Niagara. Wherever this stream or that stream started the colossal cataract of absurdity went roaring night and day. The volume of his invention overwhelmed all doubt of his inventiveness; Dickens was evidently a great man; unless he was a thousand men.

The actual circumstances of the writing and publishing of "Pickwick" shows that while Seymour's specific claim was absurd, Dickens's indignant exactitude about every jot and tittle of authorship was also inappropriate and misleading. "The Pickwick Papers," when all is said and done, did emerge out of a haze of suggestions and proposals in which more than one person was involved. The publishers failed to base the story on a Nimrod Club, but they succeeded in basing it on a club. Seymour, by virtue of his idiosyncrasy, if he did not create, brought about the creation of Mr. Winkle. Seymour sketched Mr. Pickwick as a tall, thin man. Mr. Chapman (apparently without any word from Dickens) boldly turned him into a short, fat man. Chapman took the type from a corpulent old dandy named Foster, who wore tights and gaiters and lived at Richmond. In this sense, were we affected by this idle aspect of the thing, we might call Chapman the real originator of "Pickwick." But as I have suggested, originating "Pickwick" is not the point. It was quite easy to originate "Pickwick." The difficulty was to write it.

However such things may be, there can be no question of the result of this chaos. In "The Pickwick Papers" Dickens sprang suddenly from a comparatively low level to a very high one. To the level of "Sketches by Boz" he never afterwards descended. To the level of "The Pickwick Papers" it is doubtful if he ever afterwards rose. "Pickwick," indeed, is not a good novel; but it is not a bad novel, for it is not a novel at all. In one sense, indeed, it is something nobler than a novel, for no novel with a plot and a proper termination could emit that sense of everlasting youth —a sense as of the gods gone wandering in England. This is not a novel, for all novels have an end; and "Pickwick," properly speaking, has no end-he is equal unto the angels. The point at which, as a fact, we find the printed matter terminates is not an end in any artistic sense of the word. Even as a boy I believed there were some more pages that were torn out of my copy, and I am looking for them still. The book might have been cut short anywhere else. It might have been cut short after Mr. Pickwick was released by Mr. Nupkins, or after Mr. Pickwick was fished out of the water, or at a hundred other places. And we should still have known that this was not really the story's end. We should have known that Mr. Pickwick was still having the same high adventures on the same high roads. As it happens the book ends after Mr. Pickwick has taken a house in the neighbourhood of Dulwich. But we know he did not stop there. We know he broke out, that he took again the road of the high adventures; we know that if we take it ourselves in any acre of England, we may come suddenly upon him in a lane.

But this relation of "Pickwick" to the strict form of fiction demands a further word, which should indeed be said in any case before the consideration of any or all of the Dickens tales. Dickens's work is not to be reckoned in novels at all. Dickens's work is to be reckoned always by characters, sometimes by groups, oftener by episodes, but never by novels. You cannot discuss whether "Nicholas Nickleby" is a good novel, or whether "Our Mutual Friend" is a bad novel. Strictly, there is no such novel as "Nicholas Nickleby." There is no such novel as "Our Mutual Friend." They are simply lengths cut from the flowing and mixed substance called Dickens —a substance of which any given length will be certain to contain a given proportion of brilliant and of bad stuff. You can say, according to your opinions, "the Crummles part is perfect," or "the Boffins are a mistake," just as a man watching a river go by him could count here a floating flower, and there a streak of scum. But you cannot artistically divide the output into books. The best of his work can be found in the worst of his works. "The Tale of Two Cities" is a good novel; "Little Dorrit" is not a good novel. But the description of "The Circumlocution Office" in "Little Dorrit" is quite as good as the description of "Tellson's Bank" in "The Tale of Two Cities." "The Old Curiosity Shop" is not so good as "David Copperfield," but Swiveller is quite as good as Micawber. Nor is there any reason why these superb creatures, as a general rule, should be in one novel any more than another. There is no reason why Sam Weller, in the course of his wanderings, should not wander into "Nicholas Nickleby." There is no reason why Major Bagstock, in his brisk way, should not walk straight out of "Dombey and Son" and straight into "Martin Chuzzlewit." To this generalisation some modification should be added.

"Pickwick" stands by itself, and has even a sort of unity in not pretending to unity. "David Copperfield," in a less degree, stands by itself, as being the only book in which Dickens wrote of himself; and "The Tale of Two Cities" stands by itself as being the only book in which Dickens slightly altered himself. But as a whole, this should be firmly grasped, that the units of Dickens, the primary elements, are not the stories, but the characters who affect the stories-or, more often still, the characters who do not affect the stories.

This is a plain matter; but, unless it be stated and felt, Dickens may be greatly misunderstood and greatly underrated. For not only is his whole machinery directed to facilitating the self-display of certain characters, but something more deep and more unmodern still is also true of him. It is also true that all the moving machinery exists only to display entirely static character. Things in the Dickens story shift and change only in order to give us glimpses of great characters that do not change at all. If we had a sequel of Pickwick ten years afterwards, Pickwick would be exactly the same age. We know he would not have fallen into that strange and beautiful second childhood which soothed and simplified the end of Colonel Newcome. Newcome, throughout the book, is in an atmosphere of time: Pickwick, throughout the book, is not. This will probably be taken by most modern people as praise of Thackeray and dispraise of Dickens. But this only shows how few modern people understand Dickens. It also shows how few understand the faiths and the fables of mankind. The matter can only be roughly stated in one way. Dickens did not strictly make a literature; he made a mythology.

For a few years our corner of Western Europe has had a fancy for this thing we call fiction; that is, for writing down our own lives or similar lives in order to look at them. But though we call it fiction, it differs from older literatures chiefly in being less fictitious. It imitates not only life, but the limitations of life it not only reproduces life, it reproduces death. But outside us, in every other country, in every other age, there has been going on from the beginning a more fictitious kind of fiction. I mean the kind now called folklore, the literature of the people. Our modern novels, which deal with men as they are, are chiefly produced by a small and educated section of society. But this other literature deals with men greater than they are-with demi-gods and heroes; and that is far too important a matter to be trusted to the educated classes. The fashioning of these portents is a popular trade, like ploughing or bricklaying; the men who made hedges, the men who made ditches, were the men who made deities. Men could not elect their kings, but they could elect their gods. So we find ourselves faced with a fundamental contrast between what is called fiction and what is called folklore. The one exhibits an abnormal degree of dexterity operating within our daily limitations; the other exhibits quite normal desires extended beyond those limitations. Fiction means the common things as seen by the uncommon people. Fairy tales mean the uncommon things as seen by the common people.

As our world advances through history towards its present epoch, it becomes more specialist, less democratic, and folklore turns gradually into fiction. But it is only slowly that the old elfin fire fades into the light of common realism. For ages after our characters have dressed up in the clothes of mortals they betray the blood of the gods. Even our phraseology is full of relics of this. When a modern novel is devoted to the bewilderments of a weak young clerk who cannot decide which woman he wants to marry, or which new religion he believes in, we still give this knock-kneed cad the name of "the hero"—the name which is the crown of Achilles. The popular preference for a story with "a happy ending" is not, or at least was not, a mere sweet-stuff optimism; it is the remains of the old idea of the triumph of the dragon-slayer, the ultimate apotheosis of the man beloved of heaven.

But there is another and more intangible trace of this fading supernaturalism—a trace very vivid to the reader, but very elusive to the critic. It is a certain air of endlessness in the episodes, even in the shortest episodes—a sense that, although we leave them, they still go on. Our modern attraction to short stories is not an accident of form; it is the sign of a real sense of fleetingness and fragility; it means that existence is only an impression, and, perhaps, only an illusion. A short story of today has the air of a dream; it has the irrevocable beauty of a falsehood; we get a glimpse of grey streets of London or red plains of India, as in an opium vision; we see people-arresting people with fiery and appealing faces. But when the story is ended, the people are ended. We have no instinct of anything ultimate and enduring behind the episodes. The moderns, in a word, describe life in short stories because they are possessed with the sentiment that life itself is an uncommonly short story, and perhaps not a true one. But in this elder literature, even in the comic literature (indeed, especially in the comic literature), the reverse is true. The characters are felt to be fixed things of which we have fleeting glimpses; that is, they are felt to be divine. Uncle Toby is talking for ever, as the elves are dancing for ever. We feel that whenever we hammer on the house of Falstaff, Falstaff will be at home. We feel it as a Pagan would feel that, if a cry broke the silence after ages of unbelief, Apollo would still be listening in his temple. These writers may tell short stories, but we feel they are only parts of a long story. And herein lies the peculiar significance, the peculiar sacredness even, of penny dreadfuls and the common printed matter made for our errand-boys. Here in dim and desperate forms, under the ban of our base culture, stormed at by silly magistrates, sneered at by silly schoolmasters,—here is the old popular literature still popular; here is the unmistakable voluminousness, the thousand and one tales of Dick Deadshot, like the thousand and one tales of Robin Hood. Here is the splendid and static boy, the boy who remains a boy through a thousand volumes and a thousand years. Here in mean alleys and dim shops, shadowed and shamed by the police, mankind is still driving its dark trade in heroes. And elsewhere, and in all other ages, in braver fashion, under cleaner skies, the same eternal tale-telling goes on, and the whole mortal world is a factory of immortals.

Dickens was a mythologist rather than a novelist; he was the last of the mythologists, and perhaps the greatest. He did not always manage to make his characters men, but he always managed, at the least, to make them gods. They are creatures like Punch or Father Christmas. They live statically, in a perpetual summer of being themselves. It was not the aim of Dickens to show the effect of time and circumstance upon a character; it was not even his aim to show the effect of a character on time and circumstance. It is worth remark, in passing, that whenever he tried to describe change in a character, he made a mess of it, as in the repentance of Dombey or the apparent deterioration of Boffin. It was his aim to show character hung in a kind of happy void, in a world apart from time-yes, and essentially apart from circumstance, though the phrase may seem odd in connection with the godlike horse-play of "Pickwick." But all the Pickwickian events, wild as they often are, were only designed to display the greater wildness of souls, or sometimes merely to bring the reader within touch, so to speak, of that wildness. The author would have fired Mr. Pickwick out of a can non to get him to Wardle's by Christmas; he would have taken the roof off to drop him into Bob Sawyer's party. But once put Pickwick at Wardle's, with his punch and a group of gorgeous personalities, and nothing will move him from his chair. Once he is at Sawyer's party, he forgets how he got there; he forgets Mrs. Bardell and all his story. For the story was but an incantation to call up a god, and the god (Mr. Jack Hopkins) is present in divine power. Once the great characters are face to face, the ladder by which they climbed is forgotten and falls down, the structure of the story drops to pieces, the plot is abandoned; the other characters deserted at every kind of crisis; the whole crowded thoroughfare of the tale is blocked by two or three talkers, who take their immortal ease as if they were already in Paradise. For they do not exist for the story; the story exists for them; and they know it.

To every man alive, one must hope, it has in some manner happened that he has talked with his more fascinating friends round a table on some night when all the numerous personalities unfolded themselves like great tropical flowers. All fell into their parts as in some delightful impromptu play. Every man was more himself than he had ever been in this vale of tears. Every man was a beautiful caricature of himself. The man who has known such nights will understand the exaggerations of "Pickwick." The man who has not known such nights will not enjoy "Pickwick" nor (I imagine) heaven. For, as I have said, Dickens is, in this matter, close to popular religion, which is the ultimate and reliable religion. He conceives an endless joy; he conceives creatures as permanent as Puck or Pan-creatures whose will to live aeons upon aeons cannot satisfy. He is not come, as a writer, that his creatures may copy life and copy its narrowness; he is come that they may have life, and that they may have it more abundantly. It is absurd indeed that Christians should be called the enemies of life because they wish life to last for ever; it is more absurd still to call the old comic writers dull because they wished their unchanging characters to last for ever. Both popular religion, with its endless joys, and the old comic story, with its endless jokes, have in our time faded together. We are too weak to desire that undying vigour. We believe that you can have too much of a good thing—a blasphemous belief, which at one blow wrecks all the heavens that men have hoped for. The grand old defiers of God were not afraid of an eternity of torment. We have come to be afraid of an eternity of joy. It is not my business here to take sides in this division between those who like life and long novels and those who like death and short stories; my only business is to point out that those who see in Dickens's unchanging characters and recurring catch-words a mere stiffness and lack of living movement miss the point and nature of his work. His tradition is another tradition altogether; his aim is another aim altogether to those of the modern novelists who trace the alchemy of experience and the autumn tints of character. He is there, like the common people of all ages, to make deities; he is there, as I have said, to exaggerate life in the direction of life. The spirit he at bottom celebrates is that of two friends drinking wine together and talking through the night. But for him they are two deathless friends talking through an endless night and pouring wine from an inexhaustible bottle.

This, then, is the first firm fact to grasp about "Pickwick"—about "Pickwick" more than about any of the other stories. It is, first and foremost, a supernatural story. Mr. Pickwick was a fairy. So was old Mr. Weller. This does not imply that they were suited to swing in a trapeze of gossamer; it merely implies that if they had fallen out of it on their heads they would not have died. But, to speak more strictly, Mr. Samuel Pickwick is not the fairy; he is the fairy prince; that is to say, he is the abstract wanderer and wonderer, the Ulysses of comedy; the half-human and half-elfin creature-human enough to wander, human enough to wonder, but still sustained with that merry fatalism that is natural to immortal beings-sustained by that hint of divinity which tells him in the darkest hour that he is doomed to live happily ever afterwards. He has set out walking to the end of the world, but he knows he will find an inn there.

And this brings us to the best and boldest element of originality in "Pickwick." It has not, I think, been observed, and it may be that Dickens did not observe it. Certainly he did not plan it; it grew gradually, perhaps out of the unconscious part of his soul, and warmed the whole story like a slow fire. Of course it transformed the whole story also; transformed it out of all likeness to itself. About this latter point was waged one of the numberless little wars of Dickens. It was a part of his pugnacious vanity that he refused to admit the truth of the mildest criticism. Moreover, he used his inexhaustible ingenuity to find an apologia that was generally an afterthought. Instead of laughingly admitting, in answer to criticism, the glorious improbability of Pecksniff, he retorted with a sneer, clever and very unjust, that he was not surprised that the Pecksniffs should deny the portrait of Pecksniff. When it was objected that the pride of old Paul Dombey breaks as abruptly as a stick, he tried to make out that there had been an absorbing psychological struggle going on in that gentleman all the time, which the reader was too stupid to perceive. Which is, I am afraid, rubbish. And so, in a similar vein, he answered those who pointed out to him the obvious and not very shocking fact that our sentiments about Pickwick are very different in the second part of the book from our sentiments in the first; that we find ourselves at the beginning setting out in the company of a farcical old fool, if not a farcical old humbug, and that we find ourselves at the end saying farewell to a fine old England merchant, a monument of genial sanity. Dickens answered with the same ingenious self-justification as in the other cases-that surely it often happened that a man met us first arrayed in his more grotesque qualities, and that fuller acquaintance unfolded his more serious merits. This, of course, is quite true; but I think any honest admirer of "Pickwick" will feel that it is not an answer. For the fault in "Pickwick" (if it be a fault) is a change not in the hero but in the whole atmosphere. The point is not that Pickwick turns into a different kind of man; it is that "The Pickwick Papers" turns into a different kind of book. And however artistic both parts may be, this combination must, in strict art, be called inartistic. A man is quite artistically justified in writing a tale in which a man as cowardly as Bob Acres becomes a man as brave as Hector. But a man is not artistically justified in writing a tale which begins in the style of "The Rivals" and ends in the style of the "Iliad." In other words, we do not mind the hero changing in the course of a book; but we are not prepared for the author changing in the course of the book. And the author did change in the course of this book. He made, in the midst of this book, a great discovery, which was the discovery of his destiny, or, what is more important, of his duty. That discovery turned him from the author of "Sketches by Boz" to the author of "David Copperfield." And that discovery constituted the thing of which I have spoken-the outstanding and arresting original feature in "The Pickwick Papers."

"Pickwick," I have said, is a romance of adventure, and Samuel Pickwick is the romantic adventurer. So much is indeed obvious. But the strange and stirring discovery which Dickens made was this-that having chosen a fat old man of the middle classes as a good thing of which to make a butt, he found that a fat old man of the middle classes is the very best thing of which to make a romantic adventurer. "Pickwick" is supremely original in that it is the adventures of an old man. It is a fairy tale in which the victor is not the youngest of the three brothers, but one of the oldest of their uncles. The result is both noble and new and true. There is nothing which so much needs simplicity as adventure. And there is no one who so much possesses simplicity as an honest and elderly man of business. For romance he is better than a troop of young troubadours; for the swaggering young fellow anticipates his adventures, just as he anticipates his income. Hence both the adventures and the income, when he comes up to them, are not there. But a man in late middle-age has grown used to the plain necessities, and his first holiday is a second youth. A good man, as Thackeray said with such thorough and searching truth, grows simpler as he grows older. Samuel Pickwick in his youth was probably an insufferable young coxcomb. He knew then, or thought he knew, all about the confidence tricks of swindlers like Jingle. He knew then, or thought he knew, all about the amatory designs of sly ladies like Mrs. Bardell. But years and real life have relieved him of this idle and evil knowledge. He has had the high good luck in losing the follies of youth to lose the wisdom of youth also. Dickens has caught, in a manner at once wild and convincing, this queer innocence of the afternoon of life. The round, moonlike face, the round, moon-like spectacles of Samuel Pickwick move through the tale as emblems of a certain spherical simplicity. They are fixed in that grave surprise that may be seen in babies; that grave surprise which is the only real happiness that is possible to man. Pickwick's round face is like a round and honourable mirror, in which are reflected all the fantasies of earthly existence; for surprise is, strictly speaking, the only kind of reflection. All this grew gradually on Dickens. It is odd to recall to our minds the original plan, the plan of the Nimrod Club, and the author who was to be wholly occupied in playing practical jokes on his characters. He had chosen (or somebody else had chosen) that corpulent old simpleton as a person peculiarly fitted to fall down trapdoors, to shoot over butter slides, to struggle with apple-pie beds, to be tipped out of carts and dipped into horse-ponds. But Dickens, and Dickens only, discovered as he went on how fitted the fat old man was to rescue ladies, to defy tyrants, to dance, to leap, to experiment with life, to be a deus ex machinâ and even a knight errant. Dickens made this discovery. Dickens went into the Pickwick Club to scoff, and Dickens remained to pray.

Molière and his marquises are very much amused when M. Jourdain, the fat old middle-class fellow, discovers with delight that he has been talking prose all his life. I have often wondered whether Molière saw how in this fact M. Jourdain towers above them all and touches the stars. He has the freshness to enjoy a fresh fact, the freshness to enjoy even an old one. He can feel that the common thing prose is an accomplishment like verse; and it is an accomplishment like verse; it is the miracle of language. He can feel the subtle taste of water, and roll it on his tongue like wine. His simple vanity and voracity, his innocent love of living, his ignorant love of learning, are things far fuller of romance than the weariness and foppishness of the sniggering cavaliers. When he consciously speaks prose, he unconsciously thinks poetry. It would be better for us all if we were as conscious that supper is supper or that life is life, as this true romantic was that prose is actually prose. M. Jourdain is here the type, Mr. Pickwick is elsewhere the type, of this true and neglected thing, the romance of the middle classes. It is the custom in our little epoch to sneer at the middle classes. Cockney artists profess to find the bourgeoisie dull, as if artists had any business to find anything dull. Decadents talk contemptuously of its conventions and its set tasks; it never occurs to them that conventions and set tasks are the very way to keep that greenness in the grass and that redness in the roses-which they have lost for ever. Stevenson, in his incomparable "Lantern Bearers," describes the ecstasy of a schoolboy in the mere fact of buttoning a dark lantern under a dark great-coat. If you wish for that ecstasy of the schoolboy, you must have the boy; but you must also have the school. Strict opportunities and defined hours are the very outline of that enjoyment. A man like Mr. Pickwick has been at school all his life, and when he comes out he astonishes the youngsters. His heart, as that acute psychologist, Mr. Weller, points out, had been born later than his body. It will be remembered that Mr. Pickwick also, when on the escapade of Winkle and Miss Allen, took immoderate pleasure in the performances of a dark lantern which was not dark enough, and was nothing but a nuisance to everybody. His soul also was with Stevenson's boys on the grey sands of Haddington, talking in the dark by the sea. He also was of the league of the "Lantern Bearers." Stevenson, I remember, says that in the shops of that town they could purchase "penny Pickwicks (that remarkable cigar)." Let us hope they smoked them, and that the rotund ghost of Pickwick hovered over the rings of smoke.

Pickwick goes through life with that god-like gullibility which is the key to all adventures. The greenhorn is the ultimate victor in everything; it is he that gets the most out of life. Because Pickwick is led away by Jingle, he will be led to the White Hart Inn, and see the only Weller cleaning boots in the courtyard. Because he is bamboozled by Dodson and Fogg, he will enter the prison house like a paladin, and rescue the man and the woman who have wronged him most. His soul will never starve for exploits or excitements who is wise enough to be made a fool of. He will make himself happy in the traps that have been laid for him; he will roll in their nets and sleep. All doors will fly open to him who has a mildness more defiant than mere courage. The whole is unerringly expressed in one fortunate phrase-he will be always "taken in." To be taken in everywhere is to see the inside of everything. It is the hospitality of circumstance. With torches and trumpets, like a guest, the greenhorn is taken in by Life. And the sceptic is cast out by it.

Chapter 5
The great Popularity

There is one aspect of Charles Dickens which must be of interest even to that subterranean race which does not admire his books. Even if we are not interested in Dickens as a great event in English literature, we must still be interested in him as a great event in English history. If he had not his place with Fielding and Thackeray, he would still have his place with Wat Tyler and Wilkes; for the man led a mob. He did what no English statesman, perhaps, has really done; he called out the people. He was popular in a sense of which we moderns have not even a notion. In that sense there is no popularity now. There are no popular authors today. We call such authors as Mr. Guy Boothby or Mr. William Le Queux popular authors. But this is popularity altogether in a weaker sense; not only in quantity, but in quality. The old popularity was positive; the new is negative. There is a great deal of difference between the eager man who wants to read a book, and the tired man who wants a book to read. A man reading a Le Queux mystery wants to get to the end of it. A man reading the Dickens novel wished that it might never end. Men read a Dickens story six times because they knew it so well. If a man can read a Le Queux story six times it is only because he can forget it six times. In short, the Dickens novel was popular not because it was an unreal world, but because it was a real world; a world in which the soul could live. The modern "shocker" at its very best is an interlude in life. But in the days when Dickens's work was coming out in serial, people talked as if real life were itself the interlude between one issue of "Pickwick" and another.

In reaching the period of the publication of "Pickwick," we reach this sudden apotheosis of Dickens. Henceforward he filled the literary world in a way hard to imagine. Fragments of that huge fashion remain in our daily language; in the talk of every trade or public question are embedded the wrecks of that enormous religion. Men give out the airs of Dickens without even opening his books; just as Catholics can live in a tradition of Christianity without having looked at the New Testament. The man in the street has more memories of Dickens, whom he has not read, than of Marie Corelli, whom he has. There is nothing in any way parallel to this omnipresence and vitality in the great comic characters of Boz. There are no modern Bumbles and Pecksniffs, no modern Gamps and Micawbers. Mr. Rudyard Kipling (to take an author of a higher type than those before mentioned) is called, and called justly, a popular author; that is to say, he is widely read, greatly enjoyed, and highly remunerated; he has achieved the paradox of at once making poetry and making money. But let anyone who wishes to see the difference try the experiment of assuming the Kipling characters to be common property like the Dickens characters. Let anyone go into an average parlour and allude to Strickland as he would allude to Mr. Bumble, the Beadle. Let anyone say that somebody is "a perfect Learoyd," as he would say "a perfect Pecksniff." Let anyone write a comic paragraph for a halfpenny paper, and allude to Mrs. Hawksbee instead of to Mrs. Gamp. He will soon discover that the modern world has forgotten its own fiercest booms more completely than it has forgotten this formless tradition from its fathers. The mere dregs of it come to more than any contemporary excitement; the gleaning of the grapes of "Pickwick" is more than the whole vintage of "Soldiers Three." There is one instance, and I think only one, of an exception to this generalisation; there is one figure in our popular literature which would really be recognised by the populace. Ordinary men would understand you if you referred currently to Sherlock Holmes. Sir Arthur Conan Doyle would no doubt be justified in rearing his head to the stars, remembering that Sherlock Holmes is the only really familiar figure in modern fiction. But let him droop that head again with a gentle sadness, remembering that if Sherlock Holmes is the only familiar figure in modern fiction Sherlock Holmes is also the only familiar figure in the Sherlock Holmes tales. Not many people could say offhand what was the name of the owner of Silver Blaze, or whether Mrs. Watson was dark or fair. But if Dickens had written the Sherlock Holmes stories, every character in them would have been equally arresting and memorable. A Sherlock Holmes would have cooked the dinner for Sherlock Holmes; a Sherlock Holmes would have driven his cab. If

Dickens brought in a man merely to carry a letter, he had time for a touch or two, and made him a giant. Dickens not only conquered the world, he conquered it with minor characters. Mr. John Smauker, the servant of Mr. Cyrus Bantam, though he merely passes across the stage, is almost as vivid to us as Mr. Samuel Weller, the servant of Mr. Samuel Pickwick. The young man with the lumpy forehead, who only says "Esker" to Mr. Podsnap's foreign gentleman, is as good as Mr. Podsnap himself. They appear only for a fragment of time, but they belong to eternity. We have them only for an instant, but they have us for ever.

In dealing with Dickens, then, we are dealing with a man whose public success was a marvel and almost a monstrosity. And here I perceive that my friend, the purely artistic critic, primed himself with Flaubert and Turgenev, can contain himself no longer. He leaps to his feet, upsetting his cup of cocoa, and asks contemptuously what all this has to do with criticism. "Why begin your study of an author," he says, "with trash about popularity? Boothby is popular, and Le Queux is popular, and Mother Siegel is popular. If Dickens was even more popular, it may only mean that Dickens was even worse. The people like bad literature. If your object is to show that Dickens was good literature, you should rather apologise for his popularity, and try to explain it away. You should seek to show that Dickens's work was good literature, although it was popular. Yes, that is your task, to prove that Dickens was admirable, although he was admired!"

I ask the artistic critic to be patient for a little and to believe that I have a serious reason for registering this historic popularity. To that we shall come presently. But as a manner of approach I may perhaps ask leave to examine this actual and fashionable statement, to which I have supposed him to have recourse-the statement that the people like bad literature, and even like literature because it is bad. This way of stating the thing is an error, and in that error lies matter of much import to Dickens and his destiny in letters. The public does not like bad literature. The public likes a certain kind of literature and likes that kind of literature even when it is bad better than another kind of literature even when it is good. Nor is this unreasonable; for the line between different types of literature is as real as the line between tears and laughter; and to tell people who can only get bad comedy that you have some first-class tragedy is as irrational as to offer a man who is shivering over weak warm coffee a really superior sort of ice.

Ordinary people dislike the delicate modern work, not because it is good or because it is bad, but because it is not the thing that they asked for. If, for instance, you find them pent in sterile streets and hungering for adventure and a violent secrecy, and if you then give them their choice between "A Study in Scarlet," a good detective story, and "The Autobiography of Mark Rutherford," a good psychological monologue, no doubt they will prefer "A Study in Scarlet." But they will not do so because "The Autobiography of Mark Rutherford" is a very good monologue, but because it is evidently a very poor detective story. They will be indifferent to "Les Aveugles," not because it is good drama, but because it is bad melodrama. They do not like good introspective sonnets; but neither do they like bad introspective sonnets, of which there are many. When they walk behind the brass of the Salvation Army band, instead of listening to harmonies at Queen's Hall, it is always assumed that they prefer bad music. But it may be merely that they prefer military music, music marching down the open street, and that if Dan Godfrey's band could be smitten with salvation and lead them they would like that even better. And while they might easily get more satisfaction out of a screaming article in The War Cry than out of a page of Emerson about the Oversoul, this would not be because the page of Emerson is another and superior kind of literature. It would be because the page of Emerson is another (and inferior) kind of religion.

Dickens stands first as a defiant monument of what happens when a great literary genius has a literary taste akin to that of the community. For this kinship was deep and spiritual. Dickens was not like our ordinary demagogues and journalists. Dickens did not write what the people wanted. Dickens wanted what the people wanted. And with this was connected that other fact which must never be forgotten, and which I have more than once insisted on, that Dickens and his school had a hilarious faith in democracy and thought of the service of it as a sacred priesthood. Hence there was this vital point in his popularism, that there was no condescension in it. The belief that the rabble will only read rubbish can be read between the lines of all our contemporary writers, even of those writers whose rubbish the rabble reads. Mr. Fergus Hume has no more respect for the populace than Mr. George Moore. The only difference lies between those writers who will consent to talk down to the people, and those writers who will not consent to talk down to the people. But Dickens never talked down to the people. He talked up to the people. He approached the people like a deity and poured out his riches and his blood. This is what makes the immortal bond between him and the masses of men. He had not merely produced something they could understand, but he took it seriously, and toiled and agonised to produce it. They were not only enjoying one of the best writers, they were enjoying the best he could do. His raging and sleepless nights, his wild walks in the darkness, his note-books crowded, his nerves in rags, all this extraordinary output was but a fit sacrifice to the ordinary man. He climbed towards the lower classes. He panted upwards on weary wings to reach the heaven of the poor.

His power, then, lay in the fact that he expressed with an energy and brilliancy quite uncommon the things close to the common mind. But with this mere phrase, the common mind, we collide with a current error. Commonness and the common mind are now generally spoken of as meaning in some manner inferiority and the inferior mind; the mind of the mere mob. But the common mind means the mind of all the artists and heroes; or else it would not be common. Plato had the common mind; Dante had the common mind; or that mind was not common. Commonness means the quality common to the saint and the sinner, to the philosopher and the fool; and it was this that Dickens grasped and developed. In everybody there is a certain thing that loves babies, that fears death, that likes sunlight that thing enjoys Dickens. And everybody does not mean uneducated crowds; everybody means everybody: everybody means Mrs. Meynell. This lady, a cloistered and fastidious writer, has written one of the best eulogies of Dickens that exist, an essay in praise of his pungent perfection of epithet. And when I say that everybody understands Dickens I do not mean that he is suited to the untaught intelligence. I mean that he is so plain that even scholars can understand him.

The best expression of the fact, however, is to be found in noting the two things in which he is most triumphant. In order of artistic value, next after his humour, comes his horror. And both his humour and his horror are of a kind strictly to be called human; that is, they belong to the basic part of us, below the lowest roots of our variety. His horror for instance is a healthy churchyard horror, a fear of the grotesque defamation called death; and this every man has, even if he also has the more delicate and depraved fears that come of an evil spiritual outlook. We may be afraid of a fine shade with Henry James; that is, we may be afraid of the world. We may be afraid of a taut silence with Maeterlinck, that is, we may be afraid of our own souls. But every one will certainly be afraid of a Cock Lane Ghost, including Henry James and Maeterlinck. This latter is literally a mortal fear, a fear of death; it is not the immortal fear, or fear of damnation, which belongs to all the more refined intellects of our day. In a word, Dickens does, in the exact sense, make the flesh creep; he does not, like the decadents, make the soul crawl. And the creeping of the flesh on being reminded of its fleshly failure is a strictly universal thing which we can all feel, while some of us are as yet uninstructed in the art of spiritual crawling. In the same way the Dickens mirth is a part of man and universal. All men can laugh at broad humour, even the subtle humorists. Even the modern flâneur, who can smile at a particular combination of green and yellow, would laugh at Mr. Lammle's request for Mr. Fledgeby's nose. In a word-the common things are common-even to the uncommon people.

These two primary dispositions of Dickens, to make the flesh creep and to make the sides ache, were a sort of twins of his spirit; they were never far apart and the fact of their affinity is interestingly exhibited in the first two novels.

Generally he mixed the two up in a book and mixed a great many other things with them. As a rule he cared little if he kept six stories of quite different colours running in the same book. The effect was sometimes similar to that of playing six tunes at once. He does not mind the coarse tragic figure of Jonas Chuzzlewit crossing the mental stage which is full of the allegorical pantomime of Eden, Mr. Chollop and The Watertoast Gazette, a scene which is as much of a satire as "Gulliver," and nearly as much of a fairy tale. He does not mind binding up a rather pompous sketch of prostitution in the same book with an adorable impossibility like Bunsby. But "Pickwick" is so far a coherent thing that it is coherently comic and consistently rambling. And as a consequence his next book was, upon the whole, coherently and consistently horrible. As his natural turn for terrors was kept down in "Pickwick," so his natural turn for joy and laughter is kept down in "Oliver Twist." In "Oliver Twist" the smoke of the thieves' kitchen hangs over the whole tale, and the shadow of Fagin falls everywhere. The little lamp-lit rooms of Mr. Brownlow and Rose Maylie are to all appearance purposely kept subordinate, a mere foil to the foul darkness without. It was a strange and appropriate accident that Cruikshank and not "Phiz" should have illustrated this book. There was about Cruikshank's art a kind of cramped energy which is almost the definition of the criminal mind. His drawings have a dark strength: yet he does not only draw morbidly, he draws meanly. In the doubled-up figure and frightful eyes of Fagin in the condemned cell there is not only a baseness of subject; there is a kind of baseness in the very technique of it. It is not drawn with the free lines of a free man; it has the half-witted secrecies of a hunted thief. It does not look merely like a picture of Fagin; it looks like a picture by Fagin. Among these dark and detestable plates there is one which has, with a kind of black directness, the dreadful poetry that does inhere in the story, stumbling as it often is. It represents Oliver asleep at an open window in the house of one of his humaner patrons. And outside the window, but as big and close as if they were in the room, stand Fagin and the foul-laced Monks, staring at him with dark monstrous visages and great white wicked eyes, in the style of the simple devilry of the draughtsman. The very naïveté of the horror is horrifying: the very woodenness of the two wicked men seems to make them worse than mere men who are wicked. But this picture of big devils at the window-sill does express, as has been suggested above, the thread of poetry in the whole thing; the sense, that is, of the thieves as a kind of army of devils compassing earth and sky crying for Oliver's soul and besieging the house in which he is barred for safety. In this matter there is, I think, a difference between the author and the illustrator. In Cruikshank there was surely something morbid; but, sensitive and sentimental as Dickens was, there was nothing morbid in him. He had, as Stevenson had, more of the mere boy's love of suffocating stories of blood and darkness; of skulls, of gibbets, of all the things, in a word, that are sombre without being sad. There is a ghastly joy in remembering our boyish reading about Sikes and his flight; especially about the voice of that unbearable pedlar which went on in a monotonous and maddening sing-song, "will wash out grease-stains, mud-stains, blood-stains," until Sikes fled almost screaming. For this boyish mixture of appetite and repugnance there is a good popular phrase, "supping on horrors." Dickens supped on horrors as he supped on Christmas pudding. He supped on horrors because he was an optimist and could sup on anything. There was no saner or simpler schoolboy than Traddles, who covered all his books with skeletons.

"Oliver Twist" had begun in Bentley's Miscellany, which Dickens edited in 1837. It was interrupted by a blow that for the moment broke the author's spirit and seemed to have broken his heart. His wife's sister, Mary Hogarth, died suddenly. To Dickens his wife's family seems to have been like his own; his affections were heavily committed to the sisters, and of this one he was peculiarly fond. All his life, through much conceit and sometimes something bordering on selfishness, we can feel the redeeming note of an almost tragic tenderness; he was a man who could really have died of love or sorrow. He took up the work of "Oliver Twist" again later in the year, and finished it at the end of 1838. His work was incessant and almost bewildering. In 1838 he had already brought out the first number of "Nicholas Nickleby." But the great popularity went booming on; the whole world was roaring for books by Dickens, and more books by Dickens, and Dickens was labouring night and day like a factory. Among other things he edited the "Memoirs of Grimaldi," The incident is only worth mentioning for the sake of one more example of the silly ease with which Dickens was drawn by criticism and the clever ease with which he managed, in these small squabbles, to defend himself. Somebody mildly suggested that, after all, Dickens had never known Grimaldi. Dickens was down on him like a thunderbolt, sardonically asking how close an intimacy Lord Braybrooke had with Mr. Samuel Pepys.

"Nicholas Nickleby" is the most typical perhaps of the tone of his earlier works. It is in form a very rambling, old-fashioned romance, the kind of romance in which the hero is only a convenience for the frustration of the villain. Nicholas is what is called in theatricals a stick. But any stick is good enough to beat a Squeers with. That strong thwack, that simplified energy is the whole object of such a story; and the whole of this tale is full of a kind of highly picturesque platitude. The wicked aristocrats, Sir Mulberry Hawk, Lord Verisopht and the rest are inadequate versions of the fashionable profligate. But this is not (as some suppose) because Dickens in his vulgarity could not comprehend the refinement of patrician vice. There is no idea more vulgar or more ignorant than the notion that a gentleman is generally what is called refined. The error of the Hawk conception is that, if anything, he is too refined. Real aristocratic blackguards do not swagger and rant so well. A real fast baronet would not have defied Nicholas in the tavern with so much oratorical dignity. A real fast baronet would probably have been choked with apoplectic embarrassment and said nothing at all. But Dickens read into this aristocracy a grandiloquence and a natural poetry which, like all melodrama, is really the precious jewel of the poor.

But the book contains something which is much more Dickensian. It is exquisitely characteristic of Dickens that the truly great achievement of the story is the person who delays the story. Mrs. Nickleby, with her beautiful mazes of memory, does her best to prevent the story of Nicholas Nickleby from being told. And she does well. There is no particular necessity that we should know what happens to Madeline Bray. There is a desperate and crying necessity that we should know Mrs. Nickleby once had a foot-boy who had a wart on his nose and a driver who had a green shade over his left eye. If Mrs. Nickleby is a fool, she is one of those fools who are wiser than the world. She stands for a great truth which we must not forget; the truth that experience is not in real life a saddening thing at all. The people who have had misfortunes are generally the people who love to talk about them. Experience is really one of the gaieties of old age, one of its dissipations. Mere memory becomes a kind of debauch. Experience may be disheartening to those who are foolish enough to try to coordinate it and to draw deductions from it. But to those happy souls, like Mrs. Nickleby, to whom relevancy is nothing, the whole of their past life is like an inexhaustible fairyland. Just as we take a rambling walk because we know that a whole district is beautiful, so they indulge a rambling mind because they know that a whole existence is interesting. A boy does not plunge into his future more romantically and at random, than they plunge into their past.

Another gleam in the book is Mr. Mantalini. Of him, as of all the really great comic characters of Dickens, it is impossible to speak with any critical adequacy. Perfect absurdity is a direct thing, like physical pain, or a strong smell. A joke is a fact. However indefensible it is it cannot be attacked. However defensible it is it cannot be defended. That Mr. Mantalini should say in praising the "outline" of his wife, "The two Countesses had no outlines, and the Dowager's was a demd outline," —this can only be called an unanswerable absurdity. You may try to analyze it, as Charles Lamb did the indefensible joke about the hare; you may dwell for a moment on the dark distinctions between the negative disqualification of the Countess and the positive disqualification of the Dowager, but you will not capture the violent beauty of it in any way. "She will be a lovely widow. I shall be a body. Some handsome women will cry; she will laugh demnebly." This vision of demoniac heartlessness has the same defiant finality. I mention the matter here, but it has to be remembered in connection with all the comic masterpieces of Dickens. Dickens has greatly suffered with the critics precisely through this stunning simplicity in his best work. The critic is called upon to describe his sensations while enjoying Mantalini and Micawber, and he can no more describe them than he can describe a blow in the face, Thus Dickens, in this self-conscious, analytical and descriptive age, loses both ways.

He is doubly unfitted for the best modern criticism, His bad work is below that criticism. His good work is above it.

But gigantic as were Dickens's labours, gigantic as were the exactions from him, his own plans were more gigantic still. He had the type of mind that wishes to do every kind of work at once; to do everybody's work as well as its own. There floated before him a vision of a monstrous magazine, entirely written by himself. It is true that when this scheme came to be discussed, ho suggested that other pens might be occasionally employed; but, reading between the lines, it is sufficiently evident that he thought of the thing as a kind of vast multiplication of himself, with Dickens as editor opening letters, Dickens as leader-writer writing leaders, Dickens as reporter reporting meetings, Dickens as reviewer reviewing books, Dickens, for all I know, as office-boy opening and shutting doors. This serial, of which he spoke to Messrs. Chapman & Hall, began and broke off and remains as a colossal fragment bound together under the title of "Master Humphrey's Clock." One characteristic thing he wished to have in the periodical. He suggested an Arabian Nights of London, in which Gog and Magog, the giants of the city, should give forth chronicles as enormous as themselves. He had a taste for these schemes or frameworks for many tales. He made and abandoned many; many he half-fulfilled. I strongly suspect that he meant Major Jackman, in "Mrs. Lirriper's Lodgings" and "Mrs. Lirriper's Legacy," to start a series of studies of that lady's lodgers, a kind of history of No. 81, Norfolk Street, Strand. "The Seven Poor Travellers" was planned for seven stories; we will not say seven poor stories. Dickens had meant, probably, to write a tale for each article of "Somebody's Luggage": he only got as far as the hat and the boots. This gigantesque scale of literary architecture, huge and yet curiously cosy, is characteristic of his spirit, fond of size and yet fond of comfort. He liked to have story within story, like room within room of some labyrinthine but comfortable castle. In this spirit he wished "Master Humphrey's Clock" to begin, and to be a big frame or bookcase for numberless novels. The clock started; but the clock stopped.

In the prologue by Master Humphrey reappear Mr. Pickwick and Sam Weller, and of that resurrection many things have been said, chiefly expressions of a reasonable regret. Doubtless they do not add much to their author's reputation, but they add a great deal to their author's pleasure. It was ingrained in him to wish to meet old friends. All his characters are, so to speak, designed to be old friends; in a sense every Dickens character is an old friend, even when he first appears. He comes to us mellow out of many implied interviews, and carries the firelight on his face. Dickens was simply pleased to meet Pickwick again, and being pleased, he made the old man too comfortable to be amusing.

But "Master Humphrey's Clock" is now scarcely known except as the shell of one of the well-known novels. "The Old Curiosity Shop" was published in accordance with the original "Clock" scheme. Perhaps the most typical thing about it is the title. There seems no reason in particular, at the first and most literal glance, why the story should be called after the Old Curiosity Shop. Only two of the characters have anything to do with such a shop, and they leave it for ever in the first few pages. It is as if Thackeray had called the whole novel of "Vanity Fair" "Miss Pinkerton's Academy." It is as if Scott had given the whole story of "The Antiquary" the title of "The Hawes Inn." But when we feel the situation with more fidelity we realise that this title is something in the nature of a key to the whole Dickens romance. His tales always started from some splendid hint in the streets. And shops, perhaps the most poetical of all things, often set off his fancy galloping. Every shop, in fact, was to him the door of romance. Among all the huge serial schemes of which we have spoken, it is a matter of wonder that he never started an endless periodical called "The Street," and divided it into shops. He could have written an exquisite romance called "The Baker's Shop"; another called "The Chemist's Shop"; another called "The Oil Shop," to keep company with "The Old Curiosity Shop." Some incomparable baker he invented and forgot. Some gorgeous chemist might have been. Some more than mortal oil-man is lost to us for ever. This Old Curiosity Shop he did happen to linger by: its tale he did happen to tell.

Around "Little Nell," of course, a controversy raged and rages; some implored Dickens not to kill her at the end of the story: some regret that he did not kill her at the beginning. To me the chief interest in this young person lies in the fact that she is an example, and the most celebrated example of what must have been, I think, a personal peculiarity, perhaps, a personal experience of Dickens. There is, of course, no paradox at all in saying that if we find in a good book a wildly impossible character it is very probable indeed that it was copied from a real person. This is one of the commonplaces of good art criticism. For although people talk of the restraints of fact and the freedom of fiction, the case for most artistic purposes is quite the other way. Nature is as free as air: art is forced to look probable. There may be a million things that do happen, and yet only one thing that convinces us is likely to happen. Out of a million possible things there may be only one appropriate thing. I fancy, therefore, that many stiff, unconvincing characters are copied from the wild freak-show of real life. And in many parts of Dickens's work there is evidence of some peculiar affection on his part for a strange sort of little girl; a little girl with a premature sense of responsibility and duty; a sort of saintly precocity. Did he know some little girl of this kind? Did she die, perhaps, and remain in his memory in colours too ethereal and pale? In any case there are a great number of them in his works. Little Dorrit was one of them, and Florence Dombey with her brother, and even Agnes in infancy; and, of course, Little Nell. And, in any case, one thing is evident; whatever charm these children may have they have not the charm of childhood. They are not little children: they are "little mothers." The beauty and divinity in a child lie in his not being worried, not being conscientious, not being like Little Nell. Little Nell has never any of the sacred bewilderment of a baby. She never wears that face, beautiful but almost half-witted, with which a real child half understands that there is evil in the universe.

As usual, however, little as the story has to do with the title, the splendid and satisfying pages have even less to do with the story. Dick Swiveller is perhaps the noblest of all the noble creations of Dickens. He has all the overwhelming absurdity of Mantalini, with the addition of being human and credible, for he knows he is absurd. His high-falutin is not done because he seriously thinks it right and proper, like that of Mr. Snodgrass, nor is it done because he thinks it will serve his turn, like that of Mr. Pecksniff, for both these beliefs are improbable; it is done because he really loves high-falutin, because he has a lonely literary pleasure in exaggerative language. Great draughts of words are to him like great draughts of wine—pungent and yet refreshing, light and yet leaving him in a glow. In unerring instinct for the perfect folly of a phrase he has no equal, even among the giants of Dickens. "I am sure," says Miss Wackles, when she had been flirting with Cheggs, the market-gardener, and reduced Mr. Swiveller to Byronic renunciation, "I am sure I'm very sorry if——" "Sorry," said Mr. Swiveller, "sorry in the possession of a Cheggs!" The abyss of bitterness is unfathomable. Scarcely less precious is the poise of Mr. Swiveller when he imitates the stage brigand. After crying, "Some wine here! Ho!" he hands the flagon to himself with profound humility, and receives it haughtily. Perhaps the very best scene in the book is that between Mr. Swiveller and the single gentleman with whom he endeavours to remonstrate for having remained in bed all day: "We cannot have single gentlemen coming into the place and sleeping like double gentlemen without paying extra . . . An equal amount of slumber was never got out of one bed, and if you want to sleep like that you must pay for a double-bedded room." His relations with the Marchioness are at once purely romantic and purely genuine; there is nothing even of Dickens's legitimate exaggerations about them. A shabby, larky, good-natured clerk would, as a matter of fact, spend hours in the society of a little servant girl if he found her about the house. It would arise partly from a dim kindliness, and partly from that mysterious instinct which is sometimes called, mistakenly, a love of low company—that mysterious instinct which makes so many men of pleasure find something soothing in the society of uneducated people, particularly uneducated women. It is the instinct which accounts for the otherwise unaccountable popularity of barmaids.

And still the pot of that huge popularity boiled. In 1841 another novel was demanded, and "Barnaby Rudge" supplied. It is chiefly of interest as an embodiment of that other element in

Dickens, the picturesque or even the pictorial. Barnaby Rudge, the idiot with his rags and his feathers and his raven, the bestial hangman, the blind mob-all make a picture, though they hardly make a novel. One touch there is in it of the richer and more humorous Dickens, the boy-conspirator, Mr. Sim Tappertit. But he might have been treated with more sympathy-with as much sympathy, for instance, as Mr. Dick Swiveller; for he is only the romantic guttersnipe, the bright boy at the particular age when it is most fascinating to found a secret society and most difficult to keep a secret. And if ever there was a romantic guttersnipe on earth it was Charles Dickens. "Barnaby Rudge" is no more an historical novel than Sim's secret league was a political movement; but they are both beautiful creations. When all is said, however, the main reason for mentioning the work here is that it is the next bubble in the pot, the next thing that burst out of that whirling, seething head. The tide of it rose and smoked and sang till it boiled over the pot of Britain and poured over all America. In the January of 1842 he set out for the United States.

Chapter 6
Dickens and America

The essential of Dickens's character was the conjunction of common sense with uncommon sensibility. The two things are not, indeed, in such an antithesis as is commonly imagined. Great English literary authorities, such as Jane Austen and Mr. Chamberlain, have put the word "sense" and the word "sensibility" in a kind of opposition to each other. But not only are they not opposite words: they are actually the same word. They both mean receptiveness or approachability by the facts outside us. To have a sense of colour is the same as to have a sensibility to colour. A person who realises that beef-steaks are appetising shows his sensibility. A person who realises that moonrise is romantic shows his sense. But it is not difficult to see the meaning and need of the popular distinction between sensibility and sense, particularly in the form called common sense. Common sense is a sensibility duly distributed in all normal directions; sensibility has come to mean a specialised sensibility in one. This is unfortunate, for it is not the sensibility that is bad, but the specialising; that is, the lack of sensibility to everything else. A young lady who stays out all night to look at the stars should not be blamed for her sensibility to starlight, but for her insensibility to other people. A poet who recites his own verses from ten to five with the tears rolling down his face should decidedly be rebuked for his lack of, sensibility-his lack of sensibility to those grand rhythms of the social harmony, crudely called manners. For all politeness is a long poem, since it is full of recurrences. This balance of all the sensibilities we call sense; and it is in this capacity that it becomes of great importance as an attribute of the character of Dickens.

Dickens, I repeat, had common sense and uncommon sensibility. That is to say, the proportion of interests in him was about the same as that of an ordinary man, but he felt all of them more excitedly. This is a distinction not easy for us to keep in mind, because we hear today chiefly of two types, the dull man who likes ordinary things mildly, and the extraordinary man who likes extraordinary things wildly. But Dickens liked quiet ordinary things; he merely made an extraordinary fuss about them. His excitement was sometimes like an epileptic fit; but it must not be confused with the fury of the man of one idea or one line of ideas. He had the excess of the eccentric, but not the defects, the narrowness. Even when he raved like a maniac he did not rave like a monomaniac. He had no particular spot of sensibility or spot of insensibility: he was merely a normal man minus a normal self-command. He had no special point of mental pain or repugnance, like Ruskin's horror of steam and iron, or Mr. Bernard Shaw's permanent irritation against romantic love. He was annoyed at the ordinary annoyances: only he was more annoyed than was necessary. He did not desire strange delights, blue wine or black women with Baudelaire, or cruel sights east of Suez with Mr. Kipling. He wanted what a healthy man wants, only he was ill with wanting it. To understand him, in a word, we must keep well in mind the medical distinction between delicacy and disease. Perhaps we shall comprehend it and him more clearly if we think of a woman rather than a man. There was much that was feminine about Dickens, and nothing more so than this abnormal normality. A woman is often, in comparison with a man, at once more sensitive and more sane.

This distinction must be especially remembered in all his quarrels. And it must be most especially remembered in what may be called his great quarrel with America, which we have now to approach. The whole incident is so typical of Dickens's attitude to everything and anything, and especially of Dickens's attitude to anything political, that I may ask permission to approach the matter by another, a somewhat long and curving avenue.

Common sense is a fairy thread, thin and faint, and as easily lost as gossamer. Dickens (in large matters) never lost it. Take, as an example, his political tone, or drift throughout his life. His views, of course, may have been right or wrong; the reforms he supported may have been successful or otherwise: that is not a matter for this book. But if we compare him with the other men that wanted the same things (or the other men that wanted the other things) we feel a startling absence of cant, a startling sense of humanity as it is and of the eternal weakness.

He was a fierce democrat, but in his best vein he laughed at the cocksure Radical of common life, the red-faced man who said, "Prove it!" when anybody said anything. He fought for the right to elect: but he would not whitewash elections. He believed in Parliamentary government; but he did not, like our contemporary newspapers, pretend that Parliament is something much more heroic and imposing than it is. He fought for the rights of the grossly oppressed Nonconformists, but he spat out of his mouth the unction of that too easy seriousness with which they oiled everything, and held up to them like a horrible mirror the foul fat face of Chadband. He saw that Mr. Podsnap thought too little of places outside England. But he saw that Mrs. Jellaby thought too much of them. In the last book he wrote he gives us, in Mr. Honeythunder, a hateful and wholesome picture of all the Liberal catchwords pouring out of one illiberal man. But perhaps the best evidence of this steadiness and sanity is the fact that, dogmatic as he was, he never tied himself to any passing dogma: he never got into any cul de sac or civic or economic fanaticism: he went down the broad road of the Revolution. He never admitted that economically, we must make hells of workhouses, any more than Rousseau would have admitted it. He never said the State had no right to teach children or save their bones, any more than Danton would have said it. He was a fierce Radical; but he was never a Manchester Radical. He used the test of Utility, but he was never a Utilitarian. While economists were writing soft words he wrote "Hard Times," which Macaulay called "sullen Socialism," because it was not complacent Whiggism. But Dickens was never a Socialist any more than he was an Individualist; and, whatever else he was, he certainly was not sullen. He was not even a politician of any kind. He was simply a man of very clear, airy judgment on things that did not inflame his private temper, and he perceived that any theory that tried to run the living State entirely on one force and motive was probably nonsense. Whenever the Liberal philosophy had embedded in it something hard and heavy and lifeless, by an instinct he dropped it out. He was too romantic, perhaps, but he would have to do only with real things. He may have cared too much about Liberty. But he cared nothing about "Laissez Faire."

Now, among many interests of his contact with America this interest emerges as infinitely the largest and most striking, that it gave a final example of this queer, unexpected coolness and candour of his, this abrupt and sensational rationality. Apart altogether from any question of the accuracy of his picture of America, the American indignation was particularly natural and inevitable. For the large circumstances of the age must be taken into account. At the end of the previous epoch the whole of our Christian civilisation had been startled from its sleep by trumpets to take sides in a bewildering Armageddon, often with eyes still misty. Germany and Austria found themselves on the side of the old order, France and America on the side of the new. England, as at the Reformation, took up eventually a dark middle position, maddeningly difficult to define. She created a democracy, but she kept an aristocracy: she reformed the House of Commons, but left the magistracy (as it is still) a mere league of gentlemen against the world. But underneath all this doubt and compromise there was in England a great and perhaps growing mass of dogmatic democracy; certainly thousands, probably millions expected a Republic in fifty years. And for these the first instinct was obvious. The first instinct was to look across the Atlantic to where lay a part of ourselves already Republican, the van of the advancing English on the road to liberty. Nearly all the great Liberals of the nineteenth century enormously idealised America. On the other hand, to the Americans, fresh from their first epic of arms, the defeated mother country, with its coronets and county magistrates, was only a broken feudal keep.

So much is self-evident. But nearly half-way through the nineteenth century there came out of England the voice of a violent satirist. In its political quality it seemed like the half-choked cry of the frustrated republic. It had no patience with the pretence that England was already free, that we had gained all that was valuable from the Revolution. It poured a cataract of contempt on the so-called working compromises of England, on the oligarchic cabinets, on the two artificial parties, on the government offices, on the J.P.'s, on the vestries, on the voluntary charities. This satirist was Dickens, and it must be remembered that he was not only fierce, but uproariously readable. He really damaged the things he struck at, a very rare thing. He stepped up to the grave official of the vestry, really trusted by the rulers, really feared like a god by the poor, and he tied round his neck a name that choked him; never again now can he be anything but Bumble. He confronted the fine old English gentleman who gives his patriotic services for nothing as a local magistrate, and he nailed him up as Nupkins, an owl in open day. For to this satire there is literally no answer; it cannot be denied that a man like Nupkins can be and is a magistrate, so long as we adopt the amazing method of letting the rich man of a district actually be the judge in it. We can only avoid the vision of the fact by shutting our eyes, and imagining the nicest rich man we can think of; and that, of course, is what we do. But Dickens, in this matter, was merely realistic; he merely asked us to look on Nupkins, on the wild, strange thing that we had made. Thus Dickens seemed to see England not at all as the country where freedom slowly broadened down from precedent to precedent, but as a rubbish heap of seventeenth-century bad habits abandoned by everybody else. That is, he looked at England almost with the eyes of an American democrat.

And so, when the voice, swelling in volume, reached America and the Americans, the Americans said, "Here is a man who will hurry the old country along, and tip her kings and beadles into the sea. Let him come here, and we will show him a race of free men such as he dreams of, alive upon the ancient earth. Let him come here and tell the English of the divine democracy towards which he drives them. There he has a monarchy and an oligarchy to make game of. Here is a republic for him to praise." It seemed, indeed, a very natural sequel, that having denounced undemocratic England as the wilderness, he should announce democratic America as the promised land. Any ordinary person would have prophesied that as he had pushed his rage at the old order almost to the edge of rant, he would push his encomium of the new order almost to the edge of cant. Amid a roar of republican idealism, compliments, hope, and anticipatory gratitude, the great democrat entered the great democracy. He looked about him; he saw a complete America, unquestionably progressive, unquestionably self-governing. Then, with a more than American coolness, and a more than American impudence, he sat down and wrote "Martin Chuzzlewit." That tricky and perverse sanity of his had mutinied again. Common sense is a wild thing, savage, and beyond rules; and it had turned on them and rent them.

The main course of action was as follows; and it is right to record it before we speak of the justice of it. When I speak of his sitting down and writing "Martin Chuzzlewit," I use, of course, an elliptical expression. He wrote the notes of the American part of "Martin Chuzzlewit" while he was still in America; but it was a later decision presumably that such impressions should go into a book, and it was little better than an afterthought that they should go into "Martin Chuzzlewit." Dickens had an uncommonly bad habit (artistically speaking) of altering a story in the middle as he did in the case of "Our Mutual Friend." And it is on record that he only sent young Martin to America because he did not know what else to do with him, and because (to say truth) the sales were falling off. But the first action, which Americans regarded as an equally hostile one, was the publication of "American Notes," the history of which should first be given. His notion of visiting America had come to him as a very vague notion, even before the appearance of "The Old Curiosity Shop." But it had grown in him through the whole ensuing period in the plaguing and persistent way that ideas did grow in him and live with him. He contended against the idea in a certain manner. He had much to induce him to contend against it. Dickens was by this time not only a husband, but a father, the father of several children, and their existence made a difficulty in itself. His wife, he said, cried whenever the project was mentioned. But it was a point in him that he could never, with any satisfaction, part with a project. He had that restless optimism, that kind of nervous optimism, which would always tend to say "Yes;" which is stricken with an immortal repentance, if ever it says "No." The idea of seeing America might be doubtful, but the idea of not seeing America was dreadful. "To miss this opportunity would be a sad thing," he says. " . . . God willing, I think it must be managed somehow!" It was managed somehow. First of all he wanted to take his children as well as his wife. Final obstacles to this fell upon him, but they did not frustrate him. A serious illness fell on him; but that did not frustrate him. He sailed for America in 1842.

He landed in America, and he liked it. As John Forster very truly says, it is due to him, as well as to the great country that welcomed him, that his first good impression should be recorded, and that it should be "considered independently of any modification it afterwards underwent." But the modification it afterwards underwent was, as I have said above, simply a sudden kicking against cant, that is, against repetition. He was quite ready to believe that all Americans were free men. He would have believed it if they had not all told him so. He was quite prepared to be pleased with America. He would have been pleased with it if it had not been so much pleased with itself. The "modification" his views underwent did not arise from any modification of America as he first saw it. His admiration did not change because America changed. It changed because America did not change. The Yankees enraged him at last, not by saying different things, but by saying the same things. They were a republic; they were a new and vigorous nation; it seemed natural that they should say so to a famous foreigner first stepping on to their shore. But it seemed maddening that they should say so to each other in every car and drinking saloon from morning till night. It was not that the Americans in any way ceased from praising him. It was rather that they went on praising him. It was not merely that their praises of him sounded beautiful when he first heard them. Their praises of themselves sounded beautiful when he first heard them. That democracy was grand, and that Charles Dickens was a remarkable person, were two truths that he certainly never doubted to his dying day. But, as I say, it was a soulless repetition that stung his sense of humour out of sleep; it woke like a wild beast for hunting, the lion of his laughter. He had heard the truth once too often. He had heard the truth for the nine hundred and ninety-ninth time, and he suddenly saw that it was falsehood.

It is true that a particular circumstance sharpened and defined his disappointment. He felt very hotly, as he felt everything, whether selfish or unselfish, the injustice of the American piracies of English literature, resulting from the American copyright laws. He did not go to America with any idea of discussing this; when, some time afterwards, somebody said that he did, he violently rejected the view as only describable "in one of the shortest words in the English language." But his entry into America was almost triumphal; the rostrum or pulpit was ready for him; he felt strong enough to say anything. He had been most warmly entertained by many American men of letters, especially by Washington Irving, and in his consequent glow of confidence he stepped up to the dangerous question of American copyright. He made many speeches attacking the American law and theory of the matter as unjust to English writers and to American readers. The effect appears to have astounded him. "I believe there is no country," he writes, "on the face of the earth where there is less freedom of opinion on any subject in reference to which there is a broad difference of opinion than in this. There! I write the words with reluctance, disappointment, and sorrow; but I believe it from the bottom of my soul . . . The notion that I, a man alone by myself in America, should venture to suggest to the Americans that there was one point on which they were neither just to their own countrymen nor to us, actually struck the boldest dumb! Washington Irving, Prescott, Hoffman, Bryant, Halleck, Dana, Washington Allston-every man who writes in this country is devoted to the question, and not one of them dares to raise his voice and complain of the atrocious state of the law . . . The wonder is that a breathing man can be found with temerity enough to suggest to the Americans the possibility of their having done wrong. I wish you could have seen the faces that I saw down both sides of the table at Hartford when I began to talk about Scott. I wish you could have heard how I gave it out. My blood so boiled when I thought of the monstrous injustice that I felt as if I were twelve feet high when I thrust it down their throats."

That is almost a portrait of Dickens. We can almost see the erect little figure, its face and hair like a flame.

For such reasons, among others, Dickens was angry with America. But if America was angry with Dickens, there were also reasons for it. I do not think that the rage against his copyright speeches was, as he supposed, merely national insolence and self-satisfaction. America is a mystery to any good Englishman; but I think Dickens managed somehow to touch it on a queer nerve. There is one thing, at any rate, that must strike all Englishmen who have the good fortune to have American friends; that is, that while there is no materialism so crude or so material as American materialism, there is also no idealism so crude or so ideal as American idealism. America will always affect an Englishman as being soft in the wrong place and hard in the wrong place; coarse exactly where all civilised men are delicate, delicate exactly where all grown-up men are coarse. Some beautiful ideal runs through this people, but it runs aslant. The only existing picture in which the thing I mean has been embodied is in Stevenson's "Wrecker," in the blundering delicacy of Jim Pinkerton. America has a new delicacy, a coarse, rank refinement. But there is another way of embodying the idea, and that is to say this-that nothing is more likely than that the Americans thought it very shocking in Dickens, the divine author, to talk about being done out of money. Nothing would be more American than to expect a genius to be too high-toned for trade. It is certain that they deplored his selfishness in the matter; it is probable that they deplored his indelicacy. A beautiful young dreamer, with flowing brown hair, ought not to be even conscious of his copyrights. For it is quite unjust to say that the Americans worship the dollar. They really do worship intellect-another of the passing superstitions of our time.

If America had then this Pinkertonian propriety, this new, raw sensibility, Dickens was the man to rasp it. He was its precise opposite in every way. The decencies he did respect were old-fashioned and fundamental. On top of these he had that lounging liberty and comfort which can only be had on the basis of very old conventions, like the carelessness of gentlemen and the deliberation of rustics. He had no fancy for being strung up to that taut and quivering ideality demanded by American patriots and public speakers. And there was something else also, connected especially with the question of copyright and his own pecuniary claims. Dickens was not in the least desirous of being thought too "high-souled" to want his wages, nor was he in the least ashamed of asking for them. Deep in him (whether the modern reader likes the quality or no) was a sense very strong in the old Radicals-very strong especially in the old English Radical —a sense of personal rights, one's own rights included, as something not merely useful but sacred. He did not think a claim any less just and solemn because it happened to be selfish; he did not divide claims into selfish and unselfish, but into right and wrong. It is significant that when he asked for his money, he never asked for it with that shamefaced cynicism, that sort of embarrassed brutality, with which the modern man of the world mutters something about business being business or looking after number one. He asked for his money in a valiant and ringing voice, like a man asking for his honour. While his American critics were moaning and sneering at his interested motives as a disqualification, he brandished his interested motives like a banner. "It is nothing to them," he cries in astonishment, "that, of all men living, I am the greatest loser by it" (the Copyright Law). "It is nothing that I have a claim to speak and be heard." The thing they set up as a barrier he actually presents as a passport. They think that he, of all men, ought not to speak because he is interested. He thinks that he, of all men, ought to speak because he is wronged.

But this particular disappointment with America in the matter of the tyranny of its public opinion was not merely the expression of the fact that Dickens was a typical Englishman; that is a man with a very sharp insistence upon individual freedom. It also worked back ultimately to that larger and vaguer disgust of which I have spoken-the disgust at the perpetual posturing of the people before a mirror. The tyranny was irritating, not so much because of the suffering it inflicted on the minority, but because of the awful glimpses that it gave of the huge and imbecile happiness of the majority. The very vastness of the vain race enraged him, its immensity, its unity, its peace. He was annoyed more with its contentment than with any of its discontents. The thought of that unthinkable mass of millions, every one of them saying that Washington was the greatest man on earth, and that the Queen lived in the Tower of London, rode his riotous fancy like a nightmare. But to the end he retained the outlines of his original republican ideal and lamented over America not as being too Liberal, but as not being Liberal enough. Among others, he used these somewhat remarkable words: "I tremble for a Radical coming here, unless he is a Radical on principle, by reason and reflection, and from the sense of right. I fear that if he were anything else he would return home a Tory . . . I say no more on that head for two months from this time, save that I do fear that the heaviest blow ever dealt at liberty will be dealt by this country, in the failure of its example on the earth."

We are still waiting to see if that prediction has been fulfilled; but nobody can say that it has been falsified.

He went west on the great canals; he went south and touched the region of slavery; he saw America superficially indeed, but as a whole. And the great mass of his experience was certainly pleasant, though he vibrated with anticipatory passion against slave-holders, though he swore he would accept no public tribute in the slave country (a resolve which he broke under the pressure of the politeness of the South), yet his actual collisions with slavery and its upholders were few and brief. In these he bore himself with his accustomed vivacity and fire, but it would be a great mistake to convey the impression that his mental reaction against America was chiefly, or even largely, due to his horror at the negro problem. Over and above the cant of which we have spoken; the weary rush of words, the chief complaint he made was a complaint against bad manners; and on a large view his anti-Americanism would seem to be more founded on spitting than on slavery. When, however, it did happen that the primary morality of man-owning came up for discussion, Dickens displayed an honourable impatience. One man, full of anti-abolitionist ardour, button-holed him and bombarded him with the well-known argument in defence of slavery, that it was not to the financial interest of a slave-owner to damage or weaken his own slaves. Dickens, in telling the story of this interview, writes as follows: "I told him quietly that it was not a man's interest to get drunk, or to steal, or to game, or to indulge in any other vice; but he did indulge in it for all that. That cruelty and the abuse of irresponsible power were two of the bad passions of human nature, with the gratification of which considerations of interest or of ruin had nothing whatever to do . . . " It is hardly possible to doubt that Dickens, in telling the man this, told him something sane and logical and unanswerable. But it is perhaps permissible to doubt whether he told it to him quietly.

He returned home in the spring of 1842, and in the later part of the year his "American Notes" appeared, and the cry against him that had begun over copyright swelled into a roar in his rear. Yet when we read the "Notes" we can find little offence in them, and, to say truth, less interest than usual. They are no true picture of America, or even of his vision of America, and this for two reasons. First, that he deliberately excluded from them all mention of that copyright question which had really given him his glimpse of how tyrannical a democracy can be. Second, that here he chiefly criticises America for faults which are not, after all, especially American. For example, he is indignant with the inadequate character of the prisons, and compares them unfavourably with those in England, controlled by Lieutenant Tracey, and by Captain Chesterton at Coldbath Fields, two reformers of prison discipline for whom he had a high regard. But it was a mere accident that American gaols were inferior to English. There was and is nothing in the American spirit to prevent their effecting all the reforms of Tracey and Chesterton, nothing to prevent their doing anything that money and energy and organisation can do. America might have (for all I know, does have) a prison system cleaner and more humane and more efficient than any other in the world. And the evil genius of America might still remain-everything might remain that makes Pogram or Chollop irritating or absurd. And against the evil genius of America Dickens was now to strike a second and a very different blow.

In January, 1843, appeared the first number of the novel called "Martin Chuzzlewit." The earlier part of the book and the end, which have no connection with America or the American problem, in any case require a passing word. But except for the two gigantic grotesques on each side of the gateway of the tale, Pecksniff and Mrs. Gamp, "Martin Chuzzlewit" will be chiefly admired for its American excursion. It is a good satire embedded in an indifferent novel. Mrs. Gamp is, indeed, a sumptuous study, laid on in those rich, oily, almost greasy colours that go to make the English comic characters, that make the very diction of Falstaff fat, and quaking with jolly degradation. Pecksniff also is almost perfect, and much too good to be true. The only other thing to be noticed about him is that here, as almost everywhere else in the novels, the best figures are at their best when they have least to do. Dickens's characters are perfect as long as he can keep them out of his stories. Bumble is divine until a dark and practical secret is entrusted to him-as if anybody but a lunatic would entrust a secret to Bumble. Micawber is noble when he is doing nothing; but he is quite unconvincing when he is spying on Uriah Heep, for obviously neither Micawber nor anyone else would employ Micawber as a private detective. Similarly, while Pecksniff is the best thing in the story, the story is the worst thing in Pecksniff. His plot against old Martin can only be described by saying that it is as silly as old Martin's plot against him. His fall at the end is one of the rare falls of Dickens. Surely it was not necessary to take Pecksniff so seriously. Pecksniff is a merely laughable character; he is so laughable that he is lovable. Why take such trouble to unmask a man whose mask you have made transparent? Why collect all the characters to witness the exposure of a man in whom none of the characters believe? Why toil and triumph to have the laugh of a man who was only made to be laughed at?

But it is the American part of "Martin Chuzzlewit" which is our concern, and which is memorable. It has the air of a great satire; but if it is only a great slander it is still great. His serious book on America was merely a squib, perhaps a damp squib. In any case, we all know that America will survive such serious books. But his fantastic book may survive America. It may survive America as "The Knights" has survived Athens. "Martin Chuzzlewit" has this quality of great satire that the critic forgets to ask whether the portrait is true to the original, because the portrait is so much more important than the original. Who cares whether Aristophanes correctly described Kleon, who is dead, when he so perfectly describes the demagogue, who cannot die? Just as little, it may be, will some future age care whether the ancient civilisation of the west, the lost cities of New York and St. Louis, were fairly depicted in the colossal monument of Elijah Pogram. For there is much more in the American episodes than their intoxicating absurdity; there is more than humour in the young man who made the speech about the British Lion, and said, "I taunt that lion. Alone I dare him;" or in the other man who told Martin that when he said that Queen Victoria did not live in the Tower of London he "fell into an error not uncommon among his countrymen." He has his finger on the nerve of an evil which was not only in his enemies, but in himself. The great democrat has hold of one of the dangers of democracy. The great optimist confronts a horrible nightmare of optimism. Above all, the genuine Englishman attacks a sin that is not merely American, but English also. The eternal, complacent iteration of patriotic half-truths; the perpetual buttering of one's self all over with the same stale butter; above all, the big defiances of small enemies, or the very urgent challenges to very distant enemies; the cowardice so habitual and unconscious that it wears the plumes of courage-all this is an English temptation as well as an American one. "Martin Chuzzlewit" may be a caricature of America. America may be a caricature of England. But in the gravest college, in the quietest country house of England, there is the seed of the same essential madness that fills Dickens's book, like an asylum, with brawling Chollops and raving Jefferson Bricks. That essential madness is the idea that the good patriot is the man who feels at ease about his country. This notion of patriotism was unknown in the little pagan republics where our European patriotism began. It was unknown in the Middle Ages. In the eighteenth century, in the making of modern politics, a "patriot" meant a discontented man. It was opposed to the word "courtier," which meant an upholder of present conditions. In all other modern countries, especially in countries like France and Ireland, where real difficulties have been faced, the word "patriot" means something like a political pessimist. This view and these countries have exaggerations and dangers of their own; but the exaggeration and danger of England is the same as the exaggeration and danger of The Watertoast Gazette. The thing which is rather foolishly called the Anglo-Saxon civilisation is at present soaked through with a weak pride. It uses great masses of men not to procure discussion but to procure the pleasure of unanimity; it uses masses like bolsters. It uses its organs of public opinion not to warn the public, but to soothe it. It really succeeds not only in ignoring the rest of the world, but actually in forgetting it. And when a civilisation really forgets the rest of the world-lets it fall as something obviously dim and barbaric-then there is only one adjective for the ultimate fate of that civilisation, and that adjective is "Chinese."

Martin Chuzzlewit's America is a mad-house: but it is a mad-house we are all on the road to. For completeness and even comfort are almost the definitions of insanity. The lunatic is the man who lives in a small world but thinks it is a large one: he is the man who lives in a tenth of the truth, and thinks it is the whole. The madman cannot conceive any cosmos outside a certain tale or conspiracy or vision. Hence the more clearly we see the world divided into Saxons and non-Saxons, into our splendid selves and the rest, the more certain we may be that we are slowly and quietly going mad. The more plain and satisfying our state appears, the more we may know that we are living in an unreal world. For the real world is not satisfying. The more clear become the colours and facts of Anglo-Saxon superiority, the more surely we may know we are in a dream. For the real world is not clear or plain. The real world is full of bracing bewilderments and brutal surprises. Comfort is the blessing and the curse of the English, and of Americans of the Pogram type also. With them it is a loud comfort, a wild comfort, a screaming and capering comfort; but comfort at bottom still. For there is but an inch of difference between the cushioned chamber and the padded cell.

Chapter 7
Dickens and Christmas

In the July of 1844 Dickens went on an Italian tour, which he afterwards summarised in the book called "Pictures from Italy." They are, of course, very vivacious, but there is no great need to insist on them considered as Italian sketches; there is no need whatever to worry about them as a phase of the mind of Dickens when he travelled out of England. He never travelled out of England. There is no trace in all these amusing pages that he really felt the great foreign things which lie in wait for us in the south of Europe, the Latin civilisation, the Catholic Church, the art of the centre, the endless end of Rome. His travels are not travels in Italy, but travels in Dickensland. He sees amusing things; he describes them amusingly. But he would have seen things just as good in a street in Pimlico, and described them just as well. Few things were racier, even in his raciest novel, than his description of the marionette play of the death of Napoleon. Nothing could be more perfect than the figure of the doctor, which had something wrong with its wires, and hence "hovered about the couch and delivered medical opinions in the air." Nothing could be better as a catching of the spirit of all popular drama than the colossal depravity of the wooden image of "Sir Uudson Low." But there is nothing Italian about it. Dickens would have made just as good fun, indeed just the same fun, of a Punch and Judy show performing in Long Acre or Lincoln's Inn Fields.

Dickens uttered just and sincere satire on Plornish and Podsnap; but Dickens was as English as any Podsnap or any Plornish. He had a hearty humanitarianism, and a hearty sense of justice to all nations so far as he understood it. But that very kind of humanitarianism, that very kind of justice, were English. He was the Englishman of the type that made Free Trade, the most English of all things, since it was at once calculating and optimistic. He respected catacombs and gondolas, but that very respect was English. He wondered at brigands and volcanoes, but that very wonder was English. The very conception that Italy consists of these things was an English conception. The root things he never understood, the Roman legend, the ancient life of the Mediterranean, the world-old civilisation of the vine and olive, the mystery of the immutable Church. He never understood these things, and I am glad he never understood them: he could only have understood them by ceasing to be the inspired cockney that he was, the rousing English Radical of the great Radical age in England. That spirit of his was one of the things that we have had which were truly national. All other forces we have borrowed, especially those which flatter us most. Imperialism is foreign, socialism is foreign, militarism is foreign, education is foreign, strictly even Liberalism is foreign. But Radicalism was our own; as English as the hedgerows.

Dickens abroad, then, was for all serious purposes simply the Englishman abroad; the Englishman man abroad is for all serious purposes simply the Englishman at home. Of this generalisation one modification must be made. Dickens did feel a direct pleasure in the bright and busy exterior of the French life, the clean caps, the coloured uniforms, the skies like blue enamel, the little green trees, the little white houses, the scene picked out in primary colours, like a child's picture-book. This he felt, and this he put (by a stroke of genius) into the mouth of Mrs. Lirriper, a London landlady on a holiday: for Dickens always knew that it is the simple and not the subtle who feel differences; and he saw all his colours through the clear eyes of the poor. And in thus taking to his heart the streets, as it were, rather than the spires of the Continent, he showed beyond question that combination of which we have spoken-of common sense with common sensibility. For it is for the sake of the streets and shops and the coats and hats, that we should go abroad; they are far better worth going to see than the castles and cathedrals and Roman camps. For the wonders of the world are the same all over the world, at least all over the European world. Castles that throw valleys in shadow, minsters that strike the sky, roads so old that they seem to have been made by the gods, these are in all Christian countries. The marvels of man are at all our doors. A labourer hoeing turnips in Sussex has no need to be ignorant that the bones of Europe are the Roman roads. A clerk living in Lambeth

71

has no need not to know that there was a Christian art exuberant in the thirteenth century; for only across the river he can see the live stones of the Middle Ages surging together towards the stars. But exactly the things that do strike the traveller as extraordinary are the ordinary things, the food, the clothes, the vehicles; the strange things are cosmopolitan, the common things are national and peculiar. Cologne spire is lifted on the same arches as Canterbury; but the thing you cannot see out of Germany is a German beer-garden. There is no need for a Frenchman to go to look at Westminster Abbey as a piece of English architecture; it is not in the special sense a piece of English architecture. But a hansom cab is a piece of English architecture; a thing produced by the peculiar poetry of our cities, a symbol of a certain reckless comfort which is really English; a thing to draw a pilgrimage of the nations. The imaginative Englishman will be found all day in a café; the imaginative Frenchman in a hansom cab.

This sort of pleasure Dickens took in the Latin life; but no deeper kind. And the strongest of all possible indications of his fundamental detachment from it can be found in one fact. A great part of the time that he was in Italy he was engaged in writing "The Chimes," and such Christmas tales, tales of Christmas in the English towns, tales full of fog and snow and hail and happiness.

Dickens could find in any street divergences between man and man deeper than the divisions of nations. His fault was to exaggerate differences. He could find types almost as distinct as separate tribes of animals in his own brain and his own city, those two homes of a magnificent chaos. The only two southerners introduced prominently into his novels, the two in "Little Dorrit," are popular English foreigners, I had almost said stage foreigners. Villainy is, in English eyes, a southern trait, therefore one of the foreigners is villainous. Vivacity is, in English eyes, another southern trait, therefore the other foreigner is vivacious. But we can see from the outlines of both that Dickens did not have to go to Italy to get them. While poor panting millionaires, poor tired earls and poor God-forsaken American men of culture are plodding about Italy for literary inspiration, Charles Dickens made up the whole of that Italian romance (as I strongly suspect) from the faces of two London organ-grinders.

In the sunlight of the southern world, he was still dreaming of the firelight of the north. Among the palaces and the white campanili, he shut his eyes to see Marylebone and dreamed a lovely dream of chimney-pots. He was not happy, he said, without streets. The very foulness and smoke of London were lovable in his eyes and fill his Christmas tales with a vivid vapour. In the clear skies of the south he saw afar off the fog of London like a sunset cloud and longed to be in the core of it.

This Christmas tone of Dickens, in connection with his travels, is a matter that can only be expressed by a parallel with one of his other works. Much the same that has here been said of his "Pictures from Italy," may be said about his "Child's History of England;" with the difference that while the "Pictures from Italy" do in a sense add to his fame, the "History of England" in almost every sense detracts from it. But the nature of the limitation is the same. What Dickens was travelling in distant lands, that he was travelling in distant ages; a sturdy, sentimental English Radical with a large heart and a narrow mind. He could not help falling into that besetting sin or weakness of the modern progressive, the habit of regarding the contemporary questions as the eternal questions and the latest word as the last. He could not get out of his head the instinctive conception that the real problem before St. Dunstan was whether he should support Lord John Russell or Sir Robert Peel. He could not help seeing the remotest peaks lit up by the raging bonfire of his own passionate political crisis. He lived for the instant and its urgency; that is, he did what St. Dunstan did. He lived in an eternal present like all simple men. It is indeed "A Child's History of England;" but the child is the writer and not the reader.

But Dickens in his cheapest cockney utilitarianism was not only English, but unconsciously historic. Upon him descended the real tradition of "Merry England," and not upon the pallid mediaevalists who thought they were reviving it. The Pre-Raphaelites, the Gothicists, the admirers of the Middle Ages, had in their subtlety and sadness the spirit of the present day.

Dickens had in his buffoonery and bravery the spirit of the Middle Ages. He was much more mediaeval in his attacks on mediaevalism than they were in their defences of it. It was he who had the things of Chaucer, the love of large jokes and long stories and brown ale and all the white roads of England. Like Chaucer he loved story within story, every man telling a tale. Like Chaucer he saw something openly comic in men's motley trades. Sam Weller would have been a great gain to the Canterbury Pilgrimage and told an admirable story. Rosetti's Damozel would have been a great bore, regarded as too fast by the Prioress and too priggish by the Wife of Bath. It is said that in the somewhat sickly Victorian revival of feudalism which was called "Young England," a nobleman hired a hermit to live in his grounds. It is also said that the hermit struck for more beer. Whether this anecdote be true or not, it is always told as showing a collapse from the ideal of the Middle Ages to the level of the present day. But in the mere act of striking for beer the holy man was very much more "medieval" than the fool who employed him.

It would be hard to find a better example of this than Dickens's great defence of Christmas. In fighting for Christmas he was fighting for the old European festival. Pagan and Christian, for that trinity of eating, drinking and praying which to moderns appears irreverent, for the holy day which is really a holiday. He had himself the most babyish ideas about the past. He supposed the Middle Ages to have consisted of tournaments and torture-chambers, he supposed himself to be a brisk man of the manufacturing age, almost a Utilitarian. But for all that he defended the mediaeval feast which was going out against the Utilitarianism which was coming in. He could only see all that was bad in mediaevalism. But he fought for all that was good in it. And he was all the more really in sympathy with the old strength and simplicity because he only knew that it was good and did not know that it was old. He cared as little for mediaevalism as the mediaevals did. He cared as much as they did for lustiness and virile laughter and sad tales of good lovers and pleasant tales of good livers. He would have been very much bored by Ruskin and Walter Pater if they had explained to him the strange sunset tints of Lippi and Botticelli. He had no pleasure in looking on the dying Middle Ages. But he looked on the living Middle Ages, on a piece of the old uproarious superstition still unbroken; and he hailed it like a new religion. The Dickens character ate pudding to an extent at which the modern mediaevalists turned pale. They would do every kind of honour to an old observance, except observing it. They would pay to a Church feast every sort of compliment except feasting.

And (as I have said) as were his unconscious relations to our European past, so were his unconscious relations to England. He imagined himself to be, if anything, a sort of cosmopolitan; at any rate to be a champion of the charms and merits of continental lands against the arrogance of our island. But he was in truth very much more a champion of the old and genuine England against that comparatively cosmopolitan England which we have all lived to see. And here again the supreme example is Christmas. Christmas is, as I have said, one of numberless old European feasts of which the essence is the combination of religion with merry-making. But among those feasts it is also especially and distinctively English in the style of its merry-making and even in the style of its religion. For the character of Christmas (as distinct, for instance, from the continental Easter) lies chiefly in two things; first on the terrestrial side the note of comfort rather than the note of brightness; and on the spiritual side, Christian charity rather than Christian ecstasy. And comfort is, like charity, a very English instinct. Nay, comfort is, like charity, an English merit; though our comfort may and does degenerate into materialism, just as our charity may and does degenerate into laxity and make-believe.

This ideal of comfort belongs peculiarly to England; it belongs peculiarly to Christmas; above all, it belongs preeminently to Dickens. And it is astonishingly misunderstood. It is misunderstood by the continent of Europe; it is, if possible, still more misunderstood by the English of today. On the Continent the restaurateurs provide us with raw beef, as if we were savages; yet old English cooking takes as much care as French. And in England has arisen a parvenu patriotism which represents the English as everything but English; as a blend of Chinese stoicism, Latin militarism, Prussian rigidity, and American bad taste. And so England, whose fault is gentility and whose virtue is geniality, England with her tradition of the great gay gentlemen of

Elizabeth, is represented to the four quarters of the world (as in Mr. Kipling's religious poems) in the enormous image of a solemn cad. And because it is very difficult to be comfortable in the suburbs, the suburbs have voted that comfort is a gross and material thing. Comfort, especially this vision of Christmas comfort, is the reverse of a gross or material thing. It is far more poetical, properly speaking, than the Garden of Epicurus. It is far more artistic than the Palace of Art. It is more artistic because it is based upon a contrast, a contrast between the fire and wine within the house and the winter and the roaring rains without. It is far more poetical, because there is in it a note of defence, almost of war; a note of being besieged by the snow and hail; of making merry in the belly of a fort. The man who said that an Englishman's house is his castle said much more than he meant. The Englishman thinks of his house as something fortified and provisioned, and his very surliness is at root romantic. And this sense would naturally be strongest in wild winter nights, when the lowered portcullis and the lifted drawbridge do not merely bar people out, but bar people in. The Englishman's house is most sacred, not merely when the King cannot enter it, but when the Englishman cannot get out of it.

This comfort, then, is an abstract thing, a principle. The English poor shut all their doors and windows till their rooms reek like the Black Hole. They are suffering for an idea. Mere animal hedonism would not dream, as we English do, of winter feasts and little rooms, but of eating fruit in large and idle gardens. Mere sensuality would desire to please all its senses. But to our good dreams this dark and dangerous background is essential; the highest pleasure we can imagine is a defiant pleasure, a happiness that stands at bay. The word "comfort" is not indeed the right word, it conveys too much of the slander of mere sense; the true word is "cosiness," a word not translatable. One, at least, of the essentials of it is smallness, smallness in preference to largeness, smallness for smallness' sake. The merry-maker wants a pleasant parlour, he would not give twopence for a pleasant continent. In our difficult time, of course, a fight for mere space has become necessary. Instead of being greedy for ale and Christmas pudding we are greedy for mere air, an equally sensual appetite. In abnormal conditions this is wise; and the illimitable veldt is an excellent thing for nervous people. But our fathers were large and healthy enough to make a thing humane, and not worry about whether it was hygienic. They were big enough to get into small rooms.

Of this quite deliberate and artistic quality in the close Christmas chamber, the standing evidence is Dickens in Italy. He created these dim firelit tales like little dim red jewels, as an artistic necessity, in the centre of an endless summer. Amid the white cities of Tuscany he hungered for something romantic, and wrote about a rainy Christmas. Amid the pictures of the Uffizi he starved for something beautiful, and fed his memory on London fog. His feeling for the fog was especially poignant and typical. In the first of his Christmas tales, the popular "Christmas Carol," he suggested the very soul of it in one simile, when he spoke of the dense air, suggesting that "Nature was brewing on a large scale." This sense of the thick atmosphere as something to eat or drink, something not only solid but satisfactory, may seem almost insane, but it is no exaggeration of Dickens's emotion. We speak of a fog "that you could cut with a knife." Dickens would have liked the phrase as suggesting that the fog was a colossal cake. He liked even more his own phrase of the Titanic brewery, and no dream would have given him a wilder pleasure than to grope his way to some such tremendous vats and drink the ale of the giants.

There is a current prejudice against fogs, and Dickens, perhaps, is their only poet. Considered hygienically, no doubt this may be more or less excusable. But, considered poetically, fog is not undeserving, it has a real significance. We have in our great cities abolished the clean and sane darkness of the country. We have outlawed night and sent her wandering in wild meadows; we have lit eternal watch-fires against her return. We have made a new cosmos, and as a consequence our own sun and stars. And as a consequence also, and most justly, we have made our own darkness. Just as every lamp is a warm human moon, so every fog is a rich human nightfall. If it were not for this mystic accident we should never see darkness, and he who has never seen darkness has never seen the sun. Fog for us is the chief form of that outward pressure which compresses mere luxury into real comfort. It makes the world small, in the same spirit as in that common and happy cry that the world is small, meaning that it is full of friends. The first man that emerges out of the mist with a light, is for us Prometheus, a saviour bringing fire to men. He is that greatest and best of all men, greater than the heroes, better than the saints, Man Friday. Every rumble of a cart, every cry in the distance, marks the heart of humanity beating undaunted in the darkness. It is wholly human; man toiling in his own cloud. If real darkness is like the embrace of God, this is the dark embrace of man.

In such a sacred cloud the tale called "The Christmas Carol" begins, the first and most typical of all his Christmas tales. It is not irrelevant to dilate upon the geniality of this darkness, because it is characteristic of Dickens that his atmospheres are more important than his stories. The Christmas atmosphere is more important than Scrooge, or the ghosts either; in a sense, the background is more important than the figures. The same thing may be noticed in his dealings with that other atmosphere (besides that of good humour) which he excelled in creating, an atmosphere of mystery and wrong, such as that which gathers round Mrs. Clennam, rigid in her chair, or old Miss Havisham, ironically robed as a bride. Here again the atmosphere altogether eclipses the story, which often seems disappointing in comparison. The secrecy is sensational; the secret is tame. The surface of the thing seems more awful than the core of it. It seems almost as if these grisly figures, Mrs. Chadband and Mrs. Clennam, Miss Havisham, and Miss Flite, Nemo and Sally Brass, were keeping something back from the author as well as from the reader. When the book closes we do not know their real secret. They soothed the optimistic Dickens with something less terrible than the truth. The dark house of Arthur Clennam's childhood really depresses us; it is a true glimpse into that quiet street in hell, where live the children of that unique dispensation which theologians call Calvinism and Christians devil-worship. But some stranger crime had really been done there, some more monstrous blasphemy or human sacrifice than the suppression of some silly document advantageous to the silly Dorrits. Something worse than a common tale of jilting lay behind the masquerade and madness of the awful Miss Havisham. Something worse was whispered by the misshapen Quilp to the sinister Sally in that wild, wet summer-house by the river, something worse than the clumsy plot against the clumsy Kit. These dark pictures seem almost as if they were literally visions; things, that is, that Dickens saw but did not understand.

And as with his backgrounds of gloom, so with his backgrounds of good-will, in such tales as "The Christmas Carol." The tone of the tale is kept throughout in a happy monotony, though the tale is everywhere irregular and in some places weak. It has the same kind of artistic unity that belongs to a dream. A dream may begin with the end of the world and end with a tea-party; but either the end of the world will em as trivial as a tea-party or that tea-party will be as terrible as the day of doom. The incidents change wildly; the story scarcely changes at all. "The Christmas Carol" is a kind of philanthropic dream, an enjoyable nightmare, in which the scenes shift bewilderingly and seem as miscellaneous as the pictures in a scrap-book, but in which there is one constant state of the soul, a state of rowdy benediction and a hunger for human faces. The beginning is bout a winter day and a miser; yet the beginning is in no way bleak. The author starts with a kind of happy howl; he bangs on our door like a drunken carol singer; his style is festive and popular; he compares the snow and hail to philanthropists who "come down handsomely;" he compares the fog to unlimited beer. Scrooge is not really inhuman at the beginning any more than he is at the end. There is a heartiness in his inhospitable sentiments that is akin to humour and therefore to humanity; he is only a crusty old bachelor, and had (I strongly suspect) given away turkeys secretly all his life. The beauty and the real blessing of the story do not lie in the mechanical plot of it, the repentance of Scrooge, probable or improbable; they lie in the great furnace of real happiness that glows through Scrooge and everything around him; that great furnace, the heart of Dickens. Whether the Christmas visions would or would not convert Scrooge, they convert us. Whether or no the visions were evoked by real Spirits of the Past, Present, and Future, they were evoked by that truly exalted order of angels who are correctly called High Spirits. They are impelled and sustained by a quality which our contemporary artists ignore or almost deny, but which in a life decently lived is as normal and attainable as sleep, positive, passionate, conscious joy. The story sings from end to end like a happy man going home; and, like a happy and good man, when it cannot sing it yells. It is lyric and exclamatory, from the first exclamatory words of it. It is strictly a Christmas carol.

Dickens, as has been said, went to Italy with this kindly cloud still about him, still meditating on Yule mysteries. Among the olives and the orange-trees he wrote his second great Christmas tale, "The Chimes," at Genoa in 1844, a Christmas tale only differing from "The Christmas Carol" in being fuller of the grey rains of winter and the north. "The Chimes" is, like the "Carol," an appeal for charity and mirth, but it is a stern and fighting appeal: if the other is a Christmas carol, this is a Christmas war-song. In it Dickens hurled himself with even more than his usual militant joy and scorn into an attack upon a cant, which he said made his blood boil. This cant was nothing more nor less than the whole tone taken by three-quarters of the political and economic world towards the poor. It was a vague and vulgar Benthamism with a rollicking Tory touch in it. It explained to the poor their duties with a cold and coarse philanthropy unendurable by any free man. It had also at its command a kind of brutal banter, a loud good humour which Dickens sketches savagely in Alderman Cute. He fell furiously on all their ideas: the cheap advice to live cheaply, the base advice to live basely, above all, the preposterous primary assumption that the rich are to advise the poor and not the poor the rich. There were and are hundreds of these benevolent bullies. Some say that the poor should give up having children, which means that they should give up their great virtue of sexual sanity. Some say that they should give up "treating" each other, which means that they should give up all that remains to them of the virtue of hospitality. Against all of this Dickens thundered very thoroughly in "The Chimes." It may be remarked in passing that this affords another instance of a confusion already referred to, the confusion whereby Dickens supposed himself to be exalting the present over the past, whereas he was really dealing deadly blows at things strictly peculiar to the present. Embedded in this very book is a somewhat useless interview between Trotty Veck and the church bells, in which the latter lecture the former for having supposed (why, I don't know) that they were expressing regret for the disappearance of the Middle Ages. There is no reason why Trotty Veck or anyone else should idealise the Middle Ages, but certainly he was the last man in the world to be asked to idealise the nineteenth century, seeing that the smug and stingy philosophy, which poisons his life through the book, was an exclusive creation of that century. But, as I have said before, the fieriest mediaevalist may forgive Dickens for disliking the good things the Middle Ages took away, considering how he loved whatever good things the Middle Ages left behind. It matters very little that he hated old feudal castles when they were already old. It matters very much that he hated the New Poor Law while it was still new.

The moral of this matter in "The Chimes" is essential. Dickens had sympathy with the poor in the Greek and literal sense; he suffered with them mentally; for the things that irritated them were the things that irritated him. He did not pity the people, or even champion the people, or even merely love the people; in this matter he was the people. He alone in our literature is the voice not merely of the social substratum, but even of the subconsciousness of the substratum. He utters the secret anger of the humble. He says what the uneducated only think, or even only feel, about the educated. And in nothing is he so genuinely such a voice as in this fact of his fiercest mood being reserved for methods that are counted scientific and progressive. Pure and exalted atheists talk themselves into believing that the working-classes are turning with indignant scorn from the churches. The working-classes are not indignant against the churches in the least. The things the working-classes really are indignant against are the hospitals. The people has no definite disbelief in the temples of theology. The people has a very fiery and practical disbelief in the temples of physical science. The things the poor hate are the modern things, the rationalistic things-doctors, inspectors, poor law guardians, professional philanthropy. They never showed any reluctance to be helped by the old and corrupt monasteries. They will often die rather than be helped by the modern and efficient workhouse.

Of all this anger, good or bad, Dickens is the voice of an accusing energy. When, in "The Christmas Carol," Scrooge refers to the surplus population, the Spirit tells him, very justly, not to speak till he knows what the surplus is and where it is. The implication is severe but sound. When a group of superciliously benevolent economists look down into the abyss for the surplus population, assuredly there is only one answer that should be given to them; and that is to say, "If there is a surplus, you are a surplus." And if anyone were ever cut off, they would be. If the barricades went up in our streets and the poor became masters, I think the priests would escape, I fear the gentlemen would; but I believe the gutters would be simply running with the blood of philanthropists.

Lastly, he was at one with the poor in this chief matter of Christmas, in the matter, that is, of special festivity. There is nothing on which the poor are more criticised than on the point of spending large sums on small feasts; and though there are material difficulties, there is nothing in which they are more right. It is said that a Boston paradox-monger said, "Give us the luxuries of life and we will dispense with the necessities." But it is the whole human race that says it, from the first savage wearing feathers instead of clothes to the last costermonger having a treat instead of three meals.

The third of his Christmas stories, "The Cricket on the Hearth," calls for no extensive comment, though it is very characteristic. It has all the qualities which we have called dominant qualities in his Christmas sentiment. It has cosiness, that is the comfort that depends upon a discomfort surrounding it. It has a sympathy with the poor, and especially with the extravagance of the poor; with what may be called the temporary wealth of the poor. It has the sentiment of the hearth, that is, the sentiment of the open fire being the red heart of the room. That open fire is the veritable flame of England, still kept burning in the midst of a mean civilisation of stoves. But everything that is valuable in "The Cricket on the Hearth" is perhaps as well expressed in the title as it is in the story. The tale itself, in spite of some of those inimitable things that Dickens never failed to say, is a little too comfortable to be quite convincing. "The Christmas Carol" is the conversion of an anti-Christmas character. "The Chimes" is a slaughter of anti-Christmas characters. "The Cricket," perhaps, fails for lack of this crusading note. For everything has its weak side, and when full justice has been done to this neglected note of poetic comfort, we must remember that it has its very real weak side. The defect of it in the work of Dickens was that he tended sometimes to pile up the cushions until none of the characters could move. He is so much interested in effecting his state of static happiness that he forgets to make a story at all. His princes at the start of the story begin to live happily ever afterwards. We feel this strongly in "Master Humphrey's Clock" and we feel it sometimes in these Christmas stories. He makes his characters so comfortable that his characters begin to dream and drivel. And he makes his reader so comfortable that his reader goes to sleep.

The actual tale of the carrier and his wife sounds somewhat sleepily in our ears; we cannot keep our attention fixed on it, though we are conscious of a kind of warmth from it as from a great wood fire. We know so well that everything will soon be all right that we do not suspect when the carrier suspects, and are not frightened when the gruff Tackleton growls. The sound of the festivities at the end come fainter on our ears than did the shout of the Cratchits or the bells of Trotty Veck. All the good figures that followed Scrooge when he came growling out of the fog fade into the fog again.

Chapter 8
The Time of Transition

Dickens was back in London by the June of 1845. About this time he became the first editor of The Daily News, a paper which he had largely planned and suggested, and which, I trust, remembers its semi-divine origin. That his thoughts had been running, as suggested in the last chapter, somewhat monotonously on his Christmas domesticities, is again suggested by the rather singular fact that he originally wished The Daily News to be called The Cricket. Probably he was haunted again with his old vision of a homely, tale-telling periodical such as had broken off in "Master Humphrey's Clock." About this time, however, he was peculiarly unsettled. Almost as soon as he had taken the editorship he threw it up; and having only recently come back to England, he soon made up his mind to go back to the Continent. In the May of 1846 he ran over to Switzerland and tried to write "Dombey and Son" at Lausanne. Tried to, I say, because his letters are full of an angry impotence. He could not get on. He attributed this especially to his love of London and his loss of it, "the absence of streets and numbers of figures . . . My figures seem disposed to stagnate without crowds about them." But he also, with shrewdness, attributed it more generally to the laxer and more wandering life he had led for the last two years, the American tour, the Italian tour, diversified, generally speaking, only with slight literary productions. His ways were never punctual or healthy, but they were also never unconscientious as far as work was concerned. If he walked all night he could write all day. But in this strange exile or interregnum he did not seem able to fall into any habits, even bad habits. A restlessness beyond all his experience had fallen for a season upon the most restless of the children of men.

It may be a mere coincidence: but this break in his life very nearly coincided with the important break in his art. "Dombey and Son," planned in all probability some time before, was destined to be the last of a quite definite series, the early novels of Dickens. The difference between the books from the beginning up to "Dombey," and the books from "David Copperfield" to the end may be hard to state dogmatically, but is evident to every one with any literary sense. Very coarsely, the case may be put by saying that he diminished, in the story as a whole, the practice of pure caricature. Still more coarsely it may be put in the phrase that he began to practise realism. If we take Mr. Stiggins, say, as a clergyman depicted at the beginning of his literary career, and Mr. Crisparkle, say, as a clergyman depicted at the end of it, it is evident that the difference does not merely consist in the fact that the first is a less desirable clergyman than the second. It consists in the nature of our desire for either of them. The glory of Mr. Crisparkle partly consists in the fact that he might really exist anywhere, in any country town into which we may happen to stray. The glory of Mr. Stiggins wholly consists in the fact that he could not possibly exist anywhere except in the head of Dickens. Dickens has the secret recipe of that divine dish. In some sense, therefore, when we say that he became less of a caricaturist we mean that he became less of a creator. That original violent vision of all things which he had seen from his boyhood began to be mixed with other men's milder visions and with the light of common day. He began to understand and practise other than his own mad merits; began to have some movement towards the merits of other writers, towards the mixed emotion of Thackeray, or the solidity of George Eliot. And this must be said for the process; that the fierce wine of Dickens could endure some dilution. On the whole, perhaps, his primal personalism was all the better when surging against some saner restraints. Perhaps a flavour of strong Stiggins goes a long way. Perhaps the colossal Crummles might be cut down into six or seven quite creditable characters. For my own part, for reasons which I shall afterwards mention, I am in real doubt about the advantage of this realistic education of Dickens. I am not sure that it made his books better; but I am sure it made them less bad. He made fewer mistakes undoubtedly; he succeeded in eliminating much of the mere rant or cant of his first books; he threw away much of the old padding, all the more annoying, perhaps, in a literary sense, because he did not mean it for padding, but for essential eloquence. But he did not produce anything actually better than Mr. Chuckster. But then there is nothing better than Mr. Chuckster. Certain works of art, such as the Venus of Milo, exhaust our aspiration. Upon the whole this may, perhaps, be safely said of the transition. Those who have any doubt about Dickens can have no doubt of the superiority of the later books. Beyond question they have less of what annoys us in Dickens. But do not, if you are in the company of any ardent adorers of Dickens (as I hope for your sake you are), do not insist too urgently and exclusively on the splendour of Dickens's last works, or they will discover that you do not like him.

"Dombey and Son" is the last novel in the first manner: "David Copperfield" is the first novel in the last. The increase in care and realism in the second of the two is almost startling. Yet even in "Dombey and Son" we can see the coming of a change, however faint, if we compare it with his first fantasies such as "Nicholas Nickleby" or "The Old Curiosity Shop." The central story is still melodrama, bat it is much more tactful and effective melodrama. Melodrama is a form of art, legitimate like any other, as noble as farce, almost as noble as pantomime. The essence of melodrama is that it appeals to the moral sense in a highly simplified state, just as farce appeals to the sense of humour in a highly simplified state. Farce creates people who are so intellectually simple as to hide in packing-cases or pretend to be their own aunts. Melodrama creates people so morally simple as to kill their enemies in Oxford Street, and repent on seeing their mother's photograph. The object of the simplification in farce and melodrama is the same, and quite artistically legitimate, the object of gaining a resounding rapidity of action which subtleties would obstruct. And this can be done well or ill. The simplified villain can be a spirited charcoal sketch or a mere black smudge. Carker is a spirited charcoal sketch: Ralph Nickleby is a mere black smudge. The tragedy of Edith Dombey teems with unlikelihood, but it teems with life. That Dombey should give his own wife censure through his own business manager is impossible, I will not say in a gentleman, but in a person of ordinary sane self-conceit. But once having got the inconceivable trio before the footlights, Dickens gives us good ringing dialogue very different from the mere rants in which Ralph Nickleby figures in the unimaginable character of a rhetorical money-lender. And there is another point of technical improvement in this book over such books as "Nicholas Nickleby." It has not only a basic idea, but a good basic idea. There is a real artistic opportunity in the conception of a solemn and selfish man of affairs, feeling for his male heir, his first and last emotion, mingled of a thin flame of tenderness and a strong flame of pride. But with all these possibilities, the serious episode of the Dombeys serves ultimately only to show how unfitted Dickens was for such things, how fitted he was for something opposite.

The incurable poetic character, the hopelessly non-realistic character of Dickens's essential genius could not have a better example than the story of the Dombeys. For the story itself is probable; it is the treatment that makes it unreal. In attempting to paint the dark pagan devotion of the father (as distant from the ecstatic and Christian devotion of the mother) Dickens was painting something that was really there. This is no wild theme, like the wanderings of Nell's grandfather, or the marriage of Gride. A man of Dombey's type would love his son as he loves Paul. He would neglect his daughter as he neglects Florence. And yet we feel the utter unreality of it all, while we feel the utter reality of monsters like Stiggins or Mantalini. Dickens could only work in his own way, and that way was the wild way. We may almost say this: that he could only make his characters probable if he was allowed to make them impossible. Give him licence to say and do anything, and he could create beings as vivid as our own aunts and uncles. Keep him to likelihood and he could not tell the plainest tale so as to make it seem likely. The story of "Pickwick" is credible, although it is not possible. The story of Florence Dombey is incredible although it is true.

An excellent example can be found in the same story. Major Bagstock is a grotesque, and yet he contains touch after touch of Dickens's quiet and sane observation of things as they are. He was always most accurate when he was most fantastic. Dombey and Florence are perfectly reasonable, but we simply know that they do not exist. The Major is mountainously exaggerated, but we all feel that we have met him at Brighton. Nor is the rationale of the paradox difficult to see; Dickens exaggerated when he had found a real truth to exaggerate. It is a deadly error (an error at the back of much of the false placidity of our politics) to suppose that lies are told with excess and luxuriance, and truths told with modesty and restraint. Some of the most frantic lies on the face of life are told with modesty and restraint; for the simple reason that only modesty and restraint will save them. Many official declarations are just as dignified as Mr. Dombey, because they are just as fictitious. On the other hand, the man who has found a truth dances about like a boy who has found a shilling; he breaks into extravagances, as the Christian churches broke into gargoyles. In one sense truth alone can be exaggerated; nothing else can stand the strain. The outrageous Bagstock is a glowing and glaring exaggeration of a thing we have all seen in life-the worst and most dangerous of all its hypocrisies. For the worst and most dangerous hypocrite is not he who affects unpopular virtue, but he who affects popular vice. The jolly fellow of the saloon bar and the racecourse is the real deceiver of mankind; he has misled more than any false prophet, and his victims cry to him out of hell. The excellence of the Bagstock conception can best be seen if we compare it with the much weaker and more improbable knavery of Pecksniff. It would not be worth a man's while, with any worldly object, to pretend to be a holy and high-minded architect. The world does not admire holy and high-minded architects. The world does admire rough and tough old army men who swear at waiters and wink at women. Major Bagstock is simply the perfect prophecy of that decadent jingoism which corrupted England of late years. England has been duped, not by the cant of goodness, but by the cant of badness. It has been fascinated by a quite fictitious cynicism, and reached that last and strangest of all impostures in which the mask is as repulsive as the face.

"Dombey and Son" provides us with yet another instance of this general fact in Dickens. He could only get to the most solemn emotions adequately if he got to them through the grotesque. He could only, so to speak, really get into the inner chamber by coming down the chimney, like his own most lovable lunatic in "Nicholas Nickleby." A good example is such a character as Toots. Toots is what none of Dickens's dignified characters are, in the most serious sense, a true lover. He is the twin of Romeo. He has passion, humility, self-knowledge, a mind lifted into all magnanimous thoughts, everything that goes with the best kind of romantic love. His excellence in the art of love can only be expressed by the somewhat violent expression that he is as good a lover as Walter Gay is a bad one. Florence surely deserved her father's scorn if she could prefer Gay to Toots. It is neither a joke nor any kind of exaggeration to say that in the vacillations of Toots, Dickens not only came nearer to the psychology of true love than he ever came elsewhere, but nearer than anyone else ever came. To ask for the loved one, and then not to dare to cross the threshold, to be invited by her, to long to accept, and then to lie in order to decline, these are the funny things that Mr. Toots did, and that every honest man who yells with laughter at him has done also. For the moment, however, I only mention this matter as a pendant case to the case of Major Bagstock, an example of the way in which Dickens had to be ridiculous in order to begin to be true. His characters that begin solemn end futile; his characters that begin frivolous end solemn in the best sense. His foolish figures are not only more entertaining than his serious figures, they are also much more serious. The Marchioness is not only much more laughable than Little Nell; she is also much more of all that Little Nell was meant to be; much more really devoted, pathetic, and brave. Dick Swiveller is not only a much funnier fellow than Kit, he is also a much more genuine fellow, being free from that slight stain of "meekness," or the snobbishness of the respectable poor, which the wise and perfect Chuckster wisely and perfectly perceived in Kit. Susan Nipper is not only more of a comic character than Florence; she is more of a heroine than Florence any day of the week. In "Our Mutual Friend" we do not, for some reason or other, feel really very much excited about the fall or rescue of Lizzie Hexam. She seems too romantic to be really pathetic. But we do feel excited about the rescue of Miss Podsnap, because she is, like Toots, a holy fool; because her pink nose and pink elbows, and candid outcry and open indecent affections do convey to us a sense of innocence helpless among human dragons, of Andromeda tied naked to a rock. Dickens had to make a character humorous before he could make it human; it was the only way he knew, and he ought to have always adhered to it. Whether he knew it or not, the only two really touching figures in "Martin Chuzzlewit" are the Misses Pecksniff. Of the things he tried to treat unsmilingly and grandly we can all make game to our heart's content. But when once he has laughed at a thing it is sacred for ever.

"Dombey," however, means first and foremost the finale of the early Dickens. It is difficult to say exactly in what it is that we perceive that the old crudity ends here, and does not reappear in "David Copperfield" or in any of the novels after it. But so certainly it is. In detached scenes and characters, indeed, Dickens kept up his farcical note almost or quite to the end. But this is the last farce; this is the last work in which a farcical licence is tacitly claimed, a farcical note struck to start with. And in a sense his next novel may be called his first novel. But the growth of this great novel, "David Copperfield," is a thing very interesting, but at the same time very dark, for it is a growth in the soul. We have seen that Dickens's mind was in a stir of change; that he was dreaming of art and even of realism. Hugely delighted as he invariably was with his own books, he was humble enough to be ambitious. He was even humble enough to be envious. In the matter of art, for instance, in the narrower sense, of arrangement and proportion in fictitious things, he began to be conscious of his deficiency, and even, in a stormy sort of way, ashamed of it; he tried to gain completeness even while raging at anyone who called him incomplete. And in this manner of artistic construction, his ambition (and his success too) grew steadily up to the instant of his death. The end finds him attempting things that are at the opposite pole to the frank formlessness of "Pickwick." His last book, "The Mystery of Edwin Drood," depends entirely upon construction, even upon a centralised strategy. He staked everything upon a plot; he who had been the weakest of plotters, weaker than Sim Tappertit. He essayed a detective story, he who could never keep a secret; and he has kept it to this day. A new Dickens was really being born when Dickens died.

And as with art, so with reality. He wished to show that he could construct as well as anybody. He also wished to show that he could be as accurate as anybody. And in this connection (as in many others) we must recur constantly to the facts mentioned in connection with America and with his money-matters. We must recur, I mean, to the central fact that his desires were extravagant in quantity, but not in quality; that his wishes were excessive, but not eccentric. It must never be forgotten that sanity was his ideal, even when he seemed almost insane. It was thus with his literary aspirations. He was brilliant; but he wished sincerely to be solid. Nobody out of an asylum could deny that he was a genius and an unique writer; but he did not wish to be an unique writer, but an universal writer. Much of the manufactured pathos or rhetoric against which his enemies quite rightly rail, is really due to his desire to give all sides of life at once, to make his book a cosmos instead of a tale. He was sometimes really vulgar in his wish to be a literary Whiteley, an universal provider. Thus it was that he felt about realism and truth to live. Nothing is easier than to defend Dickens as Dickens, but Dickens wished to be everybody else. Nothing is easier than to defend Dickens's world as a fairyland, of which he alone has the key; to defend him as one defends Maeterlinck, or any other original writer. But Dickens was not content with being original, he had a wild wish to be true. He loved truth so much in the abstract that he sacrificed to the shadow of it his own glory. He denied his own divine originality, and pretended that he had plagiarised from life. He disowned his own soul's children, and said he had picked them up in the street.

And in this mixed and heated mood of anger and ambition, vanity and doubt, a new and great design was born. He loved to be romantic, yet he desired to be real. How if he wrote of a thing that was real and showed that it was romantic? He loved real life; but he also loved his own way. How if he wrote his own real life, but wrote it in his own way? How if he showed the carping critics who doubted the existence of his strange characters, his own yet stranger existence? How if he forced these pedants and unbelievers to admit that Weller and Pecksniff, Crummles and Swiveller, whom they thought so improbably wild and wonderful, were less wild and wonderful than Charles Dickens? What if he ended the quarrels about whether his romances could occur, by confessing that his romance had occurred?

For some time past, probably during the greater part of his life, he had made notes for an autobiography. I have already quoted an admirable passage from these notes, a passage reproduced in "David Copperfield," with little more alteration than a change of proper names-the passage which describes Captain Porter and the debtor's petition in the Marshalsea. But he probably perceived at last what a less keen intelligence must ultimately have perceived, that if an autobiography is really to be honest it must be turned into a work of fiction. If it is really to tell the truth, it must at all costs profess not to. No man dare say of himself, over his own name, how badly he has behaved. No man dare say of himself over his own name, how well he has behaved. Moreover, of course, a touch of fiction is almost always essential to the real conveying of fact, because fact, as experienced, has a fragmentariness which is bewildering at first hand and quite blinding at second hand. Facts have at least to be sorted into compartments and the proper head and tail given back to each. The perfection and pointedness of art are a sort of substitute for the pungency of actuality. Without this selection and completion our life seems a tangle of unfinished tales, a heap of novels, all volume one. Dickens determined to make one complete novel of it.

For though there are many other aspects of "David Copperfield," this autobiographical aspect is, after all, the greatest. The point of the book is that, unlike all the other books of Dickens, it is concerned with quite common actualities, but it is concerned with them warmly and with the warlike sympathies. It is not only both realistic and romantic; it is realistic because it is romantic. It is human nature described with the human exaggeration. We all know the actual types in the book; they are not like the turgid and preternatural types elsewhere in Dickens. They are not purely poetic creations like Mr. Kenwigs or Mr. Bunsby. We all know that they exist. We all know the stiff-necked and humorous old-fashioned nurse, so conventional and yet so original, so dependent and yet so independent. We all know the intrusive stepfather, the abstract strange male, coarse, handsome, sulky, successful, a breaker-up of homes. We all know the erect and sardonic spinster, the spinster who is so mad in small things and so sane in great ones. We all know the cock of the school; we all know Steerforth, the creature whom the gods love and even the servants respect. We know his poor and aristocratic mother, so proud, so gratified, so desolate. We know the Rosa Dartle type, the lonely woman in whom affection itself has stagnated into a sort of poison.

But while these are real characters they are real characters lit up with the colours of youth and passion. They are real people romantically felt; that is to say, they are real people felt as real people feel them. They are exaggerated, like all Dickens's figures: but they are not exaggerated as personalities are exaggerated by an artist; they are exaggerated as personalities are exaggerated by their own friends and enemies. The strong souls are seen through the glorious haze of the emotions that strong souls really create. We have Murdstone as he would be to a boy who hated him; and rightly, for a boy would hate him. We have Steerforth as he would be to a boy who adored him; and rightly, for a boy would adore him. It may be that if these persons had a mere terrestrial existence, they appeared to other eyes more insignificant. It may be that Murdstone in common life was only a heavy business man with a human side that David was too sulky to find. It may be that Steerforth was only an inch or two taller than David, and only a shade or two above him in the lower middle classes; but this does not make the book less true. In cataloguing the facts of life the author must not omit that massive fact, illusion.

When we say the book is true to life we must stipulate that it is especially true to youth: even to boyhood. All the characters seem a little larger than they really were, for David is looking up at them. And the early pages of the book are in particular astonishingly vivid. Parts of it seem like fragments of our forgotten infancy. The dark house of childhood, the loneliness, the things half understood, the nurse with her inscrutable sulks and her more inscrutable tenderness, the sudden deportations to distant places, the seaside and its childish friendships, all this stirs in us when we read it, like something out of a previous existence. Above all, Dickens has excellently depicted the child enthroned in that humble circle which only in after years he perceives to have been humble. Modern and cultured persons, I believe, object to their children seeing kitchen company or being taught by a woman like Peggotty. But surely it is more important to be educated in a sense of human dignity and equality than in anything else in the world. And a child who has once had to respect a kind and capable woman of the lower classes will respect the lower classes for ever. The true way to overcome the evil in class distinction is not to denounce them as revolutionists denounce them, but to ignore them as children ignore them.

The early youth of David Copperfield is psychologically almost as good as his childhood. In one touch especially Dickens pierced the very core of the sensibility of boyhood; it was when he made David more afraid of a manservant than of anybody or anything else. The lowering Murdstone, the awful Mrs. Steerforth are not so alarming to him as Mr. Littimer, the unimpeachable gentleman's gentleman. This is exquisitely true to the masculine emotions, especially in their undeveloped state. A youth of common courage does not fear anything violent, but he is in mortal fear of anything correct. This may or may not be the reason that so few female writers understand their male characters, but this fact remains that the more sincere and passionate and even headlong a lad is the more certain he is to be conventional. The bolder and freer he seems the more the traditions of the college or the rules of the club will hold him with their gyves of gossamer; and the less afraid he is of his enemies the more cravenly he will be afraid of his friends. Herein lies indeed the darkest period of our ethical doubt and chaos. The fear is that as morals become less urgent, manners will become more so; and men who have forgotten the fear of God will retain the fear of Littimer. We shall merely sink into a much meaner bondage. For when you break the great laws, you do not get liberty; you do not even get anarchy. You get the small laws.

The sting and strength of this piece of fiction, then, do (by a rare accident) lie in the circumstance that it was so largely founded on fact. "David Copperfield" is the great answer of a great romancer to the realists. David says in effect: "What! you say that the Dickens tales are too purple really to have happened! Why, this is what happened to me, and it seemed the most purple of all. You say that the Dickens heroes are too handsome and triumphant! Why, no prince or paladin in Ariosto was ever so handsome and triumphant as the Head Boy seemed to me walking before me in the sun. You say the Dickens villains are too black I Why, there was no ink in the devil's inkstand black enough for my own step-father when I had to live in the same house with him. The facts are quite the other way to what you suppose. This life of grey studies and half-tones, the absence of which you regret in Dickens, is only life as it is looked at. This life of heroes and villains is life as it is lived. The life a man knows best is exactly the life he finds most full of fierce certainties and battles between good and ill-his own. Oh yes, the life we do not care about may easily be a psychological comedy. Other people's lives may easily be human documents. But a man's own life is always a melodrama."

There are other effective things in "David Copperfield;" they are not all autobiographical, but they nearly all have this new note of quietude and reality. Micawber is gigantic; an immense assertion of the truth that the way to live is to exaggerate everything. But of him I shall have to speak more fully in another connection. Mrs. Micawber, artistically speaking, is even better. She is very nearly the best thing in Dickens. Nothing could be more absurd, and at the same time more true, than her clear argumentative manner of speech as she sits smiling and expounding in the midst of ruin. What could be more lucid and logical and unanswerable than her statement of the prolegomena of the Medway problem, of which the first step must be to "see the Medway," or of the coal-trade, which required talent and capital. "Talent Mr. Micawber has. Capital Mr. Micawber has not." It seems as if something should have come at last out of so clear and scientific an arrangement of the ideas. Indeed if (as has been suggested) we regard "David Copperfield" as an unconscious defence of the poetic view of life, we might regard Mrs. Micawber as an unconscious satire on the logical view of life. She sits as a monument of the hopelessness and helplessness of reason in the face of this romantic and unreasonable world.

As I have taken "Dombey and Son" as the book before the transition, and "David Copperfield" as typical of the transition itself, I may perhaps take "Bleak House" as the book after the transition, and so complete the description. Bleak House has every characteristic of his new realistic culture. Dickens never now, as in his early books, revels in the parts he likes and scamps the parts he does not, after the manner of Scott. He does not, as in previous tales, leave his heroes and heroines mere walking gentlemen and ladies with nothing at all to do but walk: he expends upon them at least ingenuity. By the expedients (successful or not) of the self-revelation of Esther or the humorous inconsistencies of Rick, he makes his younger figures if not lovable at least readable. Everywhere we see this tighter and more careful grip. He does not, for instance, when he wishes to denounce a dark institution, sandwich it in as a mere episode in a rambling story of adventure, as the debtor's prison is embedded in the body of "Pickwick" or the low Yorkshire school in the body of "Nicholas Nickleby." He puts the Court of Chancery in the centre of the stage, a sombre and sinister temple, and groups round it in artistic relation decaying and frantic figures, its offspring and its satirists, An old dipsomaniac keeps a rag and bone shop, type of futility and antiquity, and calls himself the Lord Chancellor. A little mad old maid hangs about the courts on a forgotten or imaginary lawsuit, and says with perfect and pungent irony, "I am expecting a judgment shortly. On the Day of Judgment." Rick and Ada and Esther are not mere strollers who have strayed into the court of law, they are its children, its symbols, and its victims. The righteous indignation of the book is not at the red heat of anarchy, but at the white heat of art. Its anger is patient and plodding, like some historic revenge. Moreover, it slowly and carefully creates the real psychology of oppression. The endless formality, the endless unemotional urbanity, the endless hope deferred, these things make one feel the fact of injustice more than the madness of Nero. For it is not the activeness of tyranny that maddens, but its passiveness. We hate the deafness of the god more than his strength. Silence is the unbearable repartee.

Again we can see in this book strong traces of an increase in social experience. Dickens, as his fame carried him into more fashionable circles, began really to understand something of what is strong and what is weak in the English upper class. Sir Leicester Dedlock is a far more effective condemnation of oligarchy than the ugly swagger of Sir Mulberry Hawk, because pride stands out more plainly in all its impotence and insolence as the one weakness of a good man, than as one of the million weaknesses of a bad one. Dickens, like all young Radicals, had imagined in his youth that aristocracy rested upon the hardness of somebody; he found, as we all do, that it rests upon the softness of everybody. It is very hard not to like Sir Leicester Dedlock, not to applaud his silly old speeches, so foolish, so manly, so genuinely English, so disastrous to England. It is true that the English people love a lord, but it is not true that they fear him; rather, if anything, they pity him; there creeps into their love something of the feeling they have towards a baby or a black man. In their hearts they think it admirable that Sir Leicester Dedlock should be able to speak at all. And so a system, which no iron laws and no bloody battles could possibly force upon a people, is preserved from generation to generation by pure, weak good-nature.

In "Bleak House" occurs the character of Harold Skimpole, the character whose alleged likeness to Leigh Hunt has laid Dickens open to so much disapproval. Unjust disapproval, I think, as far as fundamental morals are concerned. In method he was a little clamorous and clumsy, as, indeed, he was apt to be. But when he said that it was possible to combine a certain tone of conversation taken from a particular man with other characteristics which were not meant to be his, he surely said what all men who write stories know. A work of fiction often consists in combining a pair of whiskers seen in one street with a crime seen in another. He may quite possibly have really meant only to make Leigh Hunt's light philosophy the mask for a new kind of scamp, as a variant on the pious mask of Pecksniff or the candid mask of Bagstock. He may never once have had the unfriendly thought, "Suppose Hunt behaved like a rascal!" he may have only had the fanciful thought, "Suppose a rascal behaved like Hunt!"

But there is a good reason for mentioning Skimpole especially. In the character of Skimpole, Dickens displayed again a quality that was very admirable in him —I mean a disposition to see things sanely and to satirise even his own faults. He was commonly occupied in satirising the Gradgrinds, the economists, the men of Smiles and Self-Help. For him there was nothing poorer than their wealth, nothing more selfish than their self-denial. And against them he was in the habit of pitting the people of a more expansive habit-the happy Swivellers and Micawbers, who, if they were poor, were at least as rich as their last penny could make them. He loved that great Christian carelessness that seeks its meat from God. It was merely a kind of uncontrollable honesty that forced him into urging the other side. He could not disguise from himself or from the world that man who began by seeking his meat from his neighbour without apprising his neighbour of the fact. He had shown how good irresponsibility could be; he could not stoop to hide how bad it could be. He created Skimpole; and Skimpole is the dark underside of Micawber.

In attempting Skimpole he attempted something with a great and urgent meaning. He attempted it, I say; I do not assert that he carried it through. As has been remarked, he was never successful in describing psychological change; his characters are the same yesterday, today, and for ever. And critics have complained very justly of the crude villainy of Skimpole's action in the matter of Joe and Mr. Bucket. Certainly Skimpole had no need to commit a clumsy treachery to win a clumsy bribe; he had only to call on Mr. Jarndyce. He had lost his honour too long to need to sell it.

The effect is bad; but I repeat that the aim was great. Dickens wished, under the symbol of Skimpole, to point out a truth which is perhaps the most terrible in moral psychology. I mean the fact that it is by no means easy to draw the line between light and heavy offence. He desired to show that there are no faults, however kindly, that we can afford to flatter or to let alone; he meant that perhaps Skimpole had once been as good a man as Swiveller. If flattered or let alone, our kindliest fault can destroy our kindliest virtue. A thing may begin as a very human weakness and end as a very inhuman weakness. Skimpole means that the extremes of evil are much nearer than we think. A man may begin by being too generous to pay his debts, and end by being too mean to pay his debts. For the vices are very strangely in league, and encourage each other. A sober man may become a drunkard through being a coward. A brave man may become a coward through being a drunkard. That is the thing Dickens was darkly trying to convey in Skimpole-that a man might become a mountain of selfishness if he attended only to the Dickens virtues. There is nothing that can be neglected; there is no such thing (he meant) as a peccadillo.

I have dwelt on this consciousness of his because, alas, it had a very sharp edge for himself. Even while he was permitting a fault originally small to make a comedy of Skimpole, a fault originally small was making a tragedy of Charles Dickens. For Dickens also had a bad quality, not intrinsically very terrible, which he allowed to wreck his life. He also had a small weakness that could sometimes become stronger than all his strengths. His selfishness was not, it need hardly be said, the selfishness of Gradgrind; he was particularly compassionate and liberal. Nor was it in the least the selfishness of Skimpole. He was entirely self-dependent, industrious, and dignified. His selfishness was wholly a selfishness of the nerves. Whatever his whim or the temperature of the instant told him to do must be done. He was the type of man who would break a window if it would not open and give him air. And this weakness of his had, by the time of which we speak, led to a breach between himself and his wife which he was too exasperated and excited to heal in time. Everything must be put right, and put right at once, with him. If London bored him, he must go to the Continent at once; if the Continent bored him, he must come back to London at once. If the day was too noisy, the whole household must be quiet; if night was too quiet, the whole household must wake up. Above all, he had the supreme character of the domestic despot-that his good temper was, if possible, more despotic than his bad temper. When he was miserable (as he often was, poor fellow), they only had to listen to his railings. When he was happy they had to listen to his novels. All this, which was mainly mere excitability, did not seem to amount to much; it did not in the least mean that he had ceased to be a clean-living and kind-hearted and quiet honest man. But there was this evil about it-that he did not resist his little weakness at all; he pampered it as Skimpole pampered his. And it separated him and his wife. A mere silly trick of temperament did everything that the blackest misconduct could have done. A random sensibility, started about the shuffling of papers or the shutting of a window, ended by tearing two clean, Christian people from each other, like a blast of bigamy or adultery.

Chapter 9
Later Life and works

I have deliberately in this book mentioned only such facts in the life of Dickens as were, I will not say significant (for all facts must be significant, including the million facts that can never be mentioned by anybody), but such facts as illustrated my own immediate meaning. I have observed this method consistently and without shame because I think that we can hardly make too evident a chasm between books which profess to be statements of all the ascertainable facts, and books which (like this one) profess only to contain a particular opinion or a summary deducible from the facts. Books like Forster's exhaustive work and others exist, and are as accessible as St. Paul's Cathedral; we have them in common as we have the facts of the physical universe; and it seems highly desirable that the function of making an exhaustive catalogue and that of making an individual generalisation should not be confused. No catalogue, of course, can contain all the facts even of five minutes; every catalogue, however long and learned, must be not only a bold, but, one may say, an audacious selection. Bat if a great many facts are given, the reader gains a blurred belief that all the facts are being given. In a professedly personal judgment it is therefore clearer and more honest to give only a few illustrative facts, leaving the other obtainable facts to balance them. For thus it is made quite clear that the thing is a sketch, an affair of a few lines.

It is as well, however, to make at this point a pause sufficient to indicate the main course of the later life of the novelist. And it is best to begin with the man himself, as he appeared in those last days of popularity and public distinction. Many are still alive who remember him in his after-dinner speeches, his lectures, and his many public activities; as I am not one of these, I cannot correct my notions with that flash of the living features without which a description may be subtly and entirely wrong. Once a man is dead, if it be only yesterday, the new-comer must piece him together from descriptions really as much at random as if he were describing Caesar or Henry II. Allowing, however, for this inevitable falsity, a figure vivid and a little fantastic, does walk across the stage of Forster's "Life."

Dickens was of a middle size and his vivacity and relative physical insignificance probably gave rather the impression of small size; certainly of the absence of bulk. In early life he wore, even for that epoch, extravagant clusters of brown hair, and in later years a brown moustache and a fringe of brown beard (cut like a sort of broad and bushy imperial) sufficiently individual in shape to give him a faint air as of a foreigner. His face had a peculiar tint or quality which is hard to describe even after one has contrived to imagine it. It was the quality which Mrs. Carlyle felt to be, as it were metallic, and compared to clear steel. It was, I think, a sort of pale glitter and animation, very much alive and yet with something deathly about it, like a corpse galvanised by a god. His face (if this was so) was curiously a counterpart of his character. For the essence of all Dickens's character was that it was at once tremulous and yet hard and sharp, just as the bright blade of a sword is tremulous and yet hard and sharp. He vibrated at every touch and yet he was indestructible; you could bend him, but you could not break him. Brown of hair and beard, somewhat pale of visage (especially in his later days of excitement and ill-health), he had quite exceptionally bright and active eyes that were always darting about like brilliant birds to pick up all the tiny things of which he made more, perhaps, than any novelist has done; for he was a sort of poetical Sherlock Holmes. The mouth behind the brown beard was large and mobile, like the mouth of an actor; indeed he was an actor, in many things too much of an actor. In his lectures, in later years, he could turn his strange face into any of the innumerable mad masks that were the faces of his grotesque characters. He could make his face fall suddenly into the blank inanity of Mrs. Raddle's servant, or swell, as if to twice its size, into the apoplectic energy of Mr. Serjeant Buzfuz. But the outline of his face itself, from his youth upwards, was cut quite delicate and decisive and in repose, and in its own keen way, may even have looked effeminate.

The dress of the comfortable classes during the later years of Dickens was, compared with ours, somewhat slipshod and somewhat gaudy. It was the time of loose pegtop trousers of an almost Turkish oddity, of large ties, of loose short jackets and of loose long whiskers. Yet even this expansive period, it must be confessed, considered Dickens a little too flashy or, as some put it, too Frenchified in his dress. Such a man would wear velvet coats and wild waistcoats that were like incredible sunsets; he would wear those old white hats of an unnecessary and startling whiteness. He did not mind being seen in sensational dressing-gowns; it is said he had his portrait painted in one of them. All this is not meritorious; neither is it particularly discreditable; it is a characteristic only, but an important one. He was an absolutely independent and entirely self-respecting man. But he had none of that old lusty, half-dignified English feeling upon which Thackeray was so sensitive; I mean the desire to be regarded as a private gentleman, which means at bottom the desire to be left alone. This again is not a merit; it is only one of the milder aspects of aristocracy. But meritorious or not, Dickens did not possess it. He had no objection to being stared at, if he were also admired. He did not exactly pose in the oriental manner of Disraeli; his instincts were too clean for that; but he did pose somewhat in the French manner, of some leaders like Mirabeau and Gambetta. Nor had he the dull desire to "get on" which makes men die contented as inarticulate Under-Secretaries of State. He did not desire success so much as fame, the old human glory, the applause and wonder of the people. Such he was as he walked down the street in his Frenchified clothes, probably with a slight swagger.

His private life consisted of one tragedy and ten thousand comedies. By one tragedy I mean one real and rending moral tragedy-the failure of his marriage. He loved his children dearly, and more than one of them died; but in sorrows like these there is no violence and above all no shame. The end of life is not tragic like the end of love. And by the ten thousand comedies I mean the whole texture of his life, his letters, his conversation, which were one incessant carnival of insane and inspired improvisation So far as he could prevent it, he never permitted a day of his life to be ordinary. There was always some prank, some impetuous proposal, some practical joke, some sudden hospitality, some sudden disappearance. It is related of him (I give one anecdote out of a hundred) that in his last visit to America, when he was already reeling as it were under the blow that was to be mortal, he remarked quite casually to his companions that a row of painted cottages looked exactly like the painted shops in a pantomime. No sooner had the suggestion passed his lips than he leapt at the nearest doorway and in exact imitation of the clown in the harlequinade, beat conscientiously with his fist, not on the door (for that would have burst the canvas scenery of course), but on the side of the doorpost. Having done this he lay down ceremoniously across the doorstep for the owner to fall over him if he should come rushing out. He then got up gravely and went on his way. His whole life was full of such unexpected energies, precisely like those of the pantomime clown. Dickens had indeed a great and fundamental affinity with the landscape, or rather house-scape, of the harlequinade. He liked high houses, and sloping roofs, and deep areas. But he would have been really happy if some good fairy of the eternal pantomime had given him the power of flying off the roofs and pitching harmlessly down the height of the houses and bounding out of the areas like an indiarubber ball. The divine lunatic in "Nicholas Nickleby" comes nearest to his dream. I really think Dickens would rather have been that one of his characters than any of the others. With what excitement he would have struggled down the chimney. With what ecstatic energy he would have hurled the cucumbers over the garden wall.

His letters exhibit even more the same incessant creative force. His letters are as creative as any of his literary creation. His shortest postcard is often as good as his ablest novel; each one of them is spontaneous; each one of them is different. He varies even the form and shape of the letter as far as possible; now it is in absurd French; now it is from one of his characters; now it is an advertisement for himself as a stray dog. All of them are very funny; they are not only very funny, but they are quite as funny as his finished and published work. This is the ultimately amazing thing about Dickens; the amount there is of him. He wrote, at the very least, sixteen thick important books packed full of original creation. And if you had burnt them all he could have written sixteen more, as a man writes idle letters to his friend.

In connection with this exuberant part of his nature there is another thing to be noted, if we are to make a personal picture of him. Many modern people, chiefly women, have been heard to object to the Bacchic element in the books of Dickens, that celebration of social drinking as a supreme symbol of social living, which those books share with almost all the great literature of mankind, including the New Testament. Undoubtedly there is an abnormal amount of drinking in a page of Dickens, as there is an abnormal amount of fighting, say, in a page of Dumas. If you reckon up the beers and brandies of Mr. Bob Sawyer, with the care of an arithmetician and the deductions of a pathologist, they rise alarmingly like a rising tide at sea. Dickens did defend drink clamorously, praised it with passion, and described whole orgies of it with enormous gusto. Yet it is wonderfully typical of his prompt and impatient nature that he himself drank comparatively little. He was the type of man who could be so eager in praising the cup that he left the cup untasted. It was a part of his active and feverish temperament that he did not drink wine very much. But it was a part of his humane philosophy, of his religion, that he did drink wine. To healthy European philosophy wine is a symbol; to European religion it is a sacrament. Dickens approved it because it was a great human institution, one of the rites of civilisation, and this it certainly is. The teetotaller who stands outside it may have perfectly clear ethical reasons of his own, as a man may have who stands outside education or nationality, who refuses to go to a University or to serve in an Army. But he is neglecting one of the great social things that man has added to nature. The teetotaller has chosen a most unfortunate phrase for the drunkard when he says that the drunkard is making a beast of himself. The man who drinks ordinarily makes nothing but an ordinary man of himself. The man who drinks excessively makes a devil of himself. But nothing connected with a human and artistic thing like wine can bring one nearer to the brute life of nature. The only man who is, in the exact and literal sense of the words, making a beast of himself is the teetotaller.

The tone of Dickens towards religion, though like that of most of his contemporaries, philosophically disturbed and rather historically ignorant, had an element that was very characteristic of himself. He had all the prejudices of his time. He had, for instance, that dislike of defined dogmas, which really means a preference for unexamined dogmas. He had the usual vague notion that the whole of our human past was packed with nothing but insane Tories. He had, in a word, al the old Radical ignorances which went along with the old Radical acuteness and courage and public spirit. But this spirit tended, in almost all the others who held it, to a specific dislike of the Church of England; and a disposition to set the other sects against it, as truer types of inquiry, or of individualism. Dickens had a definite tenderness for the Church of England. He might have even called it a weakness for the Church of England, but he had it. Something in those placid services, something in that reticent and humane liturgy pleased him against all the tendencies of his time; pleased him in the best part of himself, his virile love of charity and peace. Once, in a puff of anger at the Church's political stupidity (which is indeed profound), he left it for a week or two and went to an Unitarian Chapel; in a week or two he came back. This curious and sentimental hold of the English Church upon him increased with years. In the book he was at work on when he died he describes the Minor Canon, humble, chivalrous, tender-hearted, answering with indignant simplicity the froth and platform righteousness of the sectarian philanthropist. He upholds Canon Crisparkle and satirises Mr. Honeythunder. Almost every one of the other Radicals, his friends, would have upheld Mr. Honeythunder and satirised Canon Crisparkle.

I have mentioned this matter for a special reason. It brings us back to that apparent contradiction or dualism in Dickens to which, in one connection or another, I have often adverted, and which, in one shape or another, constitutes the whole crux of his character. I mean the union of a general wildness approaching lunacy, with a sort of secret moderation almost amounting to mediocrity. Dickens was, more or less, the man I have described-sensitive, theatrical, amazing, a bit of a dandy, a bit of a buffoon. Nor are such characteristics, whether weak or wild, entirely accidents or externals. He had some false theatrical tendencies integral in his nature. For instance, he had one most unfortunate habit, a habit that often put him in the wrong, even when he happened to be in the right. He had an incurable habit of explaining himself. This reduced his admirers to the mental condition of the authentic but hitherto uncelebrated little girl who said to her mother, "I think I should understand if only you wouldn't explain." Dickens always would explain. It was a part of that instinctive publicity of his which made him at once a splendid democrat and a little too much of an actor. He carried it to the craziest lengths. He actually printed, in Household Words, an apology for his own action in the matter of his marriage. That incident alone is enough to suggest that his external offers and proposals were sometimes like screams heard from Bedlam. Yet it remains true that he had in him a central part that was pleased only by the most decent and the most reposeful rites, by things of which the Anglican Prayer-book is very typical. It is certainly true that he was often extravagant. It is most certainly equally true that he detested and despised extravagance.

The best explanation can be found in his literary genius. His literary genius consisted in a contradictory capacity at once to entertain and to deride-very ridiculous ideas. If he is a buffoon, he is laughing at buffoonery. His books were in some ways the wildest on the face of the world. Rabelais did not introduce into Paphlagonia or the Kingdom of the Coqcigrues satiric figures more frantic and misshapen than Dickens made to walk about the Strand and Lincoln's Inn. But for all that, you come, in the core of him, on a sudden quietude and good sense. Such, I think, was the core of Rabelais, such were all the far-stretching and violent satirists. This is a point essential to Dickens, though very little comprehended in our current tone of thought. Dickens was an immoderate jester, but a moderate thinker. He was an immoderate jester because he was a moderate thinker. What we moderns call the wildness of his imagination was actually created by what we moderns call the tameness of his thought. I mean that he felt the full insanity of all extreme tendencies, because he was himself so sane; he felt eccentricities, because he was in the centre. We are always, in these days, asking our violent prophets to write violent satires; but violent prophets can never possibly write violent satires. In order to write satire like that of Rabelais-satire that juggles with the stars and kicks the world about like a football-it is necessary to be one's self temperate, and even mild. A modern man like Nietzsche, a modern man like Gorky, a modern man like d'Annunzio, could not possibly write real and riotous satire. They are themselves too much on the borderlands. They could not be a success as caricaturists, for they are already a great success as caricatures.

I have mentioned his religious preference merely as an instance of this interior moderation. To say, as some have done, that he attacked Nonconformity is quite a false way of putting it. It is clean across the whole trend of the man and his time to suppose that he could have felt bitterness against any theological body as a theological body; but anything like religious extravagance, whether Protestant or Catholic, moved him to an extravagance of satire. And he flung himself into the drunken energy of Stiggins, he piled up to the stars the "verbose flights of stairs" of Mr. Chadband, exactly because his own conception of religion was the quiet and impersonal Morning Prayer. It is typical of him that he had a peculiar hatred for speeches at the grave-side.

An even clearer case of what I mean can be found in his political attitude. He seemed to some an almost anarchic satirist. He made equal fun of the system which reformers made war on, and of the instruments on which reformers relied. He made no secret of his feeling that the average English premier was an accidental ass. In two superb sentences he summed up and swept away the whole British constitution: "England, for the last week, has been in an awful state. Lord Coodle would go out, Sir Thomas Doodle wouldn't come in, and there being no people in England to speak of except Coodle and Doodle, the country has been without a government." He lumped all cabinets and all government offices together, and made the same game of them all. He created his most staggering humbugs, his most adorable and incredible idiots, and set them in the highest thrones of our national system. To many moderate and progressive people, such a satirist seemed to be insulting heaven and earth, ready to wreck society for some mad alternative, prepared to pull down St. Paul's, and on its ruins erect a gory guillotine. Yet as a matter of fact, this apparent wildness of his came from his being, if anything, a very moderate politician. It came, not at all from fanaticism, but from a rather rational detachment. He had the sense to see that the British Constitution was not democracy, but the British Constitution. It was an artificial system-like any other, good in some ways, bad in others. His satire of it sounded wild to those that worshipped it; but his satire of it arose not from his having any wild enthusiasm against it, but simply from his not having, like every one else, a wild enthusiasm for it. Alone, as far as I know, among all the great Englishmen of that age, he realised the thing that Frenchmen and Irishmen understand. I mean the fact that popular government is one thing, and representative government another. He realised that representative government has many minor disadvantages, one of them being that it is never representative. He speaks of his "hope to have made every man in England feel something of the contempt for the House of Commons that I have." He says also these two things, both of which are wonderfully penetrating as coming from a good Radical in 1855, for they contain a perfect statement of the peril in which we now stand, and which may, if it please God, sting us into avoiding the long vista at the end of which one sees so closely the dignity and the decay of Venice —"I am hourly strengthened," he says, "in my old belief, that our political aristocracy and our tuft-hunting are the death of England. In all this business I don't see a gleam of hope. As to the popular spirit, it has come to be so entirely separated from the Parliament and the Government, and so perfectly apathetic about them both, that I seriously think it a most portentous sign." And he says also this: "I really am serious in thinking-and I have given as painful consideration to the subject as a man with children to live and suffer after him can possibly give it-that representative government is become altogether a failure with us, that the English gentilities and subserviences render the people more unfit for it, and the whole thing has broken down since the great seventeenth-century time, and has no hope in it."

These are the words of a wise and perhaps melancholy man, but certainly not of an unduly excited one. It is worth noting, for instance, how much more directly Dickens goes to the point than Carlyle did, who noted many of the same evils. But Carlyle fancied that our modern English government was wordy and long-winded because it was democratic government. Dickens saw, what is certainly the fact, that it is wordy and long-winded because it is aristocratic government, the two most pleasant aristocratic qualities being a love of literature and an unconsciousness of time. But all this amounts to the same conclusion of the matter. Frantic figures like Stiggins and Chadband were created out of the quietude of his religious preference. Wild creations like the Barnacles and the Bounderbys were produced in a kind of ecstasy of the ordinary, of the obvious in political justice. His monsters were made out of his level and his moderation, as the old monsters were made out of the level sea.

Such was the man of genius we must try to imagine; violently emotional, yet with a good judgment; pugnacious, but only when he thought himself oppressed; prone to think himself oppressed, yet not cynical about human motives. He was a man remarkably hard to understand or to reanimate. He almost always had reasons for his action; his error was that he always expounded them. Sometimes his nerve snapped; and then he was mad. Unless it did so he was quite unusually sane.

Such a rough sketch at least must suffice us in order to summarise his later years. Those years were occupied, of course, in two main additions to his previous activities. The first was the series of public readings and lectures which he now began to give systematically. The second was his successive editorship of Household Words and of All the Year Round. He was of a type that enjoys every new function and opportunity. He had been so many things in his life, a reporter, an actor, a conjuror, a poet. As he had enjoyed them all, so he enjoyed being a lecturer, and enjoyed being an editor. It is certain that his audiences (who sometimes stacked themselves so thick that they lay flat on the platform all round him) enjoyed his being a lecturer. It is not so certain that the sub-editors enjoyed his being an editor. But in both connections the main matter of importance is the effect on the permanent work of Dickens himself. The readings were important for this reason, that they fixed, as if by some public and pontifical pronouncement, what was Dickens's interpretation of Dickens's work. Such a knowledge is mere tradition, but it is very forcible. My own family has handed on to me, and I shall probably hand on to the next generation, a definite memory of how Dickens made his face suddenly like the face of an idiot in impersonating Mrs. Raddle's servant, Betsy. This does serve one of the permanent purposes of tradition; it does make it a little more difficult for any ingenious person to prove that Betsy was meant to be a brilliant satire on the over-cultivation of the intellect.

As for his relation to his two magazines, it is chiefly important, first for the admirable things that he wrote in the magazines himself (one cannot forbear to mention the inimitable monologue of the waiter in "Somebody's Luggage"), and secondly for the fact that in his capacity of editor he made one valuable discovery. He discovered Wilkie Collins. Wilkie Collins was the one man of unmistakable genius who has a certain affinity with Dickens; an affinity in this respect, that they both combine in a curious way a modern and cockney and even commonplace opinion about things with a huge elemental sympathy with strange oracles and spirits and old night. There were no two men in Mid-Victorian England, with their top-hats and umbrellas, more typical of its rationality and dull reform; and there were no two men who could touch them at a ghost-story. No two men would have more contempt for superstitions; and no two men could so create the superstitious thrill. Indeed, our modern mystics make a mistake when they wear long hair or loose ties to attract the spirits. The elves and the old gods when they revisit the earth really go straight for a dull top-hat. For it means simplicity, which the gods love.

Meanwhile his books, appearing from time to time, while as brilliant as ever, bore witness to that increasing tendency to a more careful and responsible treatment which we have remarked in the transition which culminated in "Bleak House." His next important book, "Hard Times," strikes an almost unexpected note of severity. The characters are indeed exaggerated but they are bitterly and deliberately exaggerated; they are not exaggerated with the old unconscious high spirits of Nicholas Nickleby or Martin Chuzzlewit. Dickens exaggerates Bounderby because he really hates him. He exaggerated Pecksniff because he really loved him. "Hard Times" is not one of the greatest books of Dickens; but it is perhaps in a sense one of his greatest monuments. It stamps and records the reality of Dickens's emotion on a great many things that were then considered unphilosophical grumblings, but which since have swelled into the immense phenomena of the socialist philosophy. To call Dickens a Socialist is a wild exaggeration; but the truth and peculiarity of his position might be expressed thus: that even when everybody thought that Liberalism meant individualism he was emphatically a Liberal and emphatically not an individualist. Or the truth might be better still stated in this manner: that he saw that there was a secret thing, called humanity, to which both extreme socialism and extreme individualism were profoundly and inexpressibly indifferent, and that this permanent and presiding humanity was the thing he happened to understand; he knew that individualism is nothing and non-individualism is nothing but the keeping of the commandment of man. He felt, as a novelist should, that the question is too much discussed as to whether a man is in favour of this or that scientific philosophy; that there is another question, whether the scientific philosophy is in favour of the man. That is why such books as "Hard Times" will remain always a part of the power and tradition of Dickens. He saw that economic systems are not things like the stars, but things like the lamp-posts, manifestations of the human mind, and things to be judged by the human heart.

Thenceforward until the end his books grow consistently graver, and as it were, more responsible; he improves as an artist if not always as a creator. "Little Dorrit" (published in 1857) is at once in some ways so much more subtle and in every way so much more sad than the rest of his work that it bores Dickensians and especially pleases George Gissing. It is the only one of the Dickens tales which could please Gissing, not only by its genius, but also by its atmosphere. There is something a little modern and a little sad, something also out of tune with the main trend of Dickens's moral feeling, about the description of the character of Dorrit as actually and finally weakened by his wasting experiences, as not lifting any cry above the conquered years. It is but a faint fleck of shadow. But the illimitable white light of human hopefulness, of which I spoke at the beginning, is ebbing away, the work of the revolution is growing weaker everywhere; and the night of necessitarianism cometh when no man can work. For the first time in a book by Dickens perhaps we really do feel that the hero is forty-five. Clennam is certainly very much older than Mr. Pickwick.

This was indeed only a fugitive grey cloud; he went on to breezier operations. But whatever they were, they still had the note of the later days. They' have a more cautious craftsmanship; they have a more mellow and a more mixed human sentiment. Shadows fell upon his page from the other and sadder figures out of the Victorian decline. A good instance of this is his next book, "The Tale of Two Cities" (1859). In dignity and eloquence it almost stands alone among the books by Dickens. But it also stands alone among his books in this respect, that it is not entirely by Dickens. It owes its inspiration avowedly to the passionate and cloudy pages of Carlyle's "French Revolution." And there is something quite essentially inconsistent between Carlyle's disturbed and half-sceptical transcendentalism and the original school and spirit to which Dickens belonged, the lucid and laughing decisiveness of the old convinced and contented Radicalism. Hence the genius of Dickens cannot save him, just as the great genius of Carlyle could not save him from making a picture of the French Revolution, which was delicately and yet deeply erroneous. Both tend too much to represent it as a mere elemental outbreak of hunger or vengeance; they do not see enough that it was a war for intellectual principles, even for intellectual platitudes. We, the modern English, cannot easily understand the French Revolution, because we cannot easily understand the idea of bloody battle for pure common sense; we cannot understand common sense in arms and conquering. In modern England common sense appears to mean putting up with existing conditions. For us a practical politician really means a man who can be thoroughly trusted to do nothing at all; that is where his practicality comes in. The French feeling-the feeling at the back of the Revolution-was that the more sensible a man was, the more you must look out for slaughter.

In all the imitators of Carlyle, including Dickens, there is an obscure sentiment that the thing for which the Frenchmen died must have been something new and queer, a paradox, a strange idolatry. But when such blood ran in the streets, it was for the sake of a truism; when those cities were shaken to their foundations, they were shaken to their foundations by a truism.

I have mentioned this historical matter because it illustrates these later and more mingled influences which at once improve and as it were perplex the later work of Dickens. For Dickens had in his original mental composition capacities for understanding this cheery and sensible element in the French Revolution far better than Carlyle. The French Revolution was, among other things, French, and, so far as that goes, could never have a precise counterpart in so jolly and autochthonous an Englishman as Charles Dickens. But there was a great deal of the actual and unbroken tradition of the Revolution itself in his early radical indictments; in his denunciation of the Fleet Prison there was a great deal of the capture of the Bastille. There was, above all, a certain reasonable impatience which was the essence of the old Republican, and which is quite unknown to the Revolutionist in modern Europe. The old Radical did not feel exactly that he was "in revolt"; he felt if anything that a number of idiotic institutions had revolted against reason and against him. Dickens, I say, had the revolutionary idea, though an English form of it, by clear and conscious inheritance; Carlyle had to rediscover the Revolution by a violence of genius and vision. If Dickens, then, took from Carlyle (as he said he did) his image of the Revolution, it does certainly mean that he had forgotten something of his own youth and come under the more complex influences of the end of the nineteenth century. His old hilarious and sentimental view of human nature seems for a moment dimmed in "Little Dorrit." His old political simplicity has been slightly disturbed by Carlyle.

I repeat that this graver note is varied, but it remains a graver note. We see it struck, I think, with particular and remarkable success in "Great Expectations" (1860-61). This fine story is told with a consistency and quietude of individuality which is rare in Dickens. But so far had he travelled along the road of a heavier reality, that he even intended to give the tale an unhappy ending, making Pip lose Estella for ever; and he was only dissuaded from it by the robust romanticism of Bulwer Lytton. But the best part of the tale-the account of the vacillations of the hero between the humble life to which he owes everything, and the gorgeous life from which he expects something, touches a very true and somewhat tragic part of morals; for the great paradox of morality (the paradox to which only the religions have given an adequate expression) is that the very vilest kind of fault is exactly the most easy kind. We read in books and ballads about the wild fellow who might kill a man or smoke opium, but who would never stoop to lying or cowardice or to "anything mean." But for actual human beings opium and slaughter have only occasional charm; the permanent human temptation is the temptation to be mean. The one standing probability is the probability of becoming a cowardly hypocrite. The circle of the traitors is the lowest of the abyss, and it is also the easiest to fall into. That is one of the ringing realities of the Bible, that it does not make its great men commit grand sins; it makes its great men (such as David and St. Peter) commit small sins and behave like sneaks.

Dickens has dealt with this easy descent of desertion, this silent treason, with remarkable accuracy in the account of the indecisions of Pip. It contains a good suggestion of that weak romance which is the root of all snobbishness: that the mystery which belongs to patrician life excites us more than the open, even the indecent virtues of the humble. Pip is keener about Miss Havisham, who may mean well by him, than about Joe Gargery, who evidently does. All this is very strong and wholesome; but it is still a little stern. "Our Mutual Friend," 1864, brings us back a little into his merrier and more normal manner; some of the satire, such as that upon Veneering's election, is in the best of his old style, so airy and fanciful, yet hitting so suddenly and so hard. But even here we find the fuller and more serious treatment of psychology; notably in the two facts that he creates a really human villain, Bradley Headstone, and also one whom we might call a really human hero, Eugene, if it were not that he is much too human to be called a hero at all. It has been said (invariably by cads) that Dickens never described a gentleman; it is like saying that he never described a zebra. A gentleman is a very rare animal among human creatures, and to people like Dickens, interested in all humanity, not a supremely important one. But in Eugene Wrayburne he does, whether consciously or not, turn that accusation with a vengeance. For he not only describes a gentleman but describes the inner weakness and peril that belong to a gentleman, the devil that is always rending the entrails of an idle and agreeable man. In Eugene's purposeless pursuit of Lizzie Hexam, in his yet more purposeless torturing of Bradley Headstone, the author has marvellously realised that singular empty obstinacy that drives the whims and pleasures of a leisured class. He sees that there is nothing that such a man more stubbornly adheres to, than the thing that he does not particularly want to do. We are still in serious psychology.

His last book represents yet another new departure, dividing him from the chaotic Dickens of days long before. His last book is not merely an attempt to improve his power of construction in a story: it is an attempt to rely entirely on that power of construction. It not only has a plot, it is a plot. "The Mystery of Edwin Drood," 1870, was in such a sense, perhaps the most ambitious book that Dickens ever attempted. It is, as every one knows, a detective story, and certainly a very successful one, as is attested by the tumult of discussion as to its proper solution. In this, quite apart from its unfinished state, it stands, I think, alone among the author's works. Elsewhere, if he introduced a mystery, he seldom took the trouble to make it very mysterious. "Bleak House" is finished, but if it were only half finished I think anyone would guess that Lady Dedlock and Nemo had sinned in the past. "Edwin Drood" is not finished; for in the very middle of it Dickens died.

He had altogether overstrained himself in a last lecturing tour in America. He was a man in whom any serious malady would naturally make very rapid strides; for he had the temper of an irrational invalid. I have said before that there was in his curious character something that was feminine. Certainly there was nothing more entirely feminine than this, that he worked because he was tired. Fatigue bred in him a false and feverish industry, and his case increased, like the case of a man who drinks to cure the effects of drink. He died in 1870 and the whole nation mourned him as no public man has ever been mourned; for prime ministers and princes were private persons compared with Dickens. He had been a great popular king, like a king of some more primal age whom his people could come and see, giving judgment under an oak tree. He had in essence held great audiences of millions, and made proclamations to more than one of the nations of the earth. His obvious omnipresence in every part of public life was like the omnipresence of the sovereign. His secret omnipresence in every house and hut of private life was more like the omnipresence of a deity. Compared with that popular leadership all the fusses of the last forty years are diversions in idleness. Compared with such a case as his it may be said that we play with our politicians, and manage to endure our authors. We shall never have again such a popularity until we have again a people.

He left behind him this almost sombre fragment, "The Mystery of Edwin Drood." As one turns it over the tragic element of its truncation mingles somewhat with an element of tragedy in the thing itself; the passionate and predestined Landless, or the half maniacal Jasper carving devils out of his own heart. The workmanship of it is very fine; the right hand has not only not lost, but is still gaining its cunning. But as we turn the now enigmatic pages the thought creeps into us again which I have suggested earlier, and which is never far off the mind of a true lover of Dickens. Had he lost or gained by the growth of technique and probability in his later work? His later characters were more like men; but were not his earlier characters more like immortals? He has become able to perform a social scene so that it is possible at any rate; but where is that Dickens who once performed the impossible? Where is that young poet who created such majors and architects as Nature will never dare to create? Dickens learnt to describe daily life as Thackeray and Jane Austen could describe it; but Thackeray could not have thought such a thought as Crummles; and it is painful to think of Miss Austen attempting to imagine Mantalini. After all, we feel there are many able novelists; but there is only one Dickens, and whither has he fled?

He was alive to the end. And in this last dark and secretive story of Edwin Drood he makes one splendid and staggering appearance, like a magician saying farewell to mankind. In the centre of this otherwise reasonable and rather melancholy book, this grey story of a good clergyman and the quiet Cloisterham Towers, Dickens has calmly inserted one entirely delightful and entirely insane passage. I mean the frantic and inconceivable epitaph of Mrs. Sapsea, that which describes her as "the reverential wife" of Thomas Sapsea, speaks of her consistency in "looking up to him," and ends with the words, spaced out so admirably on the tombstone, "Stranger pause. And ask thyself this question, Canst thou do likewise? If not, with a blush retire." Not the wildest tale in Pickwick contains such an impossibility as that; Dickens dare scarcely have introduced it, even as one of Jingle's lies. In no human churchyard will you find that invaluable tombstone; indeed, you could scarcely find it in any world where there are churchyards. You could scarcely have such immortal folly as that in a world where there is also death. Mr. Sapsea is one of the golden things stored up for us in a better world.

Yes, there were many other Dickenses: a clever Dickens, an industrious Dickens, a public-spirited Dickens; but this was the great one. This last outbreak of insane humour reminds us wherein lay his power and his supremacy. The praise of such beatific buffoonery should be the final praise, the ultimate word in his honour. The wild epitaph of Mrs. Sapsea should be the serious epitaph of Dickens.

Chapter 10
The Great Dickens Characters

All criticism tends too much to become criticism of criticism; and the reason is very evident. It is that criticism of creation is so very staggering a thing. We see this in the difficulty of criticising any artistic creation. We see it again in the difficulty of criticising that creation which is spelt with a capital C. The pessimists who attack the Universe are always under this disadvantage. They have an exhilarating consciousness that they could make the sun and moon better; but they also have the depressing consciousness that they could not make the sun and moon at all. A man looking at a hippopotamus may sometimes be tempted to regard a hippopotamus as an enormous mistake; but he is also bound to confess that a fortunate inferiority prevents him personally from making such mistakes. It is neither a blasphemy nor an exaggeration to say that we feel something of the same difficulty in judging of the very creative element in human literature. And this is the first and last dignity of Dickens; that he was a creator. He did not point out things, he made them. We may disapprove of Mr. Guppy, but we recognise him as a creation flung down like a miracle out of an upper sphere; we can pull him to pieces, but we could not have put him together. We can destroy Mrs. Gamp in our wrath, but we could not have made her in our joy. Under this disadvantage any book about Dickens must definitely labour. Real primary creation (such as the sun or the birth of a child) calls forth not criticism, not appreciation, but a kind of incoherent gratitude. This is why most hymns about God are bad; and this is why most eulogies on Dickens are bad. The eulogists of the divine and of the human creator are alike inclined to appear sentimentalists because they are talking about something as very real. In the same way love-letters always sound florid and artificial because they are about something real.

Any chapter such as this chapter must therefore in a sense be inadequate. There is no way of dealing properly with the ultimate greatness of Dickens, except by offering sacrifice to him as a god; and this is opposed to the etiquette of our time. But something can perhaps be done in the way of suggesting what was the quality of this creation. But even in considering its quality we ought to remember that quality is not the whole question. One of the godlike things about Dickens is his quantity, his quantity as such, the enormous output, the incredible fecundity of his invention. I have said a moment ago that not one of us could have invented Mr. Guppy. But even if we could have stolen Mr. Guppy from Dickens we have still to confront the fact that Dickens would have been able to invent another quite inconceivable character to take his place. Perhaps we could have created Mr. Guppy; but the effort would certainly have exhausted us; we should be ever afterwards wheeled about in a bath-chair at Bournemouth.

Nevertheless there is something that is worth saying about the quality of Dickens. At the very beginning of this review I remarked that the reader must be in a mood, at least, of democracy. To some it may have sounded irrelevant; but the Revolution was as much behind all the books of the nineteenth century as the Catholic religion (let us say) was behind all the colours and carving of the Middle Ages. Another great name of the nineteenth century will afford an evidence of this; and will also bring us most sharply to the problem of the literary quality of Dickens.

Of all these nineteenth-century writers there is none, in the noblest sense, more democratic than Walter Scott. As this may be disputed, and as it is relevant, I will expand the remark. There are two rooted spiritual realities out of which grow all kinds of democratic conception or sentiment of human equality. There are two things in which all men are manifestly and unmistakably equal. They are not equally clever or equally muscular or equally fat, as the sages of the modern reaction (with piercing insight) perceive. But this is a spiritual certainty, that all men are tragic. And this, again, is an equally sublime spiritual certainty, that all men are comic. No special and private sorrow can be so dreadful as the fact of having to die. And no freak or deformity can be so funny as the mere fact of having two legs. Every man is important if he loses his life; and every man is funny if he loses his hat, and has to run after it. And the universal test everywhere of whether a thing is popular, of the people, is whether it employs vigorously these extremes of the tragic and the comic. Shelley, for instance, was an aristocrat, if ever there was one in this world. He was a Republican, but he was not a democrat: in his poetry there is every perfect quality except this pungent and popular stab. For the tragic and the comic you must go, say, to Burns, a poor man. And all over the world, the folk literature, the popular literature, is the same. It consists of very dignified sorrow and very undignified fun. Its sad tales are of broken hearts; its happy tales are of broken heads.

These, I say, are two roots of democratic reality. But they have in more civilised literature, a more civilised embodiment of form. In literature such as that of the nineteenth century the two elements appear somewhat thus. Tragedy becomes a profound sense of human dignity. The other and jollier element becomes a delighted sense of human variety. The first supports equality by saying that all men are equally sublime. The second supports equality by observing that all men are equally interesting.

In this democratic aspect of the interest and variety of all men, there is, of course, no democrat so great as Dickens. But in the other matter, in the idea of the dignity of all men, I repeat that there is no democrat so great as Scott. This fact, which is the moral and enduring magnificence of Scott, has been astonishingly overlooked. His rich and dramatic effects are gained in almost every case by some grotesque or beggarly figure rising into a human pride and rhetoric. The common man, in the sense of the paltry man, becomes the common man in the sense of the universal man. He declares his humanity. For the meanest of all the modernities has been the notion that the heroic is an oddity or variation, and that the things that unite us are merely flat or foul. The common things are terrible and startling, death, for instance, and first love: the things that are common are the things that are not commonplace. Into such high and central passions the comic Scott character will suddenly rise. Remember the firm and almost stately answer of the preposterous Nicol Jarvie when Helen Macgregor seeks to browbeat him into condoning lawlessness and breaking his bourgeois decency. That speech is a great monument of the middle class. Molière made M. Jourdain talk prose; but Scott made him talk poetry. Think of the rising and rousing voice of the dull and gluttonous Athelstane when he answers and overwhelms De Bracy. Think of the proud appeal of the old beggar in the "Antiquary" when he rebukes the duellists. Scott was fond of describing kings in disguise. But all his characters are kings in disguise. He was, with all his errors, profoundly possessed with the old religious conception, the only possible democratic basis, the idea that man himself is a king in disguise.

In all this Scott, though a Royalist and a Tory, had in the strangest way, the heart of the Revolution. For instance, he regarded rhetoric, the art of the orator, as the immediate weapon of the oppressed. All his poor men make grand speeches, as they did in the Jacobin Club, which Scott would have so much detested. And it is odd to reflect that he was, as an author, giving free speech to fictitious rebels while he was, as a stupid politician, denying it to real ones. But the point for us here is this that all this popular sympathy of his rests on the graver basis, on the dark dignity of man. "Can you find no way?" asks Sir Arthur Wardour of the beggar when they are cut off by the tide. "I'll give you a farm . . . I'll make you rich. . . . " "Our riches will soon be equal," says the beggar, and looks out across the advancing sea.

Now, I have dwelt on this strong point of Scott because it is the best illustration of the one weak point of Dickens. Dickens had little or none of this sense of the concealed sublimity of every separate man. Dickens's sense of democracy was entirely of the other kind; it rested on the other of the two supports of which I have spoken. It rested on the sense that all men were wildly interesting and wildly varied. When a Dickens character becomes excited he becomes more and more himself. He does not, like the Scott beggar, turn more and more into man. As he rises he grows more and more into a gargoyle or grotesque. He does not, like the fine speaker in Scott, grow more classical as he grows more passionate, more universal as he grows more intense. The thing can only be illustrated by a special case. Dickens did more than once, of course, make one of his quaint or humble characters assert himself in a serious crisis or defy the powerful. There is, for instance, the quite admirable scene in which Susan Nipper (one of the greatest of Dickens's achievements) faces and rebukes Mr. Dombey. But it is still true (and quite appropriate in its own place and manner) that Susan Nipper remains a purely comic character throughout her speech, and even grows more comic as she goes on. She is more serious than usual in her meaning, but not more serious in her style. Dickens keeps the natural diction of Nipper, but makes her grow more Nipperish as she grows more warm. But Scott keeps the natural diction of Baillie Jarvie, but insensibly sobers and uplifts the style until it reaches a plain and appropriate eloquence. This plain and appropriate eloquence was (except in a few places at the end of "Pickwick") almost unknown to Dickens. Whenever he made comic characters talk sentiment comically, as in the instance of Susan, it was a success, but an avowedly extravagant success. Whenever he made comic characters talk sentiment seriously it was an extravagant failure. Humour was his medium; his only way of approaching emotion. Wherever you do not get humour, you get unconscious humour.

As I have said elsewhere in this book Dickens was deeply and radically English; the most English of our great writers. And there is something very English in this contentment with a grotesque democracy; and in this absence of the eloquence and elevation of Scott. The English democracy is the most humorous democracy in the world. The Scotch democracy is the most dignified, while the whole abandon and satiric genius of the English populace come from its being quite undignified in every way. A comparison of the two types might be found, for instance, by putting a Scotch Labour Leader like Mr. Keir Hardie alongside an English Labour Leader like Mr. Will Crooks. Both are good men, honest, and responsible and compassionate; but we can feel that the Scotchman carries himself seriously and universally, the Englishman personally and with an obstinate humour. Mr. Keir Hardie wishes to hold up his head as Man, Mr. Crooks wishes to follow his nose as Crooks. Mr. Keir Hardie is very like a poor man in Walter Scott. Mr. Crooks is very like a poor man in Dickens.

Dickens then had this English feeling of a grotesque democracy. By that is more properly meant a vastly varying democracy. The intoxicating variety of men-that was his vision and conception of human brotherhood. And certainly it is a great part of human brotherhood. In one sense things can only be equal if they are entirely different. Thus, for instance, people talk with a quite astonishing gravity about the inequality or equality of the sexes; as if there could possibly be any inequality between a lock and a key. Wherever there is no element of variety, wherever all the items literally have an identical aim, there is at once and of necessity inequality. A woman is only inferior to man in the matter of being not so manly; she is inferior in nothing else. Man is inferior to woman in so far as he is not a woman; there is no other reason. And the same applies in some degree to all genuine differences. It is a great mistake to suppose that love unites and unifies men. Love diversifies them, because love is directed towards individuality. The thing that really unites men and makes them like to each other is hatred. Thus, for instance, the more we love Germany the more pleased we shall be that Germany should be something different from ourselves, should keep her own ritual and conviviality and we ours. But the more we hate Germany the more we shall copy German guns and German fortifications in order to be armed against Germany. The more modern nations detest each other the more meekly they follow each other; for all competition is in its nature only a furious plagiarism. As competition means always similarity, it is equally true that similarity always means inequality. If everything is trying to be green, some things will be greener than others; but there is an immortal and indestructible equality between green and red. Something of the same kind of irrefutable equality exists between the violent and varying creations of such a writer as Dickens. They are all equally ecstatic fulfilments of a separate line of development. It would be hard to say that there could be any comparison or inequality, let us say between Mr. Sapsea and Mr. Elijah Pogram. They are both in the same difficulty; they can neither of them contrive to exist in this world; they are both too big for the gate of birth.

Of the high virtue of this variation I shall speak more adequately in a moment; but certainly this love of mere variation (which I have contrasted with the classicism of Scott) is the only intelligent statement of the common case against the exaggeration of Dickens. This is the meaning, the only sane or endurable meaning, which people have in their minds when they say that Dickens is a mere caricaturist. They do not mean merely that Uncle Pumblechook does not exist. A fictitious character ought not to be a person who exists; he ought to be an entirely new combination, an addition to the creatures already existing on the earth. They do not mean that Uncle Pumblechook could not exist; for on that obviously they can have no knowledge whatever. They do not mean that Uncle Pumblechook's utterances are selected and arranged so as to bring out his essential Pumblechookery; to say that is simply to say that he occurs in a work of art. But what they do really mean is this, and there is an element of truth in it. They mean that Dickens nowhere makes the reader feel that Pumblechook has any kind of fundamental human dignity at all. It is nowhere suggested that Pumblechook will some day die. He is felt rather as one of the idle and evil fairies, who are innocuous and yet malignant, and who live for ever because they never really live at all. This dehumanised vitality, this fantasy, this irresponsibility of creation, does in some sense truly belong to Dickens. It is the lower side of his hilarious human variety. But now we come to the higher side of his human variety, and it is far more difficult to state.

Mr. George Gissing, from the point of view of the passing intellectualism of our day, has made (among his many wise tributes to Dickens) a characteristic complaint about him. He has said that Dickens, with all his undoubted sympathy for the lower classes, never made a working man, a poor man, specifically and highly intellectual. An exception does exist, which he must at least have realised —a wit, a diplomatist, a great philosopher. I mean, of course, Mr. Weller. Broadly, however, the accusation has a truth, though it is a truth that Mr. Gissing did not grasp in its entirety. It is not only true that Dickens seldom made a poor character what we call intellectual; it is also true that he seldom made any character what we call intellectual. Intellectualism was not at all present to his imagination. What was present to his imagination was character —a thing which is not only more important than intellect, but is also much more entertaining. When some English moralists write about the importance of having character, they appear to mean only the importance of having a dull character. But character is brighter than wit, and much more complex than sophistry. The whole superiority of the democracy of Dickens over the democracy of such a man as Gissing lies exactly in the fact that Gissing would have liked to prove that poor men could instruct themselves and could instruct others. It was of final importance to Dickens that poor men could amuse themselves and could amuse him. He troubled little about the mere education of that life; he declared two essential things about it-that it was laughable, and that it was livable. The humble characters of Dickens do not amuse each other with epigrams; they amuse each other with themselves. The present that each man brings in hand is his own incredible personality. In the most sacred sense, and in the most literal sense of the phrase, he "gives himself away." Now, the man who gives himself away does the last act of generosity; he is like a martyr, a lover, or a monk. But he is also almost certainly what we commonly call a fool.

The key of the great characters of Dickens is that they are all great fools. There is the same difference between a great fool and a small fool as there is between a great poet and a small poet. The great fool is a being who is above wisdom rather than below it. That element of greatness of which I spoke at the beginning of this book is nowhere more clearly indicated than in such characters. A man can be entirely great while he is entirely foolish. We see this in the epic heroes, such as Achilles. Nay, a man can be entirely great because he is entirely foolish. We see this in all the great comic characters of all the great comic writers of whom Dickens was the last. Bottom the Weaver is great because he is foolish; Mr. Toots is great because he is foolish. The thing I mean can be observed, for instance, in innumerable actual characters. Which of us has not known, for instance, a great rustic? —a character so incurably characteristic that he seemed to break through all canons about cleverness or stupidity; we do not know whether he is an enormous idiot or an enormous philosopher; we know only that he is enormous, like a hill. These great, grotesque characters are almost entirely to be found where Dickens found them-among the poorer classes. The gentry only attain this greatness by going slightly mad.

But who has not known an unfathomably personal old nurse? Who has not known an abysmal butler? The truth is that our public life consists almost exclusively of small men. Our public men are small because they have to prove that they are in the commonplace interpretation clever, because they have to pass examinations, to learn codes of manners, to imitate a fixed type. It is in private life that we find the great characters. They are too great to get into the public world. It is easier for a camel to pass through the eye of a needle than for a great man to enter into the kingdoms of the earth. The truly great and gorgeous personality, he who talks as no one else could talk and feels with an elementary fire, you will never find this man on any cabinet bench, in any literary circle, at any society dinner. Least of all will you find him in artistic society; he is utterly unknown in Bohemia. He is more than clever, he is amusing. He is more than successful, he is alive. You will find him stranded here and there in all sorts of unknown positions, almost always in unsuccessful positions. You will find him adrift as an impecunious commercial traveller like Micawber. You will find him but one of a batch of silly clerks, like Swiveller. You will find him as an unsuccessful actor, like Crummles. You will find him as an unsuccessful doctor, like Sawyer. But you will always find this rich and reeking personality where Dickens found it-among the poor. For the glory of this world is a very small and priggish affair, and these men are too large to get in line with it. They are too strong to conquer.

It is impossible to do justice to these figures because the essential of them is their multiplicity. The whole point of Dickens is that he not only made them, but made them by myriads; that he stamped his foot, and armies came out of the earth. But let us, for the sake of showing the true Dickens method, take one of them, a very sublime one, Toots. If affords a good example of the real work of Dickens, which was the revealing of a certain grotesque greatness inside an obscure and even unattractive type. It reveals the great paradox of all spiritual things; that the inside is always larger than the outside.

Toots is a type that we all know as well as we know chimney-pots. And of all conceivable human figures he is apparently the most futile and the most dull. He is the blockhead who hangs on at a private school, overgrown and under-developed. He is always backward in his lessons, but forward in certain cheap ways of the world; he can smoke before he can spell. Toots is a perfect and pungent picture of the wretched youth. Toots has, as this youth always has, a little money of his own; enough to waste in a semi-dissipation he does not enjoy, and in a gaping regard for sports in which he could not possibly excel. Toots has, as this youth always has, bits of surreptitious finery, in his case the incomparable ring. In Toots, above all, is exactly rendered the central and most startling contradiction; the contrast between a jauntiness and a certain impudence of the attire, with the profound shame and sheepishness of the visage and the character. In him, too, is expressed the larger contrast between the external gaiety of such a lad's occupations, and the infinite, disconsolate sadness of his empty eyes. This is Toots; we know him, we pity him, and we avoid him. Schoolmasters deal with him in despair or in a heart-breaking patience. His family is vague about him. His low-class hangers-on (like the Game Chicken) lead him by the nose. The very parasites that live on him despise him. But Dickens does not despise him. Without denying one of the dreary details which make us avoid the man, Dickens makes him a man whom we long to meet. He does not gloss over one of his dismal deficiencies, but he makes them seem suddenly like violent virtues that we would go to the world's end to see. Without altering one fact, he manages to alter the whole atmosphere, the whole universe of Toots. He makes us not only like, but love, not only love, but reverence this little dunce and cad. The power to do this is a power truly and literally to be called divine.

For this is the very wholesome point. Dickens does not alter Toots in any vital point. The thing he does alter is us. He makes us lively where we were bored, kind where we were cruel, and above all, free for an universal human laughter where we were cramped in a small competition about that sad and solemn tiling, the intellect. His enthusiasm fills us, as does the love of God, with a glorious shame; after all, he has only found in Toots what we might have found for ourselves. He has only made us as much interested in Toots as Toots is in himself. He does not alter the proportions of Toots; he alters only the scale; we seem as if we were staring at a rat risen to the stature of an elephant. Hitherto we have passed him by; now we feel that nothing could induce us to pass him by; that is the nearest way of putting the truth. He has not been whitewashed in the least; he has not been depicted as any cleverer than he is. He has been turned from a small fool into a great fool. We know Toots is not clever; but we are not inclined to quarrel with Toots because he is not clever. We are more likely to quarrel with cleverness because it is not Toots. All the examinations he could not pass, all the schools he could not enter, all the temporary tests of brain and culture which surrounded him shall pass, and Toots shall remain like a mountain.

It may be noticed that the great artists always choose great fools rather than great intellectuals to embody humanity. Hamlet does express the aesthetic dreams and the bewilderments of the intellect; but Bottom the Weaver expresses them much better. In the same manner Toots expresses certain permanent dignities in human nature more than any of Dickens's more dignified characters can do it. For instance, Toots expresses admirably the enduring fear, which is the very essence of falling in love. When Toots is invited by Florence to come in, when he longs to come in, but still stays out, he is embodying a sort of insane and perverse humility which is elementary in the lover.

There is an apostolic injunction to suffer fools gladly. We always lay the stress on the word "suffer," and interpret the passage as one urging resignation. It might be better, perhaps, to lay the stress upon the word "gladly," and make our familiarity with fools a delight, and almost a dissipation. Nor is it necessary that our pleasure in fools (or at least in great and godlike fools) should be merely satiric or cruel. The great fool is he in whom we cannot tell which is the conscious and which the unconscious humour; we laugh with him and laugh at him at the same time. An obvious instance is that of ordinary and happy marriage. A man and a woman cannot live together without having against each other a kind of everlasting joke. Each has discovered that the other is a fool, but a great fool. This largeness, this grossness and gorgeousness of folly is the thing which we all find about those with whom we are in intimate contact; and it is the one enduring basis of affection, and even of respect. When we know an individual named Tomkins, we know that he has succeeded where all others have failed; he has succeeded in being Tomkins. Just so Mr. Toots succeeded; he was defeated in all scholastic examinations, but he was the victor in that visionary battle in which unknown competitors vainly tried to be Toots.

If we are to look for lessons, here at least is the last and deepest lesson of Dickens. It is in our own daily life that we are to look for the portents and the prodigies. This is the truth, not merely of the fixed figures of our life; the wife, the husband, the fool that fills the sky. It is true of the whole stream and substance of our daily experience; every instant we reject a great fool merely because he is foolish. Every day we neglect Tootses and Swivellers, Guppys and Joblings, Simmerys and Flashers. Every day we lose the last sight of Jobling and Chuckster, the Analytical Chemist, or the Marchioness. Every day we are missing a monster whom we might easily love, and an imbecile whom we should certainly admire.

This is the real gospel of Dickens; the inexhaustible opportunities offered by the liberty and the variety of man. Compared with this life, all public life, all fame, all wisdom, is by its nature cramped and cold and small. For on that defined and lighted public stage men are of necessity forced to profess one set of accomplishments, to rise to one rigid standard. It is the utterly unknown people who can grow in all directions like an exuberant tree. It is in our interior lives that we find that people are too much themselves. It is in our private life that we find them swelling into the enormous contours, and taking on the colours of caricature. Many of us live publicly with featureless public puppets, images of the small public abstractions. It is when we pass our own private gate, and open our own secret door, that we step into the land of the giants.

Chapter 11
On the Alleged Optimism of Dickens

In one of the plays of the decadent period, an intellectual expressed the atmosphere of his epoch by referring to Dickens as "a vulgar optimist." I have in a previous chapter suggested something of the real strangeness of such a term. After all, the main matter of astonishment (or rather of admiration) is that optimism should be vulgar. In a world in which physical distress is almost the common lot, we actually complain that happiness is too common. In a world in which the majority is physically miserable we actually complain of the sameness of praise; we are bored with the abundance of approval. When we consider what the conditions of the vulgar really are, it is difficult to imagine a stranger or more splendid tribute to humanity than such a phrase as vulgar optimism. It is as if one spoke of "vulgar martyrdom" or "common crucifixion."

First, however, let it be said frankly that there is a foundation for the charge against Dickens which is implied in the phrase about vulgar optimism. It does not concern itself with Dickens's confidence in the value of existence and the intrinsic victory of virtue; that is not optimism but religion. It is not concerned with his habit of making bright occasions bright, and happy stories happy; that is not optimism, but literature. Nor is it concerned even with his peculiar genius for the description of an almost bloated joviality; that is not optimism, it is simply Dickens. With all these higher variations of optimism I deal elsewhere. But over and above all these there is a real sense in which Dickens laid himself open to the accusation of a vulgar optimism, and I desire to put the admission of this first, before the discussion that follows. Dickens did have a disposition to make his characters at all costs happy, or, to speak more strictly, he had a disposition to make them comfortable rather than happy. He had a sort of literary hospitality; he too often treated his characters as if they were his guests. From a host is always expected, and always ought to be expected as long as human civilisation is healthy, a strictly physical benevolence, if you will, a kind of coarse benevolence. Food and fire and such things should always be the symbols of the man entertaining men; because they are things which all men beyond question have in common. But something more than this is needed from a man who is imagining and making men, the artist, the man who is not receiving men, but rather sending them forth.

As I shall remark in a moment in the matter of the Dickens villains, it is not true that he made every one thus at home. But he did do it to a certain wide class of incongruous characters, he did it to all who had been in any way unfortunate. It had needed its origin (a very beautiful origin) in his realisation of how much a little pleasure was to such people. He knew well that the greatest happiness that has been known since Eden is the happiness of the unhappy. So far he is admirable. And as long as he was describing the ecstasy of the poor, the borderland between pain and pleasure, he was at his highest. Nothing that has ever been written about human delights, no Earthly Paradise, no Utopia has ever come so near the quick nerve of happiness as his descriptions of the rare extravagances of the poor; such an admirable description, for instance, as that of Kit Nubbles taking his family to the theatre. For he seizes on the real source of the whole pleasure; a holy fear. Kit tells the waiter to bring the beer. And the waiter, instead of saying, "Did you address that language to me," said, "Pot of beer, sir; yes, sir." That internal and quivering humility of Kit is the only way to enjoy life or banquets; and the fear of the waiter is the beginning of dining. People in this mood "take their pleasures sadly"; which is the only way of taking them at all.

So far Dickens is supremely right. As long as he was dealing with such penury and such festivity his touch was almost invariably sure. But when he came to more difficult cases, to people who for one reason or another could not be cured with one good dinner, he did develop this other evil, this genuinely vulgar optimism of which I speak. And the mark of it is this: that he gave the characters a comfort that had no especial connection with themselves; he threw comfort at them like alms. There are cases at the end of his stories in which his kindness to his characters is a careless and insolent kindness. He loses his real charity and adopts the charity of the Charity Organisation Society; the charity that is not kind, the charity that is puffed up, and that does behave itself unseemly. At the end of some of his stories he deals out his characters a kind of out-door relief. I will give two instances. The whole meaning of the character of Mr. Micawber is that a man can be always almost rich by constantly expecting riches. The lesson is a really important one in our sweeping modern sociology. We talk of the man whose life is a failure; but Micawber's life never is a failure, because it is always a crisis. We think constantly of the man who if he looked back would see that his existence was unsuccessful; but Micawber never does look back; he always looks forward, because the bailiff is coming tomorrow. You cannot say he is defeated, for his absurd battle never ends; he cannot despair of life, for he is so much occupied in living. All this is of immense importance in the understanding of the poor; it is worth all the slum novelists that ever insulted democracy. But how did it happen that the man who created this Micawber could pension him off at the end of the story and make him a successful colonial mayor? Micawber never did succeed, never ought to succeed; his kingdom is not of this world. But this is an excellent instance of Dickens's disposition to make his characters grossly and incongruously comfortable. There is another instance in the same book. Dora, the first wife of David Copperfield, is a very genuine and amusing figure; she has certainly far more force of character than Agnes. She represents the infinite and divine irrationality of the human heart. What possessed Dickens to make her such a dehumanised prig as to recommend her husband to marry another woman? One could easily respect a husband who after time and development made such a marriage, but surely not a wife who desired it. If Dora had died hating Agnes we should know that everything was right, and that God would reconcile the irreconcilable. When Dora dies recommending Agnes we know that everything is wrong, at least if hypocrisy and artificiality and moral vulgarity are wrong. There, again, Dickens yields to a mere desire to give comfort. He wishes to pile up pillows round Dora; and he smothers her with them, like Othello.

This is the real vulgar optimism of Dickens: it does exist; and I have deliberately put it first. Let us admit that Dickens's mind was far too much filled with pictures of satisfaction and cosiness and repose. Let us admit that he thought principally of the pleasures of the oppressed classes; let us admit that it hardly cost him any artistic pang to make out human beings as much happier than they are. Let us admit all this, and a curious fact remains.

For it was this too easily contented Dickens, this man with cushions at his back and (it sometimes seems) cotton wool in his ears; it was this happy dreamer, this vulgar optimist who alone of modern writers did really destroy some of the wrongs he hated and bring about some of the reforms he desired. Dickens did help to pull down the debtors' prisons; and if he was too much of an optimist he was quite enough of a destroyer. Dickens did drive Squeers out of his Yorkshire den; and if Dickens was too contented, it was more than Squeers was. Dickens did leave his mark on parochialism, on nursing, on funerals, on public executions, on workhouses, on the Court of Chancery. These things were altered; they are different. It may be that such reforms are not adequate remedies; that is another question altogether. The next sociologists may think these old Radical reforms quite narrow or accidental. But such as they were, the old Radicals got them done; and the new sociologists cannot get anything done at all. And in the practical doing of them Dickens played a solid and quite demonstrable part; that is the plain matter that concerns us here. If Dickens was an optimist he was an uncommonly active and useful kind of optimist. If Dickens was a sentimentalist he was a very practical sentimentalist.

And the reason of this is one that goes deep into Dickens's social reform, and like every other real and desirable thing, involves a kind of mystical contradiction. If we are to save the oppressed, we must have two apparently antagonistic emotions in us at the same time. We must think the oppressed man intensely miserable, and at the same time intensely attractive and important. We must insist with violence upon his degradation; we must insist with the same violence upon his dignity. For if we relax by one inch the one assertion, men will say he does not need saving. And if we relax by one inch the other assertion, men will say he is not worth saving. The optimists will say that reform is needless. The pessimists will say that reform is hopeless. We must apply both simultaneously to the same oppressed man; we must say that he is a worm and a god; and we must thus lay ourselves open to the accusation (or the compliment) of transcendentalism. This is, indeed, the strongest argument for the religious conception of life. If the dignity of man is an earthly dignity we shall be tempted to deny his earthly degradation. If it is a heavenly dignity we can admit the earthly degradation with all the candour of Zola. If we are idealists about the other world we can be realists about this world. But that is not here the point. What is quite evident is that if a logical praise of the poor man is pushed too far, and if a logical distress about him is pushed too far, either will involve wreckage to the central paradox of reform. If the poor man is made too admirable he ceases to be pitiable; if the poor man is made too pitiable he becomes merely contemptible. There is a school of smug optimists who will deny that he is a poor man. There is a school of scientific pessimists who will deny that he is a man.

Out of this perennial contradiction arises the fact that there are always two types of the reformer. The first we may call for convenience the pessimistic, the second the optimistic reformer. One dwells upon the fact that souls are being lost; the other dwells upon the fact that they are worth saving. Both, of course, are (so far as that is concerned) quite right, but they naturally tend to a difference of method, and sometimes to a difference of perception. The pessimistic reformer points out the good elements that oppression has destroyed; the optimistic reformer, with an even fiercer joy, points out the good elements that it has not destroyed. It is the case for the first reformer that slavery has made men slavish. It is the case for the second reformer that slavery has not made men slavish. The first describes how bad men are under bad conditions. The second describes how good men are under bad conditions. Of the first class of writers, for instance, is Gorky. Of the second class of writers is Dickens.

But here we must register a real and somewhat startling fact. In the face of all apparent probability, it is certainly true that the optimistic reformer reforms much more completely than the pessimistic reformer. People produce violent changes by being contented, by being far too contented. The man who said that "revolutions are not made with rose-water" was obviously inexperienced in practical human affairs. Men like Rousseau and Shelley do make revolutions, and do make them with rose-water; that is, with a too rosy and sentimental view of human goodness. Figures that come before and create convulsion and change (for instance, the central figure of the New Testament) always have the air of walking in an unnatural sweetness and calm. They give us their peace ultimately in blood and battle and division; not as the world giveth give they unto us.

Nor is the real reason of the triumph of the too-contented reformer particularly difficult to define. He triumphs because he keeps alive in the human soul an invincible sense of the thing being worth doing, of the war being worth winning, of the people being worth their deliverance. I remember that Mr. William Archer, some time ago, published in one of his interesting series of interviews, an interview with Mr. Thomas Hardy. That powerful writer was represented as saying, in the course of the conversation, that he did not wish at the particular moment to define his opinion with regard to the ultimate problem of whether life itself was worth living. There are, he said, hundreds of remediable evils in this world. When we have remedied all these (such was his argument), it will be time enough to ask whether existence itself under its best possible conditions is valuable or desirable. Here we have presented, with a considerable element of what can only be called unconscious humour, the plain reason of the failure of the pessimist as a reformer. Mr. Hardy is asking us, I will not say to buy a pig in a poke; he is asking us to buy a poke on the remote chance of there being a pig in it. When we have for some few frantic centuries tortured ourselves to save mankind, it will then be "time enough" to discuss whether they can possibly be saved. When, in the case of infant mortality, for example, we have exhausted ourselves with the earthshaking efforts required to save the life of every individual baby, it will then be time enough to consider whether every individual baby would not have been happier dead. We are to remove mountains and bring the millennium, because then we can have a quiet moment to discuss whether the millennium is at all desirable.

Here we have the low-water mark of the impotence of the sad reformer. And here we have the reason of the paradoxical triumph of the happy one. His triumph is a religious triumph; it rests upon his perpetual assertion of the value of the human soul and of human daily life. It rests upon his assertion that human life is enjoyable because it is human. And he will never admit, like so many compassionate pessimists, that human life ever ceases to be human. He does not merely pity the lowness of men; he feels an insult to their elevation. Brute pity should be given only to brutes. Cruelty to animals is cruelty and a vile thing; but cruelty to a man is not cruelty, it is treason. Tyranny over a man is not tyranny, it is rebellion, for man is royal. Now, the practical weakness of the vast mass of modern pity for the poor and the oppressed is precisely that it is merely pity; the pity is pitiful, but not respectful. Men feel that the cruelty to the poor is a kind of cruelty to animals. They never feel that it is justice to equals; nay, it is treachery to comrades. This dark scientific pity, this brutal pity, has an elemental sincerity of its own; but it is entirely useless for all ends of social reform. Democracy swept Europe with the sabre when it was founded upon the Rights of Man. It has done literally nothing at all since it has been founded only upon the wrongs of man. Or, more strictly speaking, its recent failure has been due to its not admitting the existence of any rights, or wrongs, or indeed of any humanity. Evolution (the sinister enemy of revolution) does not especially deny the existence of God; what it does deny is the existence of man. And all the despair about the poor, and the cold and repugnant pity for them, has been largely due to the vague sense that they have literally relapsed into the state of the lower animals.

A writer sufficiently typical of recent revolutionism-Gorky-has called one of his books by the eerie and effective title "Creatures that once were Men." That title explains the whole failure of the Russian revolution. And the reason why the English writers, such as Dickens, did with all their limitations achieve so many of the actual things at which they aimed was that they could not possibly have put such a title upon a human book. Dickens really helped the unfortunate in the matters to which he set himself. And the reason is that across all his books and sketches about the unfortunate might be written the common title, "Creatures that Still are Men."

There does exist, then, this strange optimistic reformer; the man whose work begins with approval and ends with earthquake. Jesus Christ was destined to found a faith which made the rich poorer and the poor rich; but even when He was going to enrich them, He began with the phrase, "Blessed are the poor." The Gissings and the Gorkys say, as an universal literary motto, "Cursed are the poor." Among a million who have faintly followed Christ in this divine contradiction, Dickens stands out especially. He said, in all his reforming utterances, "Cure poverty;" but he said in all his actual descriptions, "Blessed are the poor." He described their happiness, and men rushed to remove their sorrow. He described them as human, and men resented the insults to their humanity. It is not difficult to see why, as I said at an earlier stage of this book, Dickens's denunciations have had so much more practical an effect than the denunciations of such a man as Gissing. Both agreed that the souls of the people were in a kind of prison. But Gissing said that the prison was full of dead souls. Dickens said that the prison was full of living souls. And the fiery cavalcade of rescuers felt that they had not come too late.

Of this general fact about Dickens's descriptions of poverty there will not, I suppose, be any serious dispute. The dispute will only be about the truth of those descriptions. It is clear that whereas Gissing would say, "See how their poverty depresses the Smiths or the Browns," Dickens says, "See how little, after all, their poverty can depress the Cratchits." No one will deny that he made a special feature of the poor. We will come to the discussion of the veracity of these scenes in a moment. It is here sufficient to register in conclusion of our examination of the reforming optimist, that Dickens certainly was such an optimist, and that he made it his business to insist upon what happiness there is in the lives of the unhappy. His poor man is always a Mark Tapley, a man the optimism of whose spirit increases if anything with the pessimism of his experience. It can also be registered as a fact equally solid and quite equally demonstrable that this optimistic Dickens did effect great reforms.

The reforms in which Dickens was instrumental were indeed, from the point of view of our sweeping social panaceas, special and limited. But perhaps, for that reason especially, they afford a compact and concrete instance of the psychological paradox of which we speak. Dickens did definitely destroy-or at the very least help to destroy-certain institutions; he destroyed those institutions simply by describing them. But the crux and peculiarity of the whole matter is this, that, in a sense, it can really be said that he described these things too optimistically. In a real sense, he described Dotheboys Hall as a better place than it is. In a real sense, he made out the workhouse as a pleasanter place than it can ever be. For the chief glory of Dickens is that he made these places interesting; and the chief infamy of England is that it has made these places dull. Dullness was the thing that Dickens's genius could never succeed in describing; his vitality was so violent that he could not introduce into his books the genuine impression even of a moment of monotony. If there is anywhere in his novels an instant of silence, we only hear more clearly the hero whispering with the heroine, the villain sharpening his dagger, or the creaking of the machinery that is to give out the god from the machine. He could splendidly describe gloomy places, but he could not describe dreary places. He could describe miserable marriages, but not monotonous marriages. It must have been genuinely entertaining to be married to Mr. Quilp. This sense of a still incessant excitement he spreads over every inch of his story, and over every dark tract of his landscape. His idea of a desolate place is a place where anything can happen, he has no idea of that desolate place where nothing can happen. This is a good thing for his soul, for the place where nothing can happen is hell. But still, it might reasonably be maintained by the modern mind that he is hampered in describing human evil and sorrow by this inability to imagine tedium, this dullness in the matter of dullness. For, after all, it is certainly true that the worst part of the lot of the unfortunate is the fact that they have long spaces in which to review the irrevocability of their doom. It is certainly true that the worst days of the oppressed man are the nine days out of ten in which he is not oppressed. This sense of sickness and sameness Dickens did certainly fail or refuse to give. When we read such a description as that excellent one-in detail-of Dotheboys Hall, we feel that, while everything else is accurate, the author does, in the words of the excellent Captain Nares in Stevenson's "Wrecker," "draw the dreariness rather mild." The boys at Dotheboys were, perhaps, less bullied, but they were certainly more bored. For, indeed, how could anyone be bored with the society of so sumptuous a creature as Mr. Squeers? Who would not put up with a few illogical floggings in order to enjoy the conversation of a man who could say, "She's a rum 'un is Natur' . . . Natur' is more easier conceived than described." The same principle applies to the workhouse in "Oliver Twist." We feel vaguely that neither Oliver nor anyone else could be entirely unhappy in the presence of the purple personality of Mr. Bumble. The one thing he did not describe in any of the abuses he denounced was the soul-destroying potency of routine. He made out the bad school, the bad parochial system, the bad debtor's prison as very much jollier and more exciting than they may really have been. In a sense, then, he flattered them; but he destroyed them with the flattery. By making Mrs. Gamp delightful he made her impossible. He gave every one an interest in Mr. Bumble's existence; and by the same act gave every one an interest in his destruction. It would be difficult to find a stronger instance of the utility and energy of the method which we have, for the sake of argument, called the method of the optimistic reformer. As long as low Yorkshire schools were entirely colourless and dreary, they continued quietly tolerated by the public and quietly intolerable to the victims. So long as Squeers was dull as well as cruel he was permitted; the moment he became amusing as well as cruel he was destroyed. As long as Bumble was merely inhuman he was allowed. When he became human, humanity wiped him right out. For in order to do these great acts of justice we must always realise not only the humanity of the oppressed, but even the humanity of the oppressor. The satirist had, in a sense, to create the images in the mind before, as an iconoclast, he could destroy them. Dickens had to make Squeers live before be could make him die.

In connection with the accusation of vulgar optimism, which I have taken as a text for this chapter, there is another somewhat odd thing to notice. Nobody in the world was ever less optimistic than Dickens in his treatment of evil or the evil man. When I say optimist in this matter I mean optimism, in the modern sense, of an attempt to whitewash evil. Nobody ever made less attempt to whitewash evil than Dickens. Nobody black was ever less white than Dickens's black. He painted his villains and lost characters more black than they really are. He crowds his stories with a kind of villain rare in modern fiction-the villain really without any "redeeming point." There is no redeeming point in Squeers, or in Monks, or in Ralph Nickleby, or in Bill Sikes, or in Quilp, or in Brass, or in Mr. Chester, or in Mr. Pecksniff, or in Jonas Chuzzlewit, or in Carker, or in Uriah Heep, or in Blandois, or in a hundred more. So far as the balance of good and evil in human characters is concerned, Dickens certainly could not be called a vulgar optimist. His emphasis on evil was melodramatic. He might be called a vulgar pessimist.

Some will dismiss this lurid villainy as a detail of his artificial romance. I am not inclined to do so. He inherited, undoubtedly, this unqualified villain as he inherited so many other things, from the whole history of European literature. But he breathed into the blackguard a peculiar and vigorous life of his own. He did not show any tendency to modify his black-guardism in accordance with the increasing considerateness of the age; he did not seem to wish to make his villain less villainous; he did not wish to imitate the analysis of George Eliot, or the reverent scepticism of Thackeray. And all this works back, I think, to a real thing in him, that he wished to have an obstreperous and incalculable enemy. He wished to keep alive the idea of combat, which means, of necessity, a combat against something individual and alive. I do not know whether, in the kindly rationalism of his epoch, he kept any belief in a personal devil in his theology, but he certainly created a personal devil in every one of his books.

A good example of my meaning can be found, for instance, in such a character as Quilp. Dickens may, for all I know, have had originally some idea of describing Quilp as the bitter and unhappy cripple, a deformity whose mind is stunted along with his body. But if he had such an idea, he soon abandoned it. Quilp is not in the least unhappy. His whole picturesqueness consists in the fact that he has a kind of hellish happiness, an atrocious hilarity that makes him go bounding about like an indiarubber ball. Quilp is not in the least bitter; he has an unaffected gaiety, an expansiveness, an universality. He desires to hurt people in the same hearty way that a good-natured man desires to help them. He likes to poison people with the same kind of clamorous camaraderie with which an honest man likes to stand them drink. Quilp is not in the least stunted in mind; he is not in reality even stunted in body-his body, that is, does not in any way fall short of what he wants it to do. His smallness gives him rather the promptitude of a bird or the precipitance of a bullet. In a word, Quilp is precisely the devil of the Middle Ages; he belongs to that amazingly healthy period when even lost spirits were hilarious.

This heartiness and vivacity in the villains of Dickens is worthy of note because it is directly connected with his own cheerfulness. This is a truth little understood in our time, but it is a very essential one. If optimism means a general approval, it is certainly true that the more a man becomes an optimist the more he becomes a melancholy man. If he manages to praise everything, his praise will develop an alarming resemblance to a polite boredom. He will say that the marsh is as good as the garden; he will mean that the garden is as dull as the marsh. He may force himself to say that emptiness is good, but he will hardly prevent himself from asking what is the good of such good. This optimism does exist-this optimism which is more hopeless than pessimism-this optimism which is the very heart of hell.

Against such an aching vacuum of joyless approval there is only one antidote —a sudden and pugnacious belief in positive evil. This world can be made beautiful again by beholding it as a battlefield. When we have defined and isolated the evil thing, the colours come back into everything else. When evil things have become evil, good things, in a blazing apocalypse, become good. There are some men who are dreary because they do not believe in God; but there are many others who are dreary because they do not believe in the devil. The grass grows green again when we believe in the devil, the roses grow red again when we believe in the devil.

No man was more filled with the sense of this bellicose basis of all cheerfulness than Dickens. He knew very well the essential truth, that the true optimist can only continue an optimist so long as he is discontented. For the full value of this life can only be got by fighting; the violent take it by storm. And if we have accepted everything, we have missed something–war. This life of ours is a very enjoyable fight, but a very miserable truce. And it appears strange to me that so few critics of Dickens or of other romantic writers have noticed this philosophical meaning in the undiluted villain. The villain is not in the story to be a character; he is there to be a danger —a ceaseless, ruthless, and uncompromising menace, like that of wild beasts or the sea. For the full satisfaction of the sense of combat, which everywhere and always involves a sense of equality, it is necessary to make the evil thing a man; but it is not always necessary, it is not even always artistic, to make him a mixed and probable man. In any tale, the tone of which is at all symbolic, he may quite legitimately be made an aboriginal and infernal energy. He must be a man only in the sense that he must have a wit and will to be matched with the wit and will of the man chiefly fighting. The evil may be inhuman, but it must not be impersonal, which is almost exactly the position occupied by Satan in the theological scheme.

But when all is said, as I have remarked before, the chief fountain in Dickens of what I have called cheerfulness, and some prefer to call optimism, is something deeper than a verbal philosophy. It is, after all, an incomparable hunger and pleasure for the vitality and the variety, for the infinite eccentricity of existence. And this word "eccentricity" brings us, perhaps, nearer to the matter than any other. It is, perhaps, the strongest mark of the divinity of man that he talks of this world as "a strange world," though he has seen no other. We feel that all there is is eccentric, though we do not know what is the centre. This sentiment of the grotesqueness of the universe ran through Dickens's brain and body like the mad blood of the elves. He saw all his streets in fantastic perspectives, he saw all his cockney villas as top heavy and wild, he saw every man's nose twice as big as it was, and very man's eyes like saucers. And this was the basis of his gaiety-the only real basis of any philosophical gaiety. This world is not to be justified as it is justified by the mechanical optimists; it is not to be justified as the best of all possible worlds. Its merit is not that it is orderly and explicable; its merit is that it is wild and utterly unexplained. Its merit is precisely that none of us could have conceived such a thing, that we should have rejected the bare idea of it as miracle and unreason. It is the best of all impossible worlds.

Chapter 12
A Note on the Future of Dickens

The hardest thing to remember about our own time, of course, is simply that it is a time; we all instinctively think of it as the Day of Judgment. But all the things in it which belong to it merely as this time will probably be rapidly turned upside down; all the things that can pass will pass. It is not merely true that all old things are already dead; it is also true that all new things are already dead; for the only undying things are the things that are neither new nor old. The more you are up with this year's fashion, the more (in a sense) you are already behind next year's. Consequently, in attempting to decide whether an author will, as it is cantly expressed, live, it is necessary to have very firm convictions about what part, if any part, of man is unchangeable. And it is very hard to have this if you have not a religion or, at least, a dogmatic philosophy.

The equality of men needs preaching quite as much as regards the ages as regards the classes of men. To feel infinitely superior to a man in the twelfth century is just precisely as snobbish as to feel infinitely superior to a man in the Old Kent Road. There are differences between the man and us, there may be superiorities in us over the man; but our sin in both cases consists in thinking of the small things wherein we differ when we ought to be confounded and intoxicated by the terrible and joyful matters in which we are at one. But here again the difficulty always is that the things near us seem larger than they are, and so seem to be a permanent part of mankind, when they may really be only one of its parting modes of expression. Few people, for instance, realise that a time may easily come when we shall see the great outburst of Science in the nineteenth century as something quite as splendid, brief, unique, and ultimately abandoned, as the outburst of Art at the Renascence. Few people realise that the general habit of fiction, of telling tales in prose, may fade, like the general habit of the ballad, of telling tales in verse, has for the time faded. Few people realise that reading and writing are only arbitrary, and perhaps temporary sciences, like heraldry.

The immortal mind will remain, and by that writers like Dickens will be securely judged. That Dickens will have a high place in permanent literature there is, I imagine, no prig surviving to deny. But though all prediction is in the dark, I would devote this chapter to suggesting that his place in nineteenth-century England will not only be high, but altogether the highest. At a certain period of his contemporary fame, an average Englishman would have said that there were at that moment in England about five or six able and equal novelists. He could have made a list, Dickens, Bulwer Lytton, Thackeray, Charlotte Brontë, George Eliot, perhaps more. Forty years or more have passed and some of them have slipped to a lower place. Some would now say that the highest platform is left to Thackeray and Dickens; some to Dickens, Thackeray, and George Eliot; some to Dickens, Thackeray, and Charlotte Brontë. I venture to offer the proposition that when more years have passed and more weeding has been effected, Dickens will dominate the whole England of the nineteenth century; he will be left on that platform alone.

I know that this is an almost impertinent thing to assert, and that its tendency is to bring in those disparaging discussions of other writers in which Mr. Swinburne brilliantly embroiled himself in his suggestive study of Dickens. But my disparagement of the other English Novelists is wholly relative and not in the least positive. It is certain that men will always return to such a writer as Thackeray, with his rich emotional autumn, his feeling that life is a sad but sacred retrospect in which at least we should forget nothing. It is not likely that wise men will forget him. So, for instance, wise and scholarly men do from time to time return to the lyrists of French Renascence, to the delicate poignancy of Du Bellay: so they will go back to Thackeray. But I mean that Dickens will bestride and dominate our time as the vast figure of Rabelais dominates Du Bellay, dominates the Renascence and the world.

Let me put a negative reason first. The particular things for which Dickens is condemned (and justly condemned) by his critics, are precisely those things which have never prevented a man from being immortal. The chief of them is the unquestionable fact that he wrote an enormous amount of bad work. This does lead to a man being put below his place in his own time: it does not affect his permanent place, to all appearance, at all. Shakespeare, for instance, and Wordsworth wrote not only an enormous amount of bad work, but an enormous amount of enormously bad work. Humanity edits such writers' works for them. Virgil was mistaken in cutting out his inferior lines; we would have undertaken the job. Moreover in the particular case of Dickens there are special reasons for regarding his bad work, as I have previously suggested, under a kind of general ambition that had nothing to do with his special genius; an ambition to be a public provider of everything, a warehouse of all human emotions. He held a kind of literary day of judgment. He distributed bad characters as punishments and good characters as rewards. My meaning can be best conveyed by one instance out of many. The character of the kind old Jew in "Our Mutual Friend" (a needless and unconvincing character) was actually introduced because some Jewish correspondent complains that the bad old Jew in "Oliver Twist" conveyed the suggestion that all Jews were bad. The principle is so light-headedly absurd that it is hard to imagine any literary man submitting to it for an instant. If ever he invented a bad auctioneer he must immediately balance him with a good auctioneer; if he should have conceived an unkind philanthropist, he must on the spot, with whatever natural agony and toil, imagine a kind philanthropist. The complaint is frantic; yet Dickens, who tore people in pieces for much fairer complaints, liked this complaint of his Jewish correspondent. It pleased him to be mistaken for a public arbiter: it pleased him to be asked (in a double sense) to judge Israel. All this is so much another thing, a non-literary vanity, that there is much less difficulty than usual in separating it from his serious genius: and by his serious genius, I need hardly say, I mean his comic genius. Such irrelevant ambitions as this are easily passed over, like the sonnets of great statesmen. We feel that such things can be set aside, as the ignorant experiments of men otherwise great, like the politics of Professor Tyndall or the philosophy of Professor Haeckel. Hence, I think, posterity will not care that Dickens has done bad work, but will know that he has done good.

Again, the other chief accusation against Dickens was that his characters and their actions were exaggerated and impossible. But this only meant that they were exaggerated and impossible as compared with the modern world and with certain writers (like Thackeray or Trollope) who were making a very exact copy of the manners of the modern world. Some people, oddly enough, have suggested that Dickens has suffered or will suffer from the change of manners. Surely this is irrational. It is not the creators of the impossible who will suffer from the process of time: Mr. Bunsby can never be any more impossible than he was when Dickens made him. The writers who will obviously suffer from time will be the careful and realistic writers, the writers who have observed every detail of the fashion of this world which passeth away. It is surely obvious that there is nothing so fragile as a fact, that a fact flies away quicker than a fancy. A fancy will endure for two thousand years. For instance, we all have fancy for an entirely fearless man, a hero; and the Achilles of Homer still remains. But exactly the thing we do not know about Achilles is how far he was possible. The realistic narrators of the time are all forgotten (thank God), so we cannot tell whether Homer slightly exaggerated or wildly exaggerated or did not exaggerate at all, the personal activity of a Mycenaean captain in battle; for the fancy has survived the facts. So the fancy of Podsnap may survive the facts of English commerce: and no one will know whether Podsnap was possible, but only know that he is desirable, like Achilles.

The positive argument for the permanence of Dickens comes back to the thing that can only be stated and cannot be discussed: creation. He made things which nobody else could possibly make. He made Dick Swiveller in a very different sense from that in which Thackeray made Colonel Newcome. Thackeray's creation was observation: Dickens's was poetry, and is therefore permanent. But there is one other test that can be added. The immortal writer, I conceive, is commonly he who does something Universal in a special manner. I mean that he does something interesting to all men in a way in which only one man or one land can do. Other men in that land, who do only what other men in other lands are doing as well, tend to have a great reputation in their day and to sink slowly into a second or a third or a fourth place. A parallel from war will make the point clear. I cannot think that anyone will doubt that, although Wellington and Nelson were always bracketed, Nelson will steadily become more important and Wellington less. For the fame of Wellington rests upon the fact that he was a good soldier in the service of England, exactly as twenty similar men were good soldiers in the service of Austria or Prussia or France. But Nelson is the symbol of a special mode of attack, which is at once universal and yet especially English, the sea. Now Dickens is at once as universal as the sea and as English as Nelson. Thackeray and George Eliot and the other great figures of that great England, were comparable to Wellington in this, that the kind of thing they were doing, —realism, the acute study of intellectual things, numerous men in France, Germany and Italy were doing as well or better than they. But Dickens was really doing something universal, yet something that no one but an Englishman could do. This is attested by the fact that he and Byron are the men who, like pinnacles, strike the eye of the continent. The points would take long to study: yet they may take only a moment to indicate. No one but an Englishman could have filled his books at once with a furious caricature and with a positively furious kindness. In more central countries, full of cruel memories of political change, caricature is always inhumane. No one but an Englishman could have described the democracy as consisting of free men, but yet of funny men. In other countries where the democratic issue has been more bitterly fought, it is felt that unless you describe a man as dignified you are describing him as a slave. This is the only final greatness of a man; that he does for all the world what all the world cannot do for itself. Dickens, I believe, did it.

The hour of absinthe is over. We shall not be much further troubled with the little artists who found Dickens too sane for their sorrows and too clean for their delights. But we have a long way to travel before we get back to what Dickens meant: and the passage is along a rambling English road, a twisting road such as Mr. Pickwick travelled. But this at least is part of what he meant; that comradeship and serious joy are not interludes in our travel; but that rather our travels are interludes in comradeship and joy, which through God shall endure for ever. The inn does not point to the road; the road points to the inn. And all roads point at last to an ultimate inn, where we shall meet Dickens and all his characters: and when we drink again it shall be from the great flagons in the tavern at the end of the world.

Appreciations and Criticisms of the Works of Charles Dickens

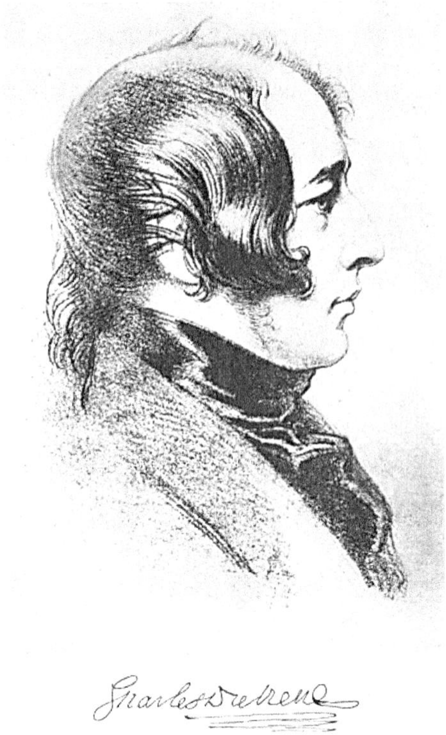

Introduction

These papers were originally published as prefaces to the separate books of Dickens in one of the most extensive of those cheap libraries of the classics which are one of the real improvements of recent times. Thus they were harmless, being diluted by, or rather drowned in Dickens. My scrap of theory was a mere dry biscuit to be taken with the grand tawny port of great English comedy; and by most people it was not taken at all-like the biscuit. Nevertheless the essays were not in intention so aimless as they appear in fact. I had a general notion of what needed saying about Dickens to the new generation, though probably I did not say it. I will make another attempt to do so in this prologue, and, possibly fail again.

There was a painful moment (somewhere about the eighties) when we watched anxiously to see whether Dickens was fading from the modern world. We have watched a little longer, and with great relief we begin to realise that it is the modern world that is fading. All that universe of ranks and respectabilities in comparison with which Dickens was called a caricaturist, all that Victorian universe in which he seemed vulgar-all that is itself breaking up like a cloudland. And only the caricatures of Dickens remain like things carved in stone. This, of course, is an old story in the case of a man reproached with any excess of the poetic. Again and again when the man of visions was pinned by the sly dog who knows the world,

> "The man recovered of the bite,
> The dog it was that died."

To call Thackeray a cynic, which means a sly dog, was indeed absurd; but it is fair to say that in comparison with Dickens he felt himself a man of the world. Nevertheless, that world of which he was a man is coming to an end before our eyes; its aristocracy has grown corrupt, its middle class insecure, and things that he never thought of are walking about the drawing-rooms of both. Thackeray has described for ever the Anglo-Indian Colonel; but what on earth would he have done with an Australian Colonel? What can it matter whether Dickens's clerks talked cockney now that half the duchesses talk American? What would Thackeray have made of an age in which a man in the position of Lord Kew may actually be the born brother of Mr. Moss of Wardour Street? Nor does this apply merely to Thackeray, but to all those Victorians who prided themselves on the realism or sobriety of their descriptions; it applies to Anthony Trollope and, as much as any one, to George Eliot. For we have not only survived that present which Thackeray described: we have even survived that future to which George Eliot looked forward. It is no longer adequate to say that Dickens did not understand that old world of gentility, of parliamentary politeness and the balance of the constitution. That world is rapidly ceasing to understand itself. It is vain to repeat the complaint of the old Quarterly Reviewers, that Dickens had not enjoyed a university education. What would the old Quarterly Reviewers themselves have thought of the Rhodes Scholarships? It is useless to repeat the old tag that Dickens could not describe a gentleman. A gentleman in our time has become something quite indescribable.

Now the interesting fact is this: That Dickens, whom so many considered to be at the best a vulgar enthusiast, saw the coming change in our society much more soberly and scientifically than did his better educated and more pretentious contemporaries. I give but one example out of many. Thackeray was a good Victorian radical, who seems to have gone to his grave quite contented with the early Victorian radical theory-the theory which Macaulay preached with unparalleled luminosity and completeness; the theory that true progress goes on so steadily through human history, that while reaction is indefensible, revolution is unnecessary. Thackeray seems to have been quite content to think that the world would grow more and more liberal in the limited sense; that Free Trade would get freer; that ballot boxes would grow more and more secret; that at last (as some satirist of Liberalism puts it) every man would have two votes instead of one. There is no trace in Thackeray of the slightest consciousness that progress could ever change its direction. There is in Dickens. The whole of *Hard Times* is the expression of just such a realisation. It is not true to say that Dickens was a Socialist, but it is not absurd to say so. And it would be simply absurd to say it of any of the great Individualist novelists of the Victorian time. Dickens saw far enough ahead to know that the time was coming when the people would be imploring the State to save them from mere freedom, as from some frightful foreign oppressor. He felt the society changing; and Thackeray never did.

As talking about Socialism and Individualism is one of the greatest bores ever endured among men, I will take another instance to illustrate my meaning, even though the instance be a queer and even a delicate one. Even if the reader does not agree with my deduction, I ask his attention to the fact itself, which I think a curiosity of literature. In the last important work of Dickens, that excellent book *Our Mutual Friend*, there is an odd thing about which I cannot make up my mind; I do not know whether it is unconscious observation or fiendish irony. But it is this. In *Our Mutual Friend* is an old patriarch named Aaron, who is a saintly Jew made to do the dirty work of an abominable Christian usurer. In an artistic sense I think the patriarch Aaron as much of a humbug as the patriarch Casby. In a moral sense there is no doubt at all that Dickens introduced the Jew with a philanthropic idea of doing justice to Judaism, which he was told he had affronted by the great gargoyle of Fagin. If this was his motive, it was morally a most worthy one. But it is certainly unfortunate for the Hebrew cause that the bad Jew should be so very much more convincing than the good one. Old Aaron is not an exaggeration of Jewish virtues; he is simply not Jewish, because he is not human. There is nothing about him that in any way suggests the nobler sort of Jew, such a man as Spinoza or Mr. Zangwill. He is simply a public apology, and like most public apologies, he is very stiff and not very convincing.

So far so good. Now we come to the funny part. To describe the high visionary and mystic Jew like Spinoza or Zangwill is a great and delicate task in which even Dickens might have failed. But most of us know something of the make and manners of the low Jew, who is generally the successful one. Most of us know the Jew who calls himself De Valancourt. Now to any one who knows a low Jew by sight or hearing, the story called *Our Mutual Friend* is literally full of Jews. Like all Dickens's best characters they are vivid; we know them. And we know them to be Hebrew. Mr. Veneering, the Man from Nowhere, dark, sphinx-like, smiling, with black curling hair, and a taste in florid vulgar furniture-of what stock was he? Mr. Lammle, with "too much nose in his face, too much ginger in his whiskers, too much sparkle in his studs and manners" —of what blood was he? Mr. Lammle's friends, coarse and thick-lipped, with fingers so covered with rings that they could hardly hold their gold pencils-do they remind us of anybody? Mr. Fledgeby, with his little ugly eyes and social flashiness and craven bodily servility-might not some fanatic like M. Drumont make interesting conjectures about him? The particular types that people hate in Jewry, the types that are the shame of all good Jews, absolutely run riot in this book, which is supposed to contain an apology to them. It looks at first sight as if Dickens's apology were one hideous sneer. It looks as if he put in one good Jew whom nobody could believe in, and then balanced him with ten bad Jews whom nobody could fail to recognise. It seems as if he had avenged himself for the doubt about Fagin by introducing five or six Fagins-triumphant Fagins, fashionable Fagins, Fagins who had changed their names. The impeccable old Aaron stands up in the middle of this ironic carnival with a peculiar solemnity and silliness. He looks like one particularly stupid Englishman pretending to be a Jew, amidst all that crowd of clever Jews who are pretending to be Englishmen.

But this notion of a sneer is not admissible. Dickens was far too frank and generous a writer to employ such an elaborate plot of silence. His satire was always intended to attack, never to entrap; moreover, he was far too vain a man not to wish the crowd to see all his jokes. Vanity is more divine than pride, because it is more democratic than pride. Third, and most important, Dickens was a good Liberal, and would have been horrified at the notion of making so venomous a vendetta against one race or creed. Nevertheless the fact is there, as I say, if only as a curiosity of literature. I defy any man to read through *Our Mutual Friend* after hearing this suggestion, and to get out of his head the conviction that Lammle is the wrong kind of Jew. The explanation lies, I think, in this, that Dickens was so wonderfully sensitive to that change that has come over our society, that he noticed the type of the oriental and cosmopolitan financier without even knowing that it was oriental or cosmopolitan. He had, in fact, fallen a victim to a very simple fallacy affecting this problem. Somebody said, with great wit and truth, that treason cannot prosper, because when it prospers it cannot be called treason. The same argument soothed all possible Anti-Semitism in men like Dickens. Jews cannot be sneaks and snobs, because when they are sneaks and snobs they do not admit that they are Jews.

I have taken this case of the growth of the cosmopolitan financier, because it is not so stale in discussion as its parallel, the growth of Socialism. But as regards Dickens, the same criticism applies to both. Dickens knew that Socialism was coming, though he did not know its name. Similarly, Dickens knew that the South African millionaire was coming, though he did not know the millionaire's name. Nobody does. His was not a type of mind to disentangle either the abstract truths touching the Socialist, nor the highly personal truth about the millionaire. He was a man of impressions; he has never been equalled in the art of conveying what a man looks like at first sight-and he simply felt the two things as atmospheric facts. He felt that the mercantile power was oppressive, past all bearing by Christian men; and he felt that this power was no longer wholly in the hands even of heavy English merchants like Podsnap. It was largely in the hands of a feverish and unfamiliar type, like Lammle and Veneering. The fact that he felt these things is almost more impressive because he did not understand them.

Now for this reason Dickens must definitely be considered in the light of the changes which his soul foresaw. Thackeray has become classical; but Dickens has done more: he has remained modern. The grand retrospective spirit of Thackeray is by its nature attached to places and times; he belongs to Queen Victoria as much as Addison belongs to Queen Anne, and it is not only Queen Anne who is dead. But Dickens, in a dark prophetic kind of way, belongs to the developments. He belongs to the times since his death when Hard Times grew harder, and when Veneering became not only a Member of Parliament, but a Cabinet Minister; the times when the very soul and spirit of Fledgeby carried war into Africa. Dickens can be criticised as a contemporary of Bernard Shaw or Anatole France or C. F. G. Masterman. In talking of him one need no longer talk merely of the Manchester School or Puseyism or the Charge of the Light Brigade; his name comes to the tongue when we are talking of Christian Socialists or Mr. Roosevelt or County Council Steam Boats or Guilds of Play. He can be considered under new lights, some larger and some meaner than his own; and it is a very rough effort so to consider him which is the excuse of these pages. Of the essays in this book I desire to say as little as possible; I will discuss any other subject in preference with a readiness which reaches to avidity. But I may very curtly apply the explanation used above to the cases of two or three of them. Thus in the article on *David Copperfield* I have done far less than justice to that fine book considered in its relation to eternal literature; but I have dwelt at some length upon a particular element in it which has grown enormous in England after Dickens's death. Thus again, in introducing the *Sketches by Boz* I have felt chiefly that I am introducing them to a new generation insufficiently in sympathy with such palpable and unsophisticated fun. A Board School education, evolved since Dickens's day, has given to our people a queer and inadequate sort of refinement, one which prevents them from enjoying the raw jests of the *Sketches by Boz*, but leaves them easily open to that slight but poisonous sentimentalism which I note amid all the merits of David Copperfield. In the same way I shall speak of *Little Dorrit*, with reference to a school of pessimistic fiction which did not exist when it was written, of *Hard Times* in the light of the most modern crises of economics, and of *The Child's History of England* in the light of the most matured authority of history. In short, these criticisms are an intrinsically ephemeral comment from one generation upon work that will delight many more. Dickens was a very great man, and there are many ways of testing and stating the fact. But one permissible way is to say this, that he was an ignorant man, ill-read in the past, and often confused about the present. Yet he remains great and true, and even essentially reliable, if we suppose him to have known not only all that went before his lifetime, but also all that was to come after.

From this vanishing of the Victorian compromise (I might say the Victorian illusion) there begins to emerge a menacing and even monstrous thing-we may begin again to behold the

English people. If that strange dawn ever comes, it will be the final vindication of Dickens. It will be proved that he is hardly even a caricaturist; that he is something very like a realist. Those comic monstrosities which the critics found incredible will be found to be the immense majority of the citizens of this country. We shall find that Sweedlepipe cuts our hair and Pumblechook sells our cereals; that Sam Weller blacks our boots and Tony Weller drives our omnibus. For the exaggerated notion of the exaggerations of Dickens (as was admirably pointed out by my old friend and enemy Mr. Blatchford in a *Clarion* review) is very largely due to our mixing with only one social class, whose conventions are very strict, and to whose affectations we are accustomed. In cabmen, in cobblers, in charwomen, individuality is often pushed to the edge of insanity. But as long as the Thackerayan platform of gentility stood firm all this was, comparatively speaking, concealed. For the English, of all nations, have the most uniform upper class and the most varied democracy. In France it is the peasants who are solid to uniformity; it is the marquises who are a little mad. But in England, while good form restrains and levels the universities and the army, the poor people are the most motley and amusing creatures in the world, full of humorous affections and prejudices and twists of irony. Frenchmen tend to be alike, because they are all soldiers; Prussians because they are all something else, probably policemen; even Americans are all something, though it is not easy to say what it is; it goes with hawk-like eyes and an irrational eagerness. Perhaps it is savages. But two English cabmen will be as grotesquely different as Mr. Weller and Mr. Wegg. Nor is it true to say that I see this variety because it is in my own people. For I do not see the same degree of variety in my own class or in the class above it; there is more superficial resemblance between two Kensington doctors or two Highland dukes. No; the democracy is really composed of Dickens characters, for the simple reason that Dickens was himself one of the democracy.

There remains one thing to be added to this attempt to exhibit Dickens in the growing and changing lights of our time. God forbid that any one (especially any Dickensian) should dilute or discourage the great efforts towards social improvement. But I wish that social reformers would more often remember that they are imposing their rules not on dots and numbers, but on Bob Sawyer and Tim Linkinwater, on Mrs. Lirriper and Dr. Marigold. I wish Mr. Sidney Webb would shut his eyes until he *sees* Sam Weller.

A great many circumstances have led to the neglect in literature of these exuberant types which do actually exist in the ruder classes of society. Perhaps the principal cause is that since Dickens's time the study of the poor has ceased to be an art and become a sort of sham science. Dickens took the poor individually: all modern writing tends to take them collectively. It is said that the modern realist produces a photograph rather than a picture. But this is an inadequate objection. The real trouble with the realist is not that he produces a photograph, but that he produces a composite photograph. It is like all composite photographs, blurred; like all composite photographs, hideous; and like all composite photographs, unlike anything or anybody. The new sociological novels, which attempt to describe the abstract type of the working-classes, sin in practice against the first canon of literature, true when all others are subject to exception. Literature must always be a pointing out of what is interesting in life; but these books are duller than the life they represent. Even supposing that Dickens did exaggerate the degree to which one man differs from another-that was at least an exaggeration upon the side of literature; it was better than a mere attempt to reduce what is actually vivid and unmistakable to what is in comparison colourless or unnoticeable. Even the creditable and necessary efforts of our time in certain matters of social reform have discouraged the old distinctive Dickens treatment. People are so anxious to do something for the poor man that they have a sort of subconscious desire to think that there is only one kind of man to do it for. Thus while the old accounts were sometimes too steep and crazy, the new became too sweeping and flat. People write about the problem of drink, for instance, as if it were one problem. Dickens could have told them that there is the abyss between heaven and hell between the incongruous excesses of Mr. Pickwick and the fatalistic soaking of Mr. Wickfield. He could have shown that there was nothing in common between the brandy and water of Bob Sawyer and the rum and water of Mr. Stiggins.

People talk of imprudent marriages among the poor, as if it were all one question. Dickens could have told them that it is one thing to marry without much money, like Stephen Blackpool, and quite another to marry without the smallest intention of ever trying to get any, like Harold Skimpole. People talk about husbands in the working-classes being kind or brutal to their wives, as if that was the one permanent problem and no other possibility need be considered. Dickens could have told them that there was the case (the by no means uncommon case) of the husband of Mrs. Gargery as well as of the wife of Mr. Quilp. In short, Dickens saw the problem of the poor not as a dead and definite business, but as a living and very complex one. In some ways he would be called much more conservative than the modern sociologists, in some ways much more revolutionary.

Little Dorrit

In the time of the decline and death of Dickens, and even more strongly after it, there arose a school of criticism which substantially maintained that a man wrote better when he was ill. It was some such sentiment as this that made Mr. George Gissing, that able writer, come near to contending that *Little Dorrit* is Dickens's best book. It was the principle of his philosophy to maintain (I know not why) that a man was more likely to perceive the truth when in low spirits than when in high spirits.

Reprinted Pieces

The three articles on Sunday of which I speak are almost the last expression of an articulate sort in English literature of the ancient and existing morality of the English people. It is always asserted that Puritanism came in with the seventeenth century and thoroughly soaked and absorbed the English. We are now, it is constantly said, an incurably Puritanic people. Personally, I have my doubts about this. I shall not refuse to admit to the Puritans that they conquered and crushed the English people; but I do not think that they ever transformed it. My doubt is chiefly derived from three historical facts. First, that England was never so richly and recognisably English as in the Shakespearian age before the Puritan had appeared. Second, that ever since he did appear there has been a long unbroken line of brilliant and typical Englishmen who belonged to the Shakespearian and not the Puritanic tradition; Dryden, Johnson, Wilkes, Fox, Nelson, were hardly Puritans. And third, that the real rise of a new, cold, and illiberal morality in these matters seems to me to have occurred in the time of Queen Victoria, and not of Queen Elizabeth. All things considered, it is likely that future historians will say that the Puritans first really triumphed in the twentieth century, and that Dickens was the last cry of Merry England.

And about these additional, miscellaneous, and even inferior works of Dickens there is, moreover, another use and fascination which all Dickensians will understand; which, after a manner, is not for the profane. All who love Dickens have a strange sense that he is really inexhaustible. It is this fantastic infinity that divides him even from the strongest and healthiest romantic artists of a later day-from Stevenson, for example. I have read *Treasure Island* twenty times; nevertheless I know it. But I do not really feel as if I knew all *Pickwick*; I have not so much read it twenty times as read in it a million times; and it almost seemed as if I always read something new. We of the true faith look at each other and understand; yes, our master was a magician. I believe the books are alive; I believe that leaves still grow in them, as leaves grow on the trees. I believe that this fairy library flourishes and increases like a fairy forest: but the world is listening to us, and we will put our hand upon our mouth.

Our Mutual Friend

One thing at least seems certain. Dickens may or may not have been socialist in his tendencies; one might quote on the affirmative side his satire against Mr. Podsnap, who thought Centralisation "un-English"; one might quote in reply the fact that he satirised quite as unmercifully state and municipal officials of the most modern type. But there is one condition of affairs which Dickens would certainly have detested and denounced, and that is the condition in which we actually stand to-day. At this moment it is vain to discuss whether socialism will be a selling of men's liberty for bread. The men have already sold the liberty; only they have not yet got the bread. A most incessant and exacting interference with the poor is already in operation; they are already ruled like slaves, only they are not fed like slaves. The children are forcibly provided with a school; only they are not provided with a house. Officials give the most detailed domestic directions about the fireguard; only they do not give the fireguard. Officials bring round the most stringent directions about the milk; only they do not bring round the milk. The situation is perhaps the most humorous in the whole history of oppression. We force the nigger to dig; but as a concession to him we do not give him a spade. We compel Sambo to cook; but we consult his dignity so far as to refuse him a fire.

This state of things at least cannot conceivably endure. We must either give the workers more property and liberty, or we must feed them properly as we work them properly. If we insist on sending the menu into them, they will naturally send the bill into us. This may possibly result (it is not my purpose here to prove that it will) in the drilling of the English people into hordes of humanely herded serfs; and this again may mean the fading from our consciousness of all those elves and giants, monsters and fantastics whom we are faintly beginning to feel and remember in the land. If this be so, the work of Dickens may be considered as a great vision —a vision, as Swinburne said, between a sleep and a sleep. It can be said that between the grey past of territorial depression and the grey future of economic routine the strange clouds lifted, and we beheld the land of the living.

Lastly, Dickens is even astonishingly right about Eugene Wrayburne. So far from reproaching him with not understanding a gentleman, the critic will be astonished at the accuracy with which he has really observed the worth and the weakness of the aristocrat. He is quite right when he suggests that such a man has intelligence enough to despise the invitations which he has not the energy to refuse. He is quite right when he makes Eugene (like Mr. Balfour) constantly right in argument even when he is obviously wrong in fact. Dickens is quite right when he describes Eugene as capable of cultivating a sort of secondary and false industry about anything that is not profitable; or pursuing with passion anything that is not his business. He is quite right in making Eugene honestly appreciative of essential goodness-in other people. He is quite right in making him really good at the graceful combination of satire and sentiment, both perfectly sincere. He is also right in indicating that the only cure for this intellectual condition is a violent blow on the head.

David Copperfield

The real achievement of the earlier part of *David Copperfield* lies in a certain impression of the little Copperfield living in a land of giants. It is at once Gargantuan in its fancy and grossly vivid in its facts; like Gulliver in the land of Brobdingnag when he describes mountainous hands and faces filling the sky, bristles as big as hedges, or moles as big as molehills. To him parents and guardians are not Olympians (as in Mr. Kenneth Grahame's clever book), mysterious and dignified, dwelling upon a cloudy hill. Rather they are all the more visible for being large. They come all the closer because they are colossal. Their queer features and weaknesses stand out large in a sort of gigantic domesticity, like the hairs and freckles of a Brobdingnagian. We feel the sombre Murdstone coming upon the house like a tall storm striding through the sky. We watch every pucker of Peggotty's peasant face in its moods of flinty prejudice or whimsical hesitation. We look up and feel that Aunt Betsey in her garden gloves was really terrible-especially her garden gloves. But one cannot avoid the impression that as the boy grows larger these figures grow smaller, and are not perhaps so completely satisfactory.

Christmas Books

And there is doubtless a certain poetic unity and irony in gathering together three or four of the crudest and most cocksure of the modern theorists, with their shrill voices and metallic virtues, under the fulness and the sonorous sanity of Christian bells. But the figures satirised in *The Chimes* cross each other's path and spoil each other in some degree. The main purpose of the book was a protest against that impudent and hard-hearted utilitarianism which arranges the people only in rows of men or even in rows of figures. It is a flaming denunciation of that strange mathematical morality which was twisted often unfairly out of Bentham and Mill: a morality by which each citizen must regard himself as a fraction, and a very vulgar fraction. Though the particular form of this insolent patronage has changed, this revolt and rebuke is still of value, and may be wholesome for those who are teaching the poor to be provident. Doubtless it is a good idea to be provident, in the sense that Providence is provident, but that should mean being kind, and certainly not merely being cold.

The Cricket on the Hearth, though popular, I think, with many sections of the great army of Dickensians, cannot be spoken of in any such abstract or serious terms. It is a brief domestic glimpse; it is an interior. It must be remembered that Dickens was fond of interiors as such; he was like a romantic tramp who should go from window to window looking in at the parlours. He had that solid, indescribable delight in the mere solidity and neatness of funny little humanity in its funny little houses, like doll's houses. To him every house was a box, a Christmas box, in which a dancing human doll was tied up in bricks and slates instead of string and brown paper. He went from one gleaming window to another, looking in at the lamp-lit parlours. Thus he stood for a little while looking in at this cosy if commonplace interior of the carrier and his wife; but he did not stand there very long. He was on his way to quainter towns and villages. Already the plants were sprouting upon the balcony of Miss Tox; and the great wind was rising that flung Mr. Pecksniff against his own front door.

Tale of Two Cities

It was well for him, at any rate, that the people rose in France. It was well for him, at any rate, that the guillotine was set up in the Place de la Concorde. Unconsciously, but not accidentally, Dickens was here working out the whole true comparison between swift revolutionism in Paris and slow evolutionism in London. Sidney Carton is one of those sublime ascetics whose head offends them, and who cut it off. For him at least it was better that the blood should flow in Paris than that the wine should flow any longer in London. And if I say that even now the guillotine might be the best cure for many a London lawyer, I ask you to believe that I am not merely flippant. But you will not believe it.

Barnaby Rudge

It may be said that there is no comparison between that explosive opening of the intellect in Paris and an antiquated madman leading a knot of provincial Protestants. The Man of the Hill, says Victor Hugo somewhere, fights for an idea; the Man of the Forest for a prejudice. Nevertheless it remains true that the enemies of the red cap long attempted to represent it as a sham decoration in the style of Sim Tappertit. Long after the revolutionists had shown more than the qualities of men, it was common among lords and lacqueys to attribute to them the stagey and piratical pretentiousness of urchins. The kings called Napoleon's pistol a toy pistol even while it was holding up their coach and mastering their money or their lives; they called his sword a stage sword even while they ran away from it. Something of the same senile inconsistency can be found in an English and American habit common until recently: that of painting the South Americans at once as ruffians wading in carnage, and also as poltroons playing at war. They blame them first for the cruelty of having a fight; and then for the weakness of having a sham fight. Such, however, since the French Revolution and before it, has been the fatuous attitude of certain Anglo-Saxons towards the whole revolutionary tradition. Sim Tappertit was a sort of answer to everything; and the young men were mocked as 'prentices long after they were masters. The rising fortune of the South American republics to-day is symbolical and even menacing of many things; and it may be that the romance of riot will not be so much extinguished as extended; and nearer home we may have boys being boys again, and in London the cry of "clubs."

The Uncommercial Traveller

The Uncommercial Traveller is a collection of Dickens's memories rather than of his literary purposes; but it is due to him to say that memory is often more startling in him than prophecy in anybody else. They have the character which belongs to all his vivid incidental writing: that they attach themselves always to some text which is a fact rather than an idea. He was one of those sons of Eve who are fonder of the Tree of Life than of the Tree of Knowledge-even of the knowledge of good and of evil. He was in this profoundest sense a realist. Critics have talked of an artist with his eye on the object. Dickens as an essayist always had his eye on an object before he had the faintest notion of a subject. All these works of his can best be considered as letters; they are notes of personal travel, scribbles in a diary about this or that that really happened. But Dickens was one of the few men who have the two talents that are the whole of literature-and have them both together. First, he could make a thing happen over again; and second, he could make it happen better. He can be called exaggerative; but mere exaggeration conveys nothing of his typical talent. Mere whirlwinds of words, mere melodramas of earth and heaven do not affect us as Dickens affects us, because they are exaggerations of nothing. If asked for an exaggeration of something, their inventors would be entirely dumb. They would not know how to exaggerate a broom-stick; for the life of them they could not exaggerate a tenpenny nail. Dickens always began with the nail or the broom-stick. He always began with a fact even when he was most fanciful; and even when he drew the long bow he was careful to hit the white.

This riotous realism of Dickens has its disadvantage —a disadvantage that comes out more clearly in these casual sketches than in his constructed romances. One grave defect in his greatness is that he was altogether too indifferent to theories. On large matters he went right by the very largeness of his mind; but in small matters he suffered from the lack of any logical test and ready reckoner. Hence his comment upon the details of civilisation or reform are sometimes apt to be jerky and jarring, and even grossly inconsistent. So long as a thing was heroic enough to admire, Dickens admired it; whenever it was absurd enough to laugh at he laughed at it: so far he was on sure ground. But about all the small human projects that lie between the extremes of the sublime and the ridiculous, his criticism was apt to have an accidental quality. As Matthew Arnold said of the remarks of the Young Man from the Country about the perambulator, they are felt not to be at the heart of the situation. On a great many occasions the Uncommercial Traveller seems, like other hasty travellers, to be criticising elements and institutions which he has quite inadequately understood; and once or twice the Uncommercial Traveller might almost as well be a Commercial Traveller for all he knows of the countryside.

An instance of what I mean may be found in the amusing article about the nightmares of the nursery. Superficially read it might almost be taken to mean that Dickens disapproved of ghost stories-disapproved of that old and genial horror which nurses can hardly supply fast enough for the children who want it. Dickens, one would have thought, should have been the last man in the world to object to horrible stories, having himself written some of the most horrible that exist in the world. The author of the Madman's Manuscript, of the disease of Monk and the death of Krook, cannot be considered fastidious in the matter of revolting realism or of revolting mysticism. If artistic horror is to be kept from the young, it is at least as necessary to keep little boys from reading *Pickwick* or *Bleak House* as to refrain from telling them the story of Captain Murderer or the terrible tale of Chips. If there was something appalling in the rhyme of Chips and pips and ships, it was nothing compared to that infernal refrain of "Mudstains, bloodstains" which Dickens himself, in one of his highest moments of hellish art, put into *Oliver Twist*.

I take this one instance of the excellent article called "Nurse's Stories" because it is quite typical of all the rest. Dickens (accused of superficiality by those who cannot grasp that there is foam upon deep seas) was really deep about human beings; that is, he was original and creative about them. But about ideas he did tend to be a little superficial. He judged them by whether they hit him, and not by what they were trying to hit. Thus in this book the great wizard of the Christmas ghosts seems almost the enemy of ghost stories; thus the almost melodramatic moralist who created Ralph Nickleby and Jonas Chuzzlewit cannot see the point in original sin; thus the great denouncer of official oppression in England may be found far too indulgent to the basest aspects of the modern police. His theories were less important than his creations, because he was a man of genius. But he himself thought his theories the more important, because he was a man.

Sketches by Boz

The greatest mystery about almost any great writer is why he was ever allowed to write at all. The first efforts of eminent men are always imitations; and very often they are bad imitations. The only question is whether the publisher had (as his name would seem to imply) some subconscious connection or sympathy with the public, and thus felt instinctively the presence of something that might ultimately tell; or whether the choice was merely a matter of chance and one Dickens was chosen and another Dickens left. The fact is almost unquestionable: most authors made their reputation by bad books and afterwards supported it by good ones. This is in some degree true even in the case of Dickens. The public continued to call him "Boz" long after the public had forgotten the *Sketches by Boz*. Numberless writers of the time speak of "Boz" as having written *Martin Chuzzlewit* and "Boz" as having written *David Copperfield*. Yet if they had gone back to the original book signed "Boz" they might even have felt that it was vulgar and flippant. This is indeed the chief tragedy of publishers: that they may easily refuse at the same moment the wrong manuscript and the right man. It is easy to see of Dickens now that he was the right man; but a man might have been very well excused if he had not realised that the *Sketches* was the right book. Dickens, I say, is a case for this primary query: whether there was in the first work any clear sign of his higher creative spirit. But Dickens is much less a case for this query than almost all the other great men of his period. The very earliest works of Thackeray are much more unimpressive than those of Dickens. Nay, they are much more vulgar than those of Dickens. And worst of all, they are much more numerous than those of Dickens. Thackeray came much nearer to being the ordinary literary failure than Dickens ever came. Read some of the earliest criticisms of Mr. Yellowplush or Michael Angelo Titmarsh and you will realise that at the very beginning there was more potential clumsiness and silliness in Thackeray than there ever was in Dickens. Nevertheless there was some potential clumsiness and silliness in Dickens; and what there is of it appears here and there in the admirable *Sketches by Boz*.

Perhaps we may put the matter this way: this is the only one of Dickens's works of which it is ordinarily necessary to know the date. To a close and delicate comprehension it is indeed very important that *Nicholas Nickleby* was written at the beginning of Dickens's life, and *Our Mutual Friend* towards the end of it. Nevertheless anybody could understand or enjoy these books, whenever they were written. If *Our Mutual Friend* was written in the Latin of the Dark Ages we should still want it translated. If we thought that *Nicholas Nickleby* would not be written until thirty years hence we should all wait for it eagerly. The general impression produced by Dickens's work is the same as that produced by miraculous visions; it is the destruction of time. Thomas Aquinas said that there was no time in the sight of God; however this may be, there was no time in the sight of Dickens. As a general rule Dickens can be read in any order; not only in any order of books, but even in any order of chapters. In an average Dickens book every part is so amusing and alive that you can read the parts backwards; you can read the quarrel first and then the cause of the quarrel; you can fall in love with a woman in the tenth chapter and then turn back to the first chapter to find out who she is. This is not chaos; it is eternity. It means merely that Dickens instinctively felt all his figures to be immortal souls who existed whether he wrote of them or not, and whether the reader read of them or not. There is a peculiar quality as of celestial pre-existence about the Dickens characters. Not only did they exist before we heard of them, they existed also before Dickens heard of them. As a rule this unchangeable air in Dickens deprives any discussion about date of its point. But as I have said, this is the one Dickens work of which the date *is* essential. It is really an important part of the criticism of this book to say that it is his first book. Certain elements of clumsiness, of obviousness, of evident blunder, actually require the chronological explanation. It is biographically important that this is his first book, almost exactly in the same way that it is biographically important that *The Mystery of Edwin Drood* was his last book. Change or no change, *Edwin Drood* has this plain point of a last story about it: that it is not finished. But if the last book is unfinished, the first book is more unfinished still.

The *Sketches* divide themselves, of course, into two broad classes. One half consists of sketches that are truly and in the strict sense sketches. That is, they are things that have no story and in their outline none of the character of creation; they are merely facts from the street or the tavern or the town hall, noted down as they occurred by an intelligence of quite exceptional vivacity. The second class consists of purely creative things: farces, romances, stories in any case with a non-natural perfection, or a poetical justice, to round them off. One class is admirably represented, for instance, by the sketch describing the Charity Dinner, the other by such a story as that of *Horatio Sparkins*. These things were almost certainly written by Dickens at very various periods of his youth; and early as the harvest is, no doubt it is a harvest and had ripened during a reasonably long time. Nevertheless it is with these two types of narrative that the young Charles Dickens first enters English literature; he enters it with a number of journalistic notes of such things as he has seen happen in streets or offices, and with a number of short stories which err on the side of the extravagant and even the superficial. Journalism had not then, indeed, sunk to the low level which it has since reached. His sketches of dirty London would not have been dirty enough for the modern Imperialist press. Still these first efforts of his are journalism, and sometimes vulgar journalism. It was as a journalist that he attacked the world, as a journalist that he conquered it.

The biographical circumstances will not, of course, be forgotten. The life of Dickens had been a curious one. Brought up in a family just poor enough to be painfully conscious of its prosperity and its respectability, he had been suddenly flung by a financial calamity into a social condition far below his own. For men on that exact edge of the educated class such a transition is really tragic. A duke may become a navvy for a joke, but a clerk cannot become a navvy for a joke. Dickens's parents went to a debtors' prison; Dickens himself went to a far more unpleasant place. The debtors' prison had about it at least that element of amiable compromise and kindly decay which belonged (and belongs still) to all the official institutions of England. But Dickens was doomed to see the very blackest aspect of nineteenth-century England, something far blacker than any mere bad government. He went not to a prison but to a factory. In the musty traditionalism of the Marshalsea old John Dickens could easily remain optimistic. In the ferocious efficiency of the modern factory young Charles Dickens narrowly escaped being a pessimist. He did escape this danger; finally he even escaped the factory itself. His next step in life was, if possible, even more eccentric. He was sent to school; he was sent off like an innocent little boy in Eton collars to learn the rudiments of Latin grammar, without any reference to the fact that he had already taken his part in the horrible competition and actuality of the age of manufactures. It was like giving a sacked bank manager a satchel and sending him to a dame's school. Nor was the third stage of this career unconnected with the oddity of the others. On leaving the school he was made a clerk in a lawyer's office, as if henceforward this child of ridiculous changes was to settle down into a silent assistant for a quiet solicitor. It was exactly at this moment that his fundamental rebellion began to seethe; it seethed more against the quiet finality of his legal occupation than it had seethed against the squalor and slavery of his days of poverty. There must have been in his mind, I think, a dim feeling: "Did all my dark crises mean only this; was I crucified only that I might become a solicitor's clerk?" Whatever be the truth about this conjecture there can be no question about the facts themselves. It was about this time that he began to burst and bubble over, to insist upon his own intellect, to claim a career. It was about this time that he put together a loose pile of papers, satires on institutions, pictures of private persons, fairy tales of the vulgarity of his world, odds and ends such as come out of the facility and the fierce vanity of youth. It was about this time at any rate that he decided to publish them, and gave them the name of *Sketches by Boz*.

They must, I think, be read in the light of this youthful explosion. In some psychological sense he had really been wronged. But he had only become conscious of his wrongs as his wrongs had been gradually righted. Similarly, it has often been found that a man who can patiently endure penal servitude through a judicial blunder will nevertheless, when once his cause is well asserted, quarrel about the amount of compensation or complain of small slights in his professional existence. These are the marks of the first literary action of Dickens. It has in it all the peculiar hardness of youth; a hardness which in those who have in any way been unfairly treated reaches even to impudence. It is a terrible thing for any man to find out that his elders are wrong. And this almost unkindly courage of youth must partly be held responsible for the smartness of Dickens, that almost offensive smartness which in these earlier books of his sometimes irritates us like the showy gibes in the tall talk of a school-boy. These first pages bear witness both to the energy of his genius and also to its unenlightenment; he seems more ignorant and more cocksure than so great a man should be. Dickens was never stupid, but he was sometimes silly; and he is occasionally silly here.

All this must be said to prepare the more fastidious modern for these papers, if he has never read them before. But when all this has been said there remains in them exactly what always remains in Dickens when you have taken away everything that can be taken away by the most fastidious modern who ever dissected his grandmother. There remains that *primum mobile* of which all the mystics have spoken: energy, the power to create. I will not call it "the will to live," for that is a priggish phrase of German professors. Even German professors, I suppose, have the will to live. But Dickens had exactly what German professors have not: he had the power to live. And indeed it is most valuable to have these early specimens of the Dickens work if only because they are specimens of his spirit apart from his matured intelligence. It is well to be able to realise that contact with the Dickens world is almost like a physical contact; it is like stepping suddenly into the hot smells of a greenhouse, or into the bleak smell of the sea. We know that we are there. Let any one read, for instance, one of the foolish but amusing farces in Dickens's first volume. Let him read, for instance, such a story as that of *Horatio Sparkins* or that of *The Tuggses at Ramsgate*. He will not find very much of that verbal felicity or fantastic irony that Dickens afterwards developed; the incidents are upon the plain lines of the stock comedy of the day: sharpers who entrap simpletons, spinsters who angle for husbands, youths who try to look Byronic and only look foolish. Yet there is something in these stories which there is not in the ordinary stock comedies of that day: an indefinable flavour of emphasis and richness, a hint as of infinity of fun. Doubtless, for instance, a million comic writers of that epoch had made game of the dark, romantic young man who pretended to abysses of philosophy and despair. And it is not easy to say exactly why we feel that the few metaphysical remarks of Mr. Horatio Sparkins are in some way really much funnier than any of those old stock jokes. It is in a certain quality of deep enjoyment in the writer as well as the reader; as if the few words written had been dipped in dark nonsense and were, as it were, reeking with derision. "Because if Effect be the result of Cause and Cause be the Precursor of Effect," said Mr. Horatio Sparkins, "I apprehend that you are wrong." Nobody can get at the real secret of sentences like that; sentences which were afterwards strewed with reckless liberality over the conversation of Dick Swiveller or Mr. Mantalini, Sim Tappertit or Mr. Pecksniff. Though the joke seems most superficial one has only to read it a certain number of times to see that it is most subtle. The joke does not lie in Mr. Sparkins merely using long words, any more than the joke lies merely in Mr. Swiveller drinking, or in Mr. Mantalini deceiving his wife. It is something in the arrangement of the words; something in a last inspired turn of absurdity given to a sentence. In spite of everything Horatio Sparkins is funny. We cannot tell why he is funny. When we know why he is funny we shall know why Dickens is great.

Standing as we do here upon the threshold, as it were, of the work of Dickens, it may be well perhaps to state this truth as being, after all, the most important one. This first work had, as I have said, the faults of first work and the special faults that arose from its author's accidental history; he was deprived of education, and therefore it was in some ways uneducated; he was confronted with the folly and failure of his natural superiors and guardians, and therefore it was in some ways pert and insolent. Nevertheless the main fact about the work is worth stating here for any reader who should follow the chronological order and read the *Sketches by Boz* before embarking on the stormy and splendid sea of *Pickwick*. For the sea of *Pickwick*, though splendid, does make some people seasick. The great point to be emphasised at such an initiation is this: that people, especially refined people, are not to judge of Dickens by what they would call the coarseness or commonplaceness of his subject. It is quite true that his jokes are often on the same *subjects* as the jokes in a halfpenny comic paper. Only they happen to be good jokes. He does make jokes about drunkenness, jokes about mothers-in-law, jokes about henpecked husbands, jokes (which is much more really unpardonable) about spinsters, jokes about physical cowardice, jokes about fatness, jokes about sitting down on one's hat. He does make fun of all these things; and the reason is not very far to seek. He makes fun of all these things because all these things, or nearly all of them, are really very funny. But a large number of those who might otherwise read and enjoy Dickens are undoubtedly "put off" (as the phrase goes) by the fact that he seems to be echoing a poor kind of claptrap in his choice of incidents and images. Partly, of course, he suffers from the very fact of his success; his play with these topics was so good that every one else has played with them increasingly since; he may indeed have copied the old jokes, but he certainly renewed them. For instance, "Ally Sloper" was certainly copied from Wilkins Micawber. To this day you may see (in the front page of that fine periodical) the bald head and the high shirt collar that betray the high original from which "Ally Sloper" is derived. But exactly because "Sloper" was stolen from Micawber, for that very reason the new generation feels as if Micawber were stolen from "Sloper." Many modern readers feel as if Dickens were copying the comic papers, whereas in truth the comic papers are still copying Dickens.

Dickens showed himself to be an original man by always accepting old and established topics. There is no clearer sign of the absence of originality among modern poets than their disposition to find new themes. Really original poets write poems about the spring. They are always fresh, just as the spring is always fresh. Men wholly without originality write poems about torture, or new religions, of some perversion of obscenity, hoping that the mere sting of the subject may speak for them. But we do not sufficiently realise that what is true of the classic ode is also true of the classic joke. A true poet writes about the spring being beautiful because (after a thousand springs) the spring really is beautiful. In the same way the true humourist writes about a man sitting down on his hat, because the act of sitting down on one's hat (however often and however admirably performed) really is extremely funny. We must not dismiss a new poet because his poem is called *To a Skylark*; nor must we dismiss a humourist because his new farce is called *My Mother-in-law*. He may really have splendid and inspiring things to say upon an eternal problem. The whole question is whether he has.

Now this is exactly where Dickens, and the possible mistake about Dickens, both come in. Numbers of sensitive ladies, numbers of simple æsthetes, have had a vague shrinking from that element in Dickens which begins vaguely in *The Tuggses at Ramsgate* and culminates in *Pickwick*. They have a vague shrinking from the mere subject matter; from the mere fact that so much of the fun is about drinking or fighting, or falling down, or eloping with old ladies. It is to these that the first appeal must be made upon the threshold of Dickens criticism. Let them really read the thing and really see whether the humour is the gross and half-witted jeering which they imagine it to be. It is exactly here that the whole genius of Dickens is concerned. His subjects are indeed stock subjects; like the skylark of Shelley, or the autumn of Keats. But all the more because they are stock subjects the reader realises what a magician is at work. The notion of a clumsy fellow who falls off his horse is indeed a stock and stale subject. But Mr. Winkle is not a stock and stale subject. Nor is his horse a stock and stale subject; it is as immortal as the horses of Achilles. The notion of a fat old gentleman proud of his legs might easily be vulgar. But Mr. Pickwick proud of his legs is not vulgar; somehow we feel that they were legs to be proud of. And it is exactly this that we must look for in these *Sketches*. We must not leap to any cheap fancy that they are low farces. Rather we must see that they are not low farces; and see that nobody but Dickens could have prevented them from being so.

Pickwick Papers

There are those who deny with enthusiasm the existence of a God and are happy in a hobby which they call the Mistakes of Moses. I have not studied their labours in detail, but it seems that the chief mistake of Moses was that he neglected to write the Pentateuch. The lesser errors, apparently, were not made by Moses, but by another person equally unknown. These controversialists cover the very widest field, and their attacks upon Scripture are varied to the point of wildness. They range from the proposition that the unexpurgated Bible is almost as unfit for an American girls' school as is an unexpurgated Shakespeare; they descend to the proposition that kissing the Book is almost as hygienically dangerous as kissing the babies of the poor. A superficial critic might well imagine that there was not one single sentence left of the Hebrew or Christian Scriptures which this school had not marked with some ingenious and uneducated comment. But there is one passage at least upon which they have never pounced, at least to my knowledge; and in pointing it out to them I feel that I am, or ought to be, providing material for quite a multitude of Hyde Park orations. I mean that singular arrangement in the mystical account of the Creation by which light is created first and all the luminous bodies afterwards. One could not imagine a process more open to the elephantine logic of the Bible-smasher than this: that the sun should be created after the sunlight. The conception that lies at the back of the phrase is indeed profoundly antagonistic to much of the modern point of view. To many modern people it would sound like saying that foliage existed before the first leaf; it would sound like saying that childhood existed before a baby was born. The idea is, as I have said, alien to most modern thought, and like many other ideas which are alien to most modern thought, it is a very subtle and a very sound idea. Whatever be the meaning of the passage in the actual primeval poem, there is a very real metaphysical meaning in the idea that light existed before the sun and stars. It is not barbaric; it is rather Platonic. The idea existed before any of the machinery which made manifest the idea. Justice existed when there was no need of judges, and mercy existed before any man was oppressed.

However this may be in the matter of religion and philosophy, it can be said with little exaggeration that this truth is the very key of literature. The whole difference between construction and creation is exactly this: that a thing constructed can only be loved after it is constructed; but a thing created is loved before it exists, as the mother can love the unborn child. In creative art the essence of a book exists before the book or before even the details or main features of the book; the author enjoys it and lives in it with a kind of prophetic rapture. He wishes to write a comic story before he has thought of a single comic incident. He desires to write a sad story before he has thought of anything sad. He knows the atmosphere before he knows anything. There is a low priggish maxim sometimes uttered by men so frivolous as to take humour seriously—a maxim that a man should not laugh at his own jokes. But the great artist not only laughs at his own jokes; he laughs at his own jokes before he has made them. In the case of a man really humorous we can see humour in his eye before he has thought of any amusing words at all. So the creative writer laughs at his comedy before he creates it, and he has tears for his tragedy before he knows what it is. When the symbols and the fulfilling facts do come to him, they come generally in a manner very fragmentary and inverted, mostly in irrational glimpses of crisis or consummation. The last page comes before the first; before his romance has begun, he knows that it has ended well. He sees the wedding before the wooing; he sees the death before the duel. But most of all he sees the colour and character of the whole story prior to any possible events in it. This is the real argument for art and style, only that the artists and the stylists have not the sense to use it. In one very real sense style is far more important than either character or narrative. For a man knows what style of book he wants to write when he knows nothing else about it.

Pickwick is in Dickens's career the mere mass of light before the creation of sun or moon. It is the splendid, shapeless substance of which all his stars were ultimately made. You might split up *Pickwick* into innumerable novels as you could split up that primeval light into innumerable solar systems. The *Pickwick Papers* constitute first and foremost a kind of wild promise, a pre-natal vision of all the children of Dickens. He had not yet settled down into the plain, professional habit of picking out a plot and characters, of attending to one thing at a time, of writing a separate, sensible novel and sending it off to his publishers. He is still in the youthful whirl of the kind of world that he would like to create. He has not yet really settled what story he will write, but only what sort of story he will write. He tries to tell ten stories at once; he pours into the pot all the chaotic fancies and crude experiences of his boyhood; he sticks in irrelevant short stories shamelessly, as into a scrap-book; he adopts designs and abandons them, begins episodes and leaves them unfinished; but from the first page to the last there is a nameless and elemental ecstasy—that of the man who is doing the kind of thing that he can do. Dickens, like every other honest and effective writer, came at last to some degree of care and self-restraint. He learned how to make his *dramatis personæ* assist his drama; he learned how to write stories which were full of rambling and perversity, but which were stories. But before he wrote a single real story, he had a kind of vision. It was a vision of the Dickens world—a maze of white roads, a map full of fantastic towns, thundering coaches, clamorous market-places, uproarious inns, strange and swaggering figures. That vision was *Pickwick*.

It must be remembered that this is true even in connection with the man's contemporaneous biography. Apart from anything else about it, *Pickwick* was his first great chance. It was a big commission given in some sense to an untried man, that he might show what he could do. It was in a strict sense a sample. And just as a sample of leather can be only a piece of leather, or a sample of coal a lump of coal, so this book may most properly be regarded as simply a lump of Dickens. He was anxious to show all that was in him. He was more concerned to prove that he could write well than to prove that he could write this particular book well. And he did prove this, at any rate. No one ever sent such a sample as the sample of Dickens. His roll of leather blocked up the street; his lump of coal set the Thames on fire.

The book originated in the suggestion of a publisher; as many more good books have done than the arrogance of the man of letters is commonly inclined to admit. Very much is said in our time about Apollo and Admetus, and the impossibility of asking genius to work within prescribed limits or assist an alien design. But after all, as a matter of fact, some of the greatest geniuses have done it, from Shakespeare botching up bad comedies and dramatising bad novels down to Dickens writing a masterpiece as the mere framework for a Mr. Seymour's sketches. Nor is the true explanation irrelevant to the spirit and power of Dickens. Very delicate, slender, and *bizarre* talents are indeed incapable of being used for an outside purpose, whether of public good or of private gain. But about very great and rich talent there goes a certain disdainful generosity which can turn its hand to anything. Minor poets cannot write to order; but very great poets can write to order. The larger the man's mind, the wider his scope of vision, the more likely it will be that anything suggested to him will seem significant and promising; the more he has a grasp of everything the more ready he will be to write anything. It is very hard (if that is the question) to throw a brick at a man and ask him to write an epic; but the more he is a great man the more able he will be to write about the brick. It is very unjust (if that is all) to point to a hoarding of Colman's mustard and demand a flood of philosophical eloquence; but the greater the man is the more likely he will be to give it to you. So it was proved, not for the first time, in this great experiment of the early employment of Dickens. Messrs. Chapman and Hall came to him with a scheme for a string of sporting stories to serve as the context, and one might almost say the excuse, for a string of sketches by Seymour, the sporting artist. Dickens made some modifications in the plan, but he adopted its main feature; and its main feature was Mr. Winkle. To think of what Mr. Winkle might have been in the hands of a dull *farceur*, and then to think of what he is, is to experience the feeling that Dickens made a man out of rags and refuse. Dickens was to work splendidly and successfully in many fields, and to send forth many brilliant books and brave figures. He was destined to have the applause of continents like a statesman, and to dictate to his publishers like a despot; but perhaps he never worked again so supremely well as here, where he worked in chains. It may well be questioned whether his one hack book is not his masterpiece.

Of course it is true that as he went on his independence increased, and he kicked quite free of the influences that had suggested his story. So Shakespeare declared his independence of the original chronicle of Hamlet, Prince of Denmark, eliminating altogether (with some wisdom) another uncle called Wiglerus. At the start the Nimrod Club of Chapman and Hall may have even had equal chances with the Pickwick Club of young Mr. Dickens; but the Pickwick Club became something much better than any publisher had dared to dream of. Some of the old links were indeed severed by accident or extraneous trouble; Seymour, for whose sake the whole had perhaps been planned, blew his brains out before he had drawn ten pictures. But such things were trifles compared to *Pickwick* itself. It mattered little now whether Seymour blew his brains out, so long as Charles Dickens blew his brains in. The work became systematically and progressively more powerful and masterly. Many critics have commented on the somewhat discordant and inartistic change between the earlier part of *Pickwick* and the later; they have pointed out, not without good sense, that the character of Mr. Pickwick changes from that of a silly buffoon to that of a solid merchant. But the case, if these critics had noticed it, is much stronger in the minor characters of the great company. Mr. Winkle, who has been an idiot (even, perhaps, as Mr. Pickwick says, "an impostor"), suddenly becomes a romantic and even reckless lover, scaling a forbidden wall and planning a bold elopement. Mr. Snodgrass, who has behaved in a ridiculous manner in all serious positions, suddenly finds himself in a ridiculous position-that of a gentleman surprised in a secret love affair-and behaves in a manner perfectly manly, serious, and honourable. Mr. Tupman alone has no serious emotional development, and for this reason it is, presumably, that we hear less and less of Mr. Tupman towards the end of the book. Dickens has by this time got into a thoroughly serious mood—a mood expressed indeed by extravagant incidents, but none the less serious for that; and into this Winkle and Snodgrass, in the character of romantic lovers, could be made to fit. Mr. Tupman had to be left out of the love affairs; therefore Mr. Tupman is left out of the book.

Much of the change was due to the entrance of the greatest character in the story. It may seem strange at the first glance to say that Sam Weller helped to make the story serious. Nevertheless, this is strictly true. The introduction of Sam Weller had, to begin with, some merely accidental and superficial effects. When Samuel Weller had appeared, Samuel Pickwick was no longer the chief farcical character. Weller became the joker and Pickwick in some sense the butt of his jokes. Thus it was obvious that the more simple, solemn, and really respectable this butt could be made the better. Mr. Pickwick had been the figure capering before the footlights. But with the advent of Sam, Mr. Pickwick had become a sort of black background and had to behave as such. But this explanation, though true as far as it goes, is a mean and unsatisfactory one, leaving the great elements unexplained. For a much deeper and more righteous reason Sam Weller introduces the more serious tone of Pickwick. He introduces it because he introduces something which it was the chief business of Dickens to preach throughout his life-something which he never preached so well as when he preached it unconsciously. Sam Weller introduces the English people.

Sam Weller is the great symbol in English literature of the populace peculiar to England. His incessant stream of sane nonsense is a wonderful achievement of Dickens: but it is no great falsification of the incessant stream of sane nonsense as it really exists among the English poor. The English poor live in an atmosphere of humour; they think in humour. Irony is the very air that they breathe. A joke comes suddenly from time to time into the head of a politician or a gentleman, and then as a rule he makes the most of it; but when a serious word comes into the mind of a coster it is almost as startling as a joke. The word "chaff" was, I suppose, originally applied to badinage to express its barren and unsustaining character; but to the English poor chaff is as sustaining as grain. The phrase that leaps to their lips is the ironical phrase. I remember once being driven in a hansom cab down a street that turned out to be a *cul de sac*, and brought us bang up against a wall. The driver and I simultaneously said

135

something. But I said: "This'll never do!" and he said: "This is all right!" Even in the act of pulling back his horse's nose from a brick wall, that confirmed satirist thought in terms of his highly-trained and traditional satire; while I, belonging to a duller and simpler class, expressed my feelings in words as innocent and literal as those of a rustic or a child.

This eternal output of divine derision has never been so truly typified as by the character of Sam; he is a grotesque fountain which gushes the living waters for ever. Dickens is accused of exaggeration and he is often guilty of exaggeration; but here he does not exaggerate: he merely symbolises and sublimates like any other great artist. Sam Weller does not exaggerate the wit of the London street arab one atom more than Colonel Newcome, let us say, exaggerates the stateliness of an ordinary soldier and gentleman, or than Mr. Collins exaggerates the fatuity of a certain kind of country clergyman. And this breath from the boisterous brotherhood of the poor lent a special seriousness and smell of reality to the whole story. The unconscious follies of Winkle and Tupman are blown away like leaves before the solid and conscious folly of Sam Weller. Moreover, the relations between Pickwick and his servant Sam are in some ways new and valuable in literature. Many comic writers had described the clever rascal and his ridiculous dupe; but here, in a fresh and very human atmosphere, we have a clever servant who was not a rascal and a dupe who was not ridiculous. Sam Weller stands in some ways for a cheerful knowledge of the world; Mr. Pickwick stands for a still more cheerful ignorance of the world. And Dickens responded to a profound human sentiment (the sentiment that has made saints and the sanctity of children) when he made the gentler and less-travelled type-the type which moderates and controls. Knowledge and innocence are both excellent things, and they are both very funny. But it is right that knowledge should be the servant and innocence the master.

The sincerity of this study of Sam Weller has produced one particular effect in the book which I wonder that critics of Dickens have never noticed or discussed. Because it has no Dickens "pathos," certain parts of it are truly pathetic. Dickens, realising rightly that the whole tone of the book was fun, felt that he ought to keep out of it any great experiments in sadness and keep within limits those that he put in. He used this restraint in order not to spoil the humour; but (if he had known himself better) he might well have used it in order not to spoil the pathos. This is the one book in which Dickens was, as it were, forced to trample down his tender feelings; and for that very reason it is the one book where all the tenderness there is is quite unquestionably true. An admirable example of what I mean may be found in the scene in which Sam Weller goes down to see his bereaved father after the death of his step-mother. The most loyal admirer of Dickens can hardly prevent himself from giving a slight shudder when he thinks of what Dickens might have made of that scene in some of his more expansive and maudlin moments. For all I know old Mrs. Weller might have asked what the wild waves were saying; and for all I know old Mr. Weller might have told her. As it is, Dickens, being forced to keep the tale taut and humorous, gives a picture of humble respect and decency which is manly, dignified, and really sad. There is no attempt made by these simple and honest men, the father and son, to pretend that the dead woman was anything greatly other than she was; their respect is for death, and for the human weakness and mystery which it must finally cover. Old Tony Weller does not tell his shrewish wife that she is already a white-winged angel; he speaks to her with an admirable good nature and good sense:

> "'Susan,' I says, 'you've been a wery good vife to me altogether: keep a good heart, my dear, and you'll live to see me punch that 'ere Stiggins's 'ead yet.' She smiled at this, Samivel . . . but she died arter all."

That is perhaps the first and the last time that Dickens ever touched the extreme dignity of pathos. He is restraining his compassion, and afterwards he let it go. Now laughter is a thing that can be let go; laughter has in it a quality of liberty. But sorrow has in it by its very nature a quality of confinement; pathos by its very nature fights with itself. Humour is expansive; it bursts outwards; the fact is attested by the common expression, "holding one's sides." But sorrow is not expansive; and it was afterwards the mistake of Dickens that he tried to make it expansive. It is the one great weakness of Dickens as a great writer, that he did try to make that sudden sadness, that abrupt pity, which we call pathos, a thing quite obvious, infectious, public, as if it were journalism or the measles. It is pleasant to think that in this supreme masterpiece, done in the dawn of his career, there is not even this faint fleck upon the sun of his just splendour. Pickwick will always be remembered as the great example of everything that made Dickens great; of the solemn conviviality of great friendships, of the erratic adventures of old English roads, of the hospitality of old English inns, of the great fundamental kindliness and honour of old English manners. First of all, however, it will always be remembered for its laughter, or, if you will, for its folly. A good joke is the one ultimate and sacred thing which cannot be criticised. Our relations with a good joke are direct and even divine relations. We speak of "seeing" a joke just as we speak of "seeing" a ghost or a vision. If we have seen it, it is futile to argue with us; and we have seen the vision of *Pickwick*. *Pickwick* may be the top of Dickens's humour; I think upon the whole it is. But the broad humour of *Pickwick* he broadened over many wonderful kingdoms; the narrow pathos of *Pickwick* he never found again.

Nicholas Nickleby

Romance is perhaps the highest point of human expression, except indeed religion, to which it is closely allied. Romance resembles religion especially in this, that it is not only a simplification but a shortening of existence. Both romance and religion see everything as it were foreshortened; they see everything in an abrupt and fantastic perspective, coming to an apex. It is the whole essence of perspective that it comes to a point. Similarly, religion comes to a point-to the point. Thus religion is always insisting on the shortness of human life. But it does not insist on the shortness of human life as the pessimists insist on it. Pessimism insists on the shortness of human life in order to show that life is valueless. Religion insists on the shortness of human life in order to show that life is frightfully valuable-is almost horribly valuable. Pessimism says that life is so short that it gives nobody a chance; religion says that life is so short that it gives everybody his final chance. In the first case the word brevity means futility; in the second case, opportunity. But the case is even stronger than this. Religion shortens everything. Religion shortens even eternity. Where science, submitting to the false standard of time, sees evolution, which is slow, religion sees creation, which is sudden. Philosophically speaking, the process is neither slow nor quick since we have nothing to compare it with. Religion prefers to think of it as quick. For religion the flowers shoot up suddenly like rockets. For religion the mountains are lifted up suddenly like waves. Those who quote that fine passage which says that in God's sight a thousand years are as yesterday that is passed as a watch in the night, do not realise the full force of the meaning. To God a thousand years are not only a watch but an exciting watch. For God time goes at a gallop, as it does to a man reading a good tale.

All this is, in a humble manner, true for romance. Romance is a shortening and sharpening of the human difficulty. Where you and I have to vote against a man, or write (rather feebly) against a man, or sign illegible petitions against a man, romance does for him what we should really like to see done. It knocks him down; it shortens the slow process of historical justice. All romances consist of three characters. Other characters may be introduced; but those other characters are certainly mere scenery as far as the romance is concerned. They are bushes that wave rather excitedly; they are posts that stand up with a certain pride; they are correctly painted rocks that frown very correctly; but they are all landscape-they are all a background. In every pure romance there are three living and moving characters. For the sake of argument they may be called St. George and the Dragon and the Princess. In every romance there must be the twin elements of loving and fighting. In every romance there must be the three characters: there must be the Princess, who is a thing to be loved; there must be the Dragon, who is a thing to be fought; and there must be St. George, who is a thing that both loves and fights. There have been many symptoms of cynicism and decay in our modern civilisation. But of all the signs of modern feebleness, of lack of grasp on morals as they actually must be, there has been none quite so silly or so dangerous as this: that the philosophers of to-day have started to divide loving from fighting and to put them into opposite camps. There could be no worse sign than that a man, even Nietzsche, can be found to say that we should go in for fighting instead of loving. There can be no worse sign than that a man, even Tolstoi, can be found to tell us that we should go in for loving instead of fighting. The two things imply each other; they implied each other in the old romance and in the old religion, which were the two permanent things of humanity. You cannot love a thing without wanting to fight for it. You cannot fight without something to fight for. To love a thing without wishing to fight for it is not love at all; it is lust. It may be an airy, philosophical, and disinterested lust; it may be, so to speak, a virgin lust; but it is lust, because it is wholly self-indulgent and invites no attack. On the other hand, fighting for a thing without loving it is not even fighting; it can only be called a kind of horse-play that is occasionally fatal. Wherever human nature is human and unspoilt by any special sophistry, there exists this natural kinship between war and wooing, and that natural kinship is called romance. It comes upon a man especially in the great hour of youth; and every man who has ever been young at all has felt, if only for a moment, this ultimate and poetic paradox. He knows that loving the world is the same thing as fighting the world. It was at the very moment when he offered to like everybody he also offered to hit everybody. To almost every man that can be called a man this especial moment of the romantic culmination has come. In the first resort the man wished to live a romance. In the second resort, in the last and worst resort, he was content to write one.

Now there is a certain moment when this element enters independently into the life of Dickens. There is a particular time when we can see him suddenly realise that he wants to write a romance and nothing else. In reading his letters, in appreciating his character, this point emerges clearly enough. He was full of the afterglow of his marriage; he was still young and psychologically ignorant; above all, he was now, really for the first time, sure that he was going to be at least some kind of success. There is, I repeat, a certain point at which one feels that Dickens will either begin to write romances or go off on something different altogether. This crucial point in his life is marked by *Nicholas Nickleby*.

It must be remembered that before this issue of *Nicholas Nickleby* his work, successful as it was, had not been such as to dedicate him seriously or irrevocably to the writing of novels. He had already written three books; and at least two of them are classed among the novels under his name. But if we look at the actual origin and formation of these books we see that they came from another source and were really designed upon another plan. The three books were, of course, the *Sketches by Boz*, the *Pickwick Papers*, and *Oliver Twist*. It is, I suppose, sufficiently well understood that the *Sketches by Boz* are, as their name implies, only sketches. But surely it is quite equally clear that the *Pickwick Papers* are, as their name implies, merely papers. Nor is the case at all different in spirit and essence when we come to *Oliver Twist*. There is indeed a sort of romance in *Oliver Twist*, but it is such an uncommonly bad one that it can hardly be regarded as greatly interrupting the previous process; and if the reader chooses to pay very little attention to it, he cannot pay less attention to it than the author did. But in fact the case lies far deeper. *Oliver Twist* is so much apart from the ordinary track of Dickens, it is so gloomy, it is so much all in one atmosphere, that it can best be considered as an exception or a solitary excursus in his work. Perhaps it can best be considered as the extension of one of his old sketches, of some sketch that happened to be about a visit to a workhouse or a gaol. In the *Sketches by Boz* he might well have visited a workhouse where he saw Bumble; in the *Sketches by Boz* he might well have visited a prison where he saw Fagin. We are still in the realm of sketches and sketchiness. *The Pickwick Papers* may be called an extension of one of his bright sketches. *Oliver Twist* may be called an extension of one of his gloomy ones.

Had he continued along this line all his books might very well have been note-books. It would be very easy to split up all his subsequent books into scraps and episodes, such as those which make up the *Sketches by Boz*. It would be easy enough for Dickens, instead of publishing *Nicholas Nickleby*, to have published a book of sketches, one of which was called "A Yorkshire School," another called "A Provincial Theatre," and another called "Sir Mulberry Hawk or High Life Revealed," another called "Mrs. Nickleby or a Lady's Monologue." It would have been very easy to have thrown over the rather chaotic plan of the *Old Curiosity Shop*. He might have merely written short stories called "The Glorious Apollos," "Mrs. Quilp's Tea-Party," "Mrs. Jarley's Waxwork," "The Little Servant," and "The Death of a Dwarf." *Martin Chuzzlewit* might have been twenty stories instead of one story. *Dombey and Son* might have been twenty stories instead of one story. We might have lost all Dickens's novels; we might have lost altogether Dickens the novelist. We might have lost that steady love of a seminal and growing romance which grew on him steadily as the years advanced, and which gave us towards the end some of his greatest triumphs. All his books might have been *Sketches by Boz*. But he did turn away from this, and the turning-point is *Nicholas Nickleby*.

Everything has a supreme moment and is crucial; that is where our friends the evolutionists go wrong. I suppose that there is an instant of midsummer as there is an instant of midnight. If in the same way there is a supreme point of spring, *Nicholas Nickleby* is the supreme point of Dickens's spring. I do not mean that it is the best book that he wrote in his youth. *Pickwick* is a

139

better book. I do not mean that it contains more striking characters than any of the other books in his youth. The *Old Curiosity Shop* contains at least two more striking characters. But I mean that this book coincided with his resolution to be a great novelist and his final belief that he could be one. Henceforward his books are novels, very commonly bad novels. Previously they have not really been novels at all. There are many indications of the change I mean. Here is one, for instance, which is more or less final. *Nicholas Nickleby* is Dickens's first romantic novel because it is his first novel with a proper and dignified romantic hero; which means, of course, a somewhat chivalrous young donkey. The hero of *Pickwick* is an old man. The hero of *Oliver Twist* is a child. Even after *Nicholas Nickleby* this non-romantic custom continued. The *Old Curiosity Shop* has no hero in particular. The hero of *Barnaby Rudge* is a lunatic. But Nicholas Nickleby is a proper, formal, and ceremonial hero. He has no psychology; he has not even any particular character; but he is made deliberately a hero-young, poor, brave, unimpeachable, and ultimately triumphant. He is, in short, the hero. Mr. Vincent Crummles had a colossal intellect; and I always have a fancy that under all his pomposity he saw things more keenly than he allowed others to see. The moment he saw Nicholas Nickleby, almost in rags and limping along the high road, he engaged him (you will remember) as first walking gentleman. He was right. Nobody could possibly be more of a first walking gentleman than Nicholas Nickleby was. He was the first walking gentleman before he went on to the boards of Mr. Vincent Crummles's theatre, and he remained the first walking gentleman after he had come off.

Now this romantic method involves a certain element of climax which to us appears crudity. Nicholas Nickleby, for instance, wanders through the world; he takes a situation as assistant to a Yorkshire schoolmaster; he sees an act of tyranny of which he strongly disapproves; he cries out "Stop!" in a voice that makes the rafters ring; he thrashes the schoolmaster within an inch of his life; he throws the schoolmaster away like an old cigar, and he goes away. The modern intellect is positively prostrated and flattened by this rapid and romantic way of righting wrongs. If a modern philanthropist came to Dotheboys Hall I fear he would not employ the simple, sacred, and truly Christian solution of beating Mr. Squeers with a stick. I fancy he would petition the Government to appoint a Royal Commission to inquire into Mr. Squeers. I think he would every now and then write letters to newspapers reminding people that, in spite of all appearances to the contrary, there was a Royal Commission to inquire into Mr. Squeers. I agree that he might even go the length of calling a crowded meeting in St. James's Hall on the subject of the best policy with regard to Mr. Squeers. At this meeting some very heated and daring speakers might even go the length of alluding sternly to Mr. Squeers. Occasionally even hoarse voices from the back of the hall might ask (in vain) what was going to be done with Mr. Squeers. The Royal Commission would report about three years afterwards and would say that many things had happened which were certainly most regrettable; that Mr. Squeers was the victim of a bad system; that Mrs. Squeers was also the victim of a bad system; but that the man who sold Squeers his cane had really acted with great indiscretion and ought to be spoken to kindly. Something like this would be what, after four years, the Royal Commission would have said; but it would not matter in the least what the Royal Commission had said, for by that time the philanthropists would be off on a new tack and the world would have forgotten all about Dotheboys Hall and everything connected with it. By that time the philanthropists would be petitioning Parliament for another Royal Commission; perhaps a Royal Commission to inquire into whether Mr. Mantalini was extravagant with his wife's money; perhaps a commission to inquire into whether Mr. Vincent Crummles kept the Infant Phenomenon short by means of gin.

If we wish to understand the spirit and the period of *Nicholas Nickleby* we must endeavour to comprehend and to appreciate the old more decisive remedies, or, if we prefer to put it so, the old more desperate remedies. Our fathers had a plain sort of pity; if you will, a gross and coarse pity. They had their own sort of sentimentalism. They were quite willing to weep over Smike. But it certainly never occurred to them to weep over Squeers. Even those who opposed the French war opposed it exactly in the same way as their enemies opposed the French soldiers. They fought with fighting. Charles Fox was full of horror at the bitterness and the useless bloodshed; but if any one had insulted him over the matter, he would have gone out and shot him in a duel as coolly as any of his contemporaries. All their interference was heroic interference. All their legislation was heroic legislation. All their remedies were heroic remedies. No doubt they were often narrow and often visionary. No doubt they often looked at a political formula when they should have looked at an elemental fact. No doubt they were pedantic in some of their principles and clumsy in some of their solutions. No doubt, in short, they were all very wrong; and no doubt we are the people, and wisdom shall die with us. But when they saw something which in their eyes, such as they were, really violated their morality, such as it was, then they did not cry "Investigate!" They did not cry "Educate!" They did not cry "Improve!" They did not cry "Evolve!" Like Nicholas Nickleby they cried "Stop!" And it did stop.

This is the first mark of the purely romantic method: the swiftness and simplicity with which St. George kills the dragon. The second mark of it is exhibited here as one of the weaknesses of *Nicholas Nickleby*. I mean the tendency in the purely romantic story to regard the heroine merely as something to be won; to regard the princess solely as something to be saved from the dragon. The father of Madeline Bray is really a very respectable dragon. His selfishness is suggested with much more psychological tact and truth than that of any other of the villains that Dickens described about this time. But his daughter is merely the young woman with whom Nicholas is in love. We do not care a rap about Madeline Bray. Personally I should have preferred Cecilia Bobster. Here is one real point where the Victorian romance falls below the Elizabethan romantic drama. Shakespeare always made his heroines heroic as well as his heroes.

In Dickens's actual literary career it is this romantic quality in *Nicholas Nickleby* that is most important. It is his first definite attempt to write a young and chivalrous novel. In this sense the comic characters and the comic scenes are secondary; and indeed the comic characters and the comic scenes, admirable as they are, could never be considered as in themselves superior to such characters and such scenes in many of the other books. But in themselves how unforgettable they are. Mr. Crummles and the whole of his theatrical business is an admirable case of that first and most splendid quality in Dickens—I mean the art of making something which in life we call pompous and dull, becoming in literature pompous and delightful. I have remarked before that nearly every one of the amusing characters of Dickens is in reality a great fool. But I might go further. Almost every one of his amusing characters is in reality a great bore. The very people that we fly to in Dickens are the very people that we fly from in life. And there is more in Crummles than the mere entertainment of his solemnity and his tedium. The enormous seriousness with which he takes his art is always an exact touch in regard to the unsuccessful artist. If an artist is successful, everything then depends upon a dilemma of his moral character. If he is a mean artist success will make him a society man. If he is a magnanimous artist, success will make him an ordinary man. But only as long as he is unsuccessful will he be an unfathomable and serious artist, like Mr. Crummles. Dickens was always particularly good at expressing thus the treasures that belong to those who do not succeed in this world. There are vast prospects and splendid songs in the point of view of the typically unsuccessful man; if all the used-up actors and spoilt journalists and broken clerks could give a chorus, it would be a wonderful chorus in praise of the world. But these unsuccessful men commonly cannot even speak. Dickens is the voice of them, and a very ringing voice; because he was perhaps the only one of these unsuccessful men that was ever successful.

Oliver Twist

In considering Dickens, as we almost always must consider him, as a man of rich originality, we may possibly miss the forces from which he drew even his original energy. It is not well for man to be alone. We, in the modern world, are ready enough to admit that when it is applied to some problem of monasticism or of an ecstatic life. But we will not admit that our modern artistic claim to absolute originality is really a claim to absolute unsociability; a claim to absolute loneliness. The anarchist is at least as solitary as the ascetic. And the men of very vivid vigour in literature, the men such as Dickens, have generally displayed a large sociability towards the society of letters, always expressed in the happy pursuit of pre-existent themes, sometimes expressed, as in the case of Molière or Sterne, in downright plagiarism. For even theft is a confession of our dependence on society. In Dickens, however, this element of the original foundations on which he worked is quite especially difficult to determine. This is partly due to the fact that for the present reading public he is practically the only one of his long line that is read at all. He sums up Smollett and Goldsmith, but he also destroys them. This one giant, being closest to us, cuts off from our view even the giants that begat him. But much more is this difficulty due to the fact that Dickens mixed up with the old material, materials so subtly modern, so made of the French Revolution, that the whole is transformed. If we want the best example of this, the best example is *Oliver Twist*.

Relatively to the other works of Dickens *Oliver Twist* is not of great value, but it is of great importance. Some parts of it are so crude and of so clumsy a melodrama, that one is almost tempted to say that Dickens would have been greater without it. But even if he had been greater without it he would still have been incomplete without it. With the exception of some gorgeous passages, both of humour and horror, the interest of the book lies not so much in its revelation of Dickens's literary genius as in its revelation of those moral, personal, and political instincts which were the make-up of his character and the permanent support of that literary genius. It is by far the most depressing of all his books; it is in some ways the most irritating; yet its ugliness gives the last touch of honesty to all that spontaneous and splendid output. Without this one discordant note all his merriment might have seemed like levity.

Dickens had just appeared upon the stage and set the whole world laughing with his first great story *Pickwick*. *Oliver Twist* was his encore. It was the second opportunity given to him by those who had rolled about with laughter over Tupman and Jingle, Weller and Dowler. Under such circumstances a stagey reciter will sometimes take care to give a pathetic piece after his humorous one; and with all his many moral merits, there was much that was stagey about Dickens. But this explanation alone is altogether inadequate and unworthy. There was in Dickens this other kind of energy, horrible, uncanny, barbaric, capable in another age of coarseness, greedy for the emblems of established ugliness, the coffin, the gibbet, the bones, the bloody knife. Dickens liked these things and he was all the more of a man for liking them; especially he was all the more of a boy. We can all recall with pleasure the fact that Miss Petowker (afterwards Mrs. Lillyvick) was in the habit of reciting a poem called "The Blood Drinker's Burial." I cannot express my regret that the words of this poem are not given; for Dickens would have been quite as capable of writing "The Blood Drinker's Burial" as Miss Petowker was of reciting it. This strain existed in Dickens alongside of his happy laughter; both were allied to the same robust romance. Here as elsewhere Dickens is close to all the permanent human things. He is close to religion, which has never allowed the thousand devils on its churches to stop the dancing of its bells. He is allied to the people, to the real poor, who love nothing so much as to take a cheerful glass and to talk about funerals. The extremes of his gloom and gaiety are the mark of religion and democracy; they mark him off from the moderate happiness of philosophers, and from that stoicism which is the virtue and the creed of aristocrats. There is nothing odd in the fact that the same man who conceived the humane hospitalities of Pickwick should also have imagined the inhuman laughter of Fagin's den. They are both genuine and they are both exaggerated. And the whole human tradition has tied up together in a strange knot these strands of festivity and fear. It is over the cups of Christmas Eve that men have always competed in telling ghost stories.

This first element was present in Dickens, and it is very powerfully present in *Oliver Twist*. It had not been present with sufficient consistency or continuity in *Pickwick* to make it remain on the reader's memory at all, for the tale of "Gabriel Grubb" is grotesque rather than horrible, and the two gloomy stories of the "Madman" and the "Queer Client" are so utterly irrelevant to the tale, that even if the reader remember them he probably does not remember that they occur in *Pickwick*. Critics have complained of Shakespeare and others for putting comic episodes into a tragedy. It required a man with the courage and coarseness of Dickens actually to put tragic episodes into a farce. But they are not caught up into the story at all. In *Oliver Twist*, however, the thing broke out with an almost brutal inspiration, and those who had fallen in love with Dickens for his generous buffoonery may very likely have been startled at receiving such very different fare at the next helping. When you have bought a man's book because you like his writing about Mr. Wardle's punch-bowl and Mr. Winkle's skates, it may very well be surprising to open it and read about the sickening thuds that beat out the life of Nancy, or that mysterious villain whose face was blasted with disease.

As a nightmare, the work is really admirable. Characters which are not very clearly conceived as regards their own psychology are yet, at certain moments, managed so as to shake to its foundations our own psychology. Bill Sikes is not exactly a real man, but for all that he is a real murderer. Nancy is not really impressive as a living woman; but (as the phrase goes) she makes a lovely corpse. Something quite childish and eternal in us, something which is shocked with the mere simplicity of death, quivers when we read of those repeated blows or see Sikes cursing the tell-tale cur who will follow his bloody foot-prints. And this strange, sublime, vulgar melodrama, which is melodrama and yet is painfully real, reaches its hideous height in that fine scene of the death of Sikes, the besieged house, the boy screaming within, the crowd screaming without, the murderer turned almost a maniac and dragging his victim uselessly up and down the room, the escape over the roof, the rope swiftly running taut, and death sudden, startling and symbolic; a man hanged. There is in this and similar scenes something of the quality of Hogarth and many other English moralists of the early eighteenth century. It is not easy to define this Hogarthian quality in words, beyond saying that it is a sort of alphabetical realism, like the cruel candour of children. But it has about it these two special principles which separate it from all that we call realism in our time. First, that with us a moral story means a story about moral people; with them a moral story meant more often a story about immoral people. Second, that with us realism is always associated with some subtle view of morals; with them realism was always associated with some simple view of morals. The end of Bill Sikes exactly in the way that the law would have killed him-this is a Hogarthian incident; it carries on that tradition of startling and shocking platitude.

All this element in the book was a sincere thing in the author, but none the less it came from old soils, from the graveyard and the gallows, and the lane where the ghost walked. Dickens was always attracted to such things, and (as Forster says with inimitable simplicity) "but for his strong sense might have fallen into the follies of spiritualism." As a matter of fact, like most of the men of strong sense in his tradition, Dickens was left with a half belief in spirits which became in practice a belief in bad spirits. The great disadvantage of those who have too much strong sense to believe in supernaturalism is that they keep last the low and little forms of the supernatural, such as omens, curses, spectres, and retributions, but find a high and happy supernaturalism quite incredible. Thus the Puritans denied the sacraments, but went on burning witches. This shadow does rest, to some extent, upon the rational English writers like Dickens; supernaturalism was dying, but its ugliest roots died last. Dickens would have found it easier to believe in a ghost than in a vision of the Virgin with angels. There, for good or evil, however, was the root of the old *diablerie* in Dickens, and there it is in *Oliver Twist*. But this was only the first of the new Dickens elements, which must have surprised those Dickensians who eagerly bought his second book. The second of the new Dickens elements is equally indisputable and separate. It swelled afterwards to enormous proportions in Dickens's work; but it really has its rise here. Again, as in the case of the element of *diablerie*, it would be possible to make technical exceptions in favour of *Pickwick*. Just as there were quite inappropriate scraps of the gruesome element in *Pickwick*, so there are quite inappropriate allusions to this other topic in *Pickwick*. But nobody by merely reading *Pickwick* would even remember this topic; no one by merely reading *Pickwick* would know what this topic is; this third great subject of Dickens; this second great subject of the Dickens of *Oliver Twist*.

This subject is social oppression. It is surely fair to say that no one could have gathered from *Pickwick* how this question boiled in the blood of the author of *Pickwick*. There are, indeed, passages, particularly in connection with Mr. Pickwick in the debtor's prison, which prove to us, looking back on a whole public career, that Dickens had been from the beginning bitter and inquisitive about the problem of our civilisation. No one could have imagined at the time that this bitterness ran in an unbroken river under all the surges of that superb gaiety and exuberance. With *Oliver Twist* this sterner side of Dickens was suddenly revealed. For the very first pages of *Oliver Twist* are stern even when they are funny. They amuse, but they cannot be enjoyed, as can the passages about the follies of Mr. Snodgrass or the humiliations of Mr. Winkle. The difference between the old easy humour and this new harsh humour is a difference not of degree but of kind. Dickens makes game of Mr. Bumble because he wants to kill Mr. Bumble; he made game of Mr. Winkle because he wanted him to live for ever. Dickens has taken the sword in hand; against what is he declaring war?

It is just here that the greatness of Dickens comes in; it is just here that the difference lies between the pedant and the poet. Dickens enters the social and political war, and the first stroke he deals is not only significant but even startling. Fully to see this we must appreciate the national situation. It was an age of reform, and even of radical reform; the world was full of radicals and reformers; but only too many of them took the line of attacking everything and anything that was opposed to some particular theory among the many political theories that possessed the end of the eighteenth century. Some had so much perfected the perfect theory of republicanism that they almost lay awake at night because Queen Victoria had a crown on her head. Others were so certain that mankind had hitherto been merely strangled in the bonds of the State that they saw truth only in the destruction of tariffs or of by-laws. The greater part of that generation held that clearness, economy, and a hard common-sense, would soon destroy the errors that had been erected by the superstitions and sentimentalities of the past. In pursuance of this idea many of the new men of the new century, quite confident that they were invigorating the new age, sought to destroy the old sentimental clericalism, the old sentimental feudalism, the old-world belief in priests, the old-world belief in patrons, and among other things the old-world belief in beggars. They sought among other things to clear away the old visionary kindliness on the subject of vagrants. Hence those reformers enacted not only a new reform bill but also a new poor law. In creating many other modern things they created the modern workhouse, and when Dickens came out to fight it was the first thing that he broke with his battle-axe.

This is where Dickens's social revolt is of more value than mere politics and avoids the vulgarity of the novel with a purpose. His revolt is not a revolt of the commercialist against the feudalist, of the Nonconformist against the Churchman, of the Free-trader against the Protectionist, of the Liberal against the Tory. If he were among us now his revolt would not be the revolt of the Socialist against the Individualist, or of the Anarchist against the Socialist. His revolt was simply and solely the eternal revolt; it was the revolt of the weak against the strong. He did not dislike this or that argument for oppression; he disliked oppression. He disliked a certain look on the face of a man when he looks down on another man. And that look on the face is, indeed, the only thing in the world that we have really to fight between here and the fires of Hell. That which pedants of that time and this time would have called the sentimentalism of Dickens was really simply the detached sanity of Dickens. He cared nothing for the fugitive explanations of the Constitutional Conservatives; he cared nothing for the fugitive explanations of the Manchester School. He would have cared quite as little for the fugitive explanations of the Fabian Society or of the modern scientific Socialist. He saw that under many forms there was one fact, the tyranny of man over man; and he struck at it when he saw it, whether it was old or new. When he found that footmen and rustics were too much afraid of Sir Leicester Dedlock, he attacked Sir Leicester Dedlock; he did not care whether Sir Leicester Dedlock said he was attacking England or whether Mr. Rouncewell, the Ironmaster, said he was attacking an effete oligarchy. In that case he pleased Mr. Rouncewell, the Iron-master, and displeased Sir Leicester Dedlock, the Aristocrat. But when he found that Mr. Rouncewell's workmen were much too frightened of Mr. Rouncewell, then he displeased Mr. Rouncewell in turn; he displeased Mr. Rouncewell very much by calling him Mr. Bounderby. When he imagined himself to be fighting old laws he gave a sort of vague and general approval to new laws. But when he came to the new laws they had a bad time. When Dickens found that after a hundred economic arguments and granting a hundred economic considerations, the fact remained that paupers in modern workhouses were much too afraid of the beadle, just as vassals in ancient castles were much too afraid of the Dedlocks, then he struck suddenly and at once. This is what makes the opening chapters of *Oliver Twist* so curious and important. The very fact of Dickens's distance from, and independence of, the elaborate financial arguments of his time, makes more definite and dazzling his sudden assertion that he sees the old human tyranny in front of him as plain as the sun at noon-day. Dickens attacks the modern workhouse with a sort of inspired simplicity as of a boy in a fairy tale who had wandered about, sword in hand, looking for ogres and who had found an indisputable ogre. All the other people of his time are attacking things because they are bad economics or because they are bad politics, or because they are bad science; he alone is attacking things because they are bad. All the others are Radicals with a large R; he alone is radical with a small one. He encounters evil with that beautiful surprise which, as it is the beginning of all real pleasure, is also the beginning of all righteous indignation. He enters the workhouse just as Oliver Twist enters it, as a little child.

This is the real power and pathos of that celebrated passage in the book which has passed into a proverb; but which has not lost its terrible humour even in being hackneyed. I mean, of course, the everlasting quotation about Oliver Twist asking for more. The real poignancy that there is in this idea is a very good study in that strong school of social criticism which Dickens represented. A modern realist describing the dreary workhouse would have made all the children utterly crushed, not daring to speak at all, not expecting anything, not hoping anything, past all possibility of affording even an ironical contrast or a protest of despair. A modern, in short, would have made all the boys in the workhouse pathetic by making them all pessimists. But Oliver Twist is not pathetic because he is a pessimist. Oliver Twist is pathetic because he is an optimist. The whole tragedy of that incident is in the fact that he does expect the universe to be kind to him, that he does believe that he is living in a just world. He comes before the Guardians as the ragged peasants of the French Revolution came before the Kings and Parliaments of Europe. That is to say, he comes, indeed, with gloomy experiences, but he comes with a happy philosophy. He knows that there are wrongs of man to be reviled; but he believes also that there are rights of man to be demanded. It has often been remarked as a singular fact that the French poor, who stand in historic tradition as typical of all the desperate men who have dragged down tyranny, were, as a matter of fact, by no means worse off than the poor of many other European countries before the Revolution. The truth is that the French were tragic because they were better off. The others had known the sorrowful experiences; but they alone had known the splendid expectation and the original claims. It was just here that Dickens was so true a child of them and of that happy theory so bitterly applied. They were the one oppressed people that simply asked for justice; they were the one Parish Boy who innocently asked for more.

Old Curiosity Shop

Nothing is important except the fate of the soul; and literature is only redeemed from an utter triviality, surpassing that of naughts and crosses, by the fact that it describes not the world around us or the things on the retina of the eye or the enormous irrelevancy of encyclopædias, but some condition to which the human spirit can come. All good writers express the state of their souls, even (as occurs in some cases of very good writers) if it is a state of damnation. The first thing that has to be realised about Dickens is this ultimate spiritual condition of the man, which lay behind all his creations. This Dickens state of mind is difficult to pick out in words as are all elementary states of mind; they cannot be described, not because they are too subtle for words, but because they are too simple for words. Perhaps the nearest approach to a statement of it would be this: that Dickens expresses an eager anticipation of everything that will happen in the motley affairs of men; he looks at the quiet crowd waiting for it to be picturesque and to play the fool; he expects everything; he is torn with a happy hunger. Thackeray is always looking back to yesterday; Dickens is always looking forward to to-morrow. Both are profoundly humorous, for there is a humour of the morning and a humour of the evening; but the first guesses at what it will get, at all the grotesqueness and variety which a day may bring forth; the second looks back on what the day has been and sees even its solemnities as slightly ironical. Nothing can be too extravagant for the laughter that looks forward; and nothing can be too dignified for the laughter that looks back. It is an idle but obvious thing, which many must have noticed, that we often find in the title of one of an author's books what might very well stand for a general description of all of them. Thus all Spenser's works might be called *A Hymn to Heavenly Beauty*; or all Mr. Bernard Shaw's bound books might be called *You Never Can Tell*. In the same way the whole substance and spirit of Thackeray might be gathered under the general title *Vanity Fair*. In the same way too the whole substance and spirit of Dickens might be gathered under the general title *Great Expectations*.

In a recent criticism on this position I saw it remarked that all this is reading into Dickens something that he did not mean; and I have been told that it would have greatly surprised Dickens to be informed that he "went down the broad road of the Revolution." Of course it would. Criticism does not exist to say about authors the things that they knew themselves. It exists to say the things about them which they did not know themselves. If a critic says that the *Iliad* has a pagan rather than a Christian pity, or that it is full of pictures made by one epithet, of course he does not mean that Homer could have said that. If Homer could have said that the critic would leave Homer to say it. The function of criticism, if it has a legitimate function at all, can only be one function—that of dealing with the subconscious part of the author's mind which only the critic can express, and not with the conscious part of the author's mind, which the author himself can express. Either criticism is no good at all (a very defensible position) or else criticism means saying about an author the very things that would have made him jump out of his boots.

Doubtless the name in this case *Great Expectations* is an empty coincidence; and indeed it is not in the books of the later Dickens period (the period of *Great Expectations*) that we should look for the best examples of this sanguine and expectant spirit which is the essential of the man's genius. There are plenty of good examples of it especially in the earlier works. But even in the earlier works there is no example of it more striking or more satisfactory than *The Old Curiosity Shop*. It is particularly noticeable in the fact that its opening and original framework express the idea of a random experience, a thing come across in the street; a single face in the crowd, followed until it tells its story. Though the thing ends in a novel it begins in a sketch; it begins as one of the *Sketches by Boz*. There is something unconsciously artistic in the very clumsiness of this opening. Master Humphrey starts to keep a scrap-book of all his adventures, and he finds that he can fill the whole scrap-book with the sequels and developments of one adventure; he goes out to notice everybody and he finds himself busily and variedly occupied only in watching somebody. In this there is a very profound truth about the true excitement and inexhaustible poetry of life. The truth is not so much that eternity is full of souls as that one soul can fill eternity. In strict art there is something quite lame and lumbering about the way in which the benevolent old story-teller starts to tell many stories and then drops away altogether, while one of his stories takes his place. But in a larger art, his collision with Little Nell and his complete eclipse by her personality and narrative have a real significance. They suggest the random richness of such meetings, and their uncalculated results. It makes the whole book a sort of splendid accident.

It is not true, as is commonly said, that the Dickens pathos as pathos is bad. It is not true, as is still more commonly said, that the whole business about Little Nell is bad. The case is more complex than that. Yet complex as it is it admits of one sufficiently clear distinction. Those who have written about the death of Little Nell, have generally noticed the crudities of the character itself; the little girl's unnatural and staring innocence, her constrained and awkward piety. But they have nearly all of them entirely failed to notice that there is in the death of Little Nell one quite definite and really artistic idea. It is not an artistic idea that a little child should die rhetorically on the stage like Paul Dombey; and Little Nell does not die rhetorically upon the stage like Paul Dombey. But it is an artistic idea that all the good powers and personalities in the story should set out in pursuit of one insignificant child, to repair an injustice to her, should track her from town to town over England with all the resources of wealth, intelligence, and travel, and should all-arrive too late. All the good fairies and all the kind magicians, all the just kings and all the gallant princes, with chariots and flying dragons and armies and navies go after one little child who had strayed into a wood, and find her dead. That is the conception which Dickens's artistic instinct was really aiming at when he finally condemned Little Nell to death, after keeping her, so to speak, so long with the rope round her neck. The death of Little Nell is open certainly to the particular denial which its enemies make about it. The death of Little Nell is not pathetic. It is perhaps tragic; it is in reality ironic. Here is a very good case of the injustice to Dickens on his purely literary side. It is not that I say that Dickens achieved what he designed; it is that the critics will not see what the design was. They go on talking of the death of Little Nell as if it were a mere example of maudlin description like the death of Little Paul. As a fact it is not described at all; so it cannot be objectionable. It is not the death of Little Nell, but the life of Little Nell, that I object to.

In this, in the actual picture of her personality, if you can call it a personality, Dickens did fall into some of his facile vices. The real objection to much of his pathos belongs really to another part of his character. It is connected with his vanity, his voracity for all kinds of praise, his restive experimentalism and even perhaps his envy. He strained himself to achieve pathos. His humour was inspiration; but his pathos was ambition. His laughter was lonely; he would have laughed on a desert island. But his grief was gregarious. He liked to move great masses of men, to melt them into tenderness, to play on the people as a great pianist plays on them; to make them mad or sad. His pathos was to him a way of showing his power; and for that reason it was really powerless. He could not help making people laugh; but he tried to make them cry. We come in this novel, as we often do come in his novels, upon hard lumps of unreality, upon a phrase that suddenly sickens. That is always due to his conscious despotism over the delicate feelings; that is always due to his love of fame as distinct from his love of fun. But it is not true that all Dickens's pathos is like this; it is not even true that all the passages about Little Nell are like this; there are two strands almost everywhere and they can be differentiated as the sincere and the deliberate. There is a great difference between Dickens thinking about the tears of his characters and Dickens thinking about the tears of his audience.

When all this is allowed, however, and the exaggerated contempt for the Dickens pathos is properly corrected, the broad fact remains: that to pass from the solemn characters in this book to the comic characters in this book, is to be like some Ulysses who should pass suddenly from the land of shadows to the mountain of the gods. Little Nell has her own position in careful and reasonable criticism: even that wobbling old ass, her grandfather, has his position in it; perhaps even the dissipated Fred (whom long acquaintance with Mr. Dick Swiveller has not made any less dismal in his dissipation) has a place in it also. But when we come to Swiveller and Sampson Brass and Quilp and Mrs. Jarley, then Fred and Nell and the grandfather simply do not exist. There are no such people in the story. The real hero and heroine of *The Old Curiosity Shop* are of course Dick Swiveller and the Marchioness. It is significant in a sense that these two sane, strong, living, and lovable human beings are the only two, or almost the only two, people in the story who do not run after Little Nell. They have something better to do than to go on that shadowy chase after that cheerless phantom. They have to build up between them a true romance; perhaps the one true romance in the whole of Dickens. Dick Swiveller really has all the half-heroic characteristics which make a man respected by a woman and which are the male contribution to virtue. He is brave, magnanimous, sincere about himself, amusing, absurdly hopeful; above all, he is both strong and weak. On the other hand the Marchioness really has all the characteristics, the entirely heroic characteristics which make a woman respected by a man. She is female: that is, she is at once incurably candid and incurably loyal, she is full of terrible common-sense, she expects little pleasure for herself and yet she can enjoy bursts of it; above all, she is physically timid and yet she can face anything. All this solid rocky romanticism is really implied in the speech and action of these two characters and can be felt behind them all the time. Because they are the two most absurd people in the book they are also the most vivid, human, and imaginable. There are two really fine love affairs in Dickens; and I almost think only two. One is the happy courtship of Swiveller and the Marchioness; the other is the tragic courtship of Toots and Florence Dombey. When Dick Swiveller wakes up in bed and sees the Marchioness playing cribbage he thinks that he and she are a prince and princess in a fairy tale. He thinks right.

I speak thus seriously of such characters with a deliberate purpose; for the frivolous characters of Dickens are taken much too frivolously. It has been quite insufficiently pointed out that all the serious moral ideas that Dickens did contrive to express he expressed altogether through this fantastic medium, in such figures as Swiveller and the little servant. The warmest upholder of Dickens would not go to the solemn or sentimental passages for anything fresh or suggestive in faith or philosophy. No one would pretend that the death of little Dombey (with its "What are the wild waves saying?") told us anything new or real about death. A good Christian dying, one would imagine, not only would not know what the wild waves were saying, but would not care. No one would pretend that the repentance of old Paul Dombey throws any light on the psychology or philosophy of repentance. No doubt old Dombey, white-haired and amiable, was a great improvement on old Dombey brown-haired and unpleasant. But in his case the softening of the heart seems to bear too close a resemblance to softening of the brain. Whether these serious passages are as bad as the critical people or as good as the sentimental people find them, at least they do not convey anything in the way of an illuminating glimpse or a bold suggestion about men's moral nature. The serious figures do not tell one anything about the human soul. The comic figures do. Take anything almost at random out of these admirable speeches of Dick Swiveller. Notice, for instance, how exquisitely Dickens has caught a certain very deep and delicate quality at the bottom of this idle kind of man. I mean that odd impersonal sort of intellectual justice, by which the frivolous fellow sees things as they are and even himself as he is; and is above irritation. Mr. Swiveller, you remember, asks the Marchioness whether the Brass family ever talk about him; she nods her head with vivacity. "'Complimentary?' inquired Mr. Swiveller. The motion of the little servant's head altered. . . . 'But she says,' continued the little servant, 'that you ain't to be trusted.' 'Well, do you know, Marchioness,' said Mr. Swiveller thoughtfully, 'many people, not exactly professional people, but tradesmen, have had the same idea. The excellent citizen from whom I ordered this beer inclines strongly to that opinion.'"

This philosophical freedom from all resentment, this strange love of truth which seems actually to come through carelessness, is a very real piece of spiritual observation. Even among liars there are two classes, one immeasurably better than another. The honest liar is the man who tells the truth about his old lies; who says on Wednesday, "I told a magnificent lie on Monday."

He keeps the truth in circulation; no one version of things stagnates in him and becomes an evil secret. He does not have to live with old lies; a horrible domesticity. Mr. Swiveller may mislead the waiter about whether he has the money to pay; but he does not mislead his friend, and he does not mislead himself on the point. He is quite as well aware as any one can be of the accumulating falsity of the position of a gentleman who by his various debts has closed up all the streets into the Strand except one, and who is going to close that to-night with a pair of gloves. He shuts up the street with a pair of gloves, but he does not shut up his mind with a secret. The traffic of truth is still kept open through his soul.

It is exactly in these absurd characters, then, that we can find a mass of psychological and ethical suggestion. This cannot be found in the serious characters except indeed in some of the later experiments: there is a little of such psychological and ethical suggestion in figures like Gridley, like Jasper, like Bradley Headstone. But in these earlier books at least, such as *The Old Curiosity Shop*, the grave or moral figures throw no light upon morals. I should maintain this generalisation even in the presence of that apparent exception *The Christmas Carol* with its trio of didactic ghosts. Charity is certainly splendid, at once a luxury and a necessity; but Dickens is not most effective when he is preaching charity seriously; he is most effective when he is preaching it uproariously; when he is preaching it by means of massive personalities and vivid scenes. One might say that he is best not when he is preaching his human love, but when he is practising it. In his grave pages he tells us to love men; but in his wild pages he creates men whom we can love. By his solemnity he commands us to love our neighbours. By his caricature he makes us love them.

There is an odd literary question which I wonder is not put more often in literature. How far can an author tell a truth without seeing it himself? Perhaps an actual example will express my meaning. I was once talking to a highly intelligent lady about Thackeray's *Newcomes*. We were speaking of the character of Mrs. Mackenzie, the Campaigner, and in the middle of the conversation the lady leaned across to me and said in a low, hoarse, but emphatic voice, "She drank. Thackeray didn't know it; but she drank." And it is really astonishing what a shaft of white light this sheds on the Campaigner, on her terrible temperament, on her agonised abusiveness and her almost more agonised urbanity, on her clamour which is nevertheless not open or explicable, on her temper which is not so much bad temper as insatiable, bloodthirsty, man-eating temper. How far can a writer thus indicate by accident a truth of which he is himself ignorant? If truth is a plan or pattern of things that really are, or in other words, if truth truly exists outside ourselves, or in other words, if truth exists at all, it must be often possible for a writer to uncover a corner of it which he happens not to understand, but which his reader does happen to understand. The author sees only two lines; the reader sees where they meet and what is the angle. The author sees only an arc or fragment of a curve; the reader sees the size of the circle. The last thing to say about Dickens, and especially about books like *The Old Curiosity Shop*, is that they are full of these unconscious truths. The careless reader may miss them. The careless author almost certainly did miss them. But from them can be gathered an impression of real truth to life which is for the grave critics of Dickens an almost unknown benefit, buried treasure. Here for instance is one of them out of *The Old Curiosity Shop*. I mean the passage in which (by a blazing stroke of genius) the dashing Mr. Chuckster, one of the Glorious Apollos of whom Mr. Swiveller was the Perpetual Grand, is made to entertain a hatred bordering upon frenzy for the stolid, patient, respectful, and laborious Kit. Now in the formal plan of the story Mr. Chuckster is a fool, and Kit is almost a hero; at least he is a noble boy. Yet unconsciously Dickens made the idiot Chuckster say something profoundly suggestive on the subject. In speaking of Kit Mr. Chuckster makes use of these two remarkable phrases; that Kit is "meek" and that he is "a snob." Now Kit is really a very fresh and manly picture of a boy, firm, sane, chivalrous, reasonable, full of those three great Roman virtues which Mr. Belloc has so often celebrated, *virtus* and *verecundia* and *pietas*. He is a sympathetic but still a straightforward study of the best type of that most respectable of all human classes, the respectable poor. All this is true; all that Dickens utters in praise of Kit is true; nevertheless the awful words of Chuckster remain written on the eternal skies. Kit is meek and Kit is a snob. His natural dignity does include and is partly marred by that instinctive subservience to the employing class which has been the comfortable weakness of the whole English democracy, which has prevented their making any revolution for the last two hundred years. Kit would not serve any wicked man for money, but he would serve any moderately good man and the money would give a certain dignity and decisiveness to the goodness. All this is the English popular evil which goes along with the English popular virtues of geniality, of homeliness, tolerance and strong humour, hope and an enormous appetite for a hand-to-mouth happiness. The scene in which Kit takes his family to the theatre is a monument of the massive qualities of old English enjoyment. If what we want is Merry England, our antiquarians ought not to revive the Maypole or the Morris Dancers; they ought to revive Astley's and Sadler's Wells and the old solemn Circus and the old stupid Pantomime, and all the sawdust and all the oranges. Of all this strength and joy in the poor, Kit is a splendid and final symbol. But amid all his masculine and English virtue, he has this weak touch of meekness, or acceptance of the powers that be. It is a sound touch; it is a real truth about Kit. But Dickens did not know it. Mr. Chuckster did.

Dickens's stories taken as a whole have more artistic unity than appears at the first glance. It is the immediate impulse of a modern critic to dismiss them as mere disorderly scrap-books with very brilliant scraps. But this is not quite so true as it looks. In one of Dickens's novels there is generally no particular unity of construction; but there is often a considerable unity of sentiment and atmosphere. Things are irrelevant, but not somehow inappropriate. The whole book is written carelessly; but the whole book is generally written in one mood. To take a rude parallel from the other arts, we may say that there is not much unity of form, but there is much unity of colour. In most of the novels this can be seen. *Nicholas Nickleby*, as I have remarked, is full of a certain freshness, a certain light and open-air curiosity, which irradiates from the image of the young man swinging along the Yorkshire roads in the sun. Hence the comic characters with whom he falls in are comic characters in the same key; they are a band of strolling players, charlatans and poseurs, but too humane to be called humbugs. In the same way, the central story of *Oliver Twist* is sombre; and hence even its comic character is almost sombre; at least he is too ugly to be merely amusing. Mr. Bumble is in some ways a terrible grotesque; his apoplectic visage recalls the "fire-red Cherubimme's face," which added such horror to the height and stature of Chaucer's Sompnour. In both these cases even the riotous and absurd characters are a little touched with the tint of the whole story. But this neglected merit of Dickens can certainly be seen best in *The Old Curiosity Shop*.

The curiosity shop itself was a lumber of grotesque and sinister things, outlandish weapons, twisted and diabolic decorations. The comic characters in the book are all like images bought in an old curiosity shop. Quilp might be a gargoyle. He might be some sort of devilish door-knocker, dropped down and crawling about the pavement. The same applies to the sinister and really terrifying stiffness of Sally Brass. She is like some old staring figure cut out of wood. Sampson Brass, her brother, again is a grotesque in the same rather inhuman manner; he is especially himself when he comes in with the green shade over his eye. About all this group of bad figures in *The Old Curiosity Shop* there is a sort of *diablerie*. There is also within this atmosphere an extraordinary energy of irony and laughter. The scene in which Sampson Brass draws up the description of Quilp, supposing him to be dead, reaches a point of fiendish fun. "We will not say very bandy, Mrs. Jiniwin," he says of his friend's legs, "we will confine ourselves to bandy. He is gone, my friends, where his legs would never be called in question." They go on to the discussion of his nose, and Mrs. Jiniwin inclines to the view that it is flat. "Aquiline, you hag! Aquiline," cries Mr. Quilp, pushing in his head and striking his nose with his fist. There is nothing better in the whole brutal exuberance of the character than that gesture with which Quilp punches his own face with his own fist. It is indeed a perfect symbol; for Quilp is always fighting himself for want of anybody else. He is energy, and energy by itself is always suicidal; he is that primordial energy which tears and which destroys itself.

Barnaby Rudge

Barnaby Rudge was written by Dickens in the spring and first flowing tide of his popularity; it came immediately after *The Old Curiosity Shop*, and only a short time after *Pickwick*. Dickens was one of those rare but often very sincere men in whom the high moment of success almost coincides with the high moment of youth. The calls upon him at this time were insistent and overwhelming; this necessarily happens at a certain stage of a successful writer's career. He was just successful enough to invite offers and not successful enough to reject them. At the beginning of his career he could throw himself into *Pickwick* because there was nothing else to throw himself into. At the end of his life he could throw himself into *A Tale of Two Cities*, because he refused to throw himself into anything else. But there was an intervening period, early in his life, when there was almost too much work for his imagination, and yet not quite enough work for his housekeeping. To this period *Barnaby Rudge* belongs. And it is a curious tribute to the quite curious greatness of Dickens that in this period of youthful strain we do not feel the strain but feel only the youth. His own amazing wish to write equalled or outstripped even his readers' amazing wish to read. Working too hard did not cure him of his abstract love of work. Unreasonable publishers asked him to write ten novels at once; but he wanted to write twenty novels at once. All this period is strangely full of his own sense at once of fertility and of futility; he did work which no one else could have done, and yet he could not be certain as yet that he was anybody.

Barnaby Rudge marks this epoch because it marks the fact that he is still confused about what kind of person he is going to be. He has already struck the note of the normal romance in *Nicholas Nickleby*; he has already created some of his highest comic characters in *Pickwick* and *The Old Curiosity Shop*, but here he betrays the fact that it is still a question what ultimate guide he shall follow. *Barnaby Rudge* is a romantic, historical novel. Its design reminds us of Scott; some parts of its fulfilment remind us, alas! of Harrison Ainsworth. It is a very fine romantic historical novel; Scott would have been proud of it. But it is still so far different from the general work of Dickens that it is permissible to wonder how far Dickens was proud of it. The book, effective as it is, is almost entirely devoted to dealings with a certain artistic element, which (in its mere isolation) Dickens did not commonly affect; an element which many men of infinitely less genius have often seemed to affect more successfully; I mean the element of the picturesque.

It is the custom in many quarters to speak somewhat sneeringly of that element which is broadly called the picturesque. It is always felt to be an inferior, a vulgar, and even an artificial form of art. Yet two things may be remarked about it. The first is that, with few exceptions, the greatest literary artists have been not only particularly clever at the picturesque, but particularly fond of it. Shakespeare, for instance, delighted in certain merely pictorial contrasts which are quite distinct from, even when they are akin to, the spiritual view involved. For instance, there is admirable satire in the idea of Touchstone teaching worldly wisdom and worldly honour to the woodland yokels. There is excellent philosophy in the idea of the fool being the representative of civilisation in the forest. But quite apart from this deeper meaning in the incident, the mere figure of the jester, in his bright motley and his cap and bells, against the green background of the forest and the rude forms of the shepherds, is a strong example of the purely picturesque. There is excellent tragic irony in the confrontation of the melancholy philosopher among the tombs with the cheerful digger of the graves. It sums up the essential point, that dead bodies can be comic; it is only dead souls that can be tragic. But quite apart from such irony, the mere picture of the grotesque gravedigger, the black-clad prince, and the skull is a picture in the strongest sense picturesque. Caliban and the two shipwrecked drunkards are an admirable symbol; but they are also an admirable scene. Bottom, with the ass's head, sitting in a ring of elves, is excellent moving comedy, but also excellent still life. Falstaff with his huge body, Bardolph with his burning nose, are masterpieces of the pen; but they would be fine sketches even for the pencil. King Lear, in the storm, is a landscape as well as a character study. There is something decorative even about the insistence on the swarthiness of Othello, or the deformity of Richard 3. Shakespeare's work is much more than picturesque; but it is picturesque. And the same which is said here of him by way of example is largely true of the highest class of literature. Dante's *Divine Comedy* is supremely important as a philosophy; but it is important merely as a panorama. Spenser's *Faery Queen* pleases us as an allegory; but it would please us even as a wall-paper. Stronger still is the case of Chaucer who loved the pure picturesque, which always includes something of what we commonly call the ugly. The huge stature and startling scarlet face of the Sompnour is in just the same spirit as Shakespeare's skulls and motley; the same spirit gave Chaucer's miller bagpipes, and clad his doctor in crimson. It is the spirit which, while making many other things, loves to make a picture.

Now the second thing to be remarked in apology for the picturesque is, that the very thing which makes it seem trivial ought really to make it seem important; I mean the fact that it consists necessarily of contrasts. It brings together types that stand out from their background, but are abruptly different from each other, like the clown among the fairies or the fool in the forest. And his audacious reconciliation is a mark not of frivolity but of extreme seriousness. A man who deals in harmonies, who only matches stars with angels or lambs with spring flowers, he indeed may be frivolous; for he is taking one mood at a time, and perhaps forgetting each mood as it passes. But a man who ventures to combine an angel and an octopus must have some serious view of the universe. The man who should write a dialogue between two early Christians might be a mere writer of dialogues. But a man who should write a dialogue between an early Christian and the Missing Link would have to be a philosopher. The more widely different the types talked of, the more serious and universal must be the philosophy which talks of them. The mark of the light and thoughtless writer is the harmony of his subject matter; the mark of the thoughtful writer is its apparent diversity. The most flippant lyric poet might write a pretty poem about lambs; but it requires something bolder and graver than a poet, it requires an ecstatic prophet, to talk about the lion lying down with the lamb.

Dickens, at any rate, strongly supports this conception: that great literary men as such do not despise the purely pictorial. No man's works have so much the quality of illustrating themselves. Few men's works have been more thoroughly and eagerly illustrated; few men's works can it have been better fun to illustrate. As a rule this fascinating quality in the mere fantastic figures of the tale was inseparable from their farcical quality in the tale. Stiggins's red nose is distinctly connected with the fact that he is a member of the Ebenezer Temperance Association; Quilp is little, because a little of him goes a long way. Mr. Carker smiles and smiles and is a villain; Mr. Chadband is fat because in his case to be fat is to be hated. The story is immeasurably more important than the picture; it is not mere indulgence in the picturesque. Generally it is an intellectual love of the comic; not a pure love of the grotesque.

But in one book Dickens suddenly confesses that he likes the grotesque even without the comic. In one case he makes clear that he enjoys pure pictures with a pure love of the picturesque. That place is *Barnaby Rudge*. There had indeed been hints of it in many episodes in his books; notably, for example, in that fine scene of the death of Quilp—a scene in which the dwarf remains fantastic long after he has ceased to be in any way funny. Still, the dwarf was meant to be funny. Humour of a horrible kind, but still humour, is the purpose of Quilp's existence and position in the book. Laughter is the object of all his oddities. But laughter is not the object of Barnaby Rudge's oddities. His idiot costume and his ugly raven are used for the purpose of the pure grotesque; solely to make a certain kind of Gothic sketch.

It is commonly this love of pictures that drives men back upon the historical novel. But it is very typical of Dickens's living interest in his own time, that though he wrote two historical novels they were neither of them of very ancient history. They were both, indeed, of very recent history; only they were those parts of recent history which were specially picturesque. I do not think that this was due to any mere consciousness on his part that he knew no history. Undoubtedly he knew no history; and he may or may not have been conscious of the fact. But the consciousness did not prevent him from writing a *History of England*. Nor did it prevent him from interlarding all or any of his works with tales of the pictorial past, such as the tale of the broken swords in *Master Humphrey's Clock*, or the indefensibly delightful nightmare of the lady in the stage-coach, which helps to soften the amiable end of Pickwick. Neither, worst of all, did it prevent him from dogmatising anywhere and everywhere about the past, of which he knew nothing; it did not prevent him from telling the bells to tell Trotty Veck that the Middle Ages were a failure, nor from solemnly declaring that the best thing that the mediæval monks ever did was to create the mean and snobbish quietude of a modern cathedral city. No, it was not historical reverence that held him back from dealing with the remote past; but rather something much better —a living interest in the living century in which he was born. He would have thought himself quite intellectually capable of writing a novel about the Council of Trent or the First Crusade. He would have thought himself quite equal to analysing the psychology of Abelard or giving a bright, satiric sketch of St. Augustine. It must frankly be confessed that it was not a sense of his own unworthiness that held him back; I fear it was rather a sense of St. Augustine's unworthiness. He could not see the point of any history before the first slow swell of the French Revolution. He could understand the revolutions of the eighteenth century; all the other revolutions of history (so many and so splendid) were unmeaning to him. But the revolutions of the eighteenth century he did understand; and to them therefore he went back, as all historical novelists go back, in search of the picturesque. And from this fact an important result follows.

The result that follows is this: that his only two historical novels are both tales of revolutions-of eighteenth-century revolutions. These two eighteenth-century revolutions may seem to differ, and perhaps do differ in everything except in being revolutions and of the eighteenth century. The French Revolution, which is the theme of *A Tale of Two Cities*, was a revolt in favour of all that is now called enlightenment and liberation. The great Gordon Riot, which is the theme of *Barnaby Rudge*, was a revolt in favour of something which would now be called mere ignorant and obscurantist Protestantism. Nevertheless both belonged more typically to the age out of which Dickens came-the great sceptical and yet creative eighteenth century of Europe. Whether the mob rose on the right side or the wrong they both belonged to the time in which a mob could rise, in which a mob could conquer. No growth of intellectual science or of moral cowardice had made it impossible to fight in the streets, whether for the republic or for the Bible. If we wish to know what was the real link, existing actually in ultimate truth, existing unconsciously in Dickens's mind, which connected the Gordon Riots with the French Revolution, the link may be defined though not with any great adequacy. The nearest and truest way of stating it is that neither of the two could possibly happen in Fleet Street to-morrow evening.

Another point of resemblance between the two books might be found in the fact that they both contain the sketch of the same kind of eighteenth-century aristocrat, if indeed that kind of aristocrat really existed in the eighteenth century. The diabolical dandy with the rapier and the sneer is at any rate a necessity of all normal plays and romances; hence Mr. Chester has a right to exist in this romance, and Foulon a right to exist in a page of history almost as cloudy and disputable as a romance. What Dickens and other romancers do probably omit from the picture of the eighteenth-century oligarch is probably his liberality. It must never be forgotten that even when he was a despot in practice he was generally a liberal in theory. Dickens and romancers make the pre-revolution tyrant a sincere believer in tyranny; generally he was not. He was a sceptic about everything, even about his own position. The romantic Foulon says of the people, "Let them eat grass," with bitter and deliberate contempt. The real Foulon (if he ever said it at all) probably said it as a sort of dreary joke because he couldn't think of any other way out of the problem. Similarly Mr. Chester, a cynic as he is, believes seriously in the beauty of being a gentleman; a real man of that type probably disbelieved in that as in everything else. Dickens was too bracing, one may say too bouncing himself to understand the psychology of fatigue in a protected and leisured class. He could understand a tyrant like Quilp, a tyrant who is on his throne because he has climbed up into it, like a monkey. He could not understand a tyrant who is on his throne because he is too weary to get out of it. The old aristocrats were in a dead way quite good-natured. They were even humanitarians; which perhaps accounts for the extent to which they roused against themselves the healthy hatred of humanity. But they were tired humanitarians; tired with doing nothing. Figures like that of Mr. Chester, therefore, fail somewhat to give the true sense of something hopeless and helpless which led men to despair of the upper class. He has a boyish pleasure in play-acting; he has an interest in life; being a villain is his hobby. But the true man of that type had found all hobbies fail him. He had wearied of himself as he had wearied of a hundred women. He was graceful and could not even admire himself in the glass. He was witty and could not even laugh at his own jokes. Dickens could never understand tedium.

There is no mark more strange and perhaps sinister of the interesting and not very sane condition of our modern literature, than the fact that tedium has been admirably described in it. Our best modern writers are never so exciting as they are about dulness. Mr. Rudyard Kipling is never so powerful as when he is painting yawning deserts, aching silences, sleepless nights, or infernal isolation. The excitement in one of the stories of Mr. Henry James becomes tense, thrilling, and almost intolerable in all the half hours during which nothing whatever is said or done. We are entering again into the mind, into the real mind of Foulon and Mr. Chester. We begin to understand the deep despair of those tyrants whom our fathers pulled down. But Dickens could never have understood that despair; it was not in his soul. And it is an interesting coincidence that here, in this book of *Barnaby Rudge*, there is a character meant to be wholly grotesque, who, nevertheless, expresses much of that element in Dickens which prevented him from being a true interpreter of the tired and sceptical aristocrat.

Sim Tappertit is a fool, but a perfectly honourable fool. It requires some sincerity to pose. Posing means that one has not dried up in oneself all the youthful and innocent vanities with the slow paralysis of mere pride. Posing means that one is still fresh enough to enjoy the good opinion of one's fellows. On the other hand, the true cynic has not enough truth in him to attempt affectation; he has never even seen the truth, far less tried to imitate it. Now we might very well take the type of Mr. Chester on the one hand, and of Sim Tappertit on the other, as marking the issue, the conflict, and the victory which really ushered in the nineteenth century. Dickens was very like Sim Tappertit. The Liberal Revolution was very like a Sim Tappertit revolution. It was vulgar, it was overdone, it was absurd, but it was alive. Dickens was vulgar, was absurd, overdid everything, but he was alive. The aristocrats were perfectly correct, but quite dead; dead long before they were guillotined. The classics and critics who lamented that Dickens was no gentleman were quite right, but quite dead. The revolution thought itself rational; but so did Sim Tappertit. It was really a huge revolt of romanticism against a reason which had grown sick even of itself. Sim Tappertit rose against Mr. Chester; and, thank God! he put his foot upon his neck.

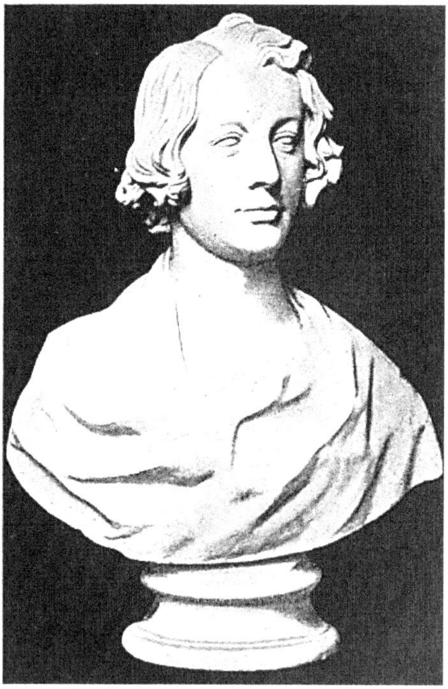

American Notes

American Notes was written soon after Dickens had returned from his first visit to America. That visit had, of course, been a great epoch in his life; but how much of an epoch men did not truly realise until, some time after, in the middle of a quiet story about Salisbury and a ridiculous architect, his feelings flamed out and flared up to the stars in *Martin Chuzzlewit*. The *American Notes* are, however, interesting, because in them he betrays his feelings when he does not know that he is betraying them. Dickens's first visit to America was, from his own point of view, and at the beginning, a happy and festive experiment. It is very characteristic of him that he went among the Americans, enjoyed them, even admired them, and then had a quarrel with them. Nothing was ever so unmistakable as his good-will, except his ill-will; and they were never far apart. And this was not, as some bloodless moderns have sneeringly insinuated, a mere repetition of the proximity between the benevolent stage and the quarrelsome stage of drink. It was a piece of pure optimism; he believed so readily that men were going to be good to him that an injury to him was something more than an injury: it was a shock. What was the exact nature of the American shock must, however, be more carefully stated.

The famous quarrel between Dickens and America, which finds its most elaborate expression in *American Notes*, though its most brilliant expression in *Martin Chuzzlewit*, is an incident about which a great deal remains to be said. But the thing which most specially remains to be said is this. This old Anglo-American quarrel was much more fundamentally friendly than most Anglo-American alliances. In Dickens's day each nation understood the other enough to argue. In our time neither nation understands itself even enough to quarrel. There was an English tradition, from Fox and eighteenth-century England; there was an American tradition from Franklin and eighteenth-century America; and they were still close enough together to discuss their differences with acrimony, perhaps, but with certain fundamental understandings. The eighteenth-century belief in a liberal civilisation was still a dogma; for dogma is the only thing that makes argument or reasoning possible. America, under all its swagger, did still really believe that Europe was its fountain and its mother, because Europe was more fully civilised. Dickens, under all his disgust, did still believe that America was in advance of Europe, because it was more democratic. It was an age, in short, in which the word "progress" could still be used reasonably; because the whole world looked to one way of escape and there was only one kind of progress under discussion. Now, of course, "progress" is a useless word; for progress takes for granted an already defined direction; and it is exactly about the direction that we disagree. Do not let us therefore be misled into any mistaken optimism or special self-congratulation upon what many people would call the improved relations between England and America. The relations are improved because America has finally become a foreign country. And with foreign countries all sane men take care to exchange a certain consideration and courtesy. But even as late as the time of Dickens's first visit to the United States, we English still felt America as a colony; an insolent, offensive, and even unintelligible colony sometimes, but still a colony; a part of our civilisation, a limb of our life. And America itself, as I have said, under all its bounce and independence, really regarded us as a mother country. This being the case it was possible for us to quarrel, like kinsmen. Now we only bow and smile, like strangers.

This tone, as a sort of family responsibility, can be felt quite specially all through the satires or suggestions of these *American Notes*. Dickens is cross with America because he is worried about America; as if he were its father. He explores its industrial, legal, and educational arrangements like a mother looking at the housekeeping of a married son; he makes suggestions with a certain acidity; he takes a strange pleasure in being pessimistic. He advises them to take note of how much better certain things are done in England. All this is very different from Dickens's characteristic way of dealing with a foreign country. In countries really foreign, such as France, Switzerland, and Italy, he had two attitudes, neither of them in the least worried or paternal. When he found a thing in Europe which he did not understand, such as the Roman Catholic Church, he simply called it an old-world superstition, and sat looking at it like a moonlit ruin. When he found something that he did understand, such as luncheon baskets, he burst into carols of praise over the superior sense in our civilisation and good management to Continental methods. An example of the first attitude may be found in one of his letters, in which he describes the backwardness and idleness of Catholics who would not build a Birmingham in Italy. He seems quite unconscious of the obvious truth, that the backwardness of Catholics was simply the refusal of Bob Cratchit to enter the house of Gradgrind. An example of the second attitude can be found in the purple patches of fun in *Mugby Junction*; in which the English waitress denounces the profligate French habit of providing new bread and clean food for people travelling by rail. The point is, however, that in neither case has he the air of one suggesting improvements or sharing a problem with the people engaged on it. He does not go carefully with a notebook through Jesuit schools nor offer friendly suggestions to the governors of Parisian prisons. Or if he does, it is in a different spirit; it is in the spirit of an ordinary tourist being shown over the Coliseum or the Pyramids. But he visited America in the spirit of a Government inspector dealing with something it was his duty to inspect. This is never felt either in his praise or blame of Continental countries. When he did not leave a foreign country to decay like a dead dog, he merely watched it at play like a kitten. France he mistook for a kitten. Italy he mistook for a dead dog.

But with America he could feel-and fear. There he could hate, because he could love. There he could feel not the past alone nor the present, but the future also; and, like all brave men, when he saw the future he was a little afraid of it. For of all tests by which the good citizen and strong reformer can be distinguished from the vague faddist or the inhuman sceptic, 1 know no better test than this-that the unreal reformer sees in front of him one certain future, the future of his fad; while the real reformer sees before him ten or twenty futures among which his country must choose, and may, in some dreadful hour, choose the wrong one. The true patriot is always doubtful of victory; because he knows that he is dealing with a living thing; a thing with free will. To be certain of free will is to be uncertain of success.

The subject matter of the real difference of opinion between Dickens and the public of America can only be understood if it is thus treated as a dispute between brothers about the destiny of a common heritage. The point at issue might be stated like this. Dickens, on his side, did not in his heart doubt for a moment that England would eventually follow America along the road towards real political equality and purely republican institutions. He lived, it must be remembered, before the revival of aristocracy, which has since overwhelmed us-the revival of aristocracy worked through popular science and commercial dictatorship, and which has nowhere been more manifest than in America itself. He knew nothing of this; in his heart he conceded to the Yankees that not only was their revolution right but would ultimately be completed everywhere. But on the other hand, his whole point against the American experiment was this-that if it ignored certain ancient English contributions it would go to pieces for lack of them. Of these the first was good manners and the second individual liberty-liberty, that is, to speak and write against the trend of the majority. In these things he was much more serious and much more sensible than it is the fashion to think he was; he was indeed one of the most serious and sensible critics England ever had of current and present problems, though his criticism is useless to the point of nonentity about all things remote from him in style of civilisation or in time. His point about good manners is really important. All his grumblings through this book of *American Notes*, all his shrieking satire in *Martin Chuzzlewit* are expressions of a grave and reasonable fear he had touching the future of democracy. And remember again what has been already remarked-instinctively he paid America the compliment of looking at her as the future of democracy.

The mistake which he attacked still exists. I cannot imagine why it is that social equality is somehow supposed to mean social familiarity. Why should equality mean that all men are equally rude? Should it not rather mean that all men are equally polite? Might it not quite reasonably mean that all men should be equally ceremonious and stately and pontifical? What is there specially Equalitarian, for instance, in calling your political friends and even your political enemies by their Christian names in public? There is something very futile in the way in which certain Socialist leaders call each other Tom, Dick, and Harry; especially when Tom is accusing Harry of having basely imposed upon the well-known imbecility of Dick. There is something quite undemocratic in all men calling each other by the special and affectionate term "comrade"; especially when they say it with a sneer and smart inquiry about the funds. Democracy would be quite satisfied if every man called every other man "sir." Democracy would have no conceivable reason to complain if every man called every other man "your excellency" or "your holiness" or "brother of the sun and moon." The only democratic essential is that it should be a term of dignity and that it should be given to all. To abolish all terms of dignity is no more specially democratic than the Roman emperor's wish to cut off everybody's head at once was specially democratic. That involved equality certainly, but it was lacking in respect.

Dickens saw America as markedly the seat of this danger. He saw that there was a perilous possibility that republican ideals might be allied to a social anarchy good neither for them nor for any other ideals. Republican simplicity, which is difficult, might be quickly turned into Bohemian brutality, which is easy. Cincinnatus, instead of putting his hand to the plough, might put his feet on the tablecloth, and an impression prevail that it was all a part of the same rugged equality and freedom. Insolence might become a tradition. Bad manners might have all the sanctity of good manners. "There you are!" cries Martin Chuzzlewit indignantly, when the American has befouled the butter. "A man deliberately makes a hog of himself and *that* is an Institution." But the thread of thought which we must always keep in hand in this matter is that he would not thus have worried about the degradation of republican simplicity into general rudeness if he had not from first to last instinctively felt that America held human democracy in her hand, to exalt it or to let it fall. In one of his gloomier moments he wrote down his fear that the greatest blow ever struck at liberty would be struck by America in the failure of her mission upon the earth.

This brings us to the other ground of his alarm-the matter of liberty of speech. Here also he was much more reasonable and philosophic than has commonly been realised. The truth is that the lurid individualism of Carlyle has, with its violent colours, "killed" the tones of most criticism of his time; and just as we can often see a scheme of decoration better if we cover some flaming picture, so you can judge nineteenth-century England much better if you leave Carlyle out. He is important to moderns because he led that return to Toryism which has been the chief feature of modernity, but his judgments were often not only spiritually false, but really quite superficial. Dickens understood the danger of democracy far better than Carlyle; just as he understood the merits of democracy far better than Carlyle. And of this fact we can produce one plain evidence in the matter of which we speak. Carlyle, in his general dislike of the revolutionary movement, lumped liberty and democracy together and said that the chief objection to democracy was that it involved the excess and misuse of liberty; he called democracy "anarchy or no-rule." Dickens, with far more philosophical insight and spiritual delicacy, saw that the real danger of democracy is that it tends to the very opposite of anarchy; even to the very opposite of liberty. He lamented in America the freedom of manners. But he lamented even more the absence of freedom of opinion. "I believe there is no country on the face of the earth," he says, "where there is less freedom of opinion on any subject in reference to which there is a broad difference of opinion than in this. There! I write the words with reluctance, disappointment, and sorrow; but I believe it from the bottom of my soul. The notion that I, a man alone by myself in America, should venture to suggest to the Americans that there was one point on which they were neither just to their own countrymen nor to us, actually struck the boldest dumb! Washington Irving, Prescott, Hoffman, Bryant, Halleck, Dana, Washington Allston-every man who writes in this country is devoted to the question, and not one of them *dares* to raise his voice and complain of the atrocious state of the law. The wonder is that a breathing man can be found with temerity enough to suggest to the Americans the possibility of their having done wrong. I wish you could have seen the faces that I saw down both sides of the table at Hartford when I began to talk about Scott. I wish you could have heard how I gave it out. My blood so boiled when I thought of the monstrous injustice that I felt as if I were twelve feet high when I thrust it down their throats." Dickens knew no history, but he had all history behind him in feeling that a pure democracy does tend, when it goes wrong, to be too traditional and absolute. The truth is indeed a singular example of the unfair attack upon democracy in our own time. Everybody can repeat the platitude that the mob can be the greatest of all tyrants. But few realise or remember the corresponding truth which goes along with it-that the mob is the only permanent and unassailable high priest. Democracy drives its traditions too hard; but democracy is the only thing that keeps any traditions. An aristocracy must always be going after some new thing. The severity of democracy is far more of a virtue than its liberty. The decorum of a democracy is far more of a danger than its lawlessness. Dickens discovered this in his great quarrels about the copyright, when a whole nation acted on a small point of opinion as if it were going to lynch him. But, fortunately for the purpose of this argument, there is no need to go back to the forties for such a case. Another great literary man has of late visited America; and it is possible that Maxim Gorky may be in a position to state how far democracy is likely to err on the side of mere liberty and laxity. He may have found, like Dickens, some freedom of manners; he did not find much freedom of morals.

Along with such American criticism should really go his very characteristic summary of the question of the Red Indian. It marks the combination between the mental narrowness and the moral justice of the old Liberal. Dickens can see nothing in the Red Indian except that he is barbaric, retrograde, bellicose, uncleanly, and superstitious-in short, that he is not a member of the special civilisation of Birmingham or Brighton. It is curious to note the contrast between the cheery, nay Cockney, contempt with which Dickens speaks of the American Indian and that chivalrous and pathetic essay in which Washington Irving celebrates the virtues of the vanishing race. Between Washington Irving and his friend Charles Dickens there was always indeed this ironical comedy of inversion. It is amusing that the Englishman should have been the pushing and even pert modernist, and the American the stately antiquarian and lover of lost causes. But while a man of more mellow sympathies may well dislike Dickens's dislike of savages, and even disdain his disdain, he ought to sharply remind himself of the admirable ethical fairness and equity which meet with that restricted outlook. In the very act of describing Red Indians as devils who, like so much dirt, it would pay us to sweep away, he pauses to deny emphatically that we have any right to sweep them away. We have no right to wrong the man, he means to say, even if he himself be a kind of wrong. Here we strike the ringing iron of the old conscience and sense of honour which marked the best men of his party and of his epoch. This rigid and even reluctant justice towers, at any rate, far above modern views of savages, above the sentimentalism of the mere humanitarian and the far weaker sentimentalism that pleads for brutality and a race war. Dickens was at least more of a man than the brutalitarian who claims to wrong people because they are nasty, or the humanitarian who cannot be just to them without pretending that they are nice.

Pictures from Italy

The *Pictures from Italy* are excellent in themselves and excellent as a foil to the *American Notes*. Here we have none of that air of giving a decision like a judge or sending in a report like an inspector; here we have only glimpses, light and even fantastic glimpses, of a world that is really alien to Dickens. It is so alien that he can almost entirely enjoy it. For no man can entirely enjoy that which he loves; contentment is always unpatriotic. The difference can indeed be put with approximate perfection in one phrase. In Italy he was on a holiday; in America he was on a tour. But indeed Dickens himself has quite sufficiently conveyed the difference in the two phrases that he did actually use for the titles of the two books. Dickens often told unconscious truths, especially in small matters. The *American Notes* really are notes, like the notes of a student or a professional witness. The *Pictures from Italy* are only pictures from Italy, like the miscellaneous pictures that all tourists bring from Italy.

To take another and perhaps closer figure of speech, almost all Dickens's works such as these may best be regarded as private letters addressed to the public. His private correspondence was quite as brilliant as his public works; and many of his public works are almost as formless and casual as his private correspondence. If he had been struck insensible for a year, I really think that his friends and family could have brought out one of his best books by themselves if they had happened to keep his letters. The homogeneity of his public and private work was indeed strange in many ways. On the one hand, there was little that was pompously and unmistakably public in the publications; on the other hand, there was very little that was private in the private letters. His hilarity had almost a kind of hardness about it; no man's letters, I should think, ever needed less expurgation on the ground of weakness or undue confession. The main part, and certainly the best part, of such a book as *Pictures from Italy* can certainly be criticised best as part of that perpetual torrent of entertaining autobiography which he flung at his children as if they were his readers and his readers as if they were his children. There are some brilliant patches of sense and nonsense in this book; but there is always something accidental in them; as if they might have occurred somewhere else. Perhaps the most attractive of them is the incomparable description of the Italian Marionette Theatre in which they acted a play about the death of Napoleon in St. Helena. The description is better than that of Codlin and Short's Punch and Judy, and almost as good as that of Mrs. Jarley's Wax Works. Indeed the humour is similar; for Punch is supposed to be funny, but Napoleon (as Mrs. Jarley said when asked if her show was funnier than Punch) was not funny at all. The idea of a really tragic scene being enacted between tiny wooden dolls with large heads is delightfully dealt with by Dickens. We can almost imagine the scene in which the wooden Napoleon haughtily rebukes his wooden jailor for calling him General Bonaparte —"Sir Hudson Low, call me not thus; I am Napoleon, Emperor of the French." There is also something singularly gratifying about the scene of Napoleon's death, in which he lay in bed with his little wooden hands outside the counterpane and the doctor (who was hung on wires too short) "delivered medical opinions in the air." It may seem flippant to dwell on such flippancies in connection with a book which contains many romantic descriptions and many moral generalisations which Dickens probably valued highly. But it is not for such things that he is valued. In all his writings, from his most reasoned and sustained novel to his maddest private note, it is always this obstreperous instinct for farce which stands out as his in the highest sense. His wisdom is at the best talent, his foolishness is genius. Just that exuberant levity which we associate with a moment we associate in his case with immortality. It is said of certain old masonry that the mortar was so hard that it has survived the stones. So if Dickens could revisit the thing he built, he would be surprised to see all the work he thought solid and responsible wasted almost utterly away, but the shortest frivolities and the most momentary jokes remaining like colossal rocks for ever.

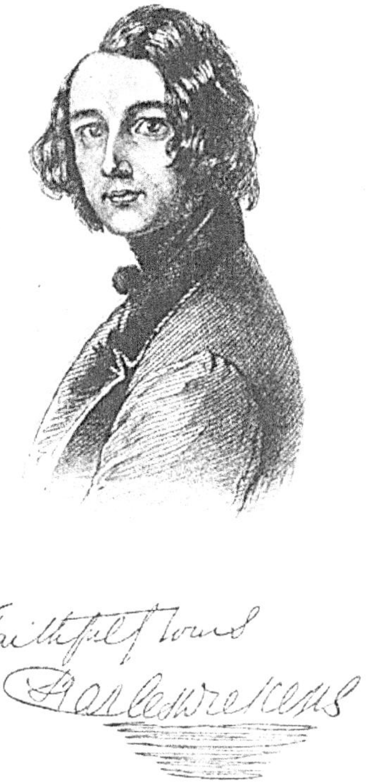
Faithfully Yours

Martin Chuzzlewit

There is a certain quality or element which broods over the whole of *Martin Chuzzlewit* to which it is difficult for either friends or foes to put a name. I think the reader who enjoys Dickens's other books has an impression that it is a kind of melancholy. There are grotesque figures of the most gorgeous kind; there are scenes that are farcical even by the standard of the farcical license of Dickens; there is humour both of the heaviest and of the lightest kind; there are two great comic personalities who run like a rich vein through the whole story, Pecksniff and Mrs. Gamp; there is one blinding patch of brilliancy, the satire on American cant; there is Todgers's boarding-house; there is Bailey; there is Mr. Mould, the incomparable undertaker. But yet in spite of everything, in spite even of the undertaker, the book is sad. No one I think ever went to it in that mixed mood of a tired tenderness and a readiness to believe and laugh in which most of Dickens's novels are most enjoyed. We go for a particular novel to Dickens as we go for a particular inn. We go to the sign of the Pickwick Papers. We go to the sign of the Rudge and Raven. We go to the sign of the Old Curiosities. We go to the sign of the Two Cities. We go to each or all of them according to what kind of hospitality and what kind of happiness we require. But it is always some kind of hospitality and some kind of happiness that we require. And as in the case of inns we also remember that while there was shelter in all and food in all and some kind of fire and some kind of wine in all, yet one has left upon us an indescribable and unaccountable memory of mortality and decay, of dreariness in the rooms and even of tastelessness in the banquet. So any one who has enjoyed the stories of Dickens as they should be enjoyed has a nameless feeling that this one story is sad and almost sodden. Dickens himself had this feeling, though his breezy vanity forbade him to express it in so many words. In spite of Pecksniff, in spite of Mrs. Gamp, in spite of the yet greater Bailey, the story went lumberingly and even lifelessly; he found the sales falling off; he fancied his popularity waning, and by a sudden impulse most inartistic and yet most artistic, he dragged in the episode of Martin's visit to America, which is the blazing jewel and the sudden redemption of the book. He wrote it at an uneasy and unhappy period of his life; when he had ceased wandering in America, but could not cease wandering altogether; when he had lost his original routine of work which was violent but regular, and had not yet settled down to the full enjoyment of his success and his later years. He poured into this book genius that might make the mountains laugh, invention that juggled with the stars. But the book was sad; and he knew it.

The just reason for this is really interesting. Yet it is one that is not easy to state without guarding one's self on the one side or the other against great misunderstandings; and these stipulations or preliminary allowances must in such a case as this of necessity be made first. Dickens was among other things a satirist, a pure satirist. I have never been able to understand why this title is always specially and sacredly reserved for Thackeray. Thackeray was a novelist; in the strict and narrow sense at any rate, Thackeray was a far greater novelist than Dickens. But Dickens certainly was the satirist. The essence of satire is that it perceives some absurdity inherent in the logic of some position, and that it draws that absurdity out and isolates it, so that all can see it. Thus for instance when Dickens says, "Lord Coodle would go out; Sir Thomas Doodle wouldn't come in; and there being no people to speak of in England except Coodle and Doodle the country has been without a Government"; when Dickens says this he suddenly pounces on and plucks out the one inherent absurdity in the English party system which is hidden behind all its paraphernalia of Parliaments and Statutes, elections and ballot papers. When all the dignity and all the patriotism and all the public interest of the English constitutional party conflict have been fully allowed for, there does remain the bold, bleak question which Dickens in substance asks, "Suppose I want somebody else who is neither Coodle nor Doodle." This is the great quality called satire; it is a kind of taunting reasonableness; and it is inseparable from a certain insane logic which is often called exaggeration. Dickens was more of a satirist than Thackeray for this simple reason: that Thackeray carried a man's principles as far as that man carried them; Dickens carried a man's principles as far as a man's principles would go. Dickens in short (as people put it) exaggerated the man and his principles; that is to say he emphasised them. Dickens drew a man's absurdity out of him; Thackeray left a man's absurdity in him. Of this last fact we can take any example we like; take for instance the comparison between the city man as treated by Thackeray in the most satiric of his novels, with the city man as treated by Dickens in one of the mildest and maturest of his. Compare the character of old Mr. Osborne in *Vanity Fair* with the character of Mr. Podsnap in *Our Mutual Friend*. In the case of Mr. Osborne there is nothing except the solid blocking in of a brutal dull convincing character. *Vanity Fair* is not a satire on the City except in so far as it happens to be true. *Vanity Fair* is not a satire on the City, in short, except in so far as the City is a satire on the City. But Mr. Podsnap is a pure satire; he is an extracting out of the City man of those purely intellectual qualities which happen to make that kind of City man a particularly exasperating fool. One might almost say that Mr. Podsnap is all Mr. Osborne's opinions separated from Mr. Osborne and turned into a character. In short the satirist is more purely philosophical than the novelist. The novelist may be only an observer; the satirist must be a thinker. He must be a thinker, he must be a philosophical thinker for this simple reason; that he exercises his philosophical thought in deciding what part of his subject he is to satirise. You may have the dullest possible intelligence and be a portrait painter; but a man must have a serious intellect in order to be a caricaturist. He has to select what thing he will caricature. True satire is always of this intellectual kind; true satire is always, so to speak, a variation or fantasia upon the air of pure logic. The satirist is the man who carries men's enthusiasm further than they carry it themselves. He outstrips the most extravagant fanatic. He is years ahead of the most audacious prophet. He sees where men's detached intellect will eventually lead them, and he tells them the name of the place-which is generally hell.

Now of this detached and rational use of satire there is one great example in this book. Even *Gulliver's Travels* is hardly more reasonable than Martin Chuzzlewit's travels in the incredible land of the Americans. Before considering the humour of this description in its more exhaustive and liberal aspects, it may be first remarked that in this American part of *Martin Chuzzlewit*, Dickens quite specially sharpens up his own more controversial and political intelligence. There are more things here than anywhere else in Dickens that partake of the nature of pamphleteering, of positive challenge, of sudden repartee, of pugnacious and exasperating query, in a word of everything that belongs to the pure art of controversy as distinct not only from the pure art of fiction but even also from the pure art of satire. I am inclined to think (to put the matter not only shortly but clumsily) that Dickens was never in all his life so strictly clever as he is in the American part of *Martin Chuzzlewit*. There are places where he was more inspired, almost in the sense of being intoxicated, as, for instance, in the Micawber feasts of *David Copperfield*; there are places where he wrote more carefully and cunningly, as, for instance, in the mystery of *The Mystery of Edwin Drood*; there are places where he wrote very much more humanly, more close to the ground and to growing things, as in the whole of that admirable book *Great Expectations*. But I do not think that his mere abstract acuteness and rapidity of thought were ever exercised with such startling exactitude as they are in this place in *Martin Chuzzlewit*. It is to be noted, for instance, that his American experience had actually worked him up to a heat and habit of argument. A slave-owner in the Southern States tells Dickens that slave-owners do not ill-treat their slaves, that it is not to the interest of slave-owners to ill-treat their slaves. Dickens flashes back that it is not to the interest of a man to get drunk, but he does get drunk. This pugnacious atmosphere of parry and riposte must first of all be allowed for and understood in all the satiric excursus of Martin in America. Dickens is arguing all the time; and, to do him justice, arguing very well. These chapters are full not merely of exuberant satire on America in the sense that Dotheboys Hall or Mr. Bumble's Workhouse are exuberant satires on England. They are full also of sharp argument with America as if the man who wrote expected retort and was prepared with rejoinder. The rest of the book, like the rest of Dickens's books, possesses humour. This part of the book, like hardly any of Dickens's books, possesses wit. The republican gentleman who receives Martin on landing is horrified on hearing an English servant speak of the employer as "the master." "There are no masters in America," says the gentleman. "All owners are they?" says Martin. This sort of verbal promptitude is out of the ordinary scope of Dickens; but we find it frequently in this particular part of *Martin Chuzzlewit*. Martin himself is constantly breaking out into a controversial lucidity, which is elsewhere not at all a part of his character. When they talk to him about the institutions of America he asks sarcastically whether bowie knives and swordsticks and revolvers are the institutions of America. All this (if I may summarise) is expressive of one main fact. Being a satirist means being a philosopher. Dickens was not always very philosophical; but he had this permanent quality of the philosopher about him, that he always remembered people by their opinions. Elijah Pogram was to him the man who said that "his boastful answer to the tyrant and the despot was that his bright home was the land of the settin' sun." Mr. Scadder and Mr. Jefferson Brick were to him the men who said (in cooperation) that "the libation of freedom must sometimes be quaffed in blood." And in these chapters more than anywhere else he falls into the extreme habit of satire, that of treating people as if there were nothing about them except their opinions. It is therefore difficult to accept these pages as pages in a novel, splendid as they are considered as pages in a parody. I do not dispute that men have said and do say that "the libation of freedom must sometimes be quaffed in blood," that "their bright homes are the land of the settin' sun," that "they taunt that lion," that "alone they dare him," or "that softly sleeps the calm ideal in the whispering chambers of imagination." I have read too much American journalism to deny that any of these sentences and any of these opinions may at some time or other have been uttered. I do not deny that there are such opinions. But I do deny that there are such people. Elijah Pogram had some other business in life besides defending defaulting postmasters; he must have been a son or a father or a husband or at least (admirable thought) a lover. Mr. Chollop had some moments in his existence when he was not threatening his fellow-creatures with his sword-stick and his revolver. Of all this human side of such American types Dickens does not really give any hint at all. He does not suggest that the bully Chollop had even such coarse good-humour as bullies almost always have. He does not suggest that the humbug Elijah Pogram had even as much greasy amiability as humbugs almost invariably have. He is not studying them as human beings, even as bad human beings; he is studying them as conceptions, as points of view, as symbols of a state of mind with which he is in violent disagreement. To put it roughly, he is not describing characters, he is satirising fads. To put it more exactly, he is not describing characters; he is persecuting heresies. There is one thing really to be said against his American satire; it is a serious thing to be said: it is an argument, and it is true. This can be said of Martin's wanderings in America, that from the time he lands in America to the time he sets sail from it he never meets a living man. He has travelled in the land of Laputa. All the people he has met have been absurd opinions walking about. The whole art of Dickens in such passages as these consisted in one thing. It consisted in finding an opinion that had not a leg to stand on, and then giving it two legs to stand on.

So much may be allowed; it may be admitted that Dickens is in this sense the great satirist, in that he can imagine absurd opinions walking by themselves about the street. It may be admitted that Thackeray would not have allowed an absurd opinion to walk about the street without at least tying a man on to it for the sake of safety. But while this first truth may be evident, the second truth which is the complement of it may easily be forgotten. On the one hand there was no man who could so much enjoy mere intellectual satire apart from humanity as Dickens. On the other hand there was no man who, with another and more turbulent part of his nature, demanded humanity, and demanded its supremacy over intellect, more than Dickens. To put it shortly: there never was a man so much fitted for saying that everything was wrong; and there never was a man who was so desirous of saying that everything was right. Thus, when he met men with whom he violently disagreed, he described them as devils or lunatics; he could not bear to describe them as men. If they could not think with him on essentials he could not stand the idea that they were human souls; he cast them out; he forgot them; and if he could not forget them he caricatured them. He was too emotional to regard them as anything but enemies, if they were not friends. He was too humane not to hate them. Charles Lamb said with his inimitable sleek pungency that he could read all the books there were; he excluded books that obviously were not books, as cookery books, chessboards bound so as to look like books, and all the works of modern historians and philosophers. One might say in much the same style that Dickens loved all the men in the world; that is he loved all the men whom he was able to recognise as men; the rest he turned into griffins and chimeras without any serious semblance to humanity. Even in his books he never hates a human being. If he wishes to hate him he adopts the simple expedient of making him an inhuman being. Now of these two strands almost the whole of Dickens is made up; they are not only different strands, they are even antagonistic strands. I mean that the whole of Dickens is made up of the strand of satire and the strand of sentimentalism; and the strand of satire is quite unnecessarily merciless and hostile, and the strand of sentimentalism is quite unnecessarily humanitarian and even maudlin. On the proper interweaving of these two things depends the great part of Dickens's success in a novel. And by the consideration of them we can probably best arrive at the solution of the particular emotional enigma of the novel called *Martin Chuzzlewit*.

Martin Chuzzlewit is, I think, vaguely unsatisfactory to the reader, vaguely sad and heavy even to the reader who loves Dickens, because in *Martin Chuzzlewit* more than anywhere else in Dickens's works, more even than in *Oliver Twist*, there is a predominance of the harsh and hostile sort of humour over the hilarious and the humane. It is absurd to lay down any such little rules for the testing of literature. But this may be broadly said and yet with confidence: that Dickens is always at his best when he is laughing at the people whom he really admires. He is at his most humorous in writing of Mr. Pickwick, who represents passive virtue. He is at his most humorous in writing of Mr. Sam Weller, who represents active virtue. He is never so funny as when he is speaking of people in whom fun itself is a virtue, like the poor people in the Fleet or the Marshalsea. And in the stories that had immediately preceded *Martin Chuzzlewit* he had consistently concerned himself in the majority of cases with the study of such genial and honourable eccentrics; if they are lunatics they are amiable lunatics. In the last important novel before *Martin Chuzzlewit*, *Barnaby Rudge*, the hero himself is an amiable lunatic. In the novel before that, *The Old Curiosity Shop*, the two comic figures, Dick Swiveller and the Marchioness, are not only the most really entertaining, but also the most really sympathetic characters in the book. Before that came *Oliver Twist* (which is, I have said, an exception), and before that *Pickwick*, where the hero is, as Mr. Weller says, "an angel in gaiters." Hitherto, then, on the whole, the central Dickens character had been the man who gave to the poor many things, gold and wine and feasting and good advice; but among other things gave them a good laugh at himself. The jolly old English merchant of the Pickwick type was popular on both counts. People liked to see him throw his money in the gutter. They also liked to see him throw himself there occasionally. In both acts they recognised a common quality of virtue.

Now I think it is certainly the disadvantage of *Martin Chuzzlewit* that none of its absurd characters are thus sympathetic. There are in the book two celebrated characters who are both especially exuberant and amusing even for Dickens, and who are both especially heartless and abominable even for Dickens—I mean of course Mr. Pecksniff on the one hand and Mrs. Gamp on the other. The humour of both of them is gigantesque. Nobody will ever forget the first time he read the words "Now I should be very glad to see Mrs. Todgers's idea of a wooden leg." It is like remembering first love: there is still some sort of ancient sweetness and sting. I am afraid that, in spite of many criticisms to the contrary, I am still unable to take Mr. Pecksniff's hypocrisy seriously. He does not seem to me so much a hypocrite as a rhetorician; he reminds me of Serjeant Buzfuz. A very capable critic, Mr. Noyes, said that I was wrong when I suggested in another place that Dickens must have loved Pecksniff. Mr. Noyes thinks it clear that Dickens hated Pecksniff. I cannot believe it. Hatred does indeed linger round its object as much as love; but not in that way. Dickens is always making Pecksniff say things which have a wild poetical truth about them. Hatred allows no such outbursts of original innocence. But however that may be the broad fact remains-Dickens may or may not have loved Pecksniff comically, but he did not love him seriously; he did not respect him as he certainly respected Sam Weller. The same of course is true of Mrs. Gamp. To any one who appreciates her unctuous and sumptuous conversation it is difficult indeed not to feel that it would be almost better to be killed by Mrs. Gamp than to be saved by a better nurse. But the fact remains. In this book Dickens has not allowed us to love the most absurd people seriously, and absurd people ought to be loved seriously. Pecksniff has to be amusing all the time; the instant he ceases to be laughable he becomes detestable. Pickwick can take his ease at his inn; he can be leisurely, he can be spacious; he can fall into moods of gravity and even of dulness; he is not bound to be always funny or to forfeit the reader's concern, for he is a good man, and therefore even his dulness is beautiful, just as is the dulness of the animal. We can leave Pickwick a little while by the fire to think; for the thoughts of Pickwick, even if they were to go slowly, would be full of all the things that all men care for-old friends and old inns and memory and the goodness of God. But we dare not leave Pecksniff alone for a moment. We dare not leave him thinking by the fire, for the thoughts of Pecksniff would be too frightful.

Christmas Books

The mystery of Christmas is in a manner identical with the mystery of Dickens. If ever we adequately explain the one we may adequately explain the other. And indeed, in the treatment of the two, the chronological or historical order must in some degree be remembered. Before we come to the question of what Dickens did for Christmas we must consider the question of what Christmas did for Dickens. How did it happen that this bustling, nineteenth-century man, full of the almost cock-sure common-sense of the utilitarian and liberal epoch, came to associate his name chiefly in literary history with the perpetuation of a half pagan and half Catholic festival which he would certainly have called an antiquity and might easily have called a superstition? Christmas has indeed been celebrated before in English literature; but it had, in the most noticeable cases, been celebrated in connection with that kind of feudalism with which Dickens would have severed his connection with an ignorant and even excessive scorn. Sir Roger de Coverley kept Christmas; but it was a feudal Christmas. Sir Walter Scott sang in praise of Christmas; but it was a feudal Christmas. And Dickens was not only indifferent to the dignity of the old country gentleman or to the genial archæology of Scott; he was even harshly and insolently hostile to it. If Dickens had lived in the neighbourhood of Sir Roger de Coverley he would undoubtedly, like Tom Touchy, have been always "having the law of him." If Dickens had stumbled in among the old armour and quaint folios of Scott's study he would certainly have read his brother novelist a lesson in no measured terms about the futility of thus fumbling in the dust-bins of old oppression and error. So far from Dickens being one of those who like a thing because it is old, he was one of those cruder kind of reformers, in theory at least, who actually dislike a thing because it is old. He was not merely the more righteous kind of Radical who tries to uproot abuses; he was partly also that more suicidal kind of Radical who tries to uproot himself. In theory at any rate, he had no adequate conception of the importance of human tradition; in his time it had been twisted and falsified into the form of an opposition to democracy. In truth, of course, tradition is the most democratic of all things, for tradition is merely a democracy of the dead as well as the living. But Dickens and his special group or generation had no grasp of this permanent position; they had been called to a special war for the righting of special wrongs. In so far as such an institution as Christmas was old, Dickens would even have tended to despise it. He could never have put the matter to himself in the correct way-that while there are some things whose antiquity does prove that they are dying, there are some other things whose antiquity only proves that they cannot die. If some Radical contemporary and friend of Dickens had happened to say to him that in defending the mince-pies and the mummeries of Christmas he was defending a piece of barbaric and brutal ritualism, doomed to disappear in the light of reason along with the Boy-Bishop and the Lord of Misrule, I am not sure that Dickens (though he was one of the readiest and most rapid masters of reply in history) would have found it very easy upon his own principles to answer. It was by a great ancestral instinct that he defended Christmas; by that sacred sub-consciousness which is called tradition, which some have called a dead thing, but which is really a thing far more living than the intellect. There is a dark kinship and brotherhood of all mankind which is much too deep to be called heredity or to be in any way explained in scientific formulæ; blood is thicker than water and is especially very much thicker than water on the brain. But this unconscious and even automatic quality in Dickens's defence of the Christmas feast, this fact that his defence might almost be called animal rather than mental, though in proper language it should be called merely virile; all this brings us back to the fact that we must begin with the atmosphere of the subject itself. We must not ask Dickens what Christmas is, for with all his heat and eloquence he does not know. Rather we must ask Christmas what Dickens is-ask how this strange child of Christmas came to be born out of due time.

Dickens devoted his genius in a somewhat special sense to the description of happiness. No other literary man of his eminence has made this central human aim so specially his subject matter. Happiness is a mystery-generally a momentary mystery-which seldom stops long enough to submit itself to artistic observation, and which, even when it is habitual, has something about it which renders artistic description almost impossible. There are twenty tiny minor poets who can describe fairly impressively an eternity of agony; there are very few even of the eternal poets who can describe ten minutes of satisfaction. Nevertheless, mankind being half divine is always in love with the impossible, and numberless attempts have been made from the beginning of human literature to describe a real state of felicity. Upon the whole, I think, the most successful have been the most frankly physical and symbolic; the flowers of Eden or the jewels of the New Jerusalem. Many writers, for instance, have called the gold and chrysolite of the Holy City a vulgar lump of jewellery. But when these critics themselves attempt to describe their conceptions of future happiness, it is always some priggish nonsense about "planes," about "cycles of fulfilment," or "spirals of spiritual evolution." Now a cycle is just as much a physical metaphor as a flower of Eden; a spiral is just as much a physical metaphor as a precious stone. But, after all, a garden is a beautiful thing; whereas this is by no means necessarily true of a cycle, as can be seen in the case of a bicycle. A jewel, after all, is a beautiful thing; but this is not necessarily so of a spiral, as can be seen in the case of a corkscrew. Nothing is gained by dropping the old material metaphors, which did hint at heavenly beauty, and adopting other material metaphors which do not even give a hint of earthly beauty. This modern or spiral method of describing indescribable happiness may, I think, be dismissed. Then there has been another method which has been adopted by many men of a very real poetical genius. It was the method of the old pastoral poets like Theocritus. It was in another way that adopted by the elegance and piety of Spenser. It was certainly expressed in the pictures of Watteau; and it had a very sympathetic and even manly expression in modern England in the decorative poetry of William Morris. These men of genius, from Theocritus to Morris, occupied themselves in endeavouring to describe happiness as a state of certain human beings, the atmosphere of a commonwealth, the enduring climate of certain cities or islands. They poured forth treasures of the truest kind of imagination upon describing the happy lives and landscapes of Utopia or Atlantis or the Earthly Paradise. They traced with the most tender accuracy the tracery of its fruit-trees or the glimmering garments of its women; they used every ingenuity of colour or intricate shape to suggest its infinite delight. And what they succeeded in suggesting was always its infinite melancholy. William Morris described the Earthly Paradise in such a way that the only strong emotional note left on the mind was the feeling of how homeless his travellers felt in that alien Elysium; and the reader sympathised with them, feeling that he would prefer not only Elizabethan England but even twentieth-century Camberwell to such a land of shining shadows. Thus literature has almost always failed in endeavouring to describe happiness as a state. Human tradition, human custom and folk-lore (though far more true and reliable than literature as a rule) have not often succeeded in giving quite the correct symbols for a real atmosphere of *camaraderie* and joy. But here and there the note has been struck with the sudden vibration of the *vox humana*. In human tradition it has been struck chiefly in the old celebrations of Christmas. In literature it has been struck chiefly in Dickens's Christmas tales.

In the historic celebration of Christmas as it remains from Catholic times in certain northern countries (and it is to be remembered that in Catholic times the northern countries were, if possible, more Catholic than anybody else), there are three qualities which explain, I think, its hold upon the human sense of happiness, especially in such men as Dickens. There are three notes of Christmas, so to speak, which are also notes of happiness, and which the pagans and the Utopians forget. If we state what they are in the case of Christmas, it will be quite sufficiently obvious how important they are in the case of Dickens.

The first quality is what may be called the dramatic quality. The happiness is not a state; it is a crisis. All the old customs surrounding the celebration of the birth of Christ are made by human instinct so as to insist and re-insist upon this crucial quality. Everything is so arranged that the whole household may feel, if possible, as a household does when a child is actually being born in it. The thing is a vigil and a vigil with a definite limit. People sit up at night until they hear the bells ring. Or they try to sleep at night in order to see their presents the next morning. Everywhere there is a limitation, a restraint; at one moment the door is shut, at the moment after it is opened. The hour has come or it has not come; the parcels are undone or they are not undone; there is no evolution of Christmas presents. This sharp and theatrical quality in pleasure, which human instinct and the mother wit of the world has wisely put into the popular celebrations of Christmas, is also a quality which is essential in such romantic literature as Dickens wrote. In romantic literature the hero and heroine must indeed be happy, but they must also be unexpectedly happy. This is the first connecting link between literature and the old religious feast; this is the first connecting link between Dickens and Christmas.

The second element to be found in all such festivity and all such romance is the element which is represented as well as it could be represented by the mere fact that Christmas occurs in the winter. It is the element not merely of contrast, but actually of antagonism. It preserves everything that was best in the merely primitive or pagan view of such ceremonies or such banquets. If we are carousing, at least we are warriors carousing. We hang above us, as it were, the shields and battle-axes with which we must do battle with the giants of the snow and hail. All comfort must be based on discomfort. Man chooses when he wishes to be most joyful the very moment when the whole material universe is most sad. It is this contradiction and mystical defiance which gives a quality of manliness and reality to the old winter feasts which is not characteristic of the sunny felicities of the Earthly Paradise. And this curious element has been carried out even in all the trivial jokes and tasks that have always surrounded such occasions as these. The object of the jovial customs was not to make everything artificially easy: on the contrary, it was rather to make everything artificially difficult. Idealism is not only expressed by shooting an arrow at the stars; the fundamental principle of idealism is also expressed by putting a leg of mutton at the top of a greasy pole. There is in all such observances a quality which can be called only the quality of divine obstruction. For instance, in the game of snapdragon (that admirable occupation) the conception is that raisins taste much nicer if they are brands saved from the burning. About all Christmas things there is something a little nobler, if only nobler in form and theory, than mere comfort; even holly is prickly. It is not hard to see the connection of this kind of historic instinct with a romantic writer like Dickens. The healthy novelist must always play snapdragon with his principal characters; he must always be snatching the hero and heroine like raisins out of the fire.

The third great Christmas element is the element of the grotesque. The grotesque is the natural expression of joy; and all the Utopias and new Edens of the poets fail to give a real impression of enjoyment, very largely because they leave out the grotesque. A man in most modern Utopias cannot really be happy; he is too dignified. A man in Morris's Earthly Paradise cannot really be enjoying himself; he is too decorative. When real human beings have real delights they tend to express them entirely in grotesques —I might almost say entirely in goblins. On Christmas Eve one may talk about ghosts so long as they are turnip ghosts. But one would not be allowed (I hope, in any decent family) to talk on Christmas Eve about astral bodies. The boar's head of old Yule-time was as grotesque as the donkey's head of Bottom the Weaver. But there is only one set of goblins quite wild enough to express the wild goodwill of Christmas. Those goblins are the characters of Dickens.

Arcadian poets and Arcadian painters have striven to express happiness by means of beautiful figures. Dickens understood that happiness is best expressed by ugly figures. In beauty, perhaps, there is something allied to sadness; certainly there is something akin to joy in the grotesque, nay, in the uncouth. There is something mysteriously associated with happiness not only in the corpulence of Falstaff and the corpulence of Tony Weller, but even in the red nose of Bardolph or the red nose of Mr. Stiggins. A thing of beauty is an inspiration for ever —a matter of meditation for ever. It is rather a thing of ugliness that is strictly a joy for ever.

All Dickens's books are Christmas books. But this is still truest of his two or three famous Yuletide tales-The *Christmas Carol* and *The Chimes* and *The Cricket on the Hearth.* Of these *The Christmas Carol* is beyond comparison the best as well as the most popular. Indeed, Dickens is in so profound and spiritual a sense a popular author that in his case, unlike most others, it can generally be said that the best work is the most popular. It is for *Pickwick* that he is best known; and upon the whole it is for Pickwick that he is best worth knowing. In any case this superiority of *The Christmas Carol* makes it convenient for us to take it as an example of the generalisations already made. If we study the very real atmosphere of rejoicing and of riotous charity in *The Christmas Carol* we shall find that all the three marks I have mentioned are unmistakably visible. *The Christmas Carol* is a happy story first, because it describes an abrupt and dramatic change. It is not only the story of a conversion, but of a sudden conversion; as sudden as the conversion of a man at a Salvation Army meeting. Popular religion is quite right in insisting on the fact of a crisis in most things. It is true that the man at the Salvation Army meeting would probably be converted from the punch bowl; whereas Scrooge was converted to it. That only means that Scrooge and Dickens represented a higher and more historic Christianity.

Again, *The Christmas Carol* owes much of its hilarity to our second source-the fact of its being a tale of winter and of a very wintry winter. There is much about comfort in the story; yet the comfort is never enervating: it is saved from that by a tingle of something bitter and bracing in the weather. Lastly, the story exemplifies throughout the power of the third principle-the kinship between gaiety and the grotesque. Everybody is happy because nobody is dignified. We have a feeling somehow that Scrooge looked even uglier when he was kind than he had looked when he was cruel. The turkey that Scrooge bought was so fat, says Dickens, that it could never have stood upright. That top-heavy and monstrous bird is a good symbol of the top-heavy happiness of the stories.

It is less profitable to criticise the other two tales in detail because they represent variations on the theme in two directions; and variations that were not, upon the whole, improvements. *The Chimes* is a monument of Dickens's honourable quality of pugnacity. He could not admire anything, even peace, without wanting to be warlike about it. That was all as it should be.

Dombey and Son

In Dickens's literary life *Dombey and Son* represents a break so important as to necessitate our casting back to a summary and a generalisation. In order fully to understand what this break is, we must say something of the previous character of Dickens's novels, and even something of the general character of novels in themselves. How essential this is we shall see shortly.

It must first be remembered that the novel is the most typical of modern forms. It is typical of modern forms especially in this, that it is essentially formless. All the ancient modes or structures of literature were definite and severe. Any one composing them had to abide by their rules; they were what their name implied. Thus a tragedy might be a bad tragedy, but it was always a tragedy. Thus an epic might be a bad epic, but it was always an epic. Now in the sense in which there is such a thing as an epic, in that sense there is no such thing as a novel. We call any long fictitious narrative in prose a novel, just as we call any short piece of prose without any narrative an essay. Both these forms are really quite formless, and both of them are really quite new. The difference between a good epic by Mr. John Milton and a bad epic by Mr. John Smith was simply the difference between the same thing done well and the same thing done badly. But it was not (for instance) like the difference between *Clarissa Harlowe* and *The Time Machine*. If we class Richardson's book with Mr. Wells's book it is really only for convenience; if we say that they are both novels we shall certainly be puzzled in that case to say what on earth a novel is. But the note of our age, both for good and evil, is a highly poetical and largely illogical faith in liberty. Liberty is not a negation or a piece of nonsense, as the cheap reactionaries say; it is a belief in variety and growth. But it is a purely poetic and even a merely romantic belief. The nineteenth century was an age of romance as certainly as the Middle Ages was an age of reason. Mediævals liked to have everything defined and defensible; the modern world prefers to run some risks for the sake of spontaneity and diversity. Consequently the modern world is full of a phenomenon peculiar to itself—I mean the spectacle of small or originally small things swollen to enormous size and power. The modern world is like a world in which toadstools should be as big as trees, and insects should walk about in the sun as large as elephants. Thus, for instance, the shopkeeper, almost an unimportant figure in carefully ordered states, has in our time become the millionaire, and has more power than ten kings. Thus again a practical knowledge of nature, of the habits of animals or the properties of fire and water, was in the old ordered state either an almost servile labour or a sort of joke; it was left to old women and gamekeepers and boys who went birds'-nesting. In our time this commonplace daily knowledge has swollen into the enormous miracle of physical size, weighing the stars and talking under the sea. In short, our age is a sort of splendid jungle in which some of the most towering weeds and blossoms have come from the smallest seed.

And this is, generally speaking, the explanation of the novel. The novel is not so much the filling up of an artistic plan, however new or fantastic. It is a thing that has grown from some germ of suggestion, and has often turned out much larger than the author intended. And this, lastly, is the final result of these facts, that the critic can generally trace in a novel what was the original artistic type or shape of thought from which the whole matter started, and he will generally find that this is different in every case. In one novel he will find that the first impulse is a character. In another novel he will find that the first impulse is a landscape, the atmosphere of some special countryside. In another novel he will find that the first impulse is the last chapter. Or it may be a thrust with sword or dagger, it may be a theology, it may be a song. Somewhere embedded in every ordinary book are the five or six words for which really all the rest will be written. Some of our enterprising editors who set their readers to hunt for banknotes and missing ladies might start a competition for finding those words in every novel. But whether or no this is possible, there is no doubt that the principle in question is of great importance in the case of Dickens, and especially in the case of *Dombey and Son*.

In all the Dickens novels can be seen, so to speak, the original thing that they were before they were novels. The same may be observed, for the matter of that, in the great novels of most of the great modern novelists. For example, Sir Walter Scott wrote poetical romances before he wrote prose romances. Hence it follows that, with all their much greater merit, his novels may still be described as poetical romances in prose. While adding a new and powerful element of popular humours and observation, Scott still retains a certain purely poetical right—a right to make his heroes and outlaws and great kings speak at the great moments with a rhetoric so rhythmical that it partakes of the nature of song, the same quite metrical rhetoric which is used in the metrical speeches of Marmion or Roderick Dhu. In the same way, although *Don Quixote* is a modern novel in its irony and subtlety, we can see that it comes from the old long romances of chivalry. In the same way, although *Clarissa* is a modern novel in its intimacy and actuality, we can see that it comes from the old polite letter-writing and polite essays of the period of the *Spectator*. Any one can see that Scott formed in *The Lay of the Last Minstrel* the style that he applied again and again afterwards, like the reappearances of a star taking leave of the stage. All his other romances were positively last appearances of the positively last Minstrel. Any one can see that Thackeray formed in fragmentary satires like *The Book of Snobs* or *The Yellowplush Papers* the style, the rather fragmentary style, in which he was to write *Vanity Fair*. In most modern cases, in short (until very lately, at any rate), the novel is an enormous outgrowth from something that was not a novel. And in Dickens this is very important. All his novels are outgrowths of the original notion of taking notes, splendid and inspired notes, of what happens in the street. Those in the modern world who cannot reconcile themselves to his method-those who feel that there is about his books something intolerably clumsy or superficial-have either no natural taste for strong literature at all, or else have fallen into their error by too persistently regarding Dickens as a modern novelist and expecting all his books to be modern novels. Dickens did not know at what exact point he really turned into a novelist. Nor do we. Dickens did not know, in his deepest soul, whether he ever really did turn into a novelist. Nor do we. The novel being a modern product is one of the few things to which we really can apply that disgusting method of thought-the method of evolution. But even in evolution there are great gaps, there are great breaks, there are great crises. I have said that the first of these breaks in Dickens may be placed at the point when he wrote *Nicholas Nickleby*. This was his first serious decision to be a novelist in any sense at all, to be anything except a maker of momentary farces. The second break, and that a far more important break, is in *Dombey and Son*. This marks his final resolution to be a novelist and nothing else, to be a serious constructor of fiction in the serious sense. Before *Dombey and Son* even his pathos had been really frivolous. After *Dombey and Son* even his absurdity was intentional and grave.

In case this transition is not understood, one or two tests may be taken at random. The episodes in *Dombey and Son*, the episodes in *David Copperfield*, which came after it, are no longer episodes merely stuck into the middle of the story without any connection with it, like most of the episodes in *Nicholas Nickleby*, or most of the episodes even in *Martin Chuzzlewit*. Take, for instance, by way of a mere coincidence, the fact that three schools for boys are described successively in *Nicholas Nickleby*, in *Dombey and Son*, and in *David Copperfield*. But the difference is enormous. Dotheboys Hall does not exist to tell us anything about Nicholas Nickleby. Rather Nicholas Nickleby exists entirely in order to tell us about Dotheboys Hall. It does not in any way affect his history or psychology; he enters Mr. Squeers's school and leaves Mr. Squeers's school with the same character, or rather absence of character. It is a mere episode, existing for itself. But when little Paul Dombey goes to an old-fashioned but kindly school, it is in a very different sense and for a very different reason from that for which Nicholas Nickleby goes to an old-fashioned and cruel school. The sending of little Paul to Dr. Blimber's is a real part of the history of little Paul, such as it is. Dickens deliberately invents all that elderly pedantry in order to show up Paul's childishness. Dickens deliberately invents all that rather heavy kindness in order to show up Paul's predestination and tragedy. Dotheboys Hall is not meant to show up anything except Dotheboys Hall. But although Dickens doubtless enjoyed Dr. Blimber quite as much as Mr. Squeers, it remains true that Dr. Blimber is really a very good foil to Paul; whereas Squeers is not a foil to Nicholas; Nicholas is merely a lame excuse for Squeers. The change can be seen continued in the school, or rather the two schools, to which David Copperfield goes. The whole idea of David Copperfield's life is that he had the dregs of life before the wine of it. He knew the worst of the world before he knew the best of it. His childhood at Dr. Strong's is a second childhood. Now for this purpose the two schools are perfectly well adapted. Mr. Creakle's school is not only, like Mr. Squeers's school, a bad school, it is a bad influence upon David Copperfield. Dr. Strong's school is not only a good school, it is a good influence upon David Copperfield. I have taken this case of the schools as a case casual but concrete. The same, however, can be seen in any of the groups or incidents of the novels on both sides of the boundary. Mr. Crummles's theatrical company is only a society that Nicholas happens to fall into. America is only a place to which Martin Chuzzlewit happens to go. These things are isolated sketches, and nothing else. Even Todgers's boarding-house is only a place where Mr. Pecksniff can be delightfully hypocritical. It is not a place which throws any new light on Mr. Pecksniff's hypocrisy. But the case is different with that more subtle hypocrite in *Dombey and Son* —I mean Major Bagstock. Dickens does mean it as a deliberate light on Mr. Dombey's character that he basks with a fatuous calm in the blazing sun of Major Bagstock's tropical and offensive flattery. Here, then, is the essence of the change. He not only wishes to write a novel; this he did as early as *Nicholas Nickleby*. He wishes to have as little as possible in the novel that does not really assist it as a novel. Previously he had asked with the assistance of what incidents could his hero wander farther and farther from the pathway. Now he has really begun to ask with the assistance of what incidents his hero can get nearer and nearer to the goal.

The change made Dickens a greater novelist. I am not sure that it made him a greater man. One good character by Dickens requires all eternity to stretch its legs in; and the characters in his later books are always being tripped up by some tiresome nonsense about the story. For instance, in *Dombey and Son*, Mrs. Skewton is really very funny. But nobody with a love of the real smell of Dickens would compare her for a moment, for instance, with Mrs. Nickleby. And the reason of Mrs. Skewton's inferiority is simply this, that she has something to do in the plot; she has to entrap or assist to entrap Mr. Dombey into marrying Edith. Mrs. Nickleby, on the other hand, has nothing at all to do in the story, except to get in everybody's way. The consequence is that we complain not of her for getting in everyone's way, but of everyone for getting in hers. What are suns and stars, what are times and seasons, what is the mere universe, that it should presume to interrupt Mrs. Nickleby? Mrs. Skewton (though supposed, of course, to be a much viler sort of woman) has something of the same quality of splendid and startling irrelevancy. In her also there is the same feeling of wild threads hung from world to world like the webs of gigantic spiders; of things connected that seem to have no connection save by this one adventurous filament of frail and daring folly. Nothing could be better than Mrs. Skewton when she finds herself, after convolutions of speech, somehow on the subject of Henry VIII., and pauses to mention with approval "his dear little peepy eyes and his benevolent chin." Nothing could be better than her attempt at Mahomedan resignation when she feels almost inclined to say "that there is no What's-his-name but Thingummy, and What-you-may-call-it is his prophet!" But she has not so much time as Mrs. Nickleby to say these good things; also she has not sufficient human virtue to say them constantly. She is always intent upon her worldly plans, among other things upon the worldly plan of assisting Charles Dickens to get a story finished. She is always "advancing her shrivelled ear" to listen to what Dombey is saying to Edith. Worldliness is the most solemn thing in the world; it is far more solemn than other-worldliness. Mrs. Nickleby can afford to ramble as a child does in a field, or as a child does to laugh at nothing, for she is like a child, innocent. It is only the good who can afford to be frivolous.

Broadly speaking, what is said here of Mrs. Skewton applies to the great part of *Dombey and Son*, even to the comic part of it. It shows an advance in art and unity; it does not show an advance in genius and creation. In some cases, in fact, I cannot help feeling that it shows a falling off. It may be a personal idiosyncrasy, but there is only one comic character really prominent in Dickens, upon whom Dickens has really lavished the wealth of his invention, and who does not amuse me at all, and that character is Captain Cuttle. But three great exceptions must be made to any such disparagement of *Dombey and Son*. They are all three of that royal order in Dickens's creation which can no more be described or criticised than strong wine. The first is Major Bagstock, the second is Cousin Feenix, the third is Toots. In Bagstock Dickens has blasted for ever that type which pretends to be sincere by the simple operation of being explosively obvious. He tells about a quarter of the truth, and then poses as truthful because a quarter of the truth is much simpler than the whole of it. He is the kind of man who goes about with posers for Bishops or for Socialists, with plain questions to which he wants a plain answer. His questions are plain only in the same sense that he himself is plain-in the sense of being uncommonly ugly. He is the man who always bursts with satisfaction because he can call a spade a spade, as if there were any kind of logical or philosophical use in merely saying the same word twice over. He is the man who wants things down in black and white, as if black and white were the only two colours; as if blue and green and red and gold were not facts of the universe. He is too selfish to tell the truth and too impatient even to hear it. He cannot endure the truth, because it is subtle. This man is almost always like Bagstock—a sycophant and a toad-eater. A man is not any the less a toad-eater because he eats his toads with a huge appetite and gobbles them up, as Bagstock did his breakfast, with the eyes starting out of his purple face. He flatters brutally. He cringes with a swagger. And men of the world like Dombey are always taken in by him, because men of the world are probably the simplest of all the children of Adam.

Cousin Feenix again is an exquisite suggestion, with his rickety chivalry and rambling compliments. It was about the period of *Dombey and Son* that Dickens began to be taken up by good society. (One can use only vulgar terms for an essentially vulgar process.) And his sketches of the man of good family in the books of this period show that he had had glimpses of what that singular world is like. The aristocrats in his earliest books are simply dragons and griffins for his heroes to fight with-monsters like Sir Mulberry Hawk or Lord Verisopht. They are merely created upon the old principle, that your scoundrel must be polite and powerful—a very sound principle. The villain must be not only a villain, but a tyrant. The giant must be larger than Jack. But in the books of the Dombey period we have many shrewd glimpses of the queer realities of English aristocracy. Of these Cousin Feenix is one of the best. Cousin Feenix is a much better sketch of the essentially decent and chivalrous aristocrat than Sir Leicester Dedlock. Both of the men are, if you will, fools, as both are honourable gentlemen. But if one may attempt a classification among fools, Sir Leicester Dedlock is a stupid fool, while Cousin Feenix is a silly fool-which is much better. The difference is that the silly fool has a folly which is always on the borderland of wit, and even of wisdom; his wandering wits come often upon undiscovered truths. The stupid fool is as consistent and as homogeneous as wood; he is as invincible as the ancestral darkness. Cousin Feenix is a good sketch of the sort of well-bred old ass who is so fundamentally genuine that he is always saying very true things by accident. His whole tone also, though exaggerated like everything in Dickens, is very true to the bewildered good nature which marks English aristocratic life. The statement that Dickens could not describe a gentleman is, like most popular animadversions against Dickens, so very thin and one-sided a truth as to be for serious purposes a falsehood. When people say that Dickens could not describe a gentleman, what they mean is this, and so far what they mean is true. They mean that Dickens could not describe a gentleman as gentlemen feel a gentleman. They mean that he could not take that atmosphere easily, accept it as the normal atmosphere, or describe that world from the inside. This is true. In Dickens's time there was such a thing as the English people, and Dickens belonged to it. Because there is no such thing as an English people now, almost all literary men drift towards what is called Society; almost all literary men either are gentlemen or pretend to be. Hence, as I say, when we talk of describing a gentleman, we always mean describing a gentleman from the point of view of one who either belongs to, or is interested in perpetuating, that type. Dickens did not describe gentlemen in the way that gentlemen describe gentlemen. He described them in the way in which he described waiters, or railway guards, or men drawing with chalk on the pavement. He described them, in short (and this we may freely concede), from the outside, as he described any other oddity or special trade. But when it comes to saying that he did not describe them well, then that is quite another matter, and that I should emphatically deny. The things that are really odd about the English upper class he saw with startling promptitude and penetration, and if the English upper class does not see these odd things in itself, it is not because they are not there, but because we are all blind to our own oddities; it is for the same reason that tramps do not feel dirty, or that niggers do not feel black. I have often heard a dear old English oligarch say that Dickens could not describe a gentleman, while every note of his own voice and turn of his own hand recalled Sir Leicester Dedlock. I have often been told by some old buck that Dickens could not describe a gentleman, and been told so in the shaky voice and with all the vague allusiveness of Cousin Feenix.

Cousin Feenix has really many of the main points of the class that governs England. Take, for an instance, his hazy notion that he is in a world where everybody knows everybody; whenever he mentions a man, it is a man "with whom my friend Dombey is no doubt acquainted." That pierces to the very helpless soul of aristocracy. Take again the stupendous gravity with which he leads up to a joke. That is the very soul of the House of Commons and the Cabinet, of the high-class English politics, where a joke is always enjoyed solemnly. Take his insistence upon the technique of Parliament, his regrets for the time when the rules of debate were perhaps better observed than they are now. Take that wonderful mixture in him (which is the real human virtue of our aristocracy) of a fair amount of personal modesty with an innocent assumption of rank. Of a man who saw all these genteel foibles so clearly it is absurd merely to say without further explanation that he could not describe a gentleman. Let us confine ourselves to saying that he did not describe a gentleman as gentlemen like to be described.

Lastly, there is the admirable study of Toots, who may be considered as being in some ways the masterpiece of Dickens. Nowhere else did Dickens express with such astonishing insight and truth his main contention, which is that to be good and idiotic is not a poor fate, but, on the contrary, an experience of primeval innocence, which wonders at all things. Dickens did not know, anymore than any great man ever knows, what was the particular thing that he had to preach. He did not know it; he only preached it. But the particular thing that he had to preach was this: That humility is the only possible basis of enjoyment; that if one has no other way of being humble except being poor, then it is better to be poor, and to enjoy; that if one has no other way of being humble except being imbecile, then it is better to be imbecile, and to enjoy. That is the deep unconscious truth in the character of Toots-that all his externals are flashy and false; all his internals unconscious, obscure, and true. He wears loud clothes, and he is silent inside them. His shirts and waistcoats are covered with bright spots of pink and purple, while his soul is always covered with the sacred shame. He always gets all the outside things of life wrong, and all the inside things right. He always admires the right Christian people, and gives them the wrong Christian names. Dimly connecting Captain Cuttle with the shop of Mr. Solomon Gills, he always addresses the astonished mariner as "Captain Gills." He turns Mr. Walter Gay, by a most improving transformation, into "Lieutenant Walters." But he always knows which people upon his own principles to admire. He forgets who they are, but he remembers what they are. With the clear eyes of humility he perceives the whole world as it is. He respects the Game Chicken for being strong, as even the Game Chicken ought to be respected for being strong. He respects Florence for being good, as even Florence ought to be respected for being good. And he has no doubt about which he admires most; he prefers goodness to strength, as do all masculine men. It is through the eyes of such characters as Toots that Dickens really sees the whole of his tales. For even if one calls him a half-wit, it still makes a difference that he keeps the right half of his wits. When we think of the unclean and craven spirit in which Toots might be treated in a psychological novel of to-day; how he might walk with a mooncalf face, and a brain of bestial darkness, the soul rises in real homage to Dickens for showing how much simple gratitude and happiness can remain in the lopped roots of the most simplified intelligence. If scientists must treat a man as a dog, it need not be always as a mad dog. They might grant him, like Toots, a little of the dog's loyalty and the dog's reward.

David Copperfield

In this book Dickens is really trying to write a new kind of book, and the enterprise is almost as chivalrous as a cavalry charge. He is making a romantic attempt to be realistic. That is almost the definition of *David Copperfield*. In his last book, *Dombey and Son*, we see a certain maturity and even a certain mild exhaustion in his earlier farcical method. He never failed to have fine things in any of his books, and Toots is a very fine thing. Still, I could never find Captain Cuttle and Mr. Sol Gills very funny, and the whole Wooden Midshipman seems to me very wooden. In *David Copperfield* he suddenly unseals a new torrent of truth, the truth out of his own life. The impulse of the thing is autobiography; he is trying to tell all the absurd things that have happened to himself, and not the least absurd thing is himself. Yet though it is Dickens's ablest and clearest book, there is in it a falling away of a somewhat singular kind.

Generally speaking there was astonishingly little of fatigue in Dickens's books. He sometimes wrote bad work; he sometimes wrote even unimportant work; but he wrote hardly a line which is not full of his own fierce vitality and fancy. If he is dull it is hardly ever because he cannot think of anything; it is because, by some silly excitement or momentary lapse of judgment, he has thought of something that was not worth thinking of. If his joke is feeble, it is as an impromptu joke at an uproarious dinner-table may be feeble; it is no indication of any lack of vitality. The joke is feeble, but it is not a sign of feebleness. Broadly speaking, this is true of Dickens. If his writing is not amusing us, at least it is amusing him. Even when he is tiring he is not tired.

But in the case of *David Copperfield* there is a real reason for noting an air of fatigue. For although this is the best of all Dickens's books, it constantly disappoints the critical and intelligent reader. The reason is that Dickens began it under his sudden emotional impulse of telling the whole truth about himself and gradually allowed the whole truth to be more and more diluted, until towards the end of the book we are back in the old pedantic and decorative art of Dickens, an art which we justly admired in its own place and on its own terms, but which we resent when we feel it gradually returning through a tale pitched originally in a more practical and piercing key. Here, I say, is the one real example of the fatigue of Dickens. He begins his story in a new style and then slips back into an old one. The earlier part is in his later manner. The later part is in his earlier manner.

There are many marks of something weak and shadowy in the end of *David Copperfield*. Here, for instance, is one of them which is not without its bearing on many tendencies of modern England. Why did Dickens at the end of this book give way to that typically English optimism about emigration? He seems to think that he can cure the souls of a whole cartload, or rather boatload, of his characters by sending them all to the Colonies. Peggotty is a desolate and insulted parent whose house has been desecrated and his pride laid low; therefore let him go to Australia. Emily is a woman whose heart is broken and whose honour is blasted; but she will be quite happy if she goes to Australia. Mr. Micawber is a man whose soul cannot be made to understand the tyranny of time or the limits of human hope; but he will understand all these things if he goes to Australia. For it must be noted that Dickens does not use this emigration merely as a mode of exit. He does not send these characters away on a ship merely as a symbol suggesting that they pass wholly out of his hearer's life. He does definitely suggest that Australia is a sort of island Valley of Avalon, where the soul may heal it of its grievous wound. It is seriously suggested that Peggotty finds peace in Australia. It is really indicated that Emily regains her dignity in Australia. It is positively explained of Mr. Micawber not that he was happy in Australia (for he would be that anywhere), but that he was definitely prosperous and practically successful in Australia; and that he would certainly be nowhere. Colonising is not talked of merely as a coarse, economic expedient for going to a new market. It is really offered as something that will cure the hopeless tragedy of Peggotty; as something that will cure the still more hopeless comedy of Micawber.

I will not dwell here on the subsequent adventures of this very sentimental and extremely English illusion. It would be an exaggeration to say that Dickens in this matter is something of a forerunner of much modern imperialism. His political views were such that he would have regarded modern imperialism with horror and contempt. Nevertheless there is here something of that hazy sentimentalism which makes some Imperialists prefer to talk of the fringe of the empire of which they know nothing, rather than of the heart of the empire which they know is diseased. It is said that in the twilight and decline of Rome, close to the dark ages, the people in Gaul believed that Britain was a land of ghosts (perhaps it was foggy), and that the dead were ferried across to it from the northern coast of France. If (as is not entirely impossible) our own century appears to future ages as a time of temporary decay and twilight, it may be said that there was attached to England a blessed island called Australia to which the souls of the socially dead were ferried across to remain in bliss for ever.

This element which is represented by the colonial optimism at the end of *David Copperfield* is a moral element. The truth is that there is something a little mean about this sort of optimism. I do not like the notion of David Copperfield sitting down comfortably to his tea-table with Agnes, having got rid of all the inconvenient or distressing characters of the story by sending them to the other side of the world. The whole thing has too much about it of the selfishness of a family which sends a scapegrace to the Colonies to starve with its blessing. There is too much in the whole thing of that element which was satirised by an ironic interpretation of the epitaph "Peace, perfect peace, with loved ones far away." We should have thought more of David Copperfield (and also of Charles Dickens) if he had endeavoured for the rest of his life, by conversation and comfort, to bind up the wounds of his old friends from the seaside. We should have thought more of David Copperfield (and also of Charles Dickens) if he had faced the possibility of going on till his dying day lending money to Mr. Wilkins Micawber. We should have thought more of David Copperfield (and also of Charles Dickens) if he had not looked upon the marriage with Dora merely as a flirtation, an episode which he survived and ought to survive. And yet the truth is that there is nowhere in fiction where we feel so keenly the primary human instinct and principle that a marriage is a marriage and irrevocable, that such things do leave a wound and also a bond as in this case of David's short connection with his silly little wife. When all is said and done, when Dickens has done his best and his worst, when he has sentimentalised for pages and tried to tie up everything in the pink tape of optimism, the fact, in the psychology of the reader, still remains. The reader does still feel that David's marriage to Dora was a real marriage; and that his marriage to Agnes was nothing, a middle-aged compromise, a taking of the second best, a sort of spiritualised and sublimated marriage of convenience. For all the readers of Dickens Dora is thoroughly avenged. The modern world (intent on anarchy in everything, even in Government) refuses to perceive the permanent element of tragic constancy which inheres in all passion, and which is the origin of marriage. Marriage rests upon the fact that you cannot have your cake and eat it; that you cannot lose your heart and have it. But, as I have said, there is perhaps no place in literature where we feel more vividly the sense of this monogamous instinct in man than in David Copperfield. A man is monogamous even if he is only monogamous for a month; love is eternal even if it is only eternal for a month. It always leaves behind it the sense of something broken and betrayed.

But I have mentioned Dora in this connection only because she illustrates the same fact which Micawber illustrates; the fact that there is at the end of this book too much tendency to bless people and get rid of them. Micawber is a nuisance. Dickens the despot condemns him to exile. Dora is a nuisance. Dickens the despot condemns her to death. But it is the whole business of Dickens in the world to express the fact that such people are the spice and interest of life. It is the whole point of Dickens that there is nobody more worth living with than a strong, splendid, entertaining, immortal nuisance. Micawber interrupts practical life; but what is practical life that it should venture to interrupt Micawber? Dora confuses the housekeeping; but we are not angry with Dora because she confuses the housekeeping. We are angry with the housekeeping because it confuses Dora. I repeat, and it cannot be too much repeated that the whole lesson of Dickens is here. It is better to know Micawber than not to know the minor worries that arise out of knowing Micawber. It is better to have a bad debt and a good friend. In the same way it is better to marry a human and healthy personality which happens to attract you than to marry a mere housewife; for a mere housewife is a mere housekeeper. All this was what Dickens stood for; that the very people who are most irritating in small business circumstances are often the people who are most delightful in long stretches of experience of life. It is just the man who is maddening when he is ordering a cutlet or arranging an appointment who is probably the man in whose company it is worth while to journey steadily towards the grave. Distribute the dignified people and the capable people and the highly business-like people among all the situations which their ambition or their innate corruption may demand; but keep close to your heart, keep deep in your inner councils the absurd people. Let the clever people pretend to govern you, let the unimpeachable people pretend to advise you, but let the fools alone influence you; let the laughable people whose faults you see and understand be the only people who are really inside your life, who really come near you or accompany you on your lonely march towards the last impossibility. That is the whole meaning of Dickens; that we should keep the absurd people for our friends. And here at the end of *David Copperfield* he seems in some dim way to deny it. He seems to want to get rid of the preposterous people simply because they will always continue to be preposterous. I have a horrible feeling that David Copperfield will send even his aunt to Australia if she worries him too much about donkeys.

I repeat, then, that this wrong ending of *David Copperfield* is one of the very few examples in Dickens of a real symptom of fatigue. Having created splendid beings for whom alone life might be worth living, he cannot endure the thought of his hero living with them. Having given his hero superb and terrible friends, he is afraid of the awful and tempestuous vista of their friendship. He slips back into a more superficial kind of story and ends it in a more superficial way. He is afraid of the things he has made; of that terrible figure Micawber; of that yet more terrible figure Dora. He cannot make up his mind to see his hero perpetually entangled in the splendid tortures and sacred surprises that come from living with really individual and unmanageable people. He cannot endure the idea that his fairy prince will not have henceforward a perfectly peaceful time. But the wise old fairy tales (which are the wisest things in the world, at any rate the wisest things of worldly origin), the wise old fairy tales never were so silly as to say that the prince and the princess lived peacefully ever afterwards. The fairy tales said that the prince and princess lived happily ever afterwards: and so they did. They lived happily, although it is very likely that from time to time they threw the furniture at each other. Most marriages, I think, are happy marriages; but there is no such thing as a contented marriage. The whole pleasure of marriage is that it is a perpetual crisis. David Copperfield and Dora quarrelled over the cold mutton; and if they had gone on quarrelling to the end of their lives, they would have gone on loving each other to the end of their lives; it would have been a human marriage. But David Copperfield and Agnes would agree about the cold mutton. And that cold mutton would be very cold.

I have here endeavoured to suggest some of the main merits of Dickens within the framework of one of his faults. I have said that *David Copperfield* represents a rather sad transition from his strongest method to his weakest. Nobody would ever complain of Charles Dickens going on writing his own kind of novels, his old kind of novels. If there be anywhere a man who loves good books, that man wishes that there were four *Oliver Twists* and at least forty-four *Pickwicks*. If there be any one who loves laughter and creation, he would be glad to read a hundred of *Nicholas Nickleby* and two hundred of *The Old Curiosity Shop*. But while any one would have welcomed one of Dickens's own ordered and conventional novels, it was not in this spirit that they welcomed *David Copperfield*.

David Copperfield begins as if it were going to be a new kind of Dickens novel; then it gradually turns into an old kind of Dickens novel. It is here that many readers of this splendid book have been subtly and secretly irritated. Nicholas Nickleby is all very well; we accept him as something which is required to tie the whole affair together. Nicholas is a sort of string or clothes-line on which are hung the limp figure of Smike, the jumping-jack of Mr. Squeers and the twin dolls named Cheeryble. If we do not accept Nicholas Nickleby as the hero of the story, at least we accept him as the title of the story. But in *David Copperfield* Dickens begins something which looks for the moment fresh and startling. In the earlier chapters (the amazing earlier chapters of this book) he does seem to be going to tell the living truth about a living boy and man. It is melancholy to see that sudden fire fading. It is sad to see David Copperfield gradually turning into Nicholas Nickleby. Nicholas Nickleby does not exist at all; he is a quite colourless primary condition of the story. We look through Nicholas Nickleby at the story just as we look through a plain pane of glass at the street. But David Copperfield does begin by existing; it is only gradually that he gives up that exhausting habit.

Any fair critical account of Dickens must always make him out much smaller than he is. For any fair criticism of Dickens must take account of his evident errors, as I have taken account of one of the most evident of them during the last two or three pages. It would not even be loyal to conceal them. But no honest criticism, no criticism, though it spoke with the tongues of men and angels, could ever really talk about Dickens. In all this that I have said I have not been talking about Dickens at all. I say it with equanimity; I say it even with arrogance. I have been talking about the gaps of Dickens. I have been talking about the omissions of Dickens. I have been talking about the slumber of Dickens and the forgetfulness and unconsciousness of Dickens. In one word, I have been talking not about Dickens, but about the absence of Dickens. But when we come to him and his work itself, what is there to be said? What is there to be said about earthquake and the dawn? He has created, especially in this book of *David Copperfield*, he has created, creatures who cling to us and tyrannise over us, creatures whom we would not forget if we could, creatures whom we could not forget if we would, creatures who are more actual than the man who made them.

This is the excuse for all that indeterminate and rambling and sometimes sentimental criticism of which Dickens, more than any one else, is the victim, of which I fear that I for one have made him the victim in this place. When I was a boy I could not understand why the Dickensians worried so wearily about Dickens, about where he went to school and where he ate his dinners, about how he wore his trousers and when he cut his hair. I used to wonder why they did not write something that I could read about a man like Micawber. But I have come to the conclusion that this almost hysterical worship of the man, combined with a comparatively feeble criticism on his works, is just and natural. Dickens was a man like ourselves; we can see where he went wrong, and study him without being stunned or getting the sunstroke. But Micawber is not a man; Micawber is the superman. We can only walk round and round him wondering what we shall say. All the critics of Dickens, when all is said and done, have only walked round and round Micawber wondering what they should say. I am myself at this moment walking round and round Micawber wondering what I shall say. And I have not found out yet.

Christmas Stories

The power of Dickens is shown even in the scraps of Dickens, just as the virtue of a saint is said to be shown in fragments of his property or rags from his robe. It is with such fragments that we are chiefly concerned in the *Christmas Stories*. Many of them are fragments in the literal sense; Dickens began them and then allowed some one else to carry them on; they are almost rejected notes. In all the other cases we have been considering the books that he wrote; here we have rather to consider the books that he might have written. And here we find the final evidence and the unconscious stamp of greatness, as we might find it in some broken bust or some rejected moulding in the studio of Michael Angelo.

These sketches or parts of sketches all belong to that period in his later life when he had undertaken the duties of an editor, the very heavy duties of a very popular editor. He was not by any means naturally fitted for that position. He was the best man in the world for founding papers; but many people wished that he could have been buried under the foundations, like the first builder in some pagan and prehistoric pile. He called the *Daily News* into existence, but when once it existed, it objected to him strongly. It is not easy, and perhaps it is not important, to state truly the cause of this incapacity. It was not in the least what is called the ordinary fault or weakness of the artist. It was not that he was careless; rather it was that he was too conscientious. It was not that he had the irresponsibility of genius; rather it was that he had the irritating responsibility of genius; he wanted everybody to see things as he saw them. But in spite of all this he certainly ran two great popular periodicals —*Household Words* and *All the Year Round* —with enormous popular success. And he certainly so far succeeded in throwing himself into the communism of journalism, into the nameless brotherhood of a big paper, that many earnest Dickensians are still engaged in picking out pieces of Dickens from the anonymous pages of *Household Words* and *All the Year Round*, and those parts which have been already beyond question picked out and proved are often fragmentary. The genuine writing of Dickens breaks off at a certain point, and the writing of some one else begins. But when the writing of Dickens breaks off, I fancy that we know it.

The singular thing is that some of the best work that Dickens ever did, better than the work in his best novels, can be found in these slight and composite scraps of journalism. For instance, the solemn and self-satisfied account of the duty and dignity of a waiter given in the opening chapter of *Somebody's Luggage* is quite as full and fine as anything done anywhere by its author in the same vein of sumptuous satire. It is as good as the account which Mr. Bumble gives of out-door relief, which, "properly understood, is the parochial safeguard. The great thing is to give the paupers what they don't want, and then they never come again." It is as good as Mr. Podsnap's description of the British Constitution, which was bestowed on him by Providence. None of these celebrated passages is more obviously Dickens at his best than this, the admirable description of "the true principles of waitering," or the account of how the waiter's father came back to his mother in broad daylight, "in itself an act of madness on the part of a waiter," and how he expired repeating continually "two and six is three and four is nine." That waiter's explanatory soliloquy might easily have opened an excellent novel, as *Martin Chuzzlewit* is opened by the clever nonsense about the genealogy of the Chuzzlewits, or as *Bleak House* is opened by a satiric account of the damp, dim life of a law court. Yet Dickens practically abandoned the scheme of *Somebody's Luggage*; he only wrote two sketches out of those obviously intended. He may almost be said to have only written a brilliant introduction to another man's book.

Yet it is exactly in such broken outbreaks that his greatness appears. If a man has flung away bad ideas he has shown his sense, but if he has flung away good ideas he has shown his genius. He proved that he actually has that over-pressure of pure creativeness which we see in nature itself, "that of a hundred seeds, she often brings but one to bear." Dickens had to be Malthusian about his spiritual children. Critics have called Keats and others who died young "the great Might-have-beens of literary history." Dickens certainly was not merely a great Might-have-been. Dickens, to say the least of him, was a great Was. Yet this fails fully to express the richness of his talent; for the truth is that he was a great Was and also a great Might-have-been. He said what he had to say, and yet not all he had to say. Wild pictures, possible stories, tantalising and attractive trains of thought, perspectives of adventure, crowded so continually upon his mind that at the end there was a vast mass of them left over, ideas that he literally had not the opportunity to develop, tales that he literally had not the time to tell. This is shown clearly in his private notes and letters, which are full of schemes singularly striking and suggestive, schemes which he never carried out. It is indicated even more clearly by these *Christmas Stories*, collected out of the chaotic opulence of *Household Words* and *All the Year Round*. He wrote short stories actually because he had not time to write long stories. He often put into the short story a deep and branching idea which would have done very well for a long story; many of his long stories, so to speak, broke off short. This is where he differs from most who are called the Might-have-beens of literature. Marlowe and Chatterton failed because of their weakness. Dickens failed because of his force.

Examine for example this case of the waiter in *Somebody's Luggage*. Dickens obviously knew enough about that waiter to have made him a running spring of joy throughout a whole novel; as the beadle is in *Oliver Twist*, or the undertaker in *Martin Chuzzlewit*. Every touch of him tingles with truth, from the vague gallantry with which he asks, "Would'st thou know, fair reader (if of the adorable female sex)" to the official severity with which he takes the chambermaid down, "as many pegs as is desirable for the future comfort of all parties." If Dickens had developed this character at full length in a book he would have preserved for ever in literature a type of great humour and great value, and a type which may only too soon be disappearing from English history. He would have eternalised the English waiter. He still exists in some sound old taverns and decent country inns, but there is no one left really capable of singing his praises. I know that Mr. Bernard Shaw has done something of the sort in the delightfully whimsical account of William in *You Never Can Tell*. But nothing will persuade me that Mr. Bernard Shaw can really understand the English waiter. He can never have ordered wine from him for instance. And though the English waiter is by the nature of things solemn about everything, he can never reach the true height and ecstasy of his solemnity except about wine. What the real English waiter would do or say if Mr. Shaw asked him for a vegetarian meal I cannot dare to predict. I rather think that for the first time in his life he would laugh —a horrible sight.

Dickens's waiter is described by one who is not merely witty, truthful, and observant, like Mr. Bernard Shaw, but one who really knew the atmosphere of inns, one who knew and even liked the smell of beef, and beer, and brandy. Hence there is a richness in Dickens's portrait which does not exist in Mr. Shaw's. Mr. Shaw's waiter is merely a man of tact; Dickens's is a man of principle. Mr. Shaw's waiter is an opportunist, just as Mr. Shaw is an opportunist in politics. Dickens's waiter is ready to stand up seriously for "the true principles of waitering," just as Dickens was ready to stand up for the true principles of Liberalism. Mr. Shaw's waiter is agnostic; his motto is "You never can tell." Dickens's waiter is a dogmatist; his motto is "You can tell; I will tell you." And the true old-fashioned English waiter had really this grave and even moral attitude; he was the servant of the customers as a priest is the servant of the faithful, but scarcely in any less dignified sense. Surely it is not mere patriotic partiality that makes one lament the disappearance of this careful and honourable figure crowded out by meaner men at meaner wages, by the German waiter who has learnt five languages in the course of running away from his own, or the Italian waiter who regards those he serves with a darkling contempt which must certainly be that either of a dynamiter or an exiled prince. The human and hospitable English waiter is vanishing. And Dickens might perhaps have saved him, as he saved Christmas.

I have taken this case of the waiter in Dickens and his equally important counterpart in England as an example of the sincere and genial sketches scattered about these short stories. But there are many others, and one at least demands special mention; I mean Mrs. Lirriper, the London landlady. Not only did Dickens never do anything better in a literary sense, but he never performed more perfectly his main moral function, that of insisting through laughter and flippancy upon the virtue of Christian charity. There has been much broad farce against the lodging-house keeper: he alone could have written broad farce in her favour. It is fashionable to represent the landlady as a tyrant; it is too much forgotten that if she is one of the oppressors she is at least as much one of the oppressed. If she is bad-tempered it is often for the same reasons that make all women bad-tempered (I suppose the exasperating qualities of the other sex); if she is grasping it is often because when a husband makes generosity a vice it is often necessary that a wife should make avarice a virtue. All this Dickens suggested very soundly and in a few strokes in the more remote character of Miss Wozenham. But in Mrs. Lirriper he went further and did not fare worse. In Mrs. Lirriper he suggested quite truly how huge a mass of real good humour, of grand unconscious patience, of unfailing courtesy and constant and difficult benevolence is concealed behind many a lodging-house door and compact in the red-faced person of many a preposterous landlady. Any one could easily excuse the ill-humour of the poor. But great masses of the poor have not even any ill-humour to be excused. Their cheeriness is startling enough to be the foundation of a miracle play; and certainly is startling enough to be the foundation of a romance. Yet I do not know of any romance in which it is expressed except this one.

Of the landlady as of the waiter it may be said that Dickens left in a slight sketch what he might have developed through a long and strong novel. For Dickens had hold of one great truth, the neglect of which has, as it were, truncated and made meagre the work of many brilliant modern novelists. Modern novelists try to make long novels out of subtle characters. But a subtle character soon comes to an end, because it works in and in to its own centre and dies there. But a simple character goes on for ever in a fresh interest and energy, because it works out and out into the infinite universe. Mr. George Moore in France is not by any means so interesting as Mrs. Lirriper in France; for she is trying to find France and he is only trying to find George Moore. Mrs. Lirriper is the female equivalent of Mr. Pickwick. Unlike Mrs. Bardell (another and lesser landlady) she was fully worthy to be Mrs. Pickwick. For in both cases the essential truth is the same; that original innocence which alone deserves adventures and because it alone can appreciate them. We have had Mr. Pickwick in England and we can imagine him in France. We have had Mrs. Lirriper in France and we can imagine her in Mesopotamia or in heaven. The subtle character in the modern novels we cannot really imagine anywhere except in the suburbs or in Limbo.

Bleak House

Bleak House is not certainly Dickens's best book; but perhaps it is his best novel. Such a distinction is not a mere verbal trick; it has to be remembered rather constantly in connection with his work. This particular story represents the highest point of his intellectual maturity. Maturity does not necessarily mean perfection. It is idle to say that a mature potato is perfect; some people like new potatoes. A mature potato is not perfect, but it is a mature potato; the mind of an intelligent epicure may find it less adapted to his particular purpose; but the mind of an intelligent potato would at once admit it as being, beyond all doubt, a genuine, fully developed specimen of his own particular species. The same is in some degree true even of literature. We can say more or less when a human being has come to his full mental growth, even if we go so far as to wish that he had never come to it. Children are very much nicer than grown-up people; but there is such a thing as growing up. When Dickens wrote *Bleak House* he had grown up.

Like Napoleon, he had made his army on the march. He had walked in front of his mob of aggressive characters as Napoleon did in front of the half-baked battalions of the Revolution. And, like Napoleon, he won battle after battle before he knew his own plan of campaign; like Napoleon, he put the enemies' forces to rout before he had put his own force into order. Like Napoleon, he had a victorious army almost before he had an army. After his decisive victories Napoleon began to put his house in order; after his decisive victories Dickens also began to put his house in order. The house, when he had put it in order, was *Bleak House*.

There was one thing common to nearly all the other Dickens tales, with the possible exception of *Dombey and Son*. They were all rambling tales; and they all had a perfect right to be. They were all rambling tales for the very simple reason that they were all about rambling people. They were novels of adventure; they were even diaries of travel. Since the hero strayed from place to place, it did not seem unreasonable that the story should stray from subject to subject. This is true of the bulk of the novels up to and including *David Copperfield*, up to the very brink or threshold of *Bleak House*. Mr. Pickwick wanders about on the white English roads, always looking for antiquities and always finding novelties. Poor Oliver Twist wanders along the same white roads to seek his fortune and to find his misfortune. Nicholas Nickleby goes walking across England because he is young and hopeful; Little Nell's grandfather does the same thing because he is old and silly. There is not much in common between Samuel Pickwick and Oliver Twist; there is not much in common between Oliver Twist and Nicholas Nickleby; there is not much in common (let us hope) between Little Nell's grandfather and any other human being. But they all have this in common, that they may actually all have trodden in each other's footprints. They were all wanderers on the face of the same fair English land. *Martin Chuzzlewit* was only made popular by the travels of the hero in America. When we come to *Dombey and Son* we find, as I have said, an exception; but even here it is odd to note the fact that it was an exception almost by accident. In Dickens's original scheme of the story, much greater prominence was to have been given to the travels and trials of Walter Gay; in fact, the young man was to have had a deterioration of character which could only have been adequately detailed in him in his character of a vagabond and a wastrel. The most important point, however, is that when we come to *David Copperfield*, in some sense the summit of his serious literature, we find the thing still there. The hero still wanders from place to place, his genius is still gipsy. The adventures in the book are less violent and less improbable than those which wait for Pickwick and Nicholas Nickleby; but they are still adventures and not merely events; they are still things met on a road. The facts of the story fall away from David as such facts do fall away from a traveller walking fast. We are more likely perhaps, to pass by Mr. Creakle's school than to pass by Mrs. Jarley's wax-works. The only point is that we should pass by both of them. Up to this point in Dickens's development, his novel, however true, is still picaresque; his hero never really rests anywhere in the story. No one seems really to know where Mr. Pickwick lived. Here he has no abiding city.

When we come to *Bleak House*, we come to a change in artistic structure. The thing is no longer a string of incidents; it is a cycle of incidents. It returns upon itself; it has recurrent melody and poetic justice; it has artistic constancy and artistic revenge. It preserves the unities; even to some extent it preserves the unities of time and place. The story circles round two or three symbolic places; it does not go straggling irregularly all over England like one of Mr. Pickwick's coaches. People go from one place to another place; but not from one place to another place on the road to everywhere else. Mr. Jarndyce goes from Bleak House to visit Mr. Boythorn; but he comes back to Bleak House. Miss Clare and Miss Summerson go from Bleak House to visit Mr. and Mrs. Bayham Badger; but they come back to Bleak House. The whole story strays from Bleak House and plunges into the foul fogs of Chancery and the autumn mists of Chesney Wold; but the whole story comes back to Bleak House. The domestic title is appropriate; it is a permanent address.

Dickens's openings are almost always good; but the opening of *Bleak House* is good in a quite new and striking sense. Nothing could be better, for instance, than the first foolish chapter about the genealogy of the Chuzzlewits; but it has nothing to do with the Chuzzlewits. Nothing could be better than the first chapter of *David Copperfield*; the breezy entrance and banging exit of Miss Betsy Trotwood. But if there is ultimately any crisis or serious subject-matter of *David Copperfield*, it is the marred marriage with Dora, the final return to Agnes; and all this is in no way involved in the highly-amusing fact that his aunt expected him to be a girl. We may repeat that the matter is picaresque. The story begins in one place and ends in another place, and there is no real connection between the beginning and the end except a biographical connection.

A picaresque novel is only a very eventful biography; but the opening of *Bleak House* is quite another business altogether. It is admirable in quite another way. The description of the fog in the first chapter of *Bleak House* is good in itself; but it is not merely good in itself, like the description of the wind in the opening of *Martin Chuzzlewit*; it is also good in the sense that Maeterlinck is good; it is what the modern people call an atmosphere. Dickens begins in the Chancery fog because he means to end in the Chancery fog. He did not begin in the Chuzzlewit wind because he meant to end in it; he began in it because it was a good beginning. This is perhaps the best short way of stating the peculiarity of the position of *Bleak House*. In this *Bleak House* beginning we have the feeling that it is not only a beginning; we have the feeling that the author sees the conclusion and the whole. The beginning is alpha and omega: the beginning and the end. He means that all the characters and all the events shall be read through the smoky colours of that sinister and unnatural vapour.

The same is true throughout the whole tale; the whole tale is symbolic and crowded with symbols. Miss Flite is a funny character, like Miss La Creevy, but Miss La Creevy means only Miss La Creevy. Miss Flite means Chancery. The rag-and-bone man, Krook, is a powerful grotesque; so is Quilp; but in the story Quilp only means Quilp; Krook means Chancery. Rick Carstone is a kind and tragic figure, like Sidney Carton; but Sidney Carton only means the tragedy of human nature; Rick Carstone means the tragedy of Chancery. Little Jo dies pathetically like Little Paul; but for the death of Little Paul we can only blame Dickens; for the death of Little Jo we blame Chancery. Thus the artistic unity of the book, compared to all the author's earlier novels, is satisfying, almost suffocating. There is the *motif*, and again the *motif*. Almost everything is calculated to assert and re-assert the savage morality of Dickens's protest against a particular social evil. The whole theme is that which another Englishman as jovial as Dickens defined shortly and finally as the law's delay. The fog of the first chapter never lifts.

In this twilight he traced wonderful shapes. Those people who fancy that Dickens was a mere clown; that he could not describe anything delicate or deadly in the human character, —those who fancy this are mostly people whose position is explicable in many easy ways. The vast majority of the fastidious critics have, in the quite strict and solid sense of the words, never read Dickens at all; hence their opposition is due to and inspired by a hearty innocence which will certainly make them enthusiastic Dickensians if they ever, by some accident, happen to read him. In other cases it is due to a certain habit of reading books under the eye of a conventional critic, admiring what we expect to admire, regretting what we are told to regret, waiting for Mr. Bumble to admire him, waiting for Little Nell to despise her. Yet again, of course, it is sometimes due to that basest of all artistic indulgences (certainly far baser than the pleasure of absinthe or the pleasure of opium), the pleasure of appreciating works of art which ordinary men cannot appreciate. Surely the vilest point of human vanity is exactly that; to ask to be admired for admiring what your admirers do not admire. But whatever be the reason, whether rude or subtle, which has prevented any particular man from personally admiring Dickens, there is in connection with a book like *Bleak House* something that may be called a solid and impressive challenge. Let anyone who thinks that Dickens could not describe the semi-tones and the abrupt instincts of real human nature simply take the trouble to read the stretch of chapters which detail the way in which Carstone's mind grew gradually morbid about his chances in Chancery. Let him note the manner in which the mere masculinity of Carstone is caught; how as he grows more mad he grows more logical, nay, more rational. Good women who love him come to him, and point out the fact that Jarndyce is a good man, a fact to them solid like an object of the senses. In answer he asks them to understand his position. He does not say this; he does not say that. He only urges that Jarndyce may have become cynical in the affair in the same sense that he himself may have become cynical in the affair. He is always a man; that is to say, he is always unanswerable, always wrong. The passionate certainty of the woman beats itself like battering waves against the thin smooth wall of his insane consistency. I repeat: let any one who thinks that Dickens was a gross and indelicate artist read that part of the book. If Dickens had been the clumsy journalist that such people represent, he never could have written such an episode at all. A clumsy journalist would have made Rick Carstone in his mad career cast off Esther and Ada and the others. The great artist knew better. He knew that even if all the good in a man is dying, the last sense that dies is the sense that knows a good woman from a bad; it is like the scent of a noble hound.

The clumsy journalist would have made Rick Carstone turn on John Jarndyce with an explosion of hatred, as of one who had made an exposure-who had found out what low people call "a false friend" in what they call "his true colours." The great artist knew better; he knew that a good man going wrong tries to salve his soul to the last with the sense of generosity and intellectual justice. He will try to love his enemy if only out of mere love of himself. As the wolf dies fighting, the good man gone wrong dies arguing. This is what constitutes the true and real tragedy of Richard Carstone. It is strictly the one and only great tragedy that Dickens wrote. It is like the tragedy of Hamlet. The others are not tragedies because they deal almost with dead men. The tragedy of old Dorrit is merely the sad spectacle of a dotard dragged about Europe in his last childhood. The tragedy of Steerforth is only that of one who dies suddenly; the tragedy of old Dombey only that of one who was dead all the time. But Rick is a real tragedy, for he is still alive when the quicksand sucks him down.

It is impossible to avoid putting in the first place this pall of smoke which Dickens has deliberately spread over the story. It is quite true that the country underneath is clear enough to contain any number of unconscious comedians or of merry monsters such as he was in the custom of introducing into the carnival of his tales. But he meant us to take the smoky atmosphere seriously. Charles Dickens, who was, like all men who are really funny about funny things, horribly serious about serious things, certainly meant us to read this story in terms of his protest and his insurrection against the emptiness and arrogance of law, against the folly and the pride of judges. Everything else that there is in this story entered into it through the unconscious or accidental energy of his genius, which broke in at every gap. But it was the tragedy of Richard Carstone that he meant, not the comedy of Harold Skimpole. He could not help being amusing; but he meant to be depressing.

Another case might be taken as testing the greater seriousness of this tale. The passages about Mrs. Jellyby and her philanthropic schemes show Dickens at his best in his old and more familiar satiric manner. But in the midst of the Jellyby pandemonium, which is in itself described with the same *abandon* and irrelevance as the boarding-house of Mrs. Todgers or the travelling theatre of Mr. Crummles, the elder Dickens introduced another piece of pure truth and even tenderness. I mean the account of Caddy Jellyby. If Carstone is a truly masculine study of how a man goes wrong, Caddy is a perfectly feminine study of how a girl goes right. Nowhere else perhaps in fiction, and certainly nowhere else in Dickens, is the mere female paradox so well epitomised, the unjust use of words covering so much capacity for a justice of ultimate estimate; the seeming irresponsibility in language concealing such a fixed and pitiless sense of responsibility about things; the air of being always at daggers-drawn with her own kindred, yet the confession of incurable kinship implied in pride and shame; and, above all, that thirst for order and beauty as for something physical; that strange female power of hating ugliness and waste as good men can only hate sin and bad men virtue. Every touch in her is true, from her first bewildering outbursts of hating people because she likes them, down to the sudden quietude and good sense which announces that she has slipped into her natural place as a woman. Miss Clare is a figure-head, Miss Summerson in some ways a failure; but Miss Caddy Jellyby is by far the greatest, the most human, and the most really dignified of all the heroines of Dickens.

With one or two exceptions, all the effects in this story are of this somewhat quieter kind, though none of them are so subtly successful as Rick Carstone and Caddy. Harold Skimpole begins as a sketch drawn with a pencil almost as airy and fanciful as his own. The humour of the earlier scenes is delightful-the scenes in which Skimpole looks on at other people paying his debts with the air of a kindly outsider, and suggests in formless legal phraseology that they might "sign something" or "make over something," or the scene in which he tries to explain the advantages of accepting everything to the apoplectic Mr. Boythorn. But it was one of the defects of Dickens as a novelist that his characters always became coarser and clumsier as they passed through the practical events of a story, and this would necessarily be so with Skimpole, whose position was conceivable even to himself only on the assumption that he was a mere spectator of life. Poor Skimpole only asked to be kept out of the business of this world, and Dickens ought to have kept him out of the business of *Bleak House*. By the end of the tale he has brought Skimpole to doing acts of mere low villainy. This altogether spoils the ironical daintiness of the original notion. Skimpole was meant to end with a note of interrogation. As it is, he ends with a big, black, unmistakable blot. Speaking purely artistically, we may say that this is as great a collapse or vulgarisation as if Richard Carstone had turned into a common blackguard and wife-beater, or Caddy Jellyby into a comic and illiterate landlady. Upon the whole it may, I think, be said that the character of Skimpole is rather a piece of brilliant moralising than of pure observation or creation. Dickens had a singularly just mind. He was wild in his caricatures, but very sane in his impressions. Many of his books were devoted, and this book is partly devoted, to a denunciation of aristocracy-of the idle class that lives easily upon the toil of nations. But he was fairer than many modern revolutionists, and he insisted on satirising also those who prey on society not in the name of rank or law, but in the name of intellect and beauty. Sir Leicester Dedlock and Mr. Harold Skimpole are alike in accepting with a royal unconsciousness the anomaly and evil of their position. But the idleness and insolence of the aristocrat is human and humble compared to the idleness and insolence of the artist.

With the exception of a few fine freaks, such as Turveydrop and Chadband, all the figures in this book are touched more delicately, even more faintly, than is common with Dickens. But if the figures are touched more faintly, it is partly because they are figures in a fog-the fog of Chancery. Dickens meant that twilight to be oppressive; for it was the symbol of oppression. Deliberately he did not dispel the darkness at the end of this book, as he does dispel it at the end of most of his books. Pickwick gets out of the Fleet Prison; Carstone never gets out of Chancery but by death. This tyranny, Dickens said, shall not be lifted by the light subterfuge of a fiction. This tyranny shall never be lifted till all Englishmen lift it together.

Child's History of England

There are works of great authors manifestly inferior to their typical work which are yet necessary to their fame and their figure in the world. It is not difficult to recall examples of them. No one, for instance, would talk of Scott's *Tales of a Grandfather* as indicating the power that produced *Kenilworth* and *Guy Mannering*. Nevertheless, without this chance minor compilation we should not really have the key of Scott. Without this one insignificant book we should not see his significance. For the truth was that Scott loved history more than romance, because he was so constituted as to find it more romantic than romance. He preferred the deeds of Wallace and Douglas to those of Marmion and Ivanhoe. Therefore his garrulous gossip of old times, his rambles in dead centuries, give us the real material and impulse of all his work; they represent the quarry in which he dug and the food on which he fed. Almost alone among novelists Scott actually preferred those parts of his historical novels which he had not invented himself. He exults when he can boast in an eager note that he has stolen some saying from history. Thus *The Tales of a Grandfather*, though small, is in some sense the frame of all the Waverley novels. We realise that all Scott's novels are tales of a grandfather.

What has been said here about Scott might be said in a less degree about Thackeray's *Four Georges*. Though standing higher among his works than *The Tales of a Grandfather* among Scott's they are not his works of genius; yet they seem in some way to surround, supplement, and explain such works. Without the *Four Georges* we should know less of the link that bound Thackeray to the beginning and to the end of the eighteenth century; thence we should have known less of Colonel Esmond and also less of Lord Steyne. To these two examples I have given of the slight historical experiments of two novelists a third has to be added. The third great master of English fiction whose glory fills the nineteenth century also produced a small experiment in the popularisation of history. It is separated from the other two partly by a great difference of merit but partly also by an utter difference of tone and outlook. We seem to hear it suddenly as in the first words spoken by a new voice, a voice gay, colloquial, and impatient. Scott and Thackeray were tenderly attached to the past; Dickens (in his consciousness at any rate) was impatient with everything, but especially impatient with the past.

A collection of the works of Dickens would be incomplete in an essential as well as a literal sense without his *Child's History of England*. It may not be important as a contribution to history, but it is important as a contribution to biography; as a contribution to the character and the career of the man who wrote it, a typical man of his time. That he had made no personal historical researches, that he had no special historical learning, that he had not had, in truth, even anything that could be called a good education, all this only accentuates not the merit but at least the importance of the book. For here we may read in plain popular language, written by a man whose genius for popular exposition has never been surpassed among men, a brief account of the origin and meaning of England as it seemed to the average Englishman of that age. When subtler views of our history, some more false and some more true than his, have become popular, or at least well known, when in the near future Carlylean or Catholic or Marxian views of history have spread themselves among the reading public, this book will always remain as a bright and brisk summary of the cock-sure, healthy-minded, essentially manly and essentially ungentlemanly view of history which characterised the Radicals of that particular Radical era. The history tells us nothing about the periods that it talks about; but it tells us a great deal about the period that it does not talk about; the period in which it was written. It is in no sense a history of England from the Roman invasion; but it is certainly one of the documents which will contribute to a history of England in the nineteenth century.

Of the actual nature of its philosophical and technical limitations it is, I suppose, unnecessary to speak. They all resolve themselves into one fault common in the modern world, and certainly characteristic of historians much more learned and pretentious than Dickens. That fault consists simply in ignoring or underrating the variety of strange evils and unique dangers in the world. The Radicals of the nineteenth century were engaged, and most righteously engaged, in dealing with one particular problem of human civilisation; they were shifting and apportioning more equally a load of custom that had really become unmeaning, often accidental, and nearly always unfair. Thus, for instance, a fierce and fighting penal code, which had been perfectly natural when the robbers were as strong as the Government, had become in more ordered times nothing but a base and bloody habit. Thus again Church powers and dues, which had been human when every man felt the Church as the best part of himself, were mere mean privileges when the nation was full of sects and full of freethinkers. This clearing away of external symbols that no longer symbolised anything was an honourable and needful work; but it was so difficult that to the men engaged in it it blocked up the perspective and filled the sky, so that they slid into a very natural mental mistake which coloured all their views of history. They supposed that this particular problem on which they were engaged was the one problem upon which all mankind had always been engaged. They got it into their heads that breaking away from a dead past was the perpetual process of humanity. The truth is obviously that humanity has found itself in many difficulties very different from that. Sometimes the best business of an age is to resist some alien invasion; sometimes to preach practical self-control in a world too self-indulgent and diffused; sometimes to prevent the growth in the State of great new private enterprises that would poison or oppress it. Above all it may sometimes happen that the highest task of a thinking citizen may be to do the exact opposite of the work which the Radicals had to do. It may be his highest duty to cling on to every scrap of the past that he can find, if he feels that the ground is giving way beneath him and sinking into mere savagery and forgetfulness of all human culture. This was exactly the position of all thinking men in what we call the dark ages, say from the sixth to the tenth century. The cheap progressive view of history can never make head or tail of that epoch; it was an epoch upside down. We think of the old things as barbaric and the new things as enlightened. In that age all the enlightened things were old; all the barbaric and brutally ignorant things were new and up to date. Republicanism was a fading legend; despotism was a new and successful experiment. Christianity was not only better than the clans that rebelled against it; Christianity was more rationalistic than they were. When men looked back they saw progress and reason; when they looked forward they saw shapeless tradition and tribal terror. Touching such an age it is obvious that all our modern terms describing reform or conservation are foolish and beside the mark. The Conservative was then the only possible reformer. If a man did not strengthen the remains of Roman order and the root of Roman Christianity, he was simply helping the world to roll downhill into ruin and idiotcy. Remember all these evident historical truths and then turn to the account given by Charles Dickens of that great man, St. Dunstan. It is not that the pert cockney tone of the abuse is irritating to the nerves: it is that he has got the whole hang of the thing wrong. His head is full of the nineteenth-century situation; that a priest imposing discipline is a person somehow blocking the way to equality and light. Whereas the point about such a man as Dunstan was that nobody in the place except he cared a button about equality or light: and that he was defending what was left of them against the young and growing power of darkness and division and caste.

Nevertheless the case against such books as this is commonly stated wrong. The fault of Dickens is not (as is often said) that he "applies the same moral standard to all ages." Every sane man must do that: a moral standard must remain the same or it is not a moral standard. If we call St. Anthony of Padua a good man, we must mean what we mean when we call Huxley a good man, or else there is no sense in using the word "good." The fault of the Dickens school of popular history lies, not in the application of a plain rule of right and wrong to all circumstances, but in ignorance of the circumstances to which it was applied. It is not that they wrongly enforce the fixed principle that life should be saved; it is that they take a fire-engine to a shipwreck and a lifeboat to a house on fire. The business of a good man in Dickens's time was to bring justice up to date. The business of a good man in Dunstan's time was to toil to ensure the survival of any justice at all.

And Dickens, through being a living and fighting man of his own time, kept the health of his own heart, and so saw many truths with a single eye: truths that were spoilt for subtler eyes. He was much more really right than Carlyle; immeasurably more right than Froude. He was more right precisely because he applied plain human morals to all facts as he saw them. Carlyle really had a vague idea that in coarse and cruel times it was right to be coarse and cruel; that tyranny was excusable in the twelfth century: as if the twelfth century did not denounce tyrants as much or more than any other. Carlyle, in fact, fancied that Rufus was the right sort of man; a view which was not only not shared by Anselm, but was probably not shared by Rufus. In this connection, or rather in connection with the other case of Froude, it is worth while to take another figure from Dickens's history, which illustrates the other and better side of the facile and popular method. Sheer ignorance of the environment made him wrong about Dunstan. But sheer instinct and good moral tradition made him right, for instance, about Henry 8.; right where Froude is wildly wrong. Dickens's imagination could not re-picture an age where learning and liberty were dying rather than being born: but Henry VIII. lived in a time of expanding knowledge and unrest; a time therefore somewhat like the Victorian. And Dickens in his childish but robust way does perceive the main point about him: that he was a wicked man. He misses all the fine shades, of course; he makes him every kind of wicked man at once. He leaves out the serious interests of the man: his strange but real concern for theology; his love of certain legal and moral forms; his half-unconscious patriotism. But he sees the solid bulk of definite badness simply because it was there; and Froude cannot see it at all; because Froude followed Carlyle and played tricks with the eternal conscience. Henry VIII. *was* "a blot of blood and grease upon the history of England." For he was the embodiment of the Devil in the Renascence, that wild worship of mere pleasure and scorn, which with its pictures and its palaces has enriched and ruined the world.

The time will soon come when the mere common-sense of Dickens, like the mere common-sense of Macaulay (though his was poisoned by learning and Whig politics), will appear to give a plainer and therefore truer picture of the mass of history than the mystical perversity of a man of genius writing only out of his own temperament, like Carlyle or Taine. If a man has a new theory of ethics there is one thing he must not be allowed to do. Let him give laws on Sinai, let him dictate a Bible, let him fill the world with cathedrals if he can. But he must not be allowed to write a history of England; or a history of any country. All history was conducted on ordinary morality: with his extraordinary morality he is certain to read it all askew. Thus Carlyle tries to write of the Middle Ages with a bias against humility and mercy; that is, with a bias against the whole theoretic morality of the Middle Ages. The result is that he turns into a mere turmoil of arrogant German savages what was really the most complete and logical, if not the highest, of human civilisations. Historically speaking, it is better to be Dickens than to be this; better to be ignorant, provincial, slap-dash, seeing only the passing moment, but in that moment, to be true to eternal things.

It must be remembered, of course, that Dickens deliberately offers this only as a "child's" history of England. That is, he only professes to be able to teach history as any father of a little boy of five professes to be able to teach him history. And although the history of England would certainly be taught very differently (as regards the actual criticism of events and men) in a family with a wider culture or with another religion, the general method would be the same. For the general method is quite right. This black-and-white history of heroes and villains; this history full of pugnacious ethics and of nothing else, is the right kind of history for children. I have often wondered how the scientific Marxians and the believers in "the materialist view of history" will ever manage to teach their dreary economic generalisations to children: but I suppose they will have no children. Dickens's history will always be popular with the young; almost as popular as Dickens's novels, and for the same reason: because it is full of moralising. Science and art without morality are not dangerous in the sense commonly supposed. They are not dangerous like a fire, but dangerous like a fog. A fire is dangerous in its brightness; a fog in its dulness; and thought without morals is merely dull, like a fog. The fog seems to be creeping up the street; putting out lamp after lamp. But this cockney lamp-post which the children love is still crowned with its flame; and when the fathers have forgotten ethics, their babies will turn and teach them.

Hard times

I have heard that in some debating clubs there is a rule that the members may discuss anything except religion and politics. I cannot imagine what they do discuss; but it is quite evident that they have ruled out the only two subjects which are either important or amusing. The thing is a part of a certain modern tendency to avoid things because they lead to warmth; whereas, obviously, we ought, even in a social sense, to seek those things specially. The warmth of the discussion is as much a part of hospitality as the warmth of the fire. And it is singularly suggestive that in English literature the two things have died together. The very people who would blame Dickens for his sentimental hospitality are the very people who would also blame him for his narrow political conviction. The very people who would mock him for his narrow radicalism are those who would mock him for his broad fireside. Real conviction and real charity are much nearer than people suppose. Dickens was capable of loving all men; but he refused to love all opinions. The modern humanitarian can love all opinions, but he cannot love all men; he seems, sometimes, in the ecstasy of his humanitarianism, even to hate them all. He can love all opinions, including the opinion that men are unlovable.

In feeling Dickens as a lover we must never forget him as a fighter, and a fighter for a creed; but indeed there is no other kind of fighter. The geniality which he spread over all his creations was geniality spread from one centre, from one flaming peak. He was willing to excuse Mr. Micawber for being extravagant; but Dickens and Dickens's doctrine were strictly to decide how far he was to be excused. He was willing to like Mr. Twemlow in spite of his snobbishness, but Dickens and Dickens's doctrine were alone to be judges of how far he was snobbish. There was never a more didactic writer: hence there was never one more amusing. He had no mean modern notion of keeping the moral doubtful. He would have regarded this as a mere piece of slovenliness, like leaving the last page illegible.

Everywhere in Dickens's work these angles of his absolute opinion stood up out of the confusion of his general kindness, just as sharp and splintered peaks stand up out of the soft confusion of the forests. Dickens is always generous, he is generally kind-hearted, he is often sentimental, he is sometimes intolerably maudlin; but you never know when you will not come upon one of the convictions of Dickens; and when you do come upon it you do know it. It is as hard and as high as any precipice or peak of the mountains. The highest and hardest of these peaks is *Hard Times*.

It is here more than anywhere else that the sternness of Dickens emerges as separate from his softness; it is here, most obviously, so to speak, that his bones stick out. There are indeed many other books of his which are written better and written in a sadder tone. *Great Expectations* is melancholy in a sense; but it is doubtful of everything, even of its own melancholy. *The Tale of Two Cities* is a great tragedy, but it is still a sentimental tragedy. It is a great drama, but it is still a melodrama. But this tale of *Hard Times* is in some way harsher than all these. For it is the expression of a righteous indignation which cannot condescend to humour and which cannot even condescend to pathos. Twenty times we have taken Dickens's hand and it has been sometimes hot with revelry and sometimes weak with weariness; but this time we start a little, for it is inhumanly cold; and then we realise that we have touched his gauntlet of steel.

One cannot express the real value of this book without being irrelevant. It is true that one cannot express the real value of anything without being irrelevant. If we take a thing frivolously we can take it separately, but the moment we take a thing seriously, if it were only an old umbrella, it is obvious that that umbrella opens above us into the immensity of the whole universe. But there are rather particular reasons why the value of the book called *Hard Times* should be referred back to great historic and theoretic matters with which it may appear superficially to have little or nothing to do. The chief reason can perhaps be stated thus-that English politics had for more than a hundred years been getting into more and more of a hopeless tangle (a tangle which, of course, has since become even worse) and that Dickens did in some extraordinary way see what was wrong, even if he did not see what was right.

The Liberalism which Dickens and nearly all of his contemporaries professed had begun in the American and the French Revolutions. Almost all modern English criticism upon those revolutions has been vitiated by the assumption that those revolutions burst upon a world which was unprepared for their ideas —a world ignorant of the possibility of such ideas. Somewhat the same mistake is made by those who suggest that Christianity was adopted by a world incapable of criticising it; whereas obviously it was adopted by a world that was tired of criticising everything. The vital mistake that is made about the French Revolution is merely this-that everyone talks about it as the introduction of a new idea. It was not the introduction of a new idea; there are no new ideas. Or if there are new ideas, they would not cause the least irritation if they were introduced into political society; because the world having never got used to them there would be no mass of men ready to fight for them at a moment's notice. That which was irritating about the French Revolution was this-that it was not the introduction of a new ideal, but the practical fulfilment of an old one. From the time of the first fairy tales men had always believed ideally in equality; they had always thought that something ought to be done, if anything could be done, to redress the balance between Cinderella and the ugly sisters. The irritating thing about the French was not that they said this ought to be done; everybody said that. The irritating thing about the French was that they did it. They proposed to carry out into a positive scheme what had been the vision of humanity; and humanity was naturally annoyed. The kings of Europe did not make war upon the Revolution because it was a blasphemy, but because it was a copy-book maxim which had been just too accurately copied. It was a platitude which they had always held in theory unexpectedly put into practice. The tyrants did not hate democracy because it was a paradox; they hated it because it was a truism which seemed in some danger of coming true.

Now it happens to be hugely important to have this right view of the Revolution in considering its political effects upon England. For the English, being a deeply and indeed excessively romantic people, could never be quite content with this quality of cold and bald obviousness about the republican formula. The republican formula was merely this-that the State must consist of its citizens ruling equally, however unequally they may do anything else. In their capacity of members of the State they are all equally interested in its preservation. But the English soon began to be romantically restless about this eternal truism; they were perpetually trying to turn it into something else, into something more picturesque-progress perhaps, or anarchy. At last they turned it into the highly exciting and highly unsound system of politics, which was known as the Manchester School, and which was expressed with a sort of logical flightiness, more excusable in literature, by Mr. Herbert Spencer. Of course Danton or Washington or any of the original republicans would have thought these people were mad. They would never have admitted for a moment that the State must not interfere with commerce or competition; they would merely have insisted that if the State did interfere, it must really be the State-that is, the whole people. But the distance between the common sense of Danton and the mere ecstasy of Herbert Spencer marks the English way of colouring and altering the revolutionary idea. The English people as a body went blind, as the saying is, for interpreting democracy entirely in terms of liberty. They said in substance that if they had more and more liberty it did not matter whether they had any equality or any fraternity. But this was violating the sacred trinity of true politics; they confounded the persons and they divided the substance.

Now the really odd thing about England in the nineteenth century is this-that there was one Englishman who happened to keep his head. The men who lost their heads lost highly scientific and philosophical heads; they were great cosmic systematisers like Spencer, great social philosophers like Bentham, great practical politicians like Bright, great political economists like Mill. The man who kept his head kept a head full of fantastic nonsense; he was a writer of rowdy farces, a demagogue of fiction, a man without education in any serious sense whatever, a man whose whole business was to turn ordinary cockneys into extraordinary caricatures. Yet when all these other children of the revolution went wrong he, by a mystical something in his bones, went right. He knew nothing of the Revolution; yet he struck the note of it. He returned to the original sentimental commonplace upon which it is forever founded, as the Church is founded on a rock. In an England gone mad about a minor theory he reasserted the original idea-the idea that no one in the State must be too weak to influence the State.

This man was Dickens. He did this work much more genuinely than it was done by Carlyle or Ruskin; for they were simply Tories making out a romantic case for the return of Toryism. But Dickens was a real Liberal demanding the return of real Liberalism. Dickens was there to remind people that England had rubbed out two words of the revolutionary motto, had left only Liberty and destroyed Equality and Fraternity. In this book, *Hard Times*, he specially champions equality. In all his books he champions fraternity.

The atmosphere of this book and what it stands for can be very adequately conveyed in the note on the book by Lord Macaulay, who may stand as a very good example of the spirit of England in those years of eager emancipation and expanding wealth-the years in which Liberalism was turned from an omnipotent truth to a weak scientific system. Macaulay's private comment on *Hard Times* runs, "One or two passages of exquisite pathos and the rest sullen Socialism." That is not an unfair and certainly not a specially hostile criticism, but it exactly shows how the book struck those people who were mad on political liberty and dead about everything else. Macaulay mistook for a new formula called Socialism what was, in truth, only the old formula called political democracy. He and his Whigs had so thoroughly mauled and modified the original idea of Rousseau or Jefferson that when they saw it again they positively thought that it was something quite new and eccentric. But the truth was that Dickens was not a Socialist, but an unspoilt Liberal; he was not sullen; nay, rather, he had remained strangely hopeful. They called him a sullen Socialist only to disguise their astonishment at finding still loose about the London streets a happy republican.

Dickens is the one living link between the old kindness and the new, between the good will of the past and the good works of the future. He links May Day with Bank Holiday, and he does it almost alone. All the men around him, great and good as they were, were in comparison puritanical, and never so puritanical as when they were also atheistic. He is a sort of solitary pipe down which pours to the twentieth century the original river of Merry England. And although this *Hard Times* is, as its name implies, the hardest of his works, although there is less in it perhaps than in any of the others of the *abandon* and the buffoonery of Dickens, this only emphasises the more clearly the fact that he stood almost alone for a more humane and hilarious view of democracy. None of his great and much more highly-educated contemporaries could help him in this. Carlyle was as gloomy on the one side as Herbert Spencer on the other. He protested against the commercial oppression simply and solely because it was not only an oppression but a depression. And this protest of his was made specially in the case of the book before us. It may be bitter, but it was a protest against bitterness. It may be dark, but it is the darkness of the subject and not of the author. He is by his own account dealing with hard times, but not with a hard eternity, not with a hard philosophy of the universe. Nevertheless, this is the one place in his work where he does not make us remember human happiness by example as well as by precept. This is, as I have said, not the saddest, but certainly the harshest of his stories. It is perhaps the only place where Dickens, in defending happiness, for a moment forgets to be happy.

He describes Bounderby and Gradgrind with a degree of grimness and sombre hatred very different from the half affectionate derision which he directed against the old tyrants or humbugs of the earlier nineteenth century-the pompous Dedlock or the fatuous Nupkins, the grotesque Bumble or the inane Tigg. In those old books his very abuse was benignant; in *Hard Times* even his sympathy is hard. And the reason is again to be found in the political facts of the century. Dickens could be half genial with the older generation of oppressors because it was a dying generation. It was evident, or at least it seemed evident then, that Nupkins could not go on much longer making up the law of England to suit himself; that Sir Leicester Dedlock could not go on much longer being kind to his tenants as if they were dogs and cats. And some of these evils the nineteenth century did really eliminate or improve. For the first half of the century Dickens and all his friends were justified in feeling that the chains were falling from mankind. At any rate, the chains did fall from Mr. Rouncewell the Iron-master. And when they fell from him he picked them up and put them upon the poor.

Little Dorrit

Little Dorrit stands in Dickens's life chiefly as a signal of how far he went down the road of realism, of sadness, and of what is called modernity. True, it was by no means the best of the books of his later period; some even think it the worst. *Great Expectations* is certainly the best of the later novels; some even think it the best of all the novels. Nor is it the novel most concerned with strictly recent problems; that title must be given to *Hard Times*. Nor again is it the most finely finished or well constructed of the later books; that claim can be probably made for *Edwin Drood*. By a queer verbal paradox the most carefully finished of his later tales is the tale that is not finished at all. In form, indeed, the book bears a superficial resemblance to those earlier works by which the young Dickens had set the whole world laughing long ago. Much of the story refers to a remote time early in the nineteenth century; much of it was actually recalled and copied from the life of Dickens's father in the old Marshalsea prison. Also the narrative has something of the form, or rather absence of form, which belonged to *Nicholas Nickleby* or *Martin Chuzzlewit*. It has something of the old air of being a string of disconnected adventures, like a boy's book about bears and Indians. The Dorrits go wandering for no particular reason on the Continent of Europe, just as young Martin Chuzzlewit went wandering for no particular reason on the continent of America. The story of *Little Dorrit* stops and lingers at the doors of the Circumlocution Office much in the same way that the story of Samuel Pickwick stops and lingers in the political excitement of Eatanswill. The villain, Blandois, is a very stagey villain indeed; quite as stagey as Ralph Nickleby or the mysterious Monk. The secret of the dark house of Clennam is a very silly secret; quite as silly as the secret of Ralph Nickleby or the secret of Monk. Yet all these external similarities between *Little Dorrit* and the earliest books, all this loose, melodramatic quality, only serves to make more obvious and startling the fact that some change has come over the soul of Dickens. *Hard Times* is harsh; but then *Hard Times* is a social pamphlet; perhaps it is only harsh as a social pamphlet must be harsh. *Bleak House* is a little sombre; but then *Bleak House* is almost a detective story; perhaps it is only sombre in the sense that a detective story must be sombre. *A Tale of Two Cities* is a tragedy; but then *A Tale of Two Cities* is a tale of the French Revolution; perhaps it is only a tragedy because the French Revolution was a tragedy. *The Mystery of Edwin Drood* is dark; but then the mystery of anybody must be dark. In all these other cases of the later books an artistic reason can be given—a reason of theme or of construction for the slight sadness that seems to cling to them. But exactly because *Little Dorrit* is a mere Dickens novel, it shows that something must somehow have happened to Dickens himself. Even in resuming his old liberty, he cannot resume his old hilarity. He can re-create the anarchy, but not the revelry.

It so happens that this strange difference between the new and the old mode of Dickens can be symbolised and stated in one separate and simple contrast. Dickens's father had been a prisoner in a debtors' prison, and Dickens's works contain two pictures partly suggested by the personality of that prisoner. Mr. Micawber is one picture of him. Mr. Dorrit is another. This truth is almost incredible, but it is the truth. The joyful Micawber, whose very despair was exultant, and the desolate Dorrit, whose very pride was pitiful, were the same man. The valiant Micawber and the nervous, shaking Dorrit were the same man. The defiant Micawber and the snobbish, essentially obsequious Dorrit were the same man. I do not mean of course that either of the pictures was an exact copy of anybody. The whole Dickens genius consisted of taking hints and turning them into human beings. As he took twenty real persons and turned them into one fictitious person, so he took one real person and turned him into twenty fictitious persons. This quality would suggest one character, that quality would suggest another. But in this case, at any rate, he did take one real person and turn him into two. And what is more, he turned him into two persons who seem to be quite opposite persons. To ordinary readers of Dickens, to say that Micawber and Dorrit had in any sense the same original, will appear unexpected and wild. No conceivable connection between the two would ever have occurred to anybody who had read Dickens with simple and superficial enjoyment, as all good literature ought to be read. It will seem to them just as silly as saying that the Fat Boy and Mr. Alfred Jingle were both copied from the same character. It will seem as insane as saying that the character of Smike and the character of Major Bagstock were both copied from Dickens's father. Yet it is an unquestionable historical fact that Micawber and Dorrit were both copied from Dickens's father, in the only sense that any figures in good literature are ever copied from anything or anybody. Dickens did get the main idea of Micawber from his father; and that idea is that a poor man is not conquered by the world. And Dickens did get the main idea of Dorrit from his father; and that idea is that a poor man may be conquered by the world. I shall take the opportunity of discussing, in a moment, which of these ideas is true. Doubtless old John Dickens included both the gay and the sad moral; most men do. My only purpose here is to point out that Dickens drew the gay moral in 1849, and the sad moral in 1857.

There must have been some real sadness at this time creeping like a cloud over Dickens himself. It is nothing that a man dwells on the darkness of dark things; all healthy men do that. It is when he dwells on the darkness of bright things that we have reason to fear some disease of the emotions. There must really have been some depression when a man can only see the sad side of flowers or the sad side of holidays or the sad side of wine. And there must be some depression of an uncommonly dark and genuine character when a man has reached such a point that he can see only the sad side of Mr. Wilkins Micawber.

Yet this is in reality what had happened to Dickens about this time. Staring at Wilkins Micawber he could see only the weakness and the tragedy that was made possible by his indifference, his indulgence, and his bravado. He had already indeed been slightly moved towards this study of the feebleness and ruin of the old epicurean type with which he had once sympathised, the type of Bob Sawyer or Dick Swiveller. He had already attacked the evil of it in *Bleak House* in the character of Harold Skimpole, with its essentially cowardly carelessness and its highly selfish communism. Nevertheless, as I have said before, it must have been no small degree of actual melancholia which led Dickens to look for a lesson of disaster and slavery in the very same career from which he had once taught lessons of continual recuperation and a kind of fantastic freedom. There must have been at this time some melancholy behind the writings. There must have existed on this earth at the time that portent and paradox —a somewhat depressed Dickens.

Perhaps it was a reminiscence of that metaphorical proverb which tells us that "truth lies at the bottom of a well." Perhaps these people thought that the only way to find truth in the well was to drown oneself. But on whatever thin theoretic basis, the type and period of George Gissing did certainly consider that Dickens, so far as he went, was all the worse for the optimism of the story of Micawber; hence it is not unnatural that they should think him all the better for the comparative pessimism of the story of *Little Dorrit*. The very things in the tale that would naturally displease the ordinary admirers of Dickens, are the things which would naturally please a man like George Gissing. There are many of these things, but one of them emerges pre-eminent and unmistakable. This is the fact that when all is said and done the main business of the story of *Little Dorrit* is to describe the victory of circumstances over a soul. The circumstances are the financial ruin and long imprisonment of Edward Dorrit; the soul is Edward Dorrit himself. Let it be granted that the circumstances are exceptional and oppressive, are denounced as exceptional and oppressive, are finally exploded and overthrown; still, they are circumstances. Let it be granted that the soul is that of a man perhaps weak in any case and retaining many merits to the last, still it is a soul. Let it be granted, above all, that the admission that such spiritual tragedies do occur does not decrease by so much as an iota our faith in the validity of any spiritual struggle. For example, Stevenson has made a study of the breakdown of a good man's character under a burden for which he is not to blame, in the tragedy of Henry Durie in *The Master of Ballantrae*. Yet he has added, in the mouth of Mackellar, the exact common sense and good theology of the matter, saying "It matters not a jot; for he that is to pass judgment upon the records of our life is the same that formed us in frailty." Let us concede then all this, and the fact remains that the study of the slow demoralisation of a man through mere misfortune was not a study congenial to Dickens, not in accordance with his original inspiration, not connected in any manner with the special thing that he had to say. In a word, the thing is not quite a part of himself; and he was not quite himself when he did it.

He was still quite a young man; his depression did not come from age. In fact, as far as I know, mere depression never does come from mere age. Age can pass into a beautiful reverie. Age can pass into a sort of beautiful idiocy. But I do not think that the actual decline and close of our ordinary vitality brings with it any particular heaviness of the spirits. The spirits of the old do not as a rule seem to become more and more ponderous until they sink into the earth. Rather the spirits of the old seem to grow lighter and lighter until they float away like thistledown. Wherever there is the definite phenomenon called depression, it commonly means that something else has been closer to us than so normal a thing as death. There has been disease, bodily or mental, or there has been sin, or there has been some struggle or effort, breaking past the ordinary boundaries of human custom. In the case of Dickens there had been two things that are not of the routine of a wholesome human life; there had been the quarrel with his wife, and there had been the strain of incessant and exaggerated intellectual labour. He had not an easy time; and on top of that (or perhaps rather at the bottom of it) he had not an easy nature. Not only did his life necessitate work, but his character necessitated worry about work; and that combination is always one which is very dangerous to the temperament which is exposed to it. The only people who ought to be allowed to work are the people who are able to shirk. The only people who ought to be allowed to worry are the people who have nothing to worry about. When the two are combined, as they were in Dickens, you are very likely to have at least one collapse. *Little Dorrit* is a very interesting, sincere, and fascinating book. But for all that, I fancy it is the one collapse.

The complete proof of this depression may be difficult to advance; because it will be urged, and entirely with reason, that the actual examples of it are artistic and appropriate. Dickens, the Gissing school will say, was here pointing out certain sad truths of psychology; can any one say that he ought not to point them out? That may be; in any case, to explain depression is not to remove it. But the instances of this more sombre quality of which I have spoken are not very hard to find. The thing can easily be seen by comparing a book like *Little Dorrit* with a book like *David Copperfield*. David Copperfield and Arthur Clennam have both been brought up in unhappy homes, under bitter guardians and a black, disheartening religion. It is the whole point of David Copperfield that he has broken out of a Calvinistic tyranny which he cannot forgive. But it is the whole point of Arthur Clennam that he has not broken out of the Calvinistic tyranny, but is still under its shadow. Copperfield has come from a gloomy childhood; Clennam, though forty years old, is still in a gloomy childhood. When David meets the Murdstones again it is to defy them with the health and hilarious anger that go with his happy delirium about Dora. But when Clennam re-enters his sepulchral house there is a weight upon his soul which makes it impossible for him to answer, with any spirit, the morbidities of his mother, or even the grotesque interferences of Mr. Flintwinch. This is only another example of the same quality which makes the Dickens of *Little Dorrit* insist on the degradation of the debtor, while the Dickens of *David Copperfield* insisted on his splendid irresponsibility, his essential emancipation. Imprisonments passed over Micawber like summer clouds. But the imprisonment in *Little Dorrit* is like a complete natural climate and environment; it has positively modified the shapes and functions of the animals that dwell in it. A horrible thing has happened to Dickens; he has almost become an Evolutionist. Worse still, in studying the Calvinism of Mrs. Clennam's house, he has almost become a Calvinist. He half believes (as do some of the modern scientists) that there is really such a thing as "a child of wrath," that a man on whom such an early shadow had fallen could never shake it off. For ancient Calvinism and modern Evolutionism are essentially the same things. They are both ingenious logical blasphemies against the dignity and liberty of the human soul.

The workmanship of the book in detail is often extremely good. The one passage in the older and heartier Dickens manner (I mean the description of the Circumlocution Office) is beyond praise. It is a complete picture of the way England is actually governed at this moment. The very core of our politics is expressed in the light and easy young Barnacle who told Clennam with a kindly frankness that he, Clennam, would "never go on with it." Dickens hit the mark so that the bell rang when he made all the lower officials, who were cads, tell Clennam coldly that his claim was absurd, until the last official, who is a gentleman, tells him genially that the whole business is absurd. Even here, perhaps, there is something more than the old exuberant derision of Dickens; there is a touch of experience that verges on scepticism. Everywhere else, certainly, there is the note which I have called Calvinistic; especially in the predestined passion of Tattycoram or the incurable cruelty of Miss Wade. Even Little Dorrit herself had, we are told, one stain from her prison experience; and it is spoken of like a bodily stain; like something that cannot be washed away.

There is no denying that this is Dickens's dark moment. It adds enormously to the value of his general view of life that such a dark moment came. He did what all the heroes and all the really happy men have done; he descended into Hell. Nor is it irreverent to continue the quotation from the Creed, for in the next book he was to write he was to break out of all these dreams of fate and failure, and with his highest voice to speak of the triumph of the weak of this world. His next book was to leave us saying, as Sydney Carton mounted the scaffold, words which, splendid in themselves, have never been so splendidly quoted—"I am the Resurrection and the Life; whoso believeth in Me though he be dead yet he shall live." In Sydney Carton at least, Dickens shows none of that dreary submission to the environment of the irrevocable that had for an instant lain on him like a cloud. On this occasion he sees with the old heroic clearness that to be a failure may be one step to being a saint. On the third day he rose again from the dead.

A Tale of Two Cities

As an example of Dickens's literary work, *A Tale of Two Cities* is not wrongly named. It is his most typical contact with the civic ideals of Europe. All his other tales have been tales of one city. He was in spirit a Cockney; though that title has been quite unreasonably twisted to mean a cad. By the old sound and proverbial test a Cockney was a man born within the sound of Bow bells. That is, he was a man born within the immediate appeal of high civilisation and of eternal religion. Shakespeare, in the heart of his fantastic forest, turns with a splendid suddenness to the Cockney ideal as being the true one after all. For a jest, for a reaction, for an idle summer love or still idler summer hatred, it is well to wander away into the bewildering forest of Arden. It is well that those who are sick with love or sick with the absence of love, those who weary of the folly of courts or weary yet more of their wisdom, it is natural that these should trail away into the twinkling twilight of the woods. Yet it is here that Shakespeare makes one of his most arresting and startling assertions of the truth. Here is one of those rare and tremendous moments of which one may say that there is a stage direction, "Enter Shakespeare." He has admitted that for men weary of courts, for men sick of cities, the wood is the wisest place, and he has praised it with his purest lyric ecstasy. But when a man enters suddenly upon that celestial picnic, a man who is not sick of cities, but sick of hunger, a man who is not weary of courts, but weary of walking, then Shakespeare lets through his own voice with a shattering sincerity and cries the praise of practical human civilisation:

> If ever you have looked on better days,
> If ever you have sat at good men's feasts,
> If ever been where bells have knolled to church,
> If ever from your eyelids wiped a tear
> Or know what 'tis to pity and be pitied.

There is nothing finer even in Shakespeare than that conception of the circle of rich men all pretending to rough it in the country, and the one really hungry man entering, sword in hand, and praising the city. "If ever been where bells have knolled to church"; if you have ever been within sound of Bow bells; if you have ever been happy and haughty enough to call yourself a Cockney.

We must remember this distinction always in the case of Dickens. Dickens is the great Cockney, at once tragic and comic, who enters abruptly upon the Arcadian banquet of the æsthetics and says, "Forbear and eat no more," and tells them that they shall not eat "until necessity be served." If there was one thing he would have favoured instinctively it would have been the spreading of the town as meaning the spreading of civilisation. And we should (I hope) all favour the spreading of the town if it did mean the spreading of civilisation. The objection to the spreading of the modern Manchester or Birmingham suburb is simply that such a suburb is much more barbaric than any village in Europe could ever conceivably be. And again, if there is anything that Dickens would have definitely hated it is that general treatment of nature as a dramatic spectacle, a piece of scene-painting which has become the common mark of the culture of our wealthier classes. Despite many fine pictures of natural scenery, especially along the English roadsides, he was upon the whole emphatically on the side of the town. He was on the side of bricks and mortar. He was a citizen; and, after all, a citizen means a man of the city. His strength was, after all, in the fact that he was a man of the city. But, after all, his weakness, his calamitous weakness, was that he was a man of one city.

For all practical purposes he had never been outside such places as Chatham and London. He did indeed travel on the Continent; but surely no man's travel was ever so superficial as his. He was more superficial than the smallest and commonest tourist. He went about Europe on stilts; he never touched the ground. There is one good test and one only of whether a man has travelled to any profit in Europe. An Englishman is, as such, a European, and as he approaches the central splendours of Europe he ought to feel that he is coming home. If he does not feel at home he had much better have stopped at home. England is a real home; London is a real home; and all the essential feelings of adventure or the picturesque can easily be gained by going out at night upon the flats of Essex or the cloven hills of Surrey. Your visit to Europe is useless unless it gives you the sense of an exile returning. Your first sight of Rome is futile unless you feel that you have seen it before. Thus useless and thus futile were the foreign experiments and the continental raids of Dickens. He enjoyed them as he would have enjoyed, as a boy, a scamper out of Chatham into some strange meadows, as he would have enjoyed, when a grown man, a steam in a police boat out into the fens to the far east of London. But he was the Cockney venturing far; he was not the European coming home. He is still the splendid Cockney Orlando of whom I spoke above; he cannot but suppose that any strange men, being happy in some pastoral way, are mysterious foreign scoundrels. Dickens's real speech to the lazy and laughing civilisation of Southern Europe would really have run in the Shakespearian words:

> but whoe'er you be
> Who in this desert inaccessible,
> Under the shade of melancholy boughs
> Lose and neglect the creeping hours of time.
> If ever you have looked on better things,
> If ever been where bells have knolled to church.

If, in short, you have ever had the advantage of being born within the sound of Bow bells. Dickens could not really conceive that there was any other city but his own.

It is necessary thus to insist that Dickens never understood the Continent, because only thus can we appreciate the really remarkable thing he did in *A Tale of Two Cities*. It is necessary to feel, first of all, the fact that to him London was the centre of the universe. He did not understand at all the real sense in which Paris is the capital of Europe. He had never realised that all roads lead to Rome. He had never felt (as an Englishman can feel) that he was an Athenian before he was a Londoner. Yet with everything against him he did this astonishing thing. He wrote a book about two cities, one of which he understood; the other he did not understand. And his description of the city he did not know is almost better than his description of the city he did know. This is the entrance of the unquestionable thing about Dickens; the thing called genius; the thing which every one has to talk about directly and distinctly because no one knows what it is. For a plain word (as for instance the word fool) always covers an infinite mystery.

A Tale of Two Cities is one of the more tragic tints of the later life of Dickens. It might be said that he grew sadder as he grew older; but this would be false, for two reasons. First, a man never or hardly ever does grow sad as he grows old; on the contrary, the most melancholy young lovers can be found forty years afterwards chuckling over their port wine. And second, Dickens never did grow old, even in a physical sense. What weariness did appear in him appeared in the prime of life; it was due not to age but to overwork, and his exaggerative way of doing everything. To call Dickens a victim of elderly disenchantment would be as absurd as to say the same of Keats. Such fatigue as there was, was due not to the slowing down of his blood, but rather to its unremitting rapidity. He was not wearied by his age; rather he was wearied by his youth. And though *A Tale of Two Cities* is full of sadness, it is full also of enthusiasm; that pathos is a young pathos rather than an old one. Yet there is one circumstance which does render important the fact that *A Tale of Two Cities* is one of the later works of Dickens. This fact is the fact of his dependence upon another of the great writers of the Victorian era. And it is in connection with this that we can best see the truth of which I have been speaking; the truth that his actual ignorance of France went with amazing intuitive perception of the truth about it. It is here that he has most clearly the plain mark of the man of genius; that he can understand what he does not understand.

Dickens was inspired to the study of the French Revolution and to the writing of a romance about it by the example and influence of Carlyle. Thomas Carlyle undoubtedly rediscovered for Englishmen the revolution that was at the back of all their policies and reforms. It is an entertaining side joke that the French Revolution should have been discovered for Britons by the only British writer who did not really believe in it. Nevertheless, the most authoritative and the most recent critics on that great renaissance agree in considering Carlyle's work one of the most searching and detailed power. Carlyle had read a great deal about the French Revolution. Dickens had read nothing at all, except Carlyle. Carlyle was a man who collected his ideas by the careful collation of documents and the verification of references. Dickens was a man who collected his ideas from loose hints in the streets, and those always the same streets; as I have said, he was the citizen of one city. Carlyle was in his way learned; Dickens was in every way ignorant. Dickens was an Englishman cut off from France; Carlyle was a Scotsman, historically connected with France. And yet, when all this is said and certified, Dickens is more right than Carlyle. Dickens's French Revolution is probably more like the real French Revolution than Carlyle's. It is difficult, if not impossible, to state the grounds of this strong conviction. One can only talk of it by employing that excellent method which Cardinal Newman employed when he spoke of the "notes" of Catholicism. There were certain "notes" of the Revolution. One note of the Revolution was the thing which silly people call optimism, and sensible people call high spirits. Carlyle could never quite get it, because with all his spiritual energy he had no high spirits. That is why he preferred prose to poetry. He could understand rhetoric; for rhetoric means singing with an object. But he could not understand lyrics; for the lyric means singing without an object; as every one does when he is happy. Now for all its blood and its black guillotines, the French Revolution was full of mere high spirits. Nay, it was full of happiness. This actual lilt and levity Carlyle never really found in the Revolution, because he could not find it in himself. Dickens knew less of the Revolution, but he had more of it. When Dickens attacked abuses, he battered them down with exactly that sort of cheery and quite one-sided satisfaction with which the French mob battered down the Bastille. Dickens utterly and innocently believed in certain things; he would, 1 think, have drawn the sword for them. Carlyle half believed in half a hundred things; he was at once more of a mystic and more of a sceptic. Carlyle was the perfect type of the grumbling servant; the old grumbling servant of the aristocratic comedies. He followed the aristocracy, but he growled as he followed. He was obedient without being servile, just as Caleb Balderstone was obedient without being servile. But Dickens was the type of the man who might really have rebelled instead of grumbling. He might have gone out into the street and fought, like the man who took the Bastille. It is somewhat nationally significant that when we talk of the man in the street it means a figure silent, slouching, and even feeble. When the French speak of the man in the street, it means danger in the street.

No one can fail to notice this deep difference between Dickens and the Carlyle whom he avowedly copied. Splendid and symbolic as are Carlyle's scenes of the French Revolution, we have in reading them a curious sense that everything is happening at night. In Dickens even massacre happens by daylight. Carlyle always assumes that because things were tragedies therefore the men who did them felt tragic. Dickens knows that the man who works the worst tragedies is the man who feels comic; as for example, Mr. Quilp. The French Revolution was a much simpler world than Carlyle could understand; for Carlyle was subtle and not simple. Dickens could understand it, for he was simple and not subtle. He understood that plain rage against plain political injustice; he understood again that obvious vindictiveness and that obvious brutality which followed. "Cruelty and the abuse of absolute power," he told an American slave-owner, "are two of the bad passions of human nature." Carlyle was quite incapable of rising to the height of that uplifted common-sense. He must always find something mystical about the cruelty of the French Revolution. The effect was equally bad whether he found it mystically bad and called the thing anarchy, or whether he found it mystically good and called it the rule of the strong. In both cases he could not understand the common-sense justice or the common-sense vengeance of Dickens and the French Revolution.

Yet Dickens has in this book given a perfect and final touch to this whole conception of mere rebellion and mere human nature. Carlyle had written the story of the French Revolution and had made the story a mere tragedy. Dickens writes the story about the French Revolution, and does not make the Revolution itself the tragedy at all. Dickens knows that an outbreak is seldom a tragedy; generally it is the avoidance of a tragedy. All the real tragedies are silent. Men fight each other with furious cries, because men fight each other with chivalry and an unchangeable sense of brotherhood. But trees fight each other in utter stillness; because they fight each other cruelly and without quarter. In this book, as in history, the guillotine is not the calamity, but rather the solution of the calamity. The sin of Sydney Carton is a sin of habit, not of revolution. His gloom is the gloom of London, not the gloom of Paris.

Great Expectations

Great Expectations, which was written in the afternoon of Dickens's life and fame, has a quality of serene irony and even sadness, which puts it quite alone among his other works. At no time could Dickens possibly be called cynical, he had too much vitality; but relatively to the other books this book is cynical; but it has the soft and gentle cynicism of old age, not the hard cynicism of youth. To be a young cynic is to be a young brute; but Dickens, who had been so perfectly romantic and sentimental in his youth, could afford to admit this touch of doubt into the mixed experience of his middle age. At no time could any books by Dickens have been called Thackerayan. Both of the two men were too great for that. But relatively to the other Dickensian productions this book may be called Thackerayan. It is a study in human weakness and the slow human surrender. It describes how easily a free lad of fresh and decent instincts can be made to care more for rank and pride and the degrees of our stratified society than for old affection and for honour. It is an extra chapter to *The Book of Snobs*.

The best way of stating the change which this book marks in Dickens can be put in one phrase. In this book for the first time the hero disappears. The hero had descended to Dickens by a long line which begins with the gods, nay, perhaps if one may say so, which begins with God. First comes Deity and then the image of Deity; first comes the god and then the demi-god, the Hercules who labours and conquers before he receives his heavenly crown. That idea, with continual mystery and modification, has continued behind all romantic tales; the demi-god became the hero of paganism; the hero of paganism became the knight-errant of Christianity; the knight-errant who wandered and was foiled before he triumphed became the hero of the later prose romance, the romance in which the hero had to fight a duel with the villain but always survived, in which the hero drove desperate horses through the night in order to rescue the heroine, but always rescued her.

This heroic modern hero, this demi-god in a top-hat, may be said to reach his supreme moment and typical example about the time when Dickens was writing that thundering and thrilling and highly unlikely scene in *Nicholas Nickleby*, the scene where Nicholas hopelessly denounces the atrocious Gride in his hour of grinning triumph, and a thud upon the floor above tells them that the heroine's tyrannical father has died just in time to set her free. That is the apotheosis of the pure heroic as Dickens found it, and as Dickens in some sense continued it. It may be that it does not appear with quite so much unmistakable youth, beauty, valour, and virtue as it does in Nicholas Nickleby. Walter Gay is a simpler and more careless hero, but when he is doing any of the business of the story he is purely heroic. Kit Nubbles is a humbler hero, but he is a hero, when he is good he is very good. Even David Copperfield, who confesses to boyish tremors and boyish evasions in his account of his boyhood, acts the strict stiff part of the chivalrous gentleman in all the active and determining scenes of the tale. But *Great Expectations* may be called, like *Vanity Fair*, a novel without a hero. Almost all Thackeray's novels except Esmond are novels without a hero, but only one of Dickens's novels can be so described. I do not mean that it is a novel without a *jeune premier*, a young man to make love; *Pickwick* is that and *Oliver Twist*, and, perhaps, *The Old Curiosity Shop*. I mean that it is a novel without a hero in the same far deeper and more deadly sense in which *Pendennis* is also a novel without a hero. I mean that it is a novel which aims chiefly at showing that the hero is unheroic.

All such phrases as these must appear of course to overstate the case. Pip is a much more delightful person than Nicholas Nickleby. Or to take a stronger case for the purpose of our argument, Pip is a much more delightful person than Sydney Carton. Still the fact remains. Most of Nicholas Nickleby's personal actions are meant to show that he is heroic. Most of Pip's actions are meant to show that he is not heroic. The study of Sydney Carton is meant to indicate that with all his vices Sydney Carton was a hero. The study of Pip is meant to indicate that with all his virtues Pip was a snob. The motive of the literary explanation is different. Pip and Pendennis are meant to show how circumstances can corrupt men. Sam Weller and Hercules are meant to show how heroes can subdue circumstances.

This is the preliminary view of the book which is necessary if we are to regard it as a real and separate fact in the life of Dickens. Dickens had many moods because he was an artist; but he had one great mood, because he was a great artist. Any real difference therefore from the general drift, or rather (1 apologise to Dickens) the general drive of his creation is very important. This is the one place in his work in which he does, I will not say feel like Thackeray, far less think like Thackeray, less still write like Thackeray, but this is the one of his works in which he understands Thackeray. He puts himself in some sense in the same place; he considers mankind at somewhat the same angle as mankind is considered in one of the sociable and sarcastic novels of Thackeray. When he deals with Pip he sets out not to show his strength like the strength of Hercules, but to show his weakness like the weakness of Pendennis. When he sets out to describe Pip's great expectation he does not set out, as in a fairytale, with the idea that these great expectations will be fulfilled; he sets out from the first with the idea that these great expectations will be disappointing. We might very well, as I have remarked elsewhere, apply to all Dickens's books the title *Great Expectations*. All his books are full of an airy and yet ardent expectation of everything; of the next person who shall happen to speak, of the next chimney that shall happen to smoke, of the next event, of the next ecstasy; of the next fulfilment of any eager human fancy. All his books might be called *Great Expectations*. But the only book to which he gave the name of *Great Expectations* was the only book in which the expectation was never realised. It was so with the whole of that splendid and unconscious generation to which he belonged. The whole glory of that old English middle class was that it was unconscious; its excellence was entirely in that, that it was the culture of the nation, and that it did not know it. If Dickens had ever known that he was optimistic, he would have ceased to be happy.

It is necessary to make this first point clear: that in *Great Expectations* Dickens was really trying to be a quiet, a detached, and even a cynical observer of human life. Dickens was trying to be Thackeray. And the final and startling triumph of Dickens is this: that even to this moderate and modern story, he gives an incomparable energy which is not moderate and which is not modern. He is trying to be reasonable; but in spite of himself he is inspired. He is trying to be detailed, but in spite of himself he is gigantic. Compared to the rest of Dickens this is Thackeray; but compared to the whole of Thackeray we can only say in supreme praise of it that it is Dickens.

Take, for example, the one question of snobbishness. Dickens has achieved admirably the description of the doubts and vanities of the wretched Pip as he walks down the street in his new gentlemanly clothes, the clothes of which he is so proud and so ashamed. Nothing could be so exquisitely human, nothing especially could be so exquisitely masculine as that combination of self-love and self-assertion and even insolence with a naked and helpless sensibility to the slightest breath of ridicule. Pip thinks himself better than every one else, and yet anybody can snub him; that is the everlasting male, and perhaps the everlasting gentleman. Dickens has described perfectly this quivering and defenceless dignity. Dickens has described perfectly how 1-armed it is against the coarse humour of real humanity-the real humanity which Dickens loved, but which idealists and philanthropists do not love, the humanity of cabmen and coster-mongers and men singing in a third-class carriage; the humanity of Trabb's boy. In describing Pip's weakness Dickens is as true and as delicate as Thackeray. But Thackeray might have been easily as true and as delicate as Dickens. This quick and quiet eye for the tremors of mankind is a thing which Dickens possessed, but which others possessed also. George Eliot or Thackeray could have described the weakness of Pip. Exactly what George Eliot and Thackeray could not have described was the vigour of Trabb's boy. There would have been admirable humour and observation in their accounts of that intolerable urchin. Thackeray would have given us little light touches of Trabb's boy, absolutely true to the quality and colour of the humour, just as in his novels of the eighteenth century, the glimpses of Steele or Bolingbroke or Doctor Johnson are exactly and perfectly true to the colour and quality of their humour. George Eliot in her earlier books would have given us shrewd authentic scraps of the real dialect of Trabb's boy, just as she gave us shrewd and authentic scraps of the real talk in a Midland country town. In her later books she would have given us highly rationalistic explanations of Trabb's boy; which we should not have read. But exactly what they could never have given, and exactly what Dickens does give, is the *bounce* of Trabb's boy. It is the real unconquerable rush and energy in a character which was the supreme and quite indescribable greatness of Dickens. He conquered by rushes; he attacked in masses; he carried things at the spear point in a charge of spears; he was the Rupert of Fiction. The thing about any figure of Dickens, about Sam Weller or Dick Swiveller, or Micawber, or Bagstock, or Trabb's boy, —the thing about each one of these persons is that he cannot be exhausted. A Dickens character hits you first on the nose and then in the waistcoat, and then in the eye and then in the waistcoat again, with the blinding rapidity of some battering engine. The scene in which Trabb's boy continually overtakes Pip in order to reel and stagger as at a first encounter is a thing quite within the real competence of such a character; it might have been suggested by Thackeray, or George Eliot, or any realist. But the point with Dickens is that there is a rush in the boy's rushings; the writer and the reader rush with him. They start with him, they stare with him, they stagger with him, they share an inexpressible vitality in the air which emanates from this violent and capering satirist. Trabb's boy is among other things a boy; he has a physical rapture in hurling himself like a boomerang and in bouncing to the sky like a ball. It is just exactly in describing this quality that Dickens is Dickens and that no one else comes near him. No one feels in his bones that Felix Holt was strong as he feels in his bones that little Quilp was strong. No one can feel that even Rawdon Crawley's splendid smack across the face of Lord Steyne is quite so living and life-giving as the "kick after kick" which old Mr. Weller dealt the dancing and quivering Stiggins as he drove him towards the trough. This quality, whether expressed intellectually or physically, is the profoundly popular and eternal quality in Dickens; it is the thing that no one else could do. This quality is the quality which has always given its continuous power and poetry to the common people everywhere. It is life; it is the joy of life felt by those who have nothing else but life. It is the thing that all aristocrats have always hated and dreaded in the people. And it is the thing which poor Pip really hates and dreads in Trabb's boy.

A great man of letters or any great artist is symbolic without knowing it. The things he describes are types because they are truths. Shakespeare may, or may not, have ever put it to himself that Richard the Second was a philosophical symbol; but all good criticism must necessarily see him so. It may be a reasonable question whether the artist should be allegorical. There can be no doubt among sane men that the critic should be allegorical. Spenser may have lost by being less realistic than Fielding. But any good criticism of *Tom Jones* must be as mystical as the *Faery Queen*. Hence it is unavoidable in speaking of a fine book like *Great Expectations* that we should give even to its unpretentious and realistic figures a certain massive mysticism. Pip is Pip, but he is also the well-meaning snob. And this is even more true of those two great figures in the tale which stand for the English democracy. For, indeed, the first and last word upon the English democracy is said in Joe Gargery and Trabb's boy. The actual English populace, as distinct from the French populace or the Scotch or Irish populace, may be said to lie between those two types. The first is the poor man who does not assert himself at all, and the second is the poor man who asserts himself entirely with the weapon of sarcasm. The only way in which the English now ever rise in revolution is under the symbol and leadership of Trabb's boy. What pikes and shillelahs were to the Irish populace, what guns and barricades were to the French populace, that chaff is to the English populace. It is their weapon, the use of which they really understand. It is the one way in which they can make a rich man feel uncomfortable, and they use it very justifiably for all it is worth. If they do not cut off the heads of tyrants at least they sometimes do their best to make the tyrants lose their heads. The gutter boys of the great towns carry the art of personal criticism to so rich and delicate a degree that some well-dressed persons when they walk past a file of them feel as if they were walking past a row of omniscient critics or judges with a power of life and death. Here and there only is some ordinary human custom, some natural human pleasure suppressed in deference to the fastidiousness of the rich. But all the rich tremble before the fastidiousness of the poor.

Of the other type of democracy it is far more difficult to speak. It is always hard to speak of good things or good people, for in satisfying the soul they take away a certain spur to speech. Dickens was often called a sentimentalist. In one sense he sometimes was a sentimentalist. But if sentimentalism be held to mean something artificial or theatrical, then in the core and reality of his character Dickens was the very reverse of a sentimentalist. He seriously and definitely loved goodness. To see sincerity and charity satisfied him like a meal. What some critics call his love of sweet stuff is really his love of plain beef and bread. Sometimes one is tempted to wish that in the long Dickens dinner the sweet courses could be left out; but this does not make the whole banquet other than a banquet singularly solid and simple. The critics complain of the sweet things, but not because they are so strong as to like simple things. They complain of the sweet things because they are so sophisticated as to like sour things; their tongues are tainted with the bitterness of absinthe. Yet because of the very simplicity of Dickens's moral tastes it is impossible to speak adequately of them; and Joe Gargery must stand as he stands in the book, a thing too obvious to be understood. But this may be said of him in one of his minor aspects, that he stands for a certain long-suffering in the English poor, a certain weary patience and politeness which almost breaks the heart. One cannot help wondering whether that great mass of silent virtue will ever achieve anything on this earth.

Our Mutual Friend

Our Mutual Friend marks a happy return to the earlier manner of Dickens at the end of Dickens's life. One might call it a sort of Indian summer of his farce. Those who most truly love Dickens love the earlier Dickens; and any return to his farce must be welcomed, like a young man come back from the dead. In this book indeed he does not merely return to his farce; he returns in a manner to his vulgarity. It is the old democratic and even uneducated Dickens who is writing here. The very title is illiterate. Any priggish pupil teacher could tell Dickens that there is no such phrase in English as "our mutual friend." Any one could tell Dickens that "our mutual friend" means "our reciprocal friend," and that "our reciprocal friend" means nothing. If he had only had all the solemn advantages of academic learning (the absence of which in him was lamented by the *Quarterly Review*), he would have known better. He would have known that the correct phrase for a man known to two people is "our common friend." But if one calls one's friend a common friend, even that phrase is open to misunderstanding.

I dwell with a gloomy pleasure on this mistake in the very title of the book because I, for one, am not pleased to see Dickens gradually absorbed by modern culture and good manners. Dickens, by class and genius, belonged to the kind of people who do talk about a "mutual friend"; and for that class there is a very great deal to be said. These two things can at least be said-that this class does understand the meaning of the word "friend" and the meaning of the word "mutual." I know that for some long time before he had been slowly and subtly sucked into the whirlpool of the fashionable views of later England. I know that in *Bleak House* he treats the aristocracy far more tenderly than he treats them in *David Copperfield*. I know that in *A Tale of Two Cities*, having come under the influence of Carlyle, he treats revolution as strange and weird, whereas under the influence of Cobbett he would have treated it as obvious and reasonable. I know that in *The Mystery of Edwin Drood* he not only praised the Minor Canon of Cloisterham at the expense of the dissenting demagogue, Honeythunder; I know that he even took the last and most disastrous step in the modern English reaction. While blaming the old Cloisterham monks (who were democratic), he praised the old-world peace that they had left behind them-an old-world peace which is simply one of the last amusements of aristocracy. The modern rich feel quite at home with the dead monks. They would have felt anything but comfortable with the live ones. I know, in short, how the simple democracy of Dickens was gradually dimmed by the decay and reaction of the middle of the nineteenth century. I know that he fell into some of the bad habits of aristocratic sentimentalism. I know that he used the word "gentleman" as meaning good man. But all this only adds to the unholy joy with which I realise that the very title of one of his best books was a vulgarism. It is pleasant to contemplate this last unconscious knock in the eye for the gentility with which Dickens was half impressed. Dickens is the old self-made man; you may take him or leave him. He has its disadvantages and its merits. No university man would have written the title; no university man could have written the book.

If it were a mere matter of the accident of a name it would not be worth while thus to dwell on it, even as a preface. But the title is in this respect typical of the tale. The novel called *Our Mutual Friend* is in many ways a real reaction towards the earlier Dickens manner. I have remarked that *Little Dorrit* was a reversion to the form of the first books, but not to their spirit; *Our Mutual Friend* is a reversion to the spirit as well as the form. Compare, for instance, the public figures that make a background in each book. Mr. Merdle is a commercial man having no great connection with the plot; similarly Mr. Podsnap is a commercial man having no great connection with the plot. This is altogether in the spirit of the earlier books; the whole point of an early Dickens novel was to have as many people as possible entirely unconnected with the plot. But exactly because both studies are irrelevant, the contrast between them can be more clearly perceived. Dickens goes out of his way to describe Merdle; and it is a gloomy description. But Dickens goes out of his way to describe Podsnap, and it is a happy and hilarious description. It recalls the days when he hunted great game; when he went out of his way to entrap such adorable monsters as Mr. Pecksniff or Mr. Vincent Crummles. With these wild beings we never bother about the cause of their coming. Such guests in a \ story may be uninvited, but they are never *de trop*. They earn their night's lodging in any tale by being so uproariously amusing; like little Tommy Tucker in the legend, they sing for their supper. This is really the marked truth about *Our Mutual Friend*, as a stage in the singular latter career of Dickens. It is like the leaping up and flaming of a slowly dying fire. The best things in the book are in the old best manner of the author. They have that great Dickens quality of being something which is pure farce and yet which is not superficial; an unfathomable farce —a farce that goes down to the roots of the universe. The highest compliment that can ever be paid to the humour of Dickens is paid when some lady says, with the sudden sincerity of her sex, that it is "too silly." The phrase is really a perfectly sound and acute criticism. Humour does consist in being too silly, in passing the borderland, in breaking through the floor of sense and falling into some starry abyss of nonsense far below our ordinary human life. This "too silly" quality is really present in *Our Mutual Friend*. It is present in *Our Mutual Friend* just as it is present in *Pickwick*, or *Martin Chuzzlewit*; just as it is not present in *Little Dorrit* or in *Hard Times*. Many tests might be employed. One is the pleasure in purely physical jokes-jokes about the body. The general dislike which every one felt for Mr. Stiggins's nose is of the same kind as the ardent desire which Mr. Lammle felt for Mr. Fledgeby's nose. "Give me your nose, Sir," said Mr. Lammle. That sentence alone would be enough to show that the young Dickens had never died.

The opening of a book goes for a great deal. The opening of *Our Mutual Friend* is much more instinctively energetic and light-hearted than that of any of the other novels of his concluding period. Dickens had always enough optimism to make his stories end well. He had not, in his later years, always enough optimism to make them begin well. Even *Great Expectations*, the saddest of his later books, ends well; it ends well in spite of himself, who had intended it to end badly. But if we leave the evident case of good endings and take the case of good beginnings, we see how much *Our Mutual Friend* stands out from among the other novels of the evening or the end of Dickens. The tale of *Little Dorrit* begins in a prison. One of the prisoners is a villain, and his villainy is as dreary as the prison; that might matter nothing. But the other prisoner is vivacious, and even his vivacity is dreary. The first note struck is sad. In the tale of *Edwin Drood* the first scene is in an opium den, suffocated with every sort of phantasy and falsehood. Nor is it true that these openings are merely accidental; they really cast their shadow over the tales. The people of *Little Dorrit* begin in prison; and it is the whole point of the book that people never get out of prison. The story of *Edwin Drood* begins amid the fumes of opium, and it never gets out of the fumes of opium. The darkness of that strange and horrible smoke is deliberately rolled over the whole story. Dickens, in his later years, permitted more and more his story to take the cue from its inception. All the more remarkable, therefore, is the real jerk and spurt of good spirits with which he opens *Our Mutual Friend*. It begins with a good piece of rowdy satire, wildly exaggerated and extremely true. It belongs to the same class as the first chapter of *Martin Chuzzlewit*, with its preposterous pedigree of the Chuzzlewit family, or even the first chapter of *Pickwick*, with its immortal imbecilities about the Theory of Tittlebats and Mr. Blotton of Aldgate. Doubtless the early satiric chapter in *Our Mutual Friend* is of a more strategic and ingenious kind of satire than can be found in these early and explosive parodies. Still, there is a quality common to both, and that quality is the whole of Dickens. It is a quality difficult to define-hence the whole difficulty of criticising Dickens. Perhaps it can be best stated in two separate statements or as two separate symptoms. The first is the mere fact that the reader rushes to read it. The second is the mere fact that the writer rushed to write it.

This beginning, which is like a burst of the old exuberant Dickens, is, of course, the Veneering dinner-party. In its own way it is as good as anything that Dickens ever did. There is the old faculty of managing a crowd, of making character clash with character, that had made Dickens not only the democrat but even the demagogue of fiction. For if it is hard to manage a mob, it is hardest of all to manage a swell mob. The particular kind of chaos that is created by the hospitality of a rich upstart has perhaps never been so accurately and outrageously described. Every touch about the thing is true; to this day any one can test it if he goes to a dinner of this particular kind. How admirable, for instance, is the description of the way in which all the guests ignored the host; how the host and hostess peered and gaped for some stray attention as if they had been a pair of poor relations. Again, how well, as a matter of social colour, the distinctions between the type and tone of the guests are made even in the matter of this unguestlike insolence. How well Dickens distinguishes the 1-bred indifference of Podsnap from the well-bred indifference of Mortimer Lightwood and Eugene Wrayburn. How well he distinguishes the bad manners of the merchant from the equally typical bad manners of the gentleman. Above all, how well he catches the character of the creature who is really the master of all these: the impenetrable male servant. Nowhere in literature is the truth about servants better told. For that truth is simply this: that the secret of aristocracy is hidden even from aristocrats. Servants, butlers, footmen, are the high priests who have the real dispensation; and even gentlemen are afraid of them. Dickens was never more right than when he made the new people, the Veneerings, employ a butler who despised not only them but all their guests and acquaintances. The admirable person called the Analytical Chemist shows his perfection particularly in the fact that he regards all the sham gentlemen and all the real gentlemen with the same gloomy and incurable contempt. He offers wine to the offensive Podsnap or the shrieking Tippins with a melancholy sincerity and silence; but he offers his letter to the aristocratic and unconscious Mortimer with the same sincerity and with the same silence. It is a great pity that the Analytical Chemist only occurs in two or three scenes of this excellent story. As far as I know, he never really says a word from one end of the book to the other; but he is one of the best characters in Dickens.

Round the Veneering dinner-table are collected not indeed the best characters in Dickens, but certainly the best characters in *Our Mutual Friend*. Certainly one exception must be made. Fledgeby is unaccountably absent. There was really no reason why he should not have been present at a dinner-party given by the Veneerings and including the Lammles. His money was at least more genuine than theirs. If he had been present the party would really have included all that is important in *Our Mutual Friend*. For indeed, outside Mr. Fledgeby and the people at the dinner-party, there is something a little heavy and careless about the story. Mr. Silas Wegg is really funny; and he serves the purpose of a necessary villain in the plot. But his humour and his villainy seem to have no particular connection with each other; when he is not scheming he seems the last man likely to scheme. He is rather like one of Dickens's agreeable Bohemians, a pleasant companion, a quoter of fine verses. His villainy seems an artificial thing attached to him, like his wooden leg. For while his villainy is supposed to be of a dull, mean, and bitter sort (quite unlike, for instance, the uproarious villainy of Quilp), his humour is of the sincere, flowing and lyric character, like that of Dick Swiveller or Mr. Micawber. He tells Mr. Boffin that he will drop into poetry in a friendly way. He does drop into it in a friendly way; in much too really a friendly way to make him convincing as a mere calculating knave. He and Mr. Venus are such natural and genuine companions that one does not see why if Venus repents Wegg should not repent too. In short, Wegg is a convenience for a plot and not a very good plot at that. But if he is one of the blots on the business, he is not the principal one. If the real degradation of Wegg is not very convincing, it is at least immeasurably more convincing than the pretended degradation of Boffin. The passage in which Boffin appears as a sort of miser, and then afterwards explains that he only assumed the character for reasons of his own, has something about it highly jerky and unsatisfactory. The truth of the whole matter 1 think, almost certainly, is that Dickens did not originally mean Boffin's lapse to be fictitious. He originally meant Boffin really to be corrupted by wealth, slowly to degenerate and as slowly to repent. But the story went too quickly for this long, double, and difficult process; therefore Dickens at the last moment made a sudden recovery possible by representing that the whole business had been a trick. Consequently, this episode is not an error merely in the sense that we may find many errors in a great writer like Dickens; it is a mistake patched up with another mistake. It is a case of that ossification which occurs round the healing of an actual fracture; the story had broken down and been mended.

If Dickens had fulfilled what was probably his original design, and described the slow freezing of Boffin's soul in prosperity, I do not say that he would have done the thing well. He was not good at describing change in anybody, especially not good at describing a change for the worse. The tendency of all his characters is upwards, like bubbles, never downwards, like stones. But at least it would probably have been more credible than the story as it stands; for the story as it stands is actually less credible than any conceivable kind of moral ruin for Boffin. Such a character as his-rough, simple and lumberingly unconscious-might be more easily conceived as really sinking in self-respect and honour than as keeping up, month after month, so strained and inhuman a theatrical performance. To a good man (of that particular type) it would be easier to be bad than to pretend to be bad. It might have taken years to turn Noddy Boffin into a miser; but it would have taken centuries to turn him into an actor. This unreality in the later Boffin scenes makes the end of the story of John Harmon somewhat more unimpressive perhaps than it might otherwise have been. Upon no hypothesis, however, can he be made one of the more impressive figures of Dickens. It is true that it is an unfair criticism to object, as some have done, that Dickens does not succeed in disguising the identity of John Harmon with John Rokesmith. Dickens never intended to disguise it; the whole story would be mainly unintelligible and largely uninteresting if it had been successfully disguised. But though John Harmon or Rokesmith was never intended to be merely a man of mystery, it is not quite so easy to say what he was intended to be. Bella is a possible and pretty sketch. Mrs. Wilfer, her mother, is an entirely impossible and entirely delightful one. Miss Podsnap is not only excellent, she is to a healthy taste positively attractive; there is a real suggestion in her of the fact that humility is akin to truth, even when humility takes its more comic form of shyness. There is not in all literature a more human *cri de 100œur* than that with which Georgiana Podsnap receives the information that a young man has professed himself to be attracted by her—"Oh what a Fool he must be!"

Two other figures require praise, though they are in the more tragic manner which Dickens touched from time to time in his later period. Bradley Headstone is really a successful villain; so successful that he fully captures our sympathies. Also there is something original in the very conception. It was a new notion to add to the villains of fiction, whose thoughts go quickly, this villain whose thoughts go slow but sure; and it was a new notion to combine a deadly criminality not with high life or the slums (the usual haunts for villains) but with the laborious respectability of the lower, middle classes. The other good conception is the boy, Bradley Headstone's pupil, with his dull, inexhaustible egoism, his pert, unconscious cruelty, and the strict decorum and incredible baseness of his views of life. It is singular that Dickens, who was not only a radical and a social reformer, but one who would have been particularly concerned to maintain the principle of modern popular education, should nevertheless have seen so clearly this potential evil in the mere educationalism of our time-the fact that merely educating the democracy may easily mean setting to work to despoil it of all the democratic virtues. It is better to be Lizzie Hexam and not know how to read and write than to be Charlie Hexam and not know how to appreciate Lizzie Hexam. It is not only necessary that the democracy should be taught; it is also necessary that the democracy should be taught democracy. Otherwise it will certainly fall a victim to that snobbishness and system of worldly standards which is the most natural and easy of all the forms of human corruption. This is one of the many dangers which Dickens saw before it existed. Dickens was really a prophet; far more of a prophet than Carlyle.

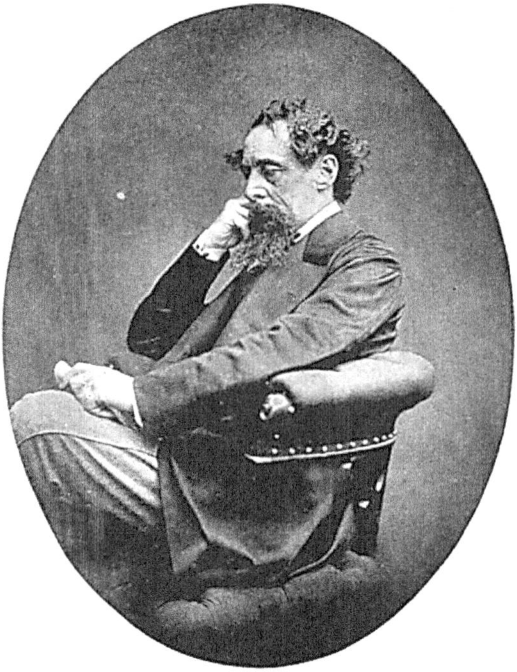

Edwin Drood

Pickwick was a work partly designed by others, but ultimately filled up by Dickens. *Edwin Drood*, the last book, was a book designed by Dickens, but ultimately filled up by others. The *Pickwick Papers* showed how much Dickens could make out of other people's suggestions; *The Mystery of Edwin Drood* shows how very little other people can make out of Dickens's suggestions.

Dickens was meant by Heaven to be the great melodramatist; so that even his literary end was melodramatic. Something more seems hinted at in the cutting short of *Edwin Drood* by Dickens than the mere cutting short of a good novel by a great man. It seems rather like the last taunt of some elf, leaving the world, that it should be this story which is not ended, this story which is only a story. The only one of Dickens's novels which he did not finish was the only one that really needed finishing. He never had but one thoroughly good plot to tell; and that he has only told in heaven. This is what separates the case in question from any parallel cases of novelists cut off in the act of creation. That great novelist, for instance, with whom Dickens is constantly compared, died also in the middle of *Denis Duval*. But any one can see in *Denis Duval* the qualities of the later work of Thackeray; the increasing discursiveness, the increasing retrospective poetry, which had been in part the charm and in part the failure of *Philip* and *The Virginians*. But to Dickens it was permitted to die at a dramatic moment and to leave a dramatic mystery. Any Thackerayan could have completed the plot of *Denis Duval*; except indeed that a really sympathetic Thackerayan might have had some doubt as to whether there was any plot to complete. But Dickens, having had far too little plot in his stories previously, had far too much plot in the story he never told. Dickens dies in the act of telling, not his tenth novel, but his first news of murder. He drops down dead as he is in the act of denouncing the assassin. It is permitted to Dickens, in short, to come to a literary end as strange as his literary beginning. He began by completing the old romance of travel. He ended by inventing the new detective story.

It is as a detective story first and last that we have to consider *The Mystery of Edwin Drood*. This does not mean, of course, that the details are not often admirable in their swift and penetrating humour; to say that of the book would be to say that Dickens did not write it. Nothing could be truer, for instance, than the manner in which the dazed and drunken dignity of Durdles illustrates a certain bitterness at the bottom of the bewilderment of the poor. Nothing could be better than the way in which the haughty and allusive conversation between Miss Twinkleton and the landlady illustrates the maddening preference of some females for skating upon thin social ice. There is an even better example than these of the original humorous insight of Dickens; and one not very often remarked, because of its brevity and its unimportance in the narrative. But Dickens never did anything better than the short account of Mr. Grewgious's dinner being brought from the tavern by two waiters: "a stationary waiter," and "a flying waiter." The "flying waiter" brought the food and the "stationary waiter" quarrelled with him; the "flying waiter" brought glasses and the "stationary waiter" looked through them. Finally, it will be remembered the "stationary waiter" left the room, casting a glance which indicated "let it be understood that all emoluments are mine, and that Nil is the reward of this slave." Still, Dickens wrote the book as a detective story; he wrote it as *The Mystery of Edwin Drood*. And alone, perhaps, among detective-story writers, he never lived to destroy his mystery. Here alone then among the Dickens novels it is necessary to speak of the plot and of the plot alone. And when we speak of the plot it becomes immediately necessary to speak of the two or three standing explanations which celebrated critics have given of the plot.

The story, so far as it was written by Dickens, can be read here. It describes, as will be seen, the disappearance of the young architect Edwin Drood after a night of festivity which was supposed to celebrate his reconciliation with a temporary enemy, Neville Landless, and was held at the house of his uncle John Jasper. Dickens continued the tale long enough to explain or explode the first and most obvious of his riddles. Long before the existing part terminates it has become evident that Drood has been put away, not by his obvious opponent, Landless, but by his uncle who professes for him an almost painful affection. The fact that we all know this, however, ought not in fairness to blind us to the fact that, considered as the first fraud in a detective story, it has been, with great skill, at once suggested and concealed. Nothing, for instance, could be cleverer as a piece of artistic mystery than the fact that Jasper, the uncle, always kept his eyes fixed on Drood's face with a dark and watchful tenderness; the thing is so told that at first we really take it as only indicating something morbid in the affection; it is only afterwards that the frightful fancy breaks upon us that it is not morbid affection but morbid antagonism. This first mystery (which is no longer a mystery) of Jasper's guilt, is only worth remarking because it shows that Dickens meant and felt himself able to mask all his batteries with real artistic strategy and artistic caution. The manner of the unmasking of Jasper marks the manner and tone in which the whole tale was to be told. Here we have not got to do with Dickens simply giving himself away, as he gave himself away in *Pickwick* or *The Christmas Carol*. Not that one complains of his giving himself away; there was no better gift.

What was the mystery of Edwin Drood from Dickens's point of view we shall never know, except perhaps from Dickens in heaven, and then he will very likely have forgotten. But the mystery of Edwin Drood from our point of view, from that of his critics, and those who have with some courage (after his death) attempted to be his collaborators, is simply this. There is no doubt that Jasper either murdered Drood or supposed that he had murdered him. This certainty we have from the fact that it is the whole point of a scene between Jasper and Drood's lawyer Grewgious in which Jasper is struck down with remorse when he realises that Drood has been killed (from his point of view) needlessly and without profit. The only question is whether Jasper's remorse was as needless as his murder. In other words the only question is whether, while he certainly thought he had murdered Drood, he had really done it. It need hardly be said that such a doubt would not have been raised for nothing; gentlemen like Jasper do not as a rule waste good remorse except upon successful crime. The origin of the doubt about the real death of Drood is this. Towards the latter end of the existing chapters there appears very abruptly, and with a quite ostentatious air of mystery, a character called Datchery. He appears for the purpose of spying upon Jasper and getting up some case against him; at any rate, if he has not this purpose in the story he has no other earthly purpose in it. He is an old gentleman of juvenile energy, with a habit of carrying his hat in his hand even in the open air; which some have interpreted as meaning that he feels the unaccustomed weight of a wig. Now there are one or two people in the story who this person might possibly be. Notably there is one person in the story who seems as if he were meant to be something, but who hitherto has certainly been nothing; I mean Bazzard, Mr. Grewgious's clerk, a sulky fellow interested in theatricals, of whom an unnecessary fuss is made. There is also Mr. Grewgious himself, and there is also another suggestion, so much more startling that I shall have to deal with it later.

For the moment, however, the point is this: That ingenious writer, Mr. Proctor, started the highly plausible theory that this Datchery was Drood himself, who had not really been killed. He adduced a most complex and complete scheme covering nearly all the details; but the strongest argument he had was rather one of general artistic effect. This argument has been quite perfectly summed up by Mr. Andrew Lang in one sentence: "If Edwin Drood is dead, there is not much mystery about him." This is quite true; Dickens, when writing in so deliberate, nay, dark and conspiratorial a manner, would surely have kept the death of Drood and the guilt of Jasper hidden a little longer if the only real mystery had been the guilt of Jasper and the death of Drood. It certainly seems artistically more likely that there was a further mystery of Edwin Drood; not the mystery that he was murdered, but the mystery that he was not murdered. It is true indeed that Mr. Cumming Walters has a theory of Datchery (to which I have already darkly alluded) a theory which is wild enough to be the centre not only of any novel but of any harlequinade. But the point is that even Mr. Cumming Walters's theory, though it makes the mystery more extraordinary, does not make it any more of a mystery of Edwin Drood. It should not have been called *The Mystery of Drood*, but *The Mystery of Datchery*.

This is the strongest case for Proctor; if the story tells of Drood coming back as Datchery, the story does at any rate fulfil the title upon its title-page.

The principal objection to Proctor's theory is that there seems no adequate reason why Jasper should not have murdered his nephew if he wanted to. And there seems even less reason why Drood, if unsuccessfully murdered, should not have raised the alarm. Happy young architects, when nearly strangled by elderly organists, do not generally stroll away and come back some time afterwards in a wig and with a false name. Superficially it would seem almost as odd to find the murderer investigating the origin of the murder, as to find the corpse investigating it. To this problem two of the ablest literary critics of our time, Mr. Andrew Lang and Mr. William Archer (both of them persuaded generally of the Proctor theory) have especially addressed themselves. Both have come to the same substantial conclusion; and I suspect that they are right. They hold that Jasper (whose mania for opium is much insisted on in the tale) had some sort of fit, or trance, or other physical seizure as he was committing the crime so that he left it unfinished; and they also hold that he had drugged Drood, so that Drood, when he recovered from the attack, was doubtful about who had been his assailant. This might really explain, if a little fancifully, his coming back to the town in the character of a detective. He might think it due to his uncle (whom he last remembered in a kind of murderous vision) to make an independent investigation as to whether he was really guilty or not. He might say, as Hamlet said of a vision equally terrifying, "I'll have grounds more relative than this." In fairness it must be said that there is something vaguely shaky about this theory; chiefly, I think, in this respect; that there is a sort of farcical cheerfulness about Datchery which does not seem altogether appropriate to a lad who ought to be in an agony of doubt as to whether his best friend was or was not his assassin. Still there are many such incongruities in Dickens; and the explanation of Mr. Archer and Mr. Lang is an explanation. I do not believe that any explanation as good can be given to account for the tale being called *The Mystery of Edwin Drood*, if the tale practically starts with his corpse.

If Drood is really dead one cannot help feeling the story ought to end where it does end, not by accident but by design. The murder is explained. Jasper is ready to be hanged, and every one else in a decent novel ought to be ready to be married. If there was to be much more of anything, it must have been of anticlimax. Nevertheless there are degrees of anticlimax. Some of the more obvious explanations of Datchery are quite reasonable, but they are distinctly tame. For instance, Datchery may be Bazzard; but it is not very exciting if he is; for we know nothing about Bazzard and care less. Again, he might be Grewgious; but there is something pointless about one grotesque character dressing up as another grotesque character actually less amusing than himself. Now, Mr. Cumming Walters has at least had the distinction of inventing a theory which makes the story at least an interesting story, even if it is not exactly the story that is promised on the cover of the book. The obvious enemy of Drood, on whom suspicion first falls, the swarthy and sulky Landless, has a sister even swarthier and, except for her queenly dignity, even sulkier than he. This barbaric princess is evidently meant to be (in a sombre way) in love with Crisparkle, the clergyman and muscular Christian who represents the breezy element in the emotions of the tale. Mr. Cumming Walters seriously maintains that it is this barbaric princess who puts on a wig and dresses up as Mr. Datchery. He urges his case with much ingenuity of detail. Helena Landless certainly had a motive; to save her brother, who was accused falsely, by accusing Jasper justly. She certainly had some of the faculties; it is elaborately stated in the earlier part of her story that she was accustomed as a child to dress up in male costume and run into the wildest adventures. There may be something in Mr. Cumming Walters's argument that the very flippancy of Datchery is the self-conscious flippancy of a strong woman in such an odd situation; certainly there is the same flippancy in Portia and in Rosalind. Nevertheless, I think, there is one final objection to the theory; and that is simply this, that it is comic. It is generally wrong to represent a great master of the grotesque as being grotesque exactly where he does not intend to be. And I am persuaded that if Dickens had really meant Helena to turn into Datchery, he would have made her from the first in some way more light, eccentric, and laughable; he would have made her at least as light and laughable as Rosa. As it is, there is something strangely stiff and incredible about the idea of a lady so dark and dignified dressing up as a swaggering old gentleman in a blue coat and grey trousers. We might almost as easily imagine Edith Dombey dressing up as Major Bagstock. We might almost as easily imagine Rebecca in *Ivanhoe* dressing up as Isaac of York.

Of course such a question can never really be settled precisely, because it is the question not merely of a mystery but of a puzzle. For here the detective novel differs from every other kind of novel. The ordinary novelist desires to keep his readers to the point; the detective novelist actually desires to keep his readers off the point. In the first case, every touch must help to tell the reader what he means; in the second case, most of the touches must conceal or even contradict what he means. You are supposed to see and appreciate the smallest gestures of a good actor; but you do not see all the gestures of a conjuror, if he is a good conjuror. Hence, into the critical estimate of such works as this, there is introduced a problem, an extra perplexity, which does not exist in other cases. I mean the problem of the things commonly called blinds. Some of the points which we pick out as suggestive may have been put in as deceptive. Thus the whole conflict between a critic with one theory, like Mr. Lang, and a critic with another theory, like Mr. Cumming Walters, becomes eternal and a trifle farcical. Mr. Walters says that all Mr. Lang's clues were blinds; Mr. Lang says that all Mr. Walters's clues were blinds. Mr. Walters can say that some passages seemed to show that Helena was Datchery; Mr. Lang can reply that those passages were only meant to deceive simple people like Mr. Walters into supposing that she was Datchery. Similarly Mr. Lang can say that the return of Drood is foreshadowed; and Mr. Walters can reply that it was foreshadowed because it was never meant to come off. There seems no end to this insane process; anything that Dickens wrote may or may not mean the opposite of what it says. Upon this principle I should be very ready for one to declare that all the suggested Datcherys were really blinds; merely because they can naturally be suggested. I would undertake to maintain that Mr. Datchery is really Miss Twinkleton, who has a mercenary interest in keeping Rosa Budd at her school. This suggestion does not seem to me to be really much more humorous than Mr. Cumming Walters's theory. Yet either may certainly be true. Dickens is dead, and a number of splendid scenes and startling adventures have died with him. Even if we get the right solution we shall not know that it is right. The tale might have been, and yet it has not been.

And I think there is no thought so much calculated to make one doubt death itself, to feel that sublime doubt which has created all religion-the doubt that found death incredible. Edwin Drood may or may not have really died; but surely Dickens did not really die. Surely our real detective liveth and shall appear in the latter days of the earth. For a finished tale may give a man immortality in the light and literary sense; but an unfinished tale suggests another immortality, more essential and more strange.

Master Humphrey's Clock

It is quite indispensable to include a criticism of *Master Humphrey's Clock* in any survey of Dickens, although it is not one of the books of which his admirers would chiefly boast; although perhaps it is almost the only one of which he would not have boasted himself. As a triumph of Dickens, at least, it is not of great importance. But as a sample of Dickens it happens to be of quite remarkable importance. The very fact that it is for the most part somewhat more level and even monotonous than most of his creations, makes us realise, as it were, against what level and monotony those creations commonly stand out. This book is the background of his mind. It is the basis and minimum of him which was always there. Alone, of all written things, this shows how he felt when he was not writing. Dickens might have written it in his sleep. That is to say, it is written by a sluggish Dickens, a half automatic Dickens, a dreaming and drifting Dickens; but still by the enduring Dickens.

But this truth can only be made evident by beginning nearer to the root of the matter. *Nicholas Nickleby* had just completed, or, to speak more strictly, confirmed, the popularity of the young author; wonderful as *Pickwick* was it might have been a nine days' wonder; *Oliver Twist* had been powerful but painful; it was *Nicholas Nickleby* that proved the man to be a great productive force of which one could ask more, of which one could ask all things. His publishers, Chapman and Hall, seem to have taken at about this point that step which sooner or later most publishers do take with regard to a half successful man who is becoming wholly successful. Instead of asking him for something, they asked him for anything. They made him, so to speak, the editor of his own works. And indeed it is literally as the editor of his own works that he next appears; for the next thing to which he proposes to put his name is not a novel, but for all practical purposes a magazine. Yet although it is a magazine, it is a magazine entirely written by himself; the publishers, in point of fact, wanted to create a kind of Dickens Miscellany, in a much more literal sense than that in which we speak of a Bentley Miscellany. Dickens was in no way disposed to dislike such a job; for the more miscellaneous he was the more he enjoyed himself. And indeed this early experiment of his bears a great deal of resemblance to those later experiences in which he was the editor of two popular periodicals. The editor of *Master Humphrey's Clock* was a kind of type or precursor of the editor of *Household Words* and *All the Year Round*. There was the same sense of absolute ease in an atmosphere of infinite gossip. There was the same great advantage gained by a man of genius who wrote best scrappily and by episodes. The omnipotence of the editor helped the eccentricities of the author. He could excuse himself for all his own shortcomings. He could begin a novel, get tired of it, and turn it into a short story. He could begin a short story, get fond of it, and turn it into a novel. Thus in the days of *Household Words* he could begin a big scheme of stories, such as *Somebody's Luggage*, or *Seven Poor Travellers*, and after writing a tale or two toss the rest to his colleagues. Thus, on the other hand, in the time of *Master Humphrey's Clock*, he could begin one small adventure of Master Humphrey and find himself unable to stop it. It is quite clear I think (though only from moral evidence, which some call reading between the lines) that he originally meant to tell many separate tales of Master Humphrey's wanderings in London, only one of which, and that a short one, was to have been concerned with a little girl going home. Fortunately for us that little girl had a grandfather, and that grandfather had a curiosity shop and also a nephew, and that nephew had an entirely irrelevant friend whom men and angels called Richard Swiveller. Once having come into the society of Swiveller it is not unnatural that Dickens stayed there for a whole book. The essential point for us here, however, is that *Master Humphrey's Clock* was stopped by the size and energy of the thing that had come out of it. It died in childbirth.

There is, however, another circumstance which, even in ordinary public opinion, makes this miscellany important, besides the great novel that came out of it. I mean that the ordinary reader can remember one great thing about *Master Humphrey's Clock*, besides the fact that it was the frame-work of *The Old Curiosity Shop*. He remembers that Mr. Pickwick and the Wellers rise again from the dead. Dickens makes Samuel Pickwick become a member of Master

Humphrey's Clock Society; and he institutes a parallel society in the kitchen under the name of Mr. Weller's Watch.

Before we consider the question of whether Dickens was wise when he did this, it is worth remarking how really odd it is that this is the only place where he did it. Dickens, one would have thought, was the one man who might naturally have introduced old characters into new stories. Dickens, as a matter of fact, was almost the one man who never did it. It would have seemed natural in him for a double reason; first, that his characters were very valuable to him, and second that they were not very valuable to his particular stories. They were dear to him, and they are dear to us; but they really might as well have turned up (within reason) in one environment as well as in another. We, I am sure, should be delighted to meet Mr. Mantalini in the story of *Dombey and Son*. And he certainly would not be much missed from the plot of Nicholas Nickleby. "I am an affectionate father," said Dickens, "to all the children of my fancy; but like many other parents I have in my heart of hearts a favourite child; and his name is David Copperfield." Yet although his heart must often have yearned backwards to the children of his fancy whose tale was already told, yet he never touched one of them again even with the point of his pen. The characters in *David Copperfield*, as in all the others, were dead for him after he had done the book; if he loved them as children, it was as dead and sanctified children. It is a curious test of the strength and even reticence that underlay the seeming exuberance of Dickens, that he never did yield at all to exactly that indiscretion or act of sentimentalism which would seem most natural to his emotions and his art. Or rather he never did yield to it except here in this one case; the case of *Master Humphrey's Clock*.

And it must be remembered that nearly everybody else did yield to it. Especially did those writers who are commonly counted Dickens's superiors in art and exactitude and closeness to connected reality. Thackeray wallowed in it; Anthony Trollope lived on it. Those modern artists who pride themselves most on the separation and unity of a work of art have indulged in it often; thus, for instance, Stevenson gave a glimpse of Alan Breck in *The Master of Ballantrae*, and meant to give a glimpse of the Master of Ballantrae in another unwritten tale called *The Rising Sun*. The habit of revising old characters is so strong in Thackeray that *Vanity Fair*, *Pendennis*, *The Newcomes*, and *Philip* are in one sense all one novel. Certainly the reader sometimes forgets which one of them he is reading. Afterwards he cannot remember whether the best description of Lord Steyne's red whiskers or Mr. Wagg's rude jokes occurred in *Vanity Fair*, or *Pendennis*; he cannot remember whether his favourite dialogue between Mr. and Mrs. Pendennis occurred in *The Newcomes*, or in *Philip*. Whenever two Thackeray characters in two Thackeray novels could by any possibility have been contemporary, Thackeray delights to connect them. He makes Major Pendennis nod to Dr. Firmin, and Colonel Newcome ask Major Dobbin to dinner. Whenever two characters could not possibly have been contemporary he goes out of his way to make one the remote ancestor of the other. Thus he created the great house of Warrington solely to connect a "blue-bearded" Bohemian journalist with the blood of Henry Esmond. It is quite impossible to conceive Dickens keeping up this elaborate connection between all his characters and all his books, especially across the ages. It would give us a kind of shock if we learnt from Dickens that Major Bagstock was the nephew of Mr. Chester. Still less can we imagine Dickens carrying on an almost systematic family chronicle as was in some sense done by Trollope. There must be some reason for such a paradox; for in itself it is a very curious one. The writers who wrote carefully were always putting, as it were, after-words and appendices to their already finished portraits; the man who did splendid and flamboyant but faulty portraits never attempted to touch them up. Or rather (we may say again) he attempted it once, and then he failed.

The reason lay, I think, in the very genius of Dickens's creation. The child he bore of his soul quitted him when his term was passed like a veritable child born of the body. It was independent of him, as a child is of its parents. It had become dead to him even in becoming alive. When Thackeray studied Pendennis or Lord Steyne he was studying something outside himself, and therefore something that might come nearer and nearer. But when Dickens brought forth

Sam Weller or Pickwick he was creating something that had once been inside himself and therefore when once created could only go further and further away. It may seem a strange thing to say of such laughable characters and of so lively an author, yet I say it quite seriously; I think it possible that there arose between Dickens and his characters that strange and almost supernatural shyness that arises often between parents and children; because they are too close to each other to be open with each other. Too much hot and high emotion had gone to the creation of one of his great figures for it to be possible for him without embarrassment ever to speak with it again. This is the thing which some fools call fickleness; but which is not the death of feeling, but rather its dreadful perpetuation; this shyness is the final seal of strong sentiment; this coldness is an eternal constancy.

This one case where Dickens broke through his rule was not such a success as to tempt him in any case to try the thing again.

There is weakness in the strict sense of the word in this particular reappearance of Samuel Pickwick and Samuel Weller. In the original *Pickwick Papers* Dickens had with quite remarkable delicacy and vividness contrived to suggest a certain fundamental sturdiness and spirit in that corpulent and complacent old gentleman. Mr. Pickwick was a mild man, a respectable man, a placid man; but he was very decidedly a man. He could denounce his enemies and fight for his nightcap. He was fat; but he had a backbone. In *Master Humphrey's Clock* the backbone seems somehow to be broken; his good nature seems limp instead of alert. He gushes out of his good heart; instead of taking a good heart for granted as a part of any decent gentleman's furniture as did the older and stronger Pickwick. The truth is, I think, that Mr. Pickwick in complete repose loses some part of the whole point of his existence. The quality which makes the *Pickwick Papers* one of the greatest of human fairy tales is a quality which all the great fairy tales possess, and which marks them out from most modern writing. A modern novelist generally endeavours to make his story interesting, by making his hero odd. The most typical modern books are those in which the central figure is himself or herself an exception, a cripple, a courtesan, a lunatic, a swindler, or a person of the most perverse temperament. Such stories, for instance, are *Sir Richard Calmady*, *Dodo*, *Quisante*, *La Bête Humaine*, even the *Egoist*. But in a fairy tale the boy sees all the wonders of fairyland because he is an ordinary boy. In the same way Mr. Samuel Pickwick sees an extraordinary England because he is an ordinary old gentleman. He does not see things through the rosy spectacles of the modern optimist or the green-smoked spectacles of the pessimist; he sees it through the crystal glasses of his own innocence. One must see the world clearly even in order to see its wildest poetry. One must see it sanely even in order to see that it is insane.

Mr. Pickwick, then, relieved against a background of heavy kindliness and quiet club life does not seem to be quite the same heroic figure as Mr. Pickwick relieved against a background of the fighting police constables at Ipswich or the roaring mobs of Eatanswill. Of the degeneration of the Wellers, though it has been commonly assumed by critics, I am not so sure. Some of the things said in the humorous assembly round Mr. Weller's Watch are really human and laughable and altogether in the old manner. Especially, I think, the vague and awful allusiveness of old Mr. Weller when he reminds his little grandson of his delinquencies under the trope or figure of their being those of another little boy, is really in the style both of the irony and the domesticity of the poorer classes. Sam also says one or two things really worthy of himself. We feel almost as if Sam were a living man, and could not appear for an instant without being amusing.

The other elements in the make-up of *Master Humphrey's Clock* come under the same paradox which I have applied to the whole work. Though not very important in literature they are somehow quite important in criticism. They show us better than anything else the whole unconscious trend of Dickens, the stuff of which his very dreams were made. If he had made up tales to amuse himself when half-awake (as I have no doubt he did) they would be just such tales as these. They would have been ghostly legends of the nooks and holes of London, echoes of old love and laughter from the taverns or the Inns of Court. In a sense also one may say that these tales are the great might-have-beens of Dickens. They are chiefly designs which he fills up here slightly and unsatisfactorily, but which he might have filled up with his own brightest and most incredible colours. Nothing, for instance, could have been nearer to the heart of Dickens than his great Gargantuan conception of Gog and Magog telling London legends to each other all through the night. Those two giants might have stood on either side of some new great city of his invention, swarming with fanciful figures and noisy with new events. But as it is, the two giants stand alone in a wilderness, guarding either side of a gate that leads nowhere.

Reprinted Pieces

Those abuses which are supposed to belong specially to religion belong to all human institutions. They are not the sins of supernaturalism, but the sins of nature. In this respect it is interesting to observe that all the evils which our Rationalist or Protestant tradition associates with the idolatrous veneration of sacred figures arises in the merely human atmosphere of literature and history. Every extravagance of hagiology can be found in hero-worship. Every folly alleged in the worship of saints can be found in the worship of poets. There are those who are honourably and intensely opposed to the atmosphere of religious symbolism or religious archæology. There are people who have a vague idea that the worship of saints is worse than the imitation of sinners. There are some, like a lady I once knew, who think that hagiology is the scientific study of hags. But these slightly prejudiced persons generally have idolatries and superstitions of their own, particularly idolatries and superstitions in connection with celebrated people. Mr. Stead preserves a pistol belonging to Oliver Cromwell in the office of the *Review of Reviews*; and I am sure he worships it in his rare moments of solitude and leisure. A man, who could not be induced to believe in God by all the arguments of all the philosophers, professed himself ready to believe if he could see it stated on a postcard in the handwriting of Mr. Gladstone. Persons not otherwise noted for their religious exercise have been known to procure and preserve portions of the hair of Paderewski. Nay, by this time blasphemy itself is a sacred tradition, and almost as much respect would be paid to the alleged relics of an atheist as to the alleged relics of a god. If any one has a fork that belonged to Voltaire, he could probably exchange it in the open market for a knife that belonged to St. Theresa.

Of all the instances of this there is none stranger than the case of Dickens. It should be pondered very carefully by those who reproach Christianity with having been easily corrupted into a system of superstitions. If ever there was a message full of what modern people call true Christianity, the direct appeal to the common heart, a faith that was simple, a hope that was infinite, and a charity that was omnivorous, if ever there came among men what they call the Christianity of Christ, it was in the message of Dickens. Christianity has been in the world nearly two thousand years, and it has not yet quite lost, its enemies being judges, its first fire and charity; but friends and enemies would agree that it was from the very first more detailed and doctrinal than the spirit of Dickens. The spirit of Dickens has been in the world about sixty years; and already it is a superstition. Already it is loaded with relics. Already it is stiff with antiquity.

Everything that can be said about the perversion of Christianity can be said about the perversion of Dickens. It is said that Christ's words are repeated by the very High Priests and Scribes whom He meant to denounce. It is just as true that the jokes in *Pickwick* are quoted with delight by the very bigwigs of bench and bar whom Dickens wished to make absurd and impossible. It is said that texts from Scripture are constantly taken in vain by Judas and Herod, by Caiaphas and Annas. It is just as true that texts from Dickens are rapturously quoted on all our platforms by Podsnap and Honeythunder, by Pardiggle and Veneering, by Tigg when he is forming a company, or Pott when he is founding a newspaper. People joke about Bumble in defence of Bumbledom; people allude playfully to Mrs. Jellyby while agitating for Borrioboola Gha. The very things which Dickens tried to destroy are preserved as relics of him. The very houses he wished to pull down are propped up as monuments of Dickens. We wish to preserve everything of him, except his perilous public spirit.

This antiquarian attitude towards Dickens has many manifestations, some of them somewhat ridiculous. I give one startling instance out of a hundred of the irony remarked upon above. In his first important book, Dickens lashed the loathsome corruption of our oligarchical politics, their blaring servility and dirty diplomacy of bribes, under the name of an imaginary town called Eatanswill. If Eatanswill, wherever it was, had been burned to the ground by its indignant neighbours the day after the exposure, it would have been not inappropriate. If it had been entirely deserted by its inhabitants, if they had fled to hide themselves in holes and caverns, one could have understood it. If it had been struck by a thunderbolt out of heaven or outlawed by the whole human race, all that would seem quite natural. What has really happened is this: that two respectable towns in Suffolk are still disputing for the honour of having been the original Eatanswill; as if two innocent hamlets each claimed to be Gomorrah. I make no comment; the thing is beyond speech.

But this strange sentimental and relic-hunting worship of Dickens has many more innocent manifestations. One of them is that which takes advantage of the fact that Dickens happened to be a journalist by trade. It occupies itself therefore with hunting through papers and magazines for unsigned articles which may possibly be proved to be his. Only a little time ago one of these enthusiasts ran up to me, rubbing his hands, and told me that he was sure he had found two and a half short paragraphs in *All the Year Round* which were certainly written by Dickens, whom he called (I regret to say) the Master. Something of this archæological weakness must cling to all mere reprints of his minor work. He was a great novelist; but he was also, among other things, a good journalist and a good man. It is often necessary for a good journalist to write bad literature. It is sometimes the first duty of a good man to write it. Pot-boilers to my feeling are sacred things; but they may well be secret as well as sacred, like the holy pot which it is their purpose to boil. In the collection called *Reprinted Pieces* there are some, I think, which demand or deserve this apology. There are many which fall below the level of his recognised books of fragments, such as *The Sketches by Boz*, and *The Uncommercial Traveller*. Two or three elements in the compilation, however, make it quite essential to any solid appreciation of the author.

Of these the first in importance is that which comes last in order. I mean the three remarkable pamphlets upon the English Sunday, called *Sunday under Three Heads*. Here, at least, we find the eternal Dickens, though not the eternal Dickens of fiction. His other political and sociological suggestions in this volume are so far unimportant that they are incidental, and even personal. Any man might have formed Dickens's opinion about flogging for garrotters, and altered it afterwards. Any one might have come to Dickens's conclusion about model prisons, or to any other conclusion equally reasonable and unimportant. These things have no colour of the great man's character. But on the subject of the English Sunday he does stand for his own philosophy. He stands for a particular view, remote at present both from Liberals and Conservatives. He was, in a conscious sense, the first of its spokesmen. He was in every sense the last.

In his appeal for the pleasures of the people, Dickens has remained alone. The pleasures of the people have now no defender, Radical or Tory. The Tories despise the people. The Radicals despise the pleasures.

Printed in Great Britain
by Amazon